I0289291

Massachusetts Society of Mayflower Descendants

The Mayflower descendant: A quarterly magazine of Pilgrim genealogy and history

Vol. 04

Massachusetts Society of Mayflower Descendants

The Mayflower descendant: A quarterly magazine of Pilgrim genealogy and history
Vol. 04

ISBN/EAN: 9783337712976

Printed in Europe, USA, Canada, Australia, Japan

Cover: Foto ©ninafisch / pixelio.de

More available books at **www.hansebooks.com**

A Quarterly Magazine

OF

Pilgrim Genealogy and History

1902

VOLUME IV

BOSTON
PUBLISHED BY THE
MASSACHUSETTS SOCIETY OF MAYFLOWER DESCENDANTS
1902

INDEX OF SUBJECTS.

Abstracts and Transcripts of Wills and Inventories of Second and Later Generations, 63, 256
Alden Research Fund, 62
Allerton, Isaac, Deposition of, 109
Allerton Research Fund, 62
"Anne," the ship, 93, 94
Arthur — Bradford Query, 64
Autographs of Mayflower Passengers, 98, 256
Autograph of Phineas Pratt, 132
Autograph of George Soule, 63, 98

Barnes, John, Will of, 98
Barnstable, Mass., Vital Records, 120, 221, 256
Barnstable County, Mass., Index Fund, 62
Barnstable County, Mass., Probate Records, 48, 62, 179, 256
Bass, John, Will and Inventory of, and the Petition against the Approval of the Will, 202
Billington Research Fund, 62
Bird, Thomas, Deed to Edward Tilson, 82
Book Note: Macdonough-Hackstaff Ancestry, 64
Bradford Meerstead, 47, 52
Bradford Query, 64
Bradford — Arthur Query, 64
Bradford — Brewster Query, 64
Bradford, Gov. William, Letter Book of, 256
Bradford Research Fund, 62, 192
Bradford, Gov. William, Letter to Gov. Winthrop, 256
Bradford, Major William, Will and Inventory of, 143
Brewster Book, 46, 256
Brewster, Mass., Records of the First Parish in, 242, 256
Brewster — Bradford Query, 64
Brewster Research Fund, 62
Brewster, William, His True Position in Our Colonial History, 100
Brewster, Wrestling, Deed from John Doty, 65
Bridgewater, Mass., Vital Records, 256
Bristol County Index Fund, 62
Bristol County Land Records, 62
Bristol County Probate Records, 62
Brown, Peter, Children of, 254, 256
Brown Research Fund, 62
Browne, James, Deed from John Browne, 84
Browne, John, Deed from Thomas Willett, 83
Browne, John, Deed to John Browne, Jr., 84
Bunker, George, Deed to Phineas Pratt, 132

Cabinet of Massachusetts Society, Donations to, 46, 56, 127, 251, 255
Calkins Family Record, 17
Cape Cod Pilgrim Memorial Association, 250
Chatham, Mass., Vital Records, 182, 198, 256
"Charity," the ship, 90
Chauncy, Charles, Deed from Church of Scituate, 85
Chilton Research Fund, 62
Church, Richard, Deposition of, 152
Church Records:
  Brewster, Mass., 242, 256
  Harwich, Mass., 242
  Plymouth, Mass., 212, 256
Colonial Research Fund, 49, 62, 63, 128, 192, 239, 254, 256
Colonial Research Work, 61, 128
Committee on Historical Research, 49, 50, 62
Committee on Marking Historic Sites, 47
Committee on Publication, 1, 50
Connecticut Society, 51, 58
Connecticut Society, Members Elected, 252
Cook, Elizabeth, Inventory of, 179
Cook, Josiah, Settlement of the Estate of, 179
Cooke, Francis, and His Descendants, 47
Cooke, Jacob, Deed from Elizabeth Hopkins, 118
Cooke, John, Deed from Phineas Pratt, 129
Cooke Research Fund, 62
Cornelius, Lawrence, Commission of, 84
Cushman, Thomas, Deed from William Paddy and Thomas Willett, 35
Cushman, Thomas, Deed to William Paddy and Thomas Willett, 36
Cushman, Elder Thomas, Will and Inventory of, and the Records of his Death, 37

Dartmouth, Purchasers of, 185
Dartmouth, Mass., Vital Records, 256
Deeds, Grantors and Grantees:
  Bird, Thomas, 82
  Brewster, Wrestling, 65
  Browne, James, 84

Deeds, etc. — *Continued.*
Browne, John, 83, 84
Bunker, George, 132
Chauncy, Charles, 85
Cooke, Jacob, 118
Cooke, John, 129
Cushman, Thomas, 35, 36
Doty, John, 65
Hopkins, Elizabeth, 118
Paddy, William, 35, 36
Pratt, Phineas, 129, 132, 133
Scituate, Church of, 85
Tilson, Edward, 82
White, Peregrine, 86
White, Resolved, 86
Willett, Thomas, 35, 36, 83, 86
Depositions:
Allerton, Isaac, 109
Church, Richard, 152
Diary of Jabez Fitch, Jr., 46, 148, 234, 256
District of Columbia Society, 51
District of Columbia Society, Members Elected, 59, 192, 253
Doty, John, Deed to Wrestling Brewster, 65
Doty, Thomas, Will and Inventory of, 233
Duxbury, Mass., Town Records, 48

Eastham, Mass., North Precinct Records, 227
Eastham and Orleans, Mass., Vital Records, 29, 140, 256

Family Records, 17, 255, 256
Fitch, Jabez, Jr., Diary of, 46, 148, 234, 256
Forefathers' Day Service of Massachusetts Society, 3, 47, 55
Foreign Research Fund, 1
"Fortune," the ship, 93, 94
"Friendship," the ship, 109

Genealogical Research, Co-operation in, 62
General Society of Mayflower Descendants, Officers Elected, 51
General Society of Mayflower Descendants, Triennial Congress of 1900, 50
Gorham, Desire (Howland), Estate of, 217
Gorham, Captain John, Estate of, 153

Halifax, Mass., Vital Records, 20, 256
Harwich, Mass., First Parish Records, 242,
Harwich, Mass., Vital Records, 175, 207, 256
Holiday Gifts, 254
Holmes, Israel, and William Sherman, Jr., Estates of, 171

Hopkins, Damaris, Her Portion of her Father's Estate, 115
Hopkins, Deborah, Her Portion of her Father's Estate, 115
Hopkins, Elizabeth, Deed to Jacob Cooke, 118
Hopkins, Elizabeth, Estate of, 114, 116, 118
Hopkins, Ruth, Her Portion of her Father's Estate, 116, 117
Hopkins, Stephen and His Descendants, 254, 256
Hopkins, Stephen, the Portions of His Daughters and the Estate of Elizabeth² Hopkins, 114

Illinois Society, 51, 58
Illinois Society, Members Elected, 59, 253
Illinois Society, Officers Elected, 58
Illinois Society, Supplemental Lines Filed, 253
Illustrations:
Gov. Edward Winslow's Will, 1
A Calkins Family Record, 18
John Doty's Deed to Wrestling Brewster, 65
George Soule's Autograph, 98
Phineas Pratt's Will, 129
Phineas Pratt's Autograph, 132
Bond of Desire (Howland) Gorham, 153
Andrew Ring's Will, 193
Inventories, see Wills, Inventories etc.

"Jacob," the ship, 94

Kemp, William, Inventory of, 75

Landing of the Pilgrims, Tri-Centennial Anniversary of, 49
Legacy to Massachusetts Society, 46
Library of Massachusetts Society, 45, 46
Library of Massachusetts Society, Donations to, 46, 56, 127, 190, 251
Little, Thomas, Will and Inventory of, and the Will of his son Thomas, 161
"Little James," the ship, 64

Macdonough-Hackstaff Ancestry, Book Note, 64
Maine Society, 60
Maine Society, Officers Elected, 60
Marriageable Women and Unidentified Wives, 63
Marshfield, Mass., Vital Records, 125, 256
Massachusetts Society, 3, 18, 43, 45, 47, 49, 51, 61, 65, 100, 126, 189, 192, 251, 255
Massachusetts Society, Cabinet of, 46, 56, 127, 251, 255

Massachusetts Society, Committees Appointed, 55
Massachusetts Society, Forefathers' Day Service of, 47, 55
Massachusetts Society, Legacy to, 46
Massachusetts Society, Library of, 45, 46, 56, 127, 190, 251
Massachusetts Society, Members Elected, 56, 127, 190, 252
Massachusetts Society, Officers Elected, 55
Massachusetts Society, Sixth Annual Report of George Ernest Bowman, Secretary, 43
Massachusetts Society, Supplemental Lines Filed, 56, 127, 190, 252
"Mayflower," the name, 256
"Mayflower," the ship, 3, 4, 6, 7, 93, 94, 100
"Mayflower Descendant," 47, 49, 54, 256
Mayflower Genealogies, 43, 48, 49, 61, 128, 254, 255
Mayflower Genealogies, Later Generations of, 255
Mayflower Lines, Finding New, 192
Mayflower Passengers, Autographs of, 98, 256
Mayflower Passengers, Vital Statistics of, 128
Mayflower Passengers, Wills and Inventories of, 2, 48
Michigan Society, 54, 60
Michigan Society, Officers Elected, 60
Middleborough, Mass., Vital Records, 67, 256
Mitchell, Experience, Will and Inventory of, 150

Negro Slave, Two Bills of Sale of a, 210
New Jersey Society, 51, 192, 254
New Jersey Society, Members Elected, 254
New York Society, 50, 57
New York Society, Members Elected, 57, 58, 191, 252
New York Society, Officers Elected, 57
Notes:
Brown, Peter, Children of, 254
Colonial Research Fund, 62, 128, 192, 254
Colonial Research Work, 61
Co-operation in Genealogical Research, 62
Finding New Mayflower Lines, 192
George Soule's Autograph, 63
Holiday Gifts, 254
Hopkins, Stephen and His Descendants, 254
Later Generations of the Mayflower Genealogies, 255
Mayflower Genealogies, 128

Notes. — *Continued.*
Supply of Back Numbers, 63
Transcripts and Abstracts of Wills of Second and Later Generations, 63
Unidentified Wives and Marriageable Women, 63

Ohio Society, 51, 59
Ohio Society, Committees Appointed, 59
Ohio Society, Members Elected, 191
Ohio Society, Officers Elected, 59
Orleans and Eastham, Mass., Vital Records, 29, 140, 256

Paddy, William, Deed from Thomas Cushman, 36
Paddy, William, Deed to Thomas Cushman, 35
Pennsylvania Society, 51, 58, 128, 252
Pennsylvania Society, Members Elected, 58
Pennsylvania Society, Officers Elected, 58
Pilgrim Notes and Queries, 61, 128, 192, 254, 256
Pilgrims, Permanent Contributions by, to the Cause of Religion, 3
Plymouth, Mass., First Church Records, 212, 256
Plymouth, Mass., Town Records, 48
Plymouth, Mass., Vital Records, 110, 256
Plymouth Colony Deeds, 35, 48, 61, 62, 82, 256
Plymouth Colony Index Fund, 62
Plymouth Colony Records, 48
Plymouth Colony Wills and Inventories, 48, 61, 62, 75, 168, 256
Plymouth County Index Fund, 62
Plymouth County Land Records, 62
Plymouth County Probate Records, 62
Plympton, Mass., Vital Records, 256
Pratt, Phineas, of Plymouth and Charlestown, 87, 129
Pratt, Phineas, Deed from George Bunker, 132
Pratt, Phineas, Deed to John Cooke, 129
Pratt, Phineas, Will and Inventory of, 139
Purchasers, The, 85, 86, 94, 185

Queries:
Arthur — Bradford, 64
Bradford, 64
Bradford—Arthur, 64
Bradford — Brewster, 64
Brewster — Bradford, 64
Soule, 64

Reports from State Societies, 55, 126, 189, 251, 256

Rhode Island, Bounds of Land near, 85
Rhode Island Society, 54, 128
Rhode Island Society, Members Elected, 192
Ring, Andrew, Will and Inventory of 193
Robinson, John, Memorial Church, 126, 189

Scituate, Church of, Deed to Charles Chauncy, 85
Scituate, Mass., Vital Records, 256
Settlements of Estates, see Wills etc.
Sherman, William, Jr., and Israel Holmes, Estates of. 171
Sixth Annual Report of George Ernest Bowman, Secretary of the Massachusetts Society, 43
Slave, Negro, Two Bills of Sale of, 210
Soule, George, Autograph of, 63, 98
Soule, John, His Inventory and the Settlement of His Estate, 159
Soule Query, 64
"Sparrow," the ship. 88–90
"Swan," the ship, 90

Tilson, Edward, Deed from Thomas Bird, 82
Tinkham, Ephraim, Will and Inventory of, 122
Tomson, Lieut. John, His Will and Inventory and the Agreement of his Heirs, 22
Town Records (See also Vital Records):
Wellfleet, Mass., 227
Transcripts and Abstracts of Wills and Inventories of Second and Later Generations, 63, 256
Tri-Centennial Anniversary of the Landing of the Pilgrims. 49
Triennial Congress Held September 15, 1900, 50

Unidentified Wives and Marriageable Women, 63

Vital Records (See also Church Records):
Barnstable, Mass., 120, 221, 256
Bridgewater, Mass., 256
Calkins Family, 17
Chatham, Mass., 182, 198, 256
Dartmouth, Mass., 256
Eastham, Mass., 29, 140, 256
Halifax, Mass., 20, 256
Harwich, Mass., 175, 207, 256
Marshfield, Mass., 125, 256
Middleborough, Mass., 67, 256
Orleans, Mass., 29, 140, 256
Plymouth, Mass., 110, 212, 256
Plympton, Mass., 256
Scituate, Mass., 256
Yarmouth, Mass., 188, 256

Vital Statistics of the Mayflower Passengers, 128

Warren, Joseph, Will and Inventory of, 14
Warren, Richard, and His Descendants, 47
Wellfleet, Mass., Records of, 227, 256
White, Peregrine, Deed to Thomas Willett, 86
White, Resolved, Deed to Thomas Willett, 86
"White Angel," the ship, 109
Willett, Thomas, Deed from Thomas Cushman, 35
Willett, Thomas, Deed from Peregrine and Resolved White, 86
Willett, Thomas, Deed to John Browne, 83
Willett, Thomas, Deed to Thomas Cushman, 36
Wills and Inventories of Second and Later Generations, 63, 256
Wills, Inventories and Settlements of Estates:
Barnes, John, 98
Bass, John, 202
Bradford, Major William, 143
Cook, Elizabeth, 179
Cook, Josiah, 179
Cushman, Elder Thomas, 37
Doty, Thomas, 233
Gorham, Desire (Howland), 217
Gorham, Captain John, 153
Holmes, Israel, 171
Hopkins, Elizabeth, 114
Hopkins, Stephen, 114
Kemp, William, 75
Little, Thomas, 161
Little, Thomas, Jr., 161
Mitchell, Experience, 150
Pratt, Phineas, 139
Ring, Andrew, 193
Sherman, William, 171
Soule, John, 159
Swift, William, 168
Tinkham, Ephraim, 122
Tomson, Lieut. John, 22
Warren, Joseph, 14
Winslow, Edward, 1
Wright, Adam, 239
Wright, Richard, 165
Winslow, Gov. Edward, Will of, 1
Wisconsin Society, 54
Wisconsin Society, Members Elected, 60,
Wright, Adam, Will and Inventory of, 239,
Wright, Richard, Will and Inventory of, 165

Yarmouth, Mass., Vital Records, 188, 256

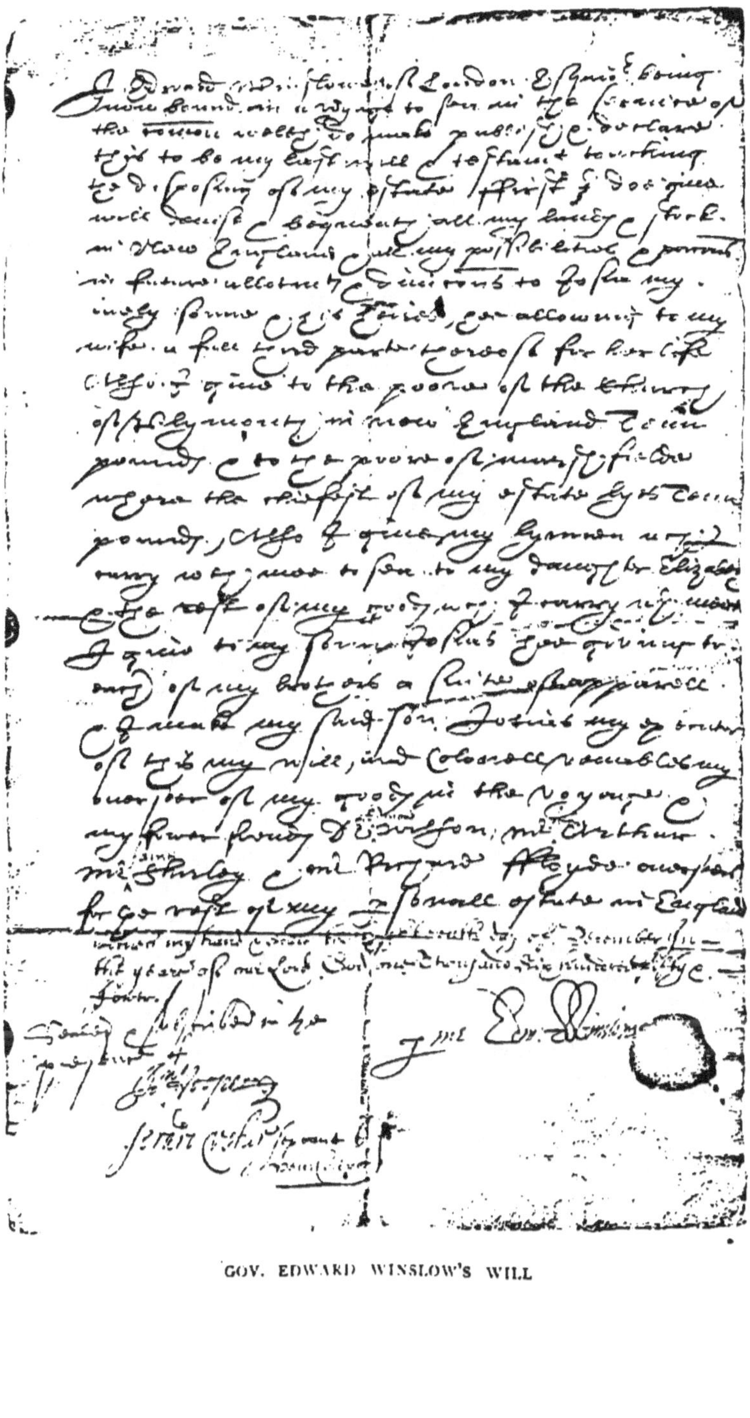
I Edward Winslow of London Esquire being
now bound on a voyage to sea in the service of
the common wealth do make publish and declare
this to be my last will and testament touching
the disposing of my estate. First I doe give
will devise and bequeath all my lands and stock
in New England and all my possibilities and portions
in future allotments and divisions to Josiah my
only sonne and his heires he allowing to my
wife a full third parte thereof for her life.
Also I give to the poore of the church
of Plymouth in New England ten
pounds and to the poore of Marshfield
where the chiefest of my estate lyes ten
pounds. Also I give my [illegible]
[illegible] to my daughter Elizabeth
and the rest of my goods [illegible]
I give to my sonne Josias he giving to
each of my brothers a suite of apparell
and I make my said son Josias my executor
of this my will, and Colonell Venables my
overseer of my goods in the voyage and
my freinds Dr Wilson, Mr [illegible]
Mr James Shirley and Mr Richard Floyd overseers
for the rest of my small estate in England
witness my hand [illegible] day of December in
the yeare of our Lord God one thousand six hundred fifty
foure.

Signed [illegible] in the presence of [illegible]

[illegible]

Edw. Winslow

GOV. EDWARD WINSLOW'S WILL

THE MAYFLOWER DESCENDANT

Vol. IV. JANUARY, 1902. No. 1.

GOVERNOR EDWARD WINSLOW'S WILL.

THE will of Governor Edward Winslow, which is preserved at Somerset House, London, is one of the three existing original wills of Mayflower passengers. The others are Mary (Chilton) Winslow's and Peregrine White's, both of which we have already reproduced. The illustration of Governor Winslow's will facing this page is from a photograph made at the expense of the Foreign Research Fund and secured by the Hon. Winslow Warren, of our Committee on Publication, with the courteous assistance of the Rev. Stopford W. Brooke, of London.

No mention of Governor Winslow's death is found on the Plymouth Colony records, and we learn the date from Nathaniel Morton's New England's Memorial, under the year 1655. We reprint his account in full, from the Rev. Thomas Prince's copy of the first edition (1669), now in the Boston Public Library.

This year that Worthy and Honourable Gentleman Mr. *Edward Winslow* deceased; of whom I have had occasion to make honourable mention formerly in this Discourse. He was the Son of *Edward VVinslow* Esq; of the Town of *Draughtwich* * in the County of *Worcester:* He travelling into the *Low-Countreys*, in his Journeys fell into acquaintance with the Church of *Leyden* in *Holland*, unto whom he joyned, and with whom he continued until they parted to come into *New-England*, he coming with that part that came first over, and became a very worthy and useful Instrument amongst them, both in the place of Government and otherwise, until his last Voyage for *England*, being sent on special Imployment for the Government of the *Massachusets*, as is forementioned in this Book; and afterwards was imployed as one of the grand Commissioners in that unhappy Design against *Domingo* in *Hispaniola*. who taking grief for the ill success of that Enterprize; on which, together with some other Infirmities that were upon him, he fell sick at Sea betwixt *Domingo* and *Jamaica*, and died the eighth day of *May*, which was about the Sixty first year of his life, and his Body was honourably committed to the Sea, with the usual Solemnity of the Discharge of Fourty two Piece of Ordnance.

* Droitwich.

One of the Company who was imployed in taking notice of the Particulars of that Tragedy, gave such Testimony of the said Mr. *VVinslow*. as followeth in this Poem:

The Eighth of May, *west from* 'Spaniola *shore,*
God took from us our Grand Commissioner,
Winslow *by Name, a man in Chiefest Trust,*
VVhose Life was sweet, and Conversation just;
VVhose Parts and wisdome most men did excell:
An honour to his Place, as all can tell.

While examining the Marshfield town records some time since, the Editor discovered a vote regarding the disposition of the ten pounds bequeathed by Governor Winslow to the poor of that town. A literal transcript of this record follows the copy of the will.

I Edward Winslowe of London. Esquio^r^. being now bound in a voyage to sea in the service of the comon welth do make publish & declare this to be my last will & testam^t^ touching the disposing of my estate. ffirst I doe give will devise & bequeath all my lands & stock. in New England & all my possibilities & porcons in future allotm^ts^ & divicons to Josia my. onely sonne & his heires, hee allowing to my wife. a full third parte thereof for her life Also. I give to the poore of the Church of Plymouth in new England Tenn pounds. & to the poore of marshfielde where the chiefest of my estate lyes Tenn pounds., Also I give my lynnen wch I carry wth me to sea. to my daughter Elizabet(h) &. the rest of. my goods wch I carry wth mee I give to my sonn Josias. hee giving to. each of my brothers a suite of apparell. & I make my said son. Josias my executor of this my will, and Colonell venables my overseer of my goods in the voyage. & my fower frends Dr Edmond wilson; m^r^ John Arthur. m^r^ James Shirley & m^r^ Richard ffloyde. overseers for the rest of my prsonall estate in England

witness my hand & Seale the Eighteenth day of December In the yeare of our Lord God one Thousand Six hundred fifty & ffower.

Sealed & subscribed pr me Edw: Winslow (seal)
in the presence of
Jo^n^ Hooper
Gerard Usher servant to Hen: Colbron

[Marshfield Records, I: 60, under date 3 Nov., 1656.]

Att ye same Townes meeting it was ordered That m^r^ Thomas Bourne and Joseph Beedell should Receave The Ten pounds which m^r Edward Winslow gave To The poore of This Towne by will and ye sayd prtyes so betrusted To Rec: & dispose of The stocke in The Townes behalfe have disposed one Cow To Edward Bumpus & John Branch one Cow & John Thomas The Remainder & These prtyes That is Edward & both The Johns To keepe These Cowes & To Returne at ye end of The Tea(rme) (as The Towne hath formerly lett out ye poore stocke) The princip(al) being living To ye Towne & The Third of The Increase The having Two Thirds of ye Increase Themselves.

PERMANENT CONTRIBUTIONS BY THE PILGRIMS TO THE CAUSE OF RELIGION.

[*An Address Delivered at the Second Annual Forefathers' Day Service of the Massachusetts Society of Mayflower Descendants, held at King's Chapel, Boston, December 21, 1901.*]

BY REV. FREDERICK BAYLIES ALLEN.

THIS is Forefathers' Day. Two hundred and eighty-one years ago, this 21st day of December, the Pilgrims first set foot on the shore of Plymouth and chose it as their home.

It was not the whole company, however, which did this. The Mayflower had cast anchor a month before (on the 21st day of November), in the harbor of what is now Provincetown, at the end of Cape Cod, and had remained there.

Three successive exploring parties went forth to find a place of settlement. It was the third party, composed of ten Pilgrims and eight seamen, which struggled into Plymouth Harbor, in a small shallop, late in the stormy evening of Friday, December 18th and landed on Clark's Island.

Bradford's history says that Saturday they dried their stuff, rested, gave thanks to God, and, this being the last day of the week, they prepared there to keep the Sabbath.

On Monday, the 21st (the day we are now observing), Bradford, who was one of the party, says: "They sounded the harbor and found it fit for shipping: and marched into the land and found divers cornfields and little running brooks: a place, (as they supposed) fit for situation; at least, it was the best they could find: and the season and their present necessitie made them glad to accept of it.

"So they returned to their ship again with this news to the rest of their people, which did much comfort their hearts."

That is the original account of the first Forefathers' Day.

The Mayflower reached Plymouth five days later (on the 26th). The second landing may be ascribed to December 30th, though the company left the ship gradually as houses were prepared for them, the last of the party going ashore as late as the month of April.

We, their descendants are met here today to commemorate by our service of prayer and song, those of whom James Russell Lowell said: "Next to the fugitives whom Moses led out of Egypt, the little shipload of outcasts who landed at Plymouth are destined to influence the future of the world."

We meet however, not at Plymouth, but at Boston, the capital of the Massachusetts Bay Colony, the original seat of Puritanism.

We worship moreover in a building whose early history is indelibly associated with the Church of England.

King's Chapel was erected (much against the will of the Puritans) under the auspices of the Royal Governors, for the express purpose of providing for public worship according to the liturgy of the English Book of Common Prayer.

It was, at one time, the only place in New England where the forms of the Court Church were used.

These triple associations of time and place: the Forefathers' Day, the Puritan city and the first Episcopal Church in New England have suggested the special theme to which I invite your attention: "The Permanent Contributions of the Pilgrims to the Cause of Religion: with incidental notice of the respective attitudes of the Pilgrims and of the Puritans to the Church of England."

I. I ask you to remember first that the Pilgrims were the earliest advocates of the separation of Church and State.

The Puritans when they crossed the ocean claimed loyal devotion to the National Church of England.

At the end of Queen Elizabeth's reign, through the popular antagonism of the people to the papacy, the great bulk of the country gentlemen and of the wealthier traders, of whom Parliament was chiefly composed, had become Puritans. Largely upon political grounds these Puritans acquired a bitter antagonism to those ceremonies which seemed to them allied to Roman Catholicism. Though called Non-Conformists, or as they preferred to call themselves Reformists, they felt themselves to be devoted members of the National Church. Owing to the personal antagonism of Elizabeth and James I. to Puritanism, it came about from the Union of Church and State that many of the appointees to the Church were persons practically destitute of religion. The spectacle of cruel and worldly ecclesiastics, performing the holiest rites of the church, stimulated the revolt against the liturgy.

This antagonism would have been comparatively feeble had the same ritual been administered by devout and earnest men.

It is generally conceded that if the demands of the Puritans had been met in a conciliatory spirit, they would have been content with moderate concessions.

The signers of the Millenary Petition, presented to King James at the beginning of his reign, asked for no change in the organization of the Church; but only "a reform of its courts, the removal of superstitious usages from the Book of Common Prayer, the disuse of lessons from the apocryphal books of Scripture, a more rigorous observance of Sundays and the provision and training of ministers who could preach to the people." How modest a request apparently.

In contemptuous scorn of these demands, three hundred Puritan clergymen who refused rigid conformity with the rubrics, were, in the spring of 1605, driven from their livings. The popular revolt deepened as they saw the church used as a machine to enforce slavish obedience to the royal will.

The very eagerness of the Puritans, however, to reform from within the Church of which they counted themselves the most loyal members, made them hate the Separatists, who looking deeper at the principles involved, withdrew, for conscience sake, from the Church.

Says John Richard Green: "To the zealot whose whole thought was of the fight with Rome, the position of those who rejected the very notion of a national Church and asserted the right of each congregation to perfect independence of faith and worship, seemed the claim of a right to mutiny in the camp, a right of breaking up Protestant England into a host of sects, too feeble to hold Rome at bay."

That explains the significance of the words of Francis Higginson, the Puritan minister of Salem, when he cried: "We will not say, as the Separatists were wont to say, at their leaving of England, Farewel Babylon! Farewel Rome! But we will say, Farewel Dear England! Farewel the Church of God in England, and all the Christian friends there! We do not go to New England as Separatists from the Church of England; though we cannot but separate from the corruptions in it. But we go to practise the positive part of church reformation, and propagate the Gospel in America."

And Governor Winthrop's Puritan company, as they sailed for America, spoke of themselves:

"As those who esteem it our honor to call the Church of England from whence we rise, our dear Mother; and cannot part from our native countrie where she specially resideth, without much sadness of heart and many tears in our eyes."

Turn now to the Pilgrims. We notice first that they were a very small company of men. Instead of the 20,000 who in less than a score of years came to Massachusetts Bay, they were but a few hundred in all. Only one hundred came over in the Mayflower and the portion of their company left behind in Holland was probably not more than twice as large.

But this small community were more homogeneous, more completely moulded into one spirit, than the mass of Puritans. They had been for thirteen years schooled and disciplined under many adversities by one man of singular force of character.

That man was their pastor in Leyden the Reverend John Robinson.

He had been the minister of the little congregation which under the fostering hospitality of William Brewster, had worshipped at Scrooby Manorhouse, England.

A man of rare piety, wisdom and thoughtfulness, he had, in the face of the tyranny and irreligion of the authorities, come to believe in the principle of the entire separation of Church and State. He states their position thus:

"As the Lord's free people, this congregation joined themselves, by a covenant of the Lord, into a church estate, in the fellowship of the Gospel, to walk in all His ways made known, or to be made known unto them, according to their best endeavors, whatever it should cost them; the Lord assisting them."

It cost them first their country, for in 1607 they were driven by the fierceness of the persecution to migrate to Holland, the only country in Europe where there was entire freedom of belief. For twelve years they dwelt there under the benign and penetrating influence of their noble pastor. It was he whose spiritual insight, wise leadership, and singular sagacity bred in these men that temper which for nearly a century characterized the Plymouth Colony.

At last in 1620, as the twelve years' truce between Holland and Spain approached its termination, as they found themselves in danger of losing their nationality in a foreign land; as they saw their children growing up under hardships and temptations which endangered both their health and their character, they came to the conclusion that it was their duty to remove, as they said, to "those vast and unpeopled countries of America, where they might at least lay the foundation for propagating and advancing the Gospel of the Kingdom of Christ."

We know well the story of that voyage across the ocean, the succession of obstacles which delayed it, the unspeakable hardships of the first winter and the gradual establishment upon firm foundations of the colony upon our shore.

The central element in the position of the Pilgrims as Separatists, was their repudiation of any official union of Church and State. The church polity called Independency or Congregationalism, though it was equally their faith, was another and distinct feature.

I shall confine what I have to say here to their protest against the mingling of the two spheres of religion and politics — the government of the Church with the administration of the State.

It was the enormities practised by the prelates of that day which forced the issue and drove them to deep and thorough searching of ultimate principles.

Had the Church of England been what it is now, Robinson and Brewster and Bradford would have gladly remained in her communion. But when a Bishop, by virtue of his office, could defy all legal restraints, and in the name of the king, who was the head of the Church, could cram the prisons of London with good Christians, who according to all modern ideas were perfectly innocent of any crime; clear thinking began to drive Robinson and Brewster into questioning the right of any such union of civil and religious functions.

This, then, was their conclusion: while they were never captious or controversial; while they said they would obey the king and his officers, and even his bishops in all secular matters — the things of man's deeper life, his faith in God, his privileges of worship were matters apart; which, with their consent, were never to be under the control of the State.

How consistently they adhered to this principle is manifest from the fact that when the ocean was crossed, unlike the Massachusetts Bay Colony, they never made church membership a condition of the franchise. So far as is known, even Myles Standish never joined the church, and some have believed that, at least nominally, he was a Roman Catholic. And these non-church members were from the beginning, regular legal members of the colony, who according to the compact signed on the Mayflower, had combined themselves into a civil (or secular) body politic. These two functions went on simply and naturally, side by side, just as they do today throughout our land. But they were the pioneers to first test this great principle.

When the Massachusetts Colony voted by its General Court—"That for time to come noe man shall be admitted to the freedom of this body pollitickc, but such as are members of some of the churches within the limits of the same." [Morton, p. 308.]—the Plymouth Colony dared to be true to its colors. A few of their number who had little in common with their noble leaders were still allowed equal political rights and absolute secular equality; and the time came when the strong, proud Massachusetts Bay Colonists were compelled to follow the lead of their humbler brethren to the south and absolutely sever Church and State.

We are all Separatists now. There is not one of us here who is not thankful that throughout the length and breadth of the land there is no established church.

It is largely because Protestants and Roman Catholics and Jews are all on precisely the same political level, in the sight of the law, that so kindly and charitable a spirit prevails between those of different faiths.

Let us never forget however, that we owe this benign result to our forefathers, who, when the title *Separatist* was a term of obloquy and reproach, exposing its bearer to persecution and loss, dared to be faithful to this fundamental principle.

II. The second tenet which we owe to the Pilgrims is their recognition of the *laity* as an integral part of the Church.

Robinson contended that "It is given to ministers to feed, guide and govern the Church, but not themselves to *be* the Church." *

In another place he says: "The officers of a church are not, by themselves, the Church. While there are *many* things in the settled and well ordered state of the Church which one would willingly leave to the administration of the officers thereof, they are or can be rightly and orderly done, but with the people's privity and consent."

The Pilgrims could not yield this point. "If," said they, "we should let the true practice of the gospel go, posterity after us, being brought into bondage, might justly blame and curse us, that we did not stand for the rights of the people in that which we acknowledge to be their due."

*These quotations from Robinson's writings are taken from "The Pilgrim Fathers of New England," by Rev. John Brown, D.D.

Robinson repeatedly asserts this root idea, though with a reasonableness and insight that shows how carefully he had studied the problem.

He says: "Wise men writing on this subject have approved as good and lawful three kinds of politics — monarchical, aristocratical and democratical, and all these three forms have their place in the Church of Christ. In respect of Christ the head, it is a monarchy; in respect of its officers, it is an aristocracy; and in respect of its body, a popular state. The governors of the Church must be in and of the church they govern, but they are not the *Church*."

Without endorsing the precise forms in which he applied this principle, its essence — that is, the representative character of the church and the rights of the laity to be duly considered in its administration is now acknowledged by all Protestant communions. We are so familiar with it, so assured of its justice and its wisdom, that it is hard for us to realize what an utter novelty it seemed in that day.

It had scant recognition at first in the Massachusetts Bay Colony. The eminent John Cotton of Boston, writing in 1636 to Lord Lay, declares: "Democracy I do not conceive that ever God did ordain as a fit government, either for church or commonwealth. If the people be governors, who shall be the governed?" Yet the day came when the Plymouth idea conquered the conservatism of the Puritan Colony.

How profound and far reaching has been the practical development of this germinal principle which our Pilgrim ancestors so fearlessly adopted.

Granting all the perverse and unlovely excesses to which it has often led in ignorant or untrained communities, it has now come to be recognized as an axiom, as a necessary and just law held by us as of priceless value. It may require both intelligence and piety for its best exercise, but it has now taken its due place as an essential and just requirement.

The *laity* are an integral part of a true church, fully entitled to a voice and due representation both in legislation and in the administering of its affairs.

III. Another Pilgrim principle, distinctive enough to merit notice, is the emphasis which they laid upon character as the supreme goal and test of religion.

At a time when Protestantism everywhere was suffering from an intense spirit of controversy, when every conceivable point of doctrine and church polity and ritual had been wrangled over until those who had forsaken the Church of Rome had become subdivided into multiplied warring sects and trifles had received more attention than essentials; it is wonderful what uniform stress was laid by the Pilgrims upon that which is central, upon personal religion and upon conduct.

This estimate of values was in one respect urged by Pilgrim and Puritan alike, when they both insisted that the church should not open wide her doors and offer her holiest rites and privileges to all men, utterly irrespective of character.

They both held that religion was something deeper than an external alliance with an institution. It was at its heart a matter of righteousness and purity and personal loyalty to the Lord. They were shocked that in the Church of England, men of notorious immorality and scandalous lives should be not only invited, but driven to the Holy Communion.

Robinson complains of England: "That all the natives there and subjects of the kingdom, although never such strangers from the show of true piety and goodness, and fraught never so full with many most heinous impieties and vices, are without difference compelled and enforced by most severe laws, civil and ecclesiastical, into the body of that church."

* * * * *

"Every subject of the kingdom dwelling in this or that parish, whether in city or country, whether in his own or other man's house, is thereby, *ipso facto*, made legally a member of the same parish in which that house is situated, and bound, will he nill he, fit or unfit, as with iron bounds, and all his with him, to participate in all holy things (and some unholy also), in that same parish church."

In this protest Pilgrims and Puritans, as I have said, shared alike; but where the former differed from the latter, was that their supreme reverence for goodness made them less critical and censorious than the Puritans as to irrelevant and secondary matters.

I believe the poet rightly judged them when he sung of the Pilgrims:

What did they want, whom high and low
Despised and persecuted so?
Little, when understood —
They wanted to be good.

To worship God in their own way;
To read their Bibles and to pray,
And save their souls! Poor men —
But poorer England then.

They proved the beauty and integrity of their religion by their example; by the lives they led before all men. Says Robinson: "God is not partial as men are; nor regards that church and chamber religion towards Him which is not accompanied in the house and in the streets with lovingkindness and mercy and all goodness towards men."

Nor was this theory merely.

Governor Bradford, recalling the days when they lived in Leyden, says: "Such was the true piety, the humble zeal and fervent love of this people towards God and his ways, and the single heartedness and the sincere affection one towards another, that they came as near the primitive pattern of the first Churches as any other Church of these later times have done according to their rank and quality."

He says in another place: "Though many of them were poor, yet there was none so poor but if they were known to be of that congregation, the Dutch (either bakers or others) would trust them in any reasonable matter when they wanted money. Because they had found by experience how careful they were to keep their word, and saw them so painful and diligent in their callings; yea, they would strive to get their custom and to employ them above others in their work, for their honesty and diligence."

This same high sense of honor and tenderness of conscience and charity towards others they carried with them into the new world. They made religion beautiful and attractive by their integrity and their cheerful kindness.

When in their sore need during one of their first explorations they took a store of corn which they found buried by the Indians, they diligently sought for the owners, and discovering them long months after, they scrupulously made them ample restitution.

The practical character of their religion is nowhere better illustrated than by their uniform fairness towards the Indians, for half a century.

Now it is not merely the fact that they were good men which is worthy of notice, but that their goodness was of so wholesome and pure a strain; so free from cant, and controversy, and perpetual argument and fault-finding. They got on amicably with all kinds of people, which was more than the so-called saints always did. They knew what was central in religion and lived it; and about the things which divided good people from one another, they were not disposed to be perpetually quarrelling.

Love towards God, purity of character, charity toward man — that was the pith of the Pilgrim faith.

IV. That brings me naturally to the remaining trait which I mention at this time, their religious tolerance.

The Pilgrims had enjoyed one advantage over the Puritans. They had sojourned for thirteen years in Holland and had seen in actual practice there, the fullest religious liberty granted to all faiths and to all nationalities.

But their practice of this principle had deeper root. Their charity to all sorts and conditions of men grew out of an openness of mind which they had learned at the feet of John Robinson. They had been taught by him to believe that they were not in the possession of all truth and that they might find something to learn from those who differed from them most fundamentally.

The memorable passage in which this hospitality to new light is enjoined, was quoted by Governor Bradford from the counsel given by John Robinson in 1620, upon the departure of the Pilgrims to America.

Familiar though it be, it can hardly be too often repeated, as it is the key to that consistent policy of religious tolerance practiced by the Plymouth Colony.

"He charged us," says Winslow, "before God and his blessed angels, to follow him no further than he followed Christ; and if God should reveal anything to us by any other instrument of His, to be as ready to receive it, as ever we were to receive any truth by his Ministry. For he was very confident the Lord had more truth and light yet to break forth out of His Holy Word."

* * * * *

"But withal he exhorted us to take heed what we received for truth: and well to examine and compare, and weigh it with other Scriptures of truth before we received it."

"For," saith he, "it is not possible the Christian world should come so lately out of such thick anti-Christian darkness; and that full perfection of knowledge should break forth at once."

Here we see how it was that these men who remembered and cherished their pastor's words were always so charitable to those of other faiths.

"Church of England people and Baptists dwelt continuously in Plymouth in peace, except such as openly sought to overturn the Independent Churches. Visitors of all beliefs and no belief

were entertained (to their host's subsequent privation), for months together, so hospitable were they."

The French Jesuit Druillette, who came to Boston in 1650, improved the opportunity to spend a day at Plymouth. He especially mentions Bradford's kindness, and the fact "that, the day being Friday, the Governor gave him an excellent dinner of *fish*."

At the Lord's table the Pilgrims communed with pious Episcopalians, with Calvinists of the French and Dutch Churches, and with Presbyterians, and recognized the spiritual fraternity of all who hold the Faith.

In 1659 Massachusetts Bay forbade keeping "any such day as Christmas, either by forbearing to labor, or feasting or in any other way," under penalty of five shillings.

Plymouth never had any such narrow and contemptible restrictions, but would have allowed anyone to feast, rest, or observe the day as they wished, provided they did not interfere with those who did not care to keep it.

Their administration of law was remarkably mild for the standards of their day. At the accession of James I., England made thirty-one crimes capital. Massachusetts Bay made thirteen crimes capital; the Virginia Colony had seventeen (including Unitarianism), Plymouth had only five classes of capital crime; and of these she actually punished but two.

As Senator Hoar says: "Their good sense kept them free from witchcraft delusions. No witch was ever hung there. They established trial by jury. They treated the Indians with justice and good faith. They held no foot of land not fairly obtained by honest purchase. Their tolerance was an example to Roger Williams himself. And when at last in 1692 Plymouth was blended with Massachusetts, the days of bigotry and tolerance and superstition as a controlling force in Massachusetts — were over."

These then were the contributions, well nigh unique in their day, which our forefathers made to the cause of religion:

1. They taught and practiced the separation of Church and State.

2. They claimed that not merely the clergy but the laity were an integral part of the Church and entitled to representation.

3. They laid stress upon character as the supreme requisite in true religion:

4. And they practiced with exquisite courtesy the principle of religious tolerance.

There is not one of these four tenets which is not cherished and defended today by all our Protestant Churches, — including the Protestant Episcopal Church to which I belong.

Yet for insisting upon these things, our forefathers suffered obloquy and persecution.

They were the pioneers who, through hardship and loss, blazed a path which has now become a smooth highway for all. We tread it with too little appreciation of the humble heroes to whose clear thought, unflinching courage and pious devotion we owe our rich privilege.

If they were not the kind of men whom the world applauds, there was One who called them "blessed," for they were poor in spirit; they mourned; they were meek; they hungered and thirsted after righteousness; they were merciful; they were pure in heart; they were peacemakers; they were persecuted for righteousness sake — and great is their reward in heaven.

JOSEPH[2] WARREN'S WILL AND INVENTORY.

Literally Transcribed from the Original Records,

BY GEORGE ERNEST BOWMAN.

JOSEPH[2] WARREN (*Richard*[1]) died at Plymouth and his wife Priscilla Faunce survived him eighteen years. The following records of their deaths are taken from the Plymouth Town Records, Volume I: "Joseph Warren Senior deceased May the 4th 1689" [p. 201] — "The Widow pricila Warren Deceased on ye 15 of May 1707 being Nea(r) 74 yeares of age" [p. 204]

Joseph Warren's will and inventory are found in the Plymouth County Probate Records, Volume I, pages 38 and 39.

To all People to whome these presents shall Come etc: Know Ye that I Joseph Warren Senr of the Town of Plimouth in the County of New Plimouth in new-England being weak of body through age & Sickness but of perfect and disposing memory & Sound understanding Blessed be God. Yet not knowing how soone it may please God to Change my Sickness & life to death do therefore make and ordaine and by these presents I do make & ordaine these presents to be my last will and Testament to stand good and to Remaine firm and Inviolable for ever in maner and forme following:

Impⁿ I Will and bequeath my Soul to God that gave it me and my body to the dust and to be decently Buried: and for that outward estate that God hath given to me I dispose of as followeth: Item I will and bequeath unto my dear and Loving wife Pricilla Warren all that my now dwelling house out housing uplands & meadow lands that I am now possessed of in the Township of Plimouth. Excepting such Lands as I shall hereafter dispose of to my Son Joseph, Together with all my household Goods and debts that is owing to me as also four Cows and two oxen which she shall have before a division of my Cattell be made, all which housing lands debts Goods and Chattels above expressed I do Give unto my dear and Loving wife Priscilla Warren to be at her disposing and for her Support during the time of her widowhoode; And farther I do give unto my loving wife all that my fifty acres of Land Lying at Monament ponds in the Township of Plimouth as alsoe Eight acres of upland at the Hoope place field So called for her to Rent out or sell if necescity Require. And I doe by these presents allow her so to doe as alsoe the one half of my uplands & meadow lands at Aggawam that is alredy divided together with a fourth part of the undivided lands. All which I do give unto my loving wife to be at her disposing to doe with it what she will during her life or widdowhoode for her Supporte and Comfort and in Case she should marrey then my will is that she shall have my best Bed and all furniture thereunto belonging to be her own for ever: Item I Give unto my son Joseph Warren all That my fifty acres of upland lying upon Sandwich Road in the Township of Plimouth this to have and possess after my decease as alsoe the one half of my share of land and meadow at Aggawam that is already divided and after my Wives decease my will is and I doe by these presents give unto my son Joseph Warren my now dwelling house outhousing uplands and meadow land that I have in the Township of Plimouth I do give to him and his Heires for ever That is begotten of his body. Item I give unto my son Benjamin Warren all my lands both uplands and meadow land that I have Lying both in Middlebury and Bridgwater Townships to belong to him and his heires for ever that is Begotten of his Body Item I give unto my daughter Mercy Bradford two Cowes. Item and it is my Will that after my Wives decease or marriage againe that then my whole Estate both movablles Chattels or debts or whatsoever or wheresoever it may be found shall be equally divided amongst four of my

Children that is to say Joseph Benjamin Patience and Elizabeth: And [p. 39] And lastly I do nominate and appoint my dear and loving wife Priscilla Warren to be the sole Executrix of this my last will and testament to administer on my s^d^ estate to pay Such debts as I owe and to Receive Such debts as is owing to me and to se that my body be decently buried and to defray the Charges thereof And I do Request my Brother Thomas ffaunce to be helpfull to my s^d^ Executrix in the acting and disposing of particulars according to the tenor hereof Thus hoping that this my last Will and Testament will be performed and kept Revoaking all other wills Either verball or written I have here unto set my hand and Seal on the 4th of May 1689:

Signed Sealed and declared to be his last will and Testament In presence of
Ephraim Morton sen^r^
Ephraim Morton jun^r^
Tho: ffaunce:

The Mark of Joseph Warren Senior and a (seal)

Leiu^t^ Ephraim Morton Thomas ffaunce and Ephraim Morton jun^r^ the witnesses herein named appeared before two of the Magistrates of this County of Plimouth Viz^t^ William Bradford dep^t^ Govr and John Cushing assistant & made oath that they were present and Saw the above named Joseph Warren deceased Signe seal & heard him declare this Instrument as his last will & testament and that to ye best of their judgment he was of a disposing mind & memory when he did ye same. September ye 4th 1689:

Attest Sam'l, Sprague Clerk

An Inventory of the Estate of Joseph Warren sen^r^ of Plimouth deceased Taken and apprised by us whose names are under written: on the 15th of May 1689:

Imp^ris^ His Wearing apparrell and Books:	15 08 00
Item in Silver	28 14 00
Item in Cattell 4 oxen at	11 00 00
Item in ten Cowes at	19 00 00
Item in four three year old Steeres	07 00 00
Item in two 4 year old Steeres	04 00 00
Item in two buls and one Steere	06 10 00
Item in 4 yearlings and two 2 year olde Heiffers	06 10 00
Item in other Small Cattel and horses and Swine	02 01 00
Item in Beds and Beding Suitable to them	30 00 00
Item in Table Linnen and new Cloth	08 01 06
Item in Pewter and Brass	04 03 00

Item in Iron pots kittles Hakes and hookes	01	10	00
Item in armes and Amunition	06	00	00
Item in Carpenters Tooles Sythes and Sickles	02	10	00
Item in Earthern Vessels and Glass Bottles	00	10	00
Item in an old fflock Bed three Blankets & Cushions	02	00	00
Item in Wooden Vessels & Spinning wheels	01	10	00
Item in Tables Chaires and Chests	02	00	00
[p. 40] Item in one paire of Stillyards Iron Hachell & Steel trapp	01	0	0
Item in an old Cart and wheels and Plows and Tacklen to them	03	0	0
Item in shingle and Boltes	06	10	0
Item in Hoes Spade and and Pitchforkes	00	12	0
Item in 3 Canooes & Cartrope	03	0	0
Item in Cotton and Linnen Yarne Woolen Yarn flax teere	03	0	0
Item in Cotton & sheeps wooll	02	0	0
Item in nailes and Razor and Case of ffleams and 2 Bells	01	0	0
Item in Wheel timber old Saddle Bridle and Pannell	01	14	0
Item in Old Cask and other Lumber	00	10	0
Item in debts due to the Estate	12	8	4
Item the Estate Indebted	20	0	0

Ephraim Morton Senr
Tho ffaunce

Priscilla Relict Widdow of the above named Joseph Warren deceased appeared at Plimouth September the 4th: 1689 before the Magistrates of this County of Plimouth and Made oath that the above written is a true Inventory of the Goods & Chattels of s^d^ deceased as far as she Knows and that if more appear she will Bring it to this Inventory

Attest Sam'l, Sprague Clerk

A CALKINS FAMILY RECORD.

By John Oviatt DeWolf.

While making some investigations into the DeWolf Genealogy, especially in the line of the Mayflower descent, I had occasion to trace the family of Stephen Calkins, and in doing so found an old memorandum book in the possession of my father, Austin DeWolf, now of Marion, Indiana, of such value that it seems worthy of reproduction in these pages, in the hopes that it may prove of interest to others.

The book was made by folding and sewing together four sheets of paper and has sixteen pages. The first eight pages have notes written in ink that, although somewhat faded, is still legible. The remaining pages are blank. On the first page is this title: "A Record Book January 24th 1799 Hillsdale district county of Columbia & State of New York."

There is nothing to show the authorship, and there seems to be no knowledge regarding it, except the following which I copy from a letter written me by my father: "I know but little of the old Record Book. After my grandfather's death I went carefully through the papers in his desk and found among them this old family record, which I put away among my papers, where it remained till sent to St. Louis to be photographed. It was not written by my grandfather, and I do not know in whose handwriting it is."

Its being sent to St. Louis, as referred to, was to have photographs of it taken in connection with the application for membership in the Society of Mayflower Descendants by Mr. Edwin A. DeWolf of that city, to whom I am indebted for certain information regarding my own ancestors.

The Stephen Calkins referred to married Sarah Calkins, daughter of Jonathan Calkins and Sarah Turner, who was daughter of Ezekiel Turner, the son of John Turner and Mary Brewster, the granddaughter of William Brewster of the Mayflower.

Jonathan and Sarah Calkins had a daughter, Lucy, who married Simon DeWolf of Lyme, Connecticut. Their son, Elisha DeWolf, married Lydia More, also of Lyme, and had a son, Simon, born in Lyme in 1776. Simon married Lydia Batchelder in 1803, and their son, Almon DeWolf, born at Deerfield, Massachusetts, in 1806, and married to Elvira Newton of the same place in 1832, had a son, Austin (my father) born at Deerfield, April 29, 1838, and married to Frances Ophelia Oviatt at Morris, Connecticut, on October 17, 1866.

The Edwin A. DeWolf of St. Louis, referred to, is also descended from Elisha DeWolf and Lydia More, of Lyme.

The illustration facing this page shows pages two and three, and is of the exact size of the book when open.

A literal copy of all the entries follows:

[p. 2] (Ste)phen Colkins was born Sepbr 5th 1701
Srah Colkins his wife was born July 7th, 1703 & they was marriaed January 2, 1723
Lucy their first child was born August 6, 1723
Elisabeth December 29, 1724

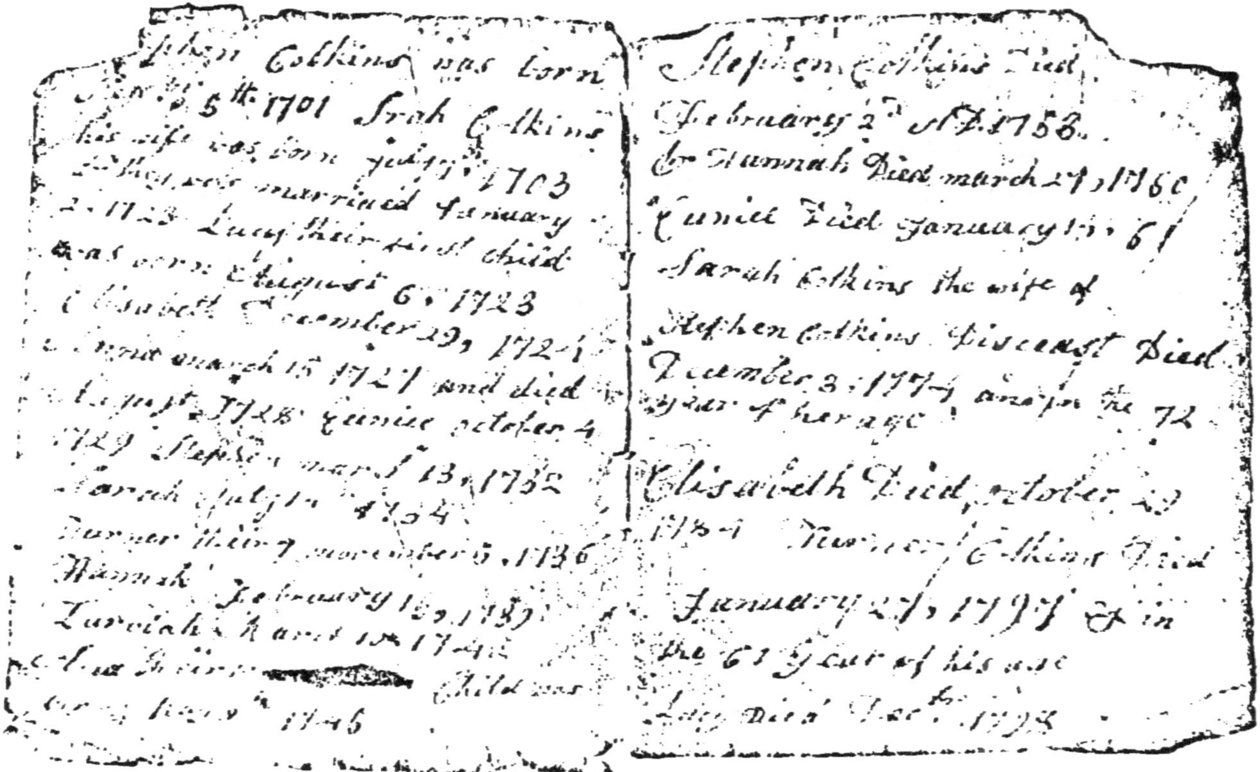
John Calkins was born
[illegible] 5th 1701 Sarah Calkins
his wife was born july [illegible] 1703
they were married January
2 1723 Lucy their first child
was born August 6 1723
Elisabeth December 29, 1724
Anne march 15 1727 and died
August 1728 Eunice october 4
1729 Stephen march 13 1732
Sarah july 1[illegible] 1734
Turner their [illegible] november 6 1736
Hannah February 1[illegible] 1737
[illegible] March 1[illegible] 1742
[illegible] Child was
born [illegible] 1746

Stephen Calkins Died
February 2d [illegible] 1758
Hannah Died march 27 1760
Eunice Died January 1[illegible] 61
Sarah Calkins the wife of
Stephen Calkins Deceast Died
December 3 1774 and in the 72
year of her age
Elisabeth Died october 29
1784 Turner Calkins Died
January 27 1797 & in
the 61 year of his age
Lucy Died Dec [illegible] 1793

A CALKINS FAMILY RECORD

Anna march 15 1727 and died August 1728
Eunice october 4 1729
Stephen march 13, 1732
Sarah July 14th 1734
Turner their 7 november 5, 1736
Hannah February 15, 1739
Zurviah March 10, 1742
Ana their 10 Child was born May 9th 1745
[p. 3] Stephen Colkins Died February 2d A D 1753.
& Hannah Died march 27, 1760
Eunice Died January 14, 61
Sarah Colkins the wife of Stephen Colkins Disceast Died December 3, 1774 and in the 72 year of her age
Elisabeth Died october 29 1784
Turner Colkins Died January 27, 1797 & in the 61 year of his age
Lucy Died Decbr, 1798
[p. 4] (Tu)rner Colkins was born November 5 1736
Mercy his wife was born may 31, 1735 and was marriaed may 21 1757
Asa their first child was born September 2, 1757
Absalom march 18, 1759
Eunice Sep 3, 1761
Matthew was born February 9, 1764
Jemima March 16, 1766
Stephen April 8, 1768
[p. 5] A Died November 12, 1768
& Sarah September 29 1769
Mercy Colkins wife of Turner Colkins Died october 6, 1771 in the 36 year of her age
[p. 6] In the year 1775 January 5th Turner Colkins was married to Phebe Cadman and She was born october 10 1753
Mercy their first child was born June 26, 1775
Stephen october 8 1776
Rebeckah July 2, 1778
Anna December 23, 1779
Hannah Sep 14, 1781
[p. 7] Daniel was born the 4 of october 1783
Elijah and Elisha the twins was born July 28, 1785
Turner July 22, 1787
Sebuary march the 2, 1789
Absalom September 2, 1790
Amos December 17, 1792
William their 13 was born march 8 1796.
[p. 8] Gallatians Chapter 4, verse 10 & Romans xiv, 5
False burdens I will cast away and follow that thats good
The example Set by thousands that gave there Lives for god
Lam 2, 14

HALIFAX, MASS., VITAL RECORDS.

(*Continued from Vol. III, page 159.*)

[Vol. I, p. 26] Published

1798. Jany. 1st. Peleg Holmes of Plympton and Eunice Woods of Halifax have been Published in Halifax as the law directs

1798 Jan^{y}: 15th Samuel Vaughan of Carver and Huldah Tomson of Halifax have been published in Halifax as the law directs

1798 June 25th Gamaliel Bolton of Raynham and Susanna Osbourn of Halifax have been Published in Halifax according to the directions of law

1798 July 23rd Joseph Bosworth and Deborah Waterman both of Halifax have been published in Halifax According to the directions of law.

[p. 214] November: 1 : 1773 Benjamin Parris of Bridgwater and Sarah Parris of Hallifax have Been Lawfully Published in Hallifax

November 15: 1773. Elisha waterman of Hallifax and Martha Benson Junr. of Bridgwater have Been Lawfully Published in Hallifax

November 15: 1773 Ezra Drew and Betty Holmes Both of Hallifax have Been Lawfully Published in Hallifax

January. 31: 1774 Rufus Barney of Taunton and Sarah Holme of Hallifax have been Lawfully Published in Hallifax

February: 14 : 1774 Isaac Tomson of Middlebrough and Lucy Sturtevant of Hallifax have been Lawfully Published in Hallifax

aprill: 4th: 1774 the Intention of marriage betwixt Giles Leach and Deborah Jackson both of Hallifax have been Lawfully Published in Hallifax

September 25th: 1774 the Intention of marriage betwixt Josiah Whitman of Bridgwater and Sarah Sturtevant Junr of Hallifax have been Lawfully Published in Hallifax

December 11th: 1774 The Intention of marriage betwixt Samuel Stafford Sturtevant and Pricilla Palmer both of Hallifax have been Lawfully Published in Hallifax

January 21st: 1775 The Intention of marriage betwixt Peleg Barrow Junr. of Plymton and Jemima Drew of Hallifax have been Lawfully Published in Hallifax

February 11th: 1775 The Intention of marriage betwixt Joshua Curtis and Phebe Waterman both of Hallifax have been Lawfully Published In Hallifax

october: 2 : 1775 : John Witherhead of Plymouth and Submit Harlow of Hallifax have been Lawfully Published in Hallifax

Nov^{r}: 20: 1775 William Waterman and Deborah Bryant Both of Hallifax Have Been Lawfully Published in Hallifax

Nov^r: 27 : 1775 the Intentions of marriage Betwixt Joseph Dunbar and Hannah Ripley Both of Hallifax have Been Lawfully Published in Hallifax

Novr 27 : 1775 the Intention of marriage Betwixt Doct^r William Batcheller of Milton and Joanna Waterman Junr of Hallifax have Been Lawfully Published in Hallifax

Dec^r: 18 : 1775 the Intentions of marriage Between David Mahuren of Easton and Ruth Dunbar of Hallifax have Been Lawfully Published in Hallifax

Decr 18 1775 the Intentions of marriage Between Benjamin Dunbar and Hannah Hathaway Both of Hallifax have Been Lawfully Published in Hallifax

January 8 : 1776 Jabez Waterman of Hallifax and Hannah Bradford of Plymton have been Lawfully Published in Hallifax

[p. 215] January 29 : 1776 the Intentions of marriage Between oliver Holmes and Lydia Tomson 3^d Both of Hallifax have Been Lawfully Published in Hallifax

January 29 : 1776 the Intentions of marriage Between Benjamin Munro of Hallifax and Abigail Munro of Hanover have Been Lawfully Published in Hallifax

February 19 : 1776 the Intentions of marriage Between Samuel Heaford of Hardwick and Bathsheba Tinkham of Hallifax have Been Lawfully Published in Hallifax

March 4 : 1776. the Intentions of marriage Between Thomas Drew and Lucy Tomson Both of Hallifax Have been Lawfully Published in Hallifax

July 29th 1776 The Intention of Marriage Between Asahel Lyon of Plimton & Fear Cushman of Hallifax have ben Lawfully Published in Hallifax

Octr 21st 1776 The Intentions of Marriage Between Ignatius Loring of Plimton and Abigail Soule of Hallifax have ben Lawfully Published in Hallifax

Novr 4th 1776 The Intentions of Marriage Between Samuel Whitman of Bridgwater and Sarah Waterman of Hallifax have Lawfully Published in Hallifax

Novr. 4th 1776 The Intentions of Marriage Between Joseph Waterman Junr of Hallifax and Lucy Josling Munro of Hanover has ben Lawfully Published in Hallifax

March 17th 1777 The Intention of Marriage Between Levi Everson of Kingston and Eunice Briggs of Hallifax has been Lawfully Published in Hallifax

March 18th 1777 The Intention of Marriage Between Doc^r Thomas Sturtevant of Middlebor^o. and Sarah Soule of Hallifax has been Lawfully Published in Hallifax

March 24th 1777 The Intention of Marriage betwen Jonathan Cortis and Moley Faxon both of Hallifax have been Lawfully Published in the Town of Hallifax

June 23: 1777 Charles Sturtevant Junr. of Rochester and Ruth Bearce of Hallifax have been Lawfully Published in Hallifax
July 14: 1777 James Faunce and Mary Cushman Both of Hallifax have Been Lawfully Published in Hallifax

(*To be continued.*)

LIEUTENANT JOHN TOMSON'S WILL AND INVENTORY AND THE AGREEMENT OF HIS HEIRS.

Literally Transcribed from the Original Records

By George Ernest Bowman.

Lieutenant John Tomson died at Middleborough 16/26 June, 1696, in the eightieth year of his age.* His wife, Mary[2] Cooke (Francis[1])†, survived him, and the agreement between the heirs regarding her share of the property is of especial interest, since it supplies the given names of the husbands of two of the daughters, Thomas Taber who married Mary Tomson, and William Read who married Esther Tomson.

The will, inventory and agreement are found in the Plymouth County Probate Records, Volume I, pages 241–245.

The spelling "Tomson" is taken from an autograph on a document which we hope to illustrate at an early date.

[p. 241] Know all men to whome these presents shall Come that I John Tomson sen^r of ye Township of Middlebury Being at this present very weak in Body through may Infirmities and diseases that are upon me but of Sound and perfect understanding & memory Do make and ordaine this to be my last will and Testament to Continue for Ever firm and Inviolable. Imprimis I Will and Bequeath unto Mary Tomson my Beloved Wife ye use of one half of my house during her Widdowhoode which half she pleaseth. And ye use of all my house hold Goods During her Widdowhoode And Six Cows and a score of Sheep And three or four Acres of land lying by my house All these to have and to use During ye time of her Widdowhoode And also my Will is that ye Executors shall se that ye said land shall be Improved for her And they shall be paid out of ye Estate And Also I will leave her one hundred pounds in money to dispose to her children as she shall se Cause but if in Case she should

* Mfr. Desc., II: 43. † Mfr. Desc., III: 105.

die Intestate my will is that this said hundred pound shall be equally divided among them all Sons and Daughters that is my own children & hers Also my will is that she shall have a Cow or a stear yearly for her provisions And if she Can not spare it out of that Stock of Cattell then it shall be provided for her out of ye Estate Also my Will is that whatsoever provisions and cloathing is left at my Decease shall belong to ye family And my wife shall have a double part of it at her disposing. And whereas I Gave unto my son John half a share of land formerly And he hath nothing to show for it I now Give it him by will and he shall have fifty Acres of land where his house standeth taking it up the whole length. Also I Give and Bequeath unto my son Jacob the House wherein he Dwelleth And ye fourth part of ye upland that is of ye two hundred Acres of upland And also I do give and Bequeath unto my sons Thomas and Peter The one half of my house wherein I do dwell during their mothers life Conditionally that they will agree to keep together and maintain their mothers stock of Cattell aforesaid And they shall have the Increase both of Cattell and sheep So that they maintain & make good ye principle And if they should Come to some extraordinary losses so that they are like to be loosers by it they shall be Considered in ye estate And my will is that there shall be meadow set apart to keep those Cattell during their mothers life. And I do Give and Bequeath unto my Son Thomas all my house and the Barn and ye orchard and ye lands Adjacent thereabout after his mothers decease that will amount to a fourth part of two hundred acres onely if my son Peter have not land enough fenced and Broaken up he shall have ye use of two or three acres of land for two years if he desire it. And also I do give and bequeath unto my son Peter That my fifty Acres of upland that I bought of John Morton And whereas I have Given to my sons John and Jacob and Thomas thre Quarters of this two hundred Acres of upland my Will is that in ye division the fourth part be left so as to be most sutably divided amongs them all four Also I Give unto my four sons aforesd A third part of land that was purchased by Captain Joseph lathrop and [p. 242] Mr Barnabas lothrop and myself. And also I Give unto my four Sons above written ye one half of that third part of upland that was purchased by Captain Church and my Self the one half of that third part next to Snipetuit pond and my one sixteene shilling purchase and that which I bought of John Irish And that Tract of land at Assawamset that I bought of ffelix ye Indian And that which I Bought of William Clarke formerly Called ye Majors purchase lying Betwixt the two paths. A fifth part of that Tract All which I Give to them to divide Equally Amongst themselves And also I Give unto my four sons aforesaid all that my two hundred Acres of upland lying Between Monponset pond and the little Herring pond with my four Acres of meadow and my two shares and half in ye Great Sedar Swamp And my two shares and half in ye undivided lands All which shall be Equally Divided Among my four sons aforesaid Also my Will is that my four sons shall Have All my Tooles of all Sorts for Carpentry or Husbandry and also all my Armes All to be Equally divided among them. Also I Give unto my Son Peter Twenty pounds in money towards ye Building of him a house besides four or five thousand foote of Boards and plank Also I do Give unto my Daughter Mary Tabor thirty and five pounds besides wt is due to me from her husband Also I do Give unto my Daughter Esther Read thirty and three pounds besides what is Due unto me from her husband likewise I do Give unto my Daughter Elizabeth Swift twenty and five pounds And also to my Grandson Thomas Swift ten pounds when he Cometh to ye age of one and twenty years And if he should dye before then it shall be forthwith paid unto his mother Also I Give unto my Daughter Sarah Tomson forty pounds Also I Give unto my Daughter Lidia Soul Thirty and four pounds Besides what she hath had already. Also I do Give unto my Daughter Mercy Tomson forty pounds likewise I do Give unto my son Jacob a yoak of steers of four years old or upwards or ye value of them. Also I Give unto my son Thomas a yoak of steers and two Cows or ye value of them Also I Give to my son Peter a yoak of steers and two Cows or ye value of them Also my will is that my four sons John and Jacob and Thomas and Peter Tomsons shall be my executors Who shall Receive what is due unto me and shall pay all my just debts And shall Se that my Body be Decently Buryed And out of my estate to defray ye charges And whatsoever is left after my and my wifes decease when all charges is cleared shall be equally divided Amongst them all my children Sons and Daughters Thus hoping that this my last will and Testament will be kept and Performed according to ye true Intent of ye same I commit my Body to ye Dust and my soul to God that Gave it me In witness whereof I Set unto my hand & Seal this Twenty third day of Aprill one thousand Six hundred ninety and six.

Witness John Tomson (seal)

Jonathan Shaw senr
Joseph King his I K mark
Anne Waterman her ∩ mark

Memorandum ye 8th day of July 1696 That Jonathan Shaw Joseph King and Anne Waterman the Witnesses hereto Subscribing made oath all of them that they were present and Saw and heard John Tomson ye Testator here named Sign Seal and declare the above Written to be his last will and Testament. And that to ye best of their judgment he was of sound disposing mind and memory when he did ye same.

Before Wm Bradford Esqr Judge.
Attest Saml Sprague Regist^{r}

[p. 243] William Bradford Esqr Commissionated &c for ye Granting of probate of Wils and letters of Administration within ye County of plimouth. To all to whome these presents shall Come or may Concern Greeting. Know ye that on the eighth day of July 1696 Before me in Duxborough the Will of John Tomson late of Middleborough deceased to these presents Annexed was Proved Approved and allowed who having while he lived and at ye time of his death Goods Chattels Rights and Credits The said deceased and his said will in any maner Concerning was Committed unto his four sons vizt John Jacob Thomas and Peter Executors in ye same will named well and truly to Administer ye same And to make a true and perfect Inventory of all & Singular the Goods Chattels Rights and Credits of ye said deceased and the same to exhibit into ye Registers office of the said County according to law Also to Render a true and Plain account of their said Administration upon oath In Testimony whereof I have here unto set my hand and ye Seal of ye said office. William Bradford
Dated at Plimouth ye 8th day of July 1696 :
Saml Sprague Regist^{r}.

Know all men by these presents that whereas our Honoured ffather John Tomson Senr of Middleborough deceased Hath made his last will and Testament Bearing date the twenty third day of Aprill one thousand six hundred ninty and Six wherein divers particulars Seemed not to be plainly expressed Wherefore to prevent future differrence we his children whose names are under written Have Joyntly agreed and Concluded to Rectifie the same as followeth that is to say That whereas in ye said will there was one hundred pounds in money Given to our loving mother onely for her to dispose among her children now we have Agreed that the same shall be hers as her own Proper Estate to use & Improve as she shall Se Cause. And whereas in said Will our said mother is to have Six Cows & a Score of sheep And that Thomas Tomson & Peter Tomson are to keep and maintain ye said stock Good for her during her widdowhood & they to have ye Increase And that she was to have a Cow or a Steer yearly for her provision We now Agree that ye said Cow or steere Shall be allowed to her yearly by the said Thomas and Peter And at her decease the abovesaid Stock is to Return to ye said Thomas and Peter And whereas there is no mention made in said Will of a horse for our said mothers own use we do now Agree that there shall be a horse allowed her out of ye estate in Generall which said Horse is to be kept and provided for by the said Thomas Tomson During her life to be for her own proper use & whereas there is Severall Tracts of meadow which did belong to our said ffather lying at Winnetuxet and no mention is made thereof in said Will we do now Agree that all ye said meadow Shall be equally divided among his four sons namely John Tomson Jacob Tomson Thomas Tomson and Peter Tomson to them and their heirs and Assigns for ever. Always provided that there shall be meadow set apart out of ye whole for ye keeping of our mothers said stock during her life. And whereas in ye said Will our father gave out the severall parcels of land which he [p. 244] was possessed of unto his four sons and no mention made of their heirs we do now agree that all ye said lands which our father dyed possessed of shall belong to ye said four sons namely John Tomson Jacob Tomson Thomas Tomson and Peter Tomson to them and their heirs and Assigns for ever And whereas in said Will It is expressed that our said mother should have ye use of three or four Acres of ye Improved land during her Widdowhood And that ye executors of said Will should Se that ye said land Should be Improved for her we do now Agree that ye said executors Shall Improve the said land for her own proper use during her naturall life And whereas we are Informed that it was our fathers mind that John Tomson Jacob Tomson and Peter Tomson should have thirty pounds in money a peece & ye same not being expressed in ye Will We do now Agree that they shall have ye same And as for what monies doth Remain after legacies are paid We do now Agree that it shall be equally divided forthwith amongst us all namely to ye four sons and ye Six daughters & their heirs or Assigns And also for what legacies are to be paid with ye Remaining part of ye Estate which by will is to be divided unto ye six daughters shall be to them and their heirs & Assigns though not so fully expressed in ye will. In Testimony whereof we whose names are under written have here unto set our hands and seals this nineteenth day of June one Thousand six hundred ninety and six.

Signed & Sealed	The mark () of	John Tomson (seal)
in yᵉ presence of us	Elizabeth Swift (seal)	Jacob Tomson (seal)
The Mark I K of	Sarah Tomson (seal)	Thomas Tomson (seal)
Joseph King	James Soul (seal)	Peter Tomson (seal)
Margaret Price	The mark TTT of	Thomas Tabor (seal)
	Marcy Tomson (seal)	William Read (seal)

Memorandum that on yᵉ first day of July 1696.

The Widdow Mary Tomson & Relict of mʳ John Tomson late of Middlebury deceased Did declare her Consent unto and acceptation of yᵉ particulars above written to her full Satisfaction In Testimony hereof yᵉ said Widdow Mary Tomson hath hereunto set her hand and seal on yᵉ day and year above mentioned.

Signed & Sealed in yᵉ presence	The II mark of yᵉ Widdow
of John Trasie	Mary Tomson (seal)
John Soul.	

Memorand yᵉ 8th day of July 1696 yᵉ within named John Tomson Jacob Tomson Thomas Tomson and Peter Tomson all of them Came personally before me yᵉ Subscriber Judge of Probate and owned and acknowledged the within written Instrument of Agreement to be their act & deed And that yᵉ same shall be good & binding to themselves and their Severall heirs for Ever

William Bradford

Memorand yᵉ same 8th day of July 1696 Joseph King one of yᵉ Witnesses to yᵉ within written Instrument appeared and made oath Before me yᵉ Subscriber Judge of Probate that he was present and saw yᵉ within Named John Tomson Jacob Tomson Thomas Tomson Peter Tomson Thomas Tabor William Read Elizabeth Swift Sarah Tomson James Soul and Mercy Tomson Every of them sign & seal the within written Instrument of Agreement as their act & deed. And yᵗ Mary yᵉ wife of Thomas Tabor and Lidia yᵉ wife of James soul were present at yᵉ doing of yᵉ same And that he said King Subscribed as a witness to said agreement and that he then saw Margaret Price yᵉ other witness Subscrib with him as a witness also

William Bradford

[p. 245] An Inventory of ye estate of Lieu^t^ John Tomson late of Middlebury deceased

Taken and Apprised by us whose names are under written on ye first of July 1696.

	£	s	d
Imp^rs^ To his wearing Apparrel and purse	.20	..	.
Item In Cash	615	12	.
Item In Books	..2	..	.
Item In Armes and Ammunition	.13	17	.
Item In Bedding one Bed in ye Parlour and furniture	..7	..	.
Item In one Bed in ye Little parlour and furniture	..6	..	.
Item In one Bed in ye kitching chamber & furniture	..6	..	.
Item In two Beds in ye Parlour Chamber and furniture	.14	..	.
Item In one pillow and pillowbeers	...	15	.
Item In sheets	..2	10	.
Item In Table Linnen	..1	.5	.
Item In pewter	..2	13	.
Item In Brass and Iron	..5	..	.
Item In Linnen and woollen yarn	..5	..	.
Item In Remnants of New Cloth and Stuff	..6	.8	.
Item In Trunks chests chairs and Little Table	..2	..	.
Item In wheeles and Cards	...	15	.
Item In sheeps wooll	..2	.7	.
Item In Wooden Vessels Cask and old Lumber	..3	..	.
Item In Provision Corne Malt and Meat	..6	..	.
Item In Meal Baggs	...	12	6
Item In Money Scales and Looking Glass	...	10	.
Item In Drest Leather	...	15	.
Item In Tobacco	..1	..	.
Item In a Compass	...	.5	.
Item In Tooles for Carpentrey and Husbandrey work	.12	11	.
Item In Boards and plank	..6	14	6
Item In Cedar Boults and Claveboard	..2	10	.
Item In Neat Cattell	.97	..	.
Item In sheep	..6	..	.
Item In Swine	..3	18	.
Item In Horse kind and furniture	.10	10	.
Item In Bees	..1	..	.
Item In ye farm on wch ye housing stands on wth all his Interest of meado on Winnatuxet River	400	..	.
Item In his two hundred Acres of land at a place Called ye herring pond wth all his Rights in ye Majors Purchasse	.50	..	.
Item In ye fifty Acres of land Bought of John Morton	.10	..	.
Item In ye land Bought of William Clarke of Duxbury deceased	..5	..	.
Item In ye land in partnership with ye Lothrops	.20	..	.

Item In his Rights in Lands purchassed by Capt Church & himself of Tuspaquin and his son at a place Called Snepetuit pond.	.40		
Item In Two Rights in ye Sixteen Shilling purchase with his Rights in Assawamset neck and lands bought of ffelix Indian in s^{d} neck & Right in lands purchassed by Henry wood	.10		
Item In Debts due to ye Estate by Bills	.46	16	.
Item In Debts due to ye Estate by Booke	.13	16	1
Item due from ye Estate for ffunerall Charges	..3	..	.
The sum totall of ye Estate is	1559	..	9
ye sum Totall of Debts due to ye estate is	..3	..	.

John Trasie John Soul Thomas ffaunce

The executors of ye last will & Testament of Lieu^{t} John Tomson above said deceased Namely John Tomson Jacob Tomson Thomas Tomson & Peter Tomson made oath July ye 8th 1696 before Wm Bradford Esqr Judge of Probate that ye above written is a true Inventory of ye goods chattells Rights & Credits of ye said deceased so far as they know & that if more shall Come to their knowledge they will discover it

Attest Saml Sprague Register

EASTHAM AND ORLEANS, MASS., VITAL RECORDS.

(*Continued from Vol. III, p. 231.*)

[Vol. I, Pt. II, p. 15] Jonnathan Bangs and Mary Mayo weare maried the 16th Day of July in the yeare 1664

Eadward Bangs the sonne of Jonnathan Bangs was borne the last Day of september in the yeare 1665

Rebeckah Bangs the Daughter of Jonnathan Bangs was borne the first Day of feburarie in the yeare 1667

Jonnathan bangs the sonne of Jonnathan Bangs was borne the last Day of aprill in the yeare 1670

Jonnathan Bangs the sonne of Jonnathan Bangs Deasessed the 11^{enth} Day of May 1670

Mary Bangs the Daughter of Jonnathan Bangs was borne the 14th of Aprill 1671

Jonathan Bangs the sonn of Jonathan Bangs Was borne the 4th day of May 1673

Hannah Bangs the daughter of Jonathan Bangs was borne the fourtenth of March 1676

Thamoson Banges the daughter of Jonathan Banges was borne in May in the yeare: 1678:

Samuel Banges the sonne of Jonathan Banges was borne the: 12th: of July in the yeare: 1680
Mercie Banges the daughter of Jonathan Banges was borne the: 7th. of Jennuarie in the yeare: 1682
Elizabeth Bangs the daughter of Jonathan Bangs was borne the 15 day of May in the year 1685
Sarah Banges the daughter of Jonnathan Banges was born in Agust in the year. 1689:
lydia Banges the daughter of Jonnathan Banges was born the Second day of october in the year. 1689:
(*worn*) Ridley and Mary Strout were Married by (Mr) Samuell Treat the third day of august Anno dom 1708
(D)aniel Hamilton and Sarah Snow were married by (Mr) Samuell Treat on the fifth day of august anno dom 1708

[p. 16] Georg godfraie the son of georg godfraie was borne the 2d of Jenuarie in the yeare: 1662
Samuel godfraie the son of george godfraie was borne the 27th of Jenuarie 1664
Moses godfraie the son of george godfraie was borne the 27th of Jenuar(y) 1667
Hannah godfraie the daughte of george godfraie was borne the 25th of aprill. 1669:
Mary godfraie the daughter of george godfraie was borne the 2nd of June in the year. 1672
Ruth godfraie the daughte of georg godfraie was borne the first day of Jenuarie: 1675
Richard godfraie the son of george godfraie was borne the 11th of June: 1677
Jonnathan godfray the son of george godfray was borne the 24th of June: 1682
Elizabeth godfrie the daughter of georg godfrie was borne the tenth day of September: 1688
Sarah Mayo the daughter of James and Sarah mayo was Born at Eastham the fourteent(h) day of Januarie 1702/3
Henry Mayo the son of James and Sarah ma(yo) was Born at Eastham the 3d day of may 1705
John Mayo the son of James and Sarah Mayo (was) Born at Eastham the fourteenth day of october 1707

[p. 17] Thomas Crosby the sonne of Mr Thomas Crosby was borne the seventh day of Aprill in the year. 1663
Simon Crosbe the sonne of Mr Thomas Crosbe was borne the 5th Day of July in the yeare 1665
Sarah Crosbe the Daughter of Mr Thomas Crosbe was borne the 24th of March in the yeare 1667
Joseph Crosbe the sonne of Mr Thomas Crosbe was borne the 27th of Jennuarie in the yeare 1668

Mr Thomas Crosbe two sonns borne at a bearth named John borne the 4th Day of December in the yeare 1670

John Crosbe the sonne of Mr Thomas Crosbe Deseased which was one of the children borne at a beirth: buried the 11^{enth} Day of feburarie 1670

William Crosby the sonne of Mr Thomas Crosby was borne in march in the year. 1673

Ebenezer Crosby the sonne of Mr Thomas Crosby was borne the twenty eight day of March in the year. 1675:

anne and mercy Crosby the daughters of Mr Thomas Crosby and a sonne that died named Increase all three at a bearth borne aprill the fourtenth an fiftenth in the year. 1678:

Eliezer Crosby the sonne of Mr Thomas Crosby was borne the one and thirtieth of March in the year: 1680:

Samuell Baker and Patience Berrie were married by Nathaniel ffreeman Esqu^{r} the Eleventh day of Januarie 1709/10

Ebenezer Severence and (*) Tomlin were married by Nathan^{ll} ffreeman Esqu^{r} febuary ye 14th 1709/10

Samuell Robins and Desire chase were married by Joseph Doane Esqu^{er} on ye 18th day of June anno Dom 1713

[p. 18] Thomas paine junior and hannah shaw wear maried the: 5: of august: 1678

hannah paine the daughter of Thomas paine was borne the: 6: of aprill: 1679

hugh paine the sonn of Tho: paine: jun: was borne the: 5th: day of July: 1680

hannah paine the daughter of Tho: paine jun: died the: 17th: of November: 1681

hugh paine the sonne of Tho: paine jun: died the: 29th: of November: 1681

Thomas paine the sonne of Tho: paine jun: was borne the: 28th: day of feburarie in the yeare: 1681/2

Thomas paine junior another daughter Named Hannah: borne the: 12th: day of May: 1684

Jonathan Paine the Sone of Thomas and Hannah Paine Jun was borne the first Day of febuary: 1685: 86

Abygaile Paine the Daughter of Thomas and Hannah Paine was borne the fourth day of march: 1687: 88 ad Shee dyed the twenty fist day of January: 1688: 9

Thomas Paine had another daughter named Abygaile borne: the tenth day of november: 1689

Phebee Paine the daughter of Tho: and Hannah Paine was borne the fourtheenth day of march: 1690: 91

Elkenah Paine the son of Thomas and Hannah Paine was borne: the first Day of febuary: 1692: 93

* The given name was omitted.

Moses Paine the Son of Thomas and Hannah Paine was Borne the twenty eighth day of September In the yeare 1695

Phebe Paine the Daughter of Thomas and Hannah Paine Dyed the 21 day of January: $169\frac{5}{6}$

Joshua Paine the Son of Thomas and Hannah Paine was Borne the twenty eighth day of august: in the year: 1697

Thomas and Hannah Paine had another daughter named Phebe borne: the eleaventh day of (*) in the year: $169\frac{8}{9}$

Lidia Paine the Daughter of Thomas and Hannah Paine was borne at Eastham the fourth day of december in the year 1700

Barnabas Paine the son of Thomas and Hannah Paine was Born y[e] 13th day of November anno 1705

[p. 19] Joshua Bangs and Hannah skuder weare Maried the first Day of December in the yeare 1669

The Children of Jabez snow recorded

Jabez snow a son Named Jabez: borne the: 6th day of september in the yeare 1670

Jabez snow a son Named Edward borne the: 26th: of March: 1672:

Jabez Snow a daughter Named Sarah borne the: 26th: of feburarie: 1673

Jabez Snow a daughter Named grace borne the first day of feburarie: 1675

Thomas Snow the son of Jabiz Snow dyed the secund day of april in the year 1697

Liu[t]: Jabiz Snow dyed the seaven and twentieth day of december: in the year 1690:

Samuell Treat Ju[r] and Joanna Vickery were married by m[r] Sam[ll] Treat the twenty-seventh day of october Ann(o) Dom 1708

Richard Stevens and Abigaile Treat were married m[r] Samuel Treat the twenty-seventh day of october Anno dom 1708

William Dyer and Hannah Strout were Married by m[r] Sam[ll] Treat the fifteenth day of aprill Anno dom 1709

Thomas Smith Jun[r] and Joanna Mayo were married by m[r] Sam[ll] Treat November y[e] 3[d] Anno dom 1709

[p. 20] Nathaniel Mayo and Elizabeth Wixam wear maried the 28th of Jenuarie 1678

Nathaniel mayo the son of nathaniel mayo was borne the 7th of July: 1681:

Bathsuah mayo the daughter of Nathanell mayo was borne the 23th of September: 1683

Nathanel Mayo a daughter borne named alis the. 29: day of aprill in the year: 1686

Nathanel Mayo a sonne borne Named Ebenezer the: 13th: of July in the year: 1689

* This appears to be "february" altered to January, but may be the reverse.

Nathanel Mayo a daughter Named Hannah borne the sixtenth day of June in the year 1692

Elisha mayo the son of Nathanel and Elizebeth mayo was Borne the twenty eight day of april In the year 1695

Robert Mayo the Son of Nathanael and Elizebeth Mayo was borne the three and twentieth day of march : $169\frac{7}{8}$

Nathanael Mayo Senr and Mercy young were Married by Nathanal ffreeman Esqu^r the tenth day of June anno dom 1708

Elisabeth Mayo the wife of Nathanael Mayo dyed in december 1799 *

Bathshebe Mayo the wife of Thomas ffreeman and Daughter of Nathanael Mayo dyed the ninth day of January 1706

Robert Young and Joanna Hix were Marryed the twenty secund day of march In the year 1693 : 4

Robert Young the son of Robert Young was borne the Eleventh day of april in the year 1695 and dyed the 23rd of June following

Robert and Joanna Young had another Son named Robert borne the eleventh day of December in the yeare 1696

Lidia Young the Daughter of Robert and Joanna Young was Borne at Eastham the nine and twentyeth day of May : 1699 :

Joannah Young the daughter of Robert and Joannah Young was Born at Eastham the first day of June in the year 1703

Jennet Young the daughter of Robert and Joannah Young was Born at Eastham the twenty second Day of may 1708

Robert Mayo the son of Nathanael Mayo dyed on the 26th day of July 1707

Ebenezer Mayo the son of Nathanael Mayo dyed on ye ninth day of November 1709

Nathanael Mayo Senr dyed on ye 30th day of November : 1709

[p. 21] John Smith and Hannah Williams weare Maried the 24th of May in the yeare 1667

Elizabeth Smith the Daughter of John Smith was Borne the 24th of feburarie in the yeare 1668

John Smith a daughter borne named Sarah the 27th day of March in the yeare 1671 ales 1672

William Nicherson and Mary Snow wear Maried the 22th of Jenuary : 1690

William Nicherson a daughter borne March the 17th : $16\frac{90}{91}$ Named Mercy

Nicholas Nicherson the son of William Nicherson was born the Nintenth day of March in the year : $169\frac{4}{5}$:

Thankfull Paine the daughter of Nicholas and Hannah Paine was borne at Eastham : the fourteenth day of march in (the) year one thousand six hundred ninety n(ine) alias seven hundred : 1699/700

Prisilla Paine the daughter of Nicholas and Hannah Pain(e) was born the sixteenth day of october Anno 1701

* This is plainly a mistake for 1699.

Phillip Paine the son of Nicholas and Hannah Paine was born at Eastham on ye eighteenth day of November: 1704

Lois Paine the daughter of Nicholas and Hannah Paine was Born at Eastham the twentyninth day of September Anno Dom 1705

Abigaile Paine the Daughter of Nicholas and Hannah Paine was Born at Eastham august ye 3^{d} 1707

Hannah Paine the Daughter of Nicholas and Hannah Paine was Born at Eastham the twenty fourth day of September Anno 1709

Philip Paine the ſon of Nicholas and Hannah Paine dyed on the tenth day of april anno dom 1725

Mrs Hannah Paine wife of Mr Nicholas Paine Died the 24 day of January 1731/2

[p. 22] Steven Twinning and Abigael younge weare Maried the: 3^{d}: day of Jenuarie in the yeare of our lord: 1683:

Steven Twining a sonne Named Steven borne the: 30th: of december in the year 1684

Eliazer Twining the sonne of Steven Twinning was borne the: 26 of November 1686

Nathanel Twining the sonne of Steven Twining was borne the 27th day of March 1689

Steven Twining a daughter Named Mercy borne the eight day of September in the year: 1690

John Twining the sonne of Steven Twinning was borne the fifth day of March: 169$\frac{2}{3}$

Sarah Rich the daughter of Richard and Anne Rich was born in Eastham January the 22^{d} 1695/6

Richard Rich the Son of Richard and Anne Rich was Born in Eastham febuary the 28th 1698/9

Rebeckah Rich the daughter of Richard and Anne Rich was Born at Eastham June the 15th 1701

Zaccheus Rich the son of Richard and Ann Rich was Born at Eastham the 2nd day of april Anno domini 1704

Obadia Rich the son of Richard and Anne Rich was Born at Eastham the fifteenth day of July: 1707

Priscilla Rich the Daughter of Richard and Anne Rich was Born at Eastham febuary ye 5th 1709/10

Huldah Rich the Daughter of Richard and anne Rich was Born at Eastham in the month of July anno Domini: 1712

Joseph Rich the son of Richard and Anne Rich was Born at Eastham on the fifth day of october anno domini: 1715:

Prissilla Rich the Daughter of Richard and Anne Rich Dyed in the beginning of July anno domini 1716

Silvanus Rich the son of Richard and anna Rich was Born at Eastham on ye fourth day of september ano dom 1720

(*To be continued.*)

PLYMOUTH COLONY DEEDS.

(*Continued from Vol. III, p. 228.*)

[Vol. II, Pt. I, p. 81]

1653 Bradford Govr

The 20th of October 1653

Memorand: That Captaine Thomas Willett of the Towne of Plymouth in the Jurisediction of New Plymouth in New England in america and Mr Willam Paddy of the Towne of Boston in the Jurisdiction of the Massachusetts marchant Doe both acknowlidg that for and in consideration of the summe of seaventy and five pounds to them in hand paied by Mr Thomas Cushman of the Towne of Plymouth in the Jurisdiction of Plymouth aforsaid yeoman wherwith they Doe acknowlidge themselves satisfyed contented and fully paied and therof and of every prte and prcell therof Doe acquite and Discharge the said Thomas Cushman hee his heires executors adminnestrators and assignes for ever by these p^{r}sents They have freely and absolutly barganed allianated and sould enfeofed and confeirmed and by these p^{r}sents Doe bargaine sell enfeofe and confeirme from them the said capt: Willett and Willam Paddy and theire heires to him the said Thomas Cushman and his heires and assignes forever All that theire house and land lying and being Scittuate att Joanses River in the Towneshipp of Plymouth aforsaid which they the said capt: Willett and Willam Paddy bought of Mr Edmond ffreeman of Sandwidge as appeers in the court records; which was formerly the house and land of Mr Thomas Prence somtimes of Plymouth aforsaid; and Originally was the house and land of Mr Isaak Allerton; being bounded with the lands of Mis ffuller on the one side and of Clement Briggs and Christopher Winter on the other side; the nether end abutting upon the river aforsaid and soe extending itselfe in the length up into the woods with all the meddow land either mersh or upland adioyneing and belonging therunto with all the outhouses barnes stables fences and all other appurtenances belonging therunto with all the additions and enlargements either of upland or meddow nearer hand or further of att any time added graunted or any way appertaining unto the said house and land with all the said capt: Willett and Willam Paddy their right title and enterest of and into the said p^{r}mises or any prte or prcell therof: To have and to hould The said house and land soe bounded as aforsaid with all the outhouses barnes stables meddowes orchyards enlargments and additions both of upland and meddow nearer hand or further of with all and singulare the privilidges apurtenances and emunities belonging unto the said p^r^mises or any prte or prcell therof unto the said Thomas Cushman his heires and assignes forever; The said p^r^mises with all and singulare the appurtenances therunto belonging to appertaine and belonge unto the onely proper use and behoofe of him the said Thomas Cushman his heires and assignes forever;

The Day and year abovewritten m^is^ Mary Willett the wife of the said capt: Willet gave her free and full consent unto the sale of the house and lands and theire severall appurtenances abovewritten;

[p. 83] 1653 Bradford Govr

The 20th of October 1653

Memorand: That Mr Thomas Cushman of the Towne of Plymouth in the Jurisdiction of New Plymouth in New Eengland in america yeoman Doth acknowlidge that ffor and in consideration of the summe of seaventy and seaven pounds to him in hand paied by capt: Thomas Willett of the Towne of Plymouth in the Jurisdiction of Plymouth and Mr Willam Paddy of the Towne of Boston in the Jurisdiction of the Massachusetts marchant wherwith hee Doth acknowlidge himselfe satisfyed contented and fully paied and therof and of every prte and prcell therof Doeth acquite and Discharg the said capt: Willett and Mr Paddy them theire heires exequitors adminnestrators and assignes forever by these p^r^sents; hee hath freely and absolutly barganed allianated and sould enfeofed and confeirmed and pr these p^r^sents Doth bargaine sell enfeofe and confeirme from him the said Thomas Cushman and his heires to them the said captaine Willett and Willam Paddy them and theire and every of theire heires and assignes forever All that his prte portion or share of land both upland and meddow belonging unto him as purchaser lying and being att Sowamsett Secunke and place or places adiacent together with all and singulare the appurtenances privilidges and emunities therunto belonging with all the said Thomas Cushman his right title and enterest of and into the said p^r^mises or any prte or prcell therof, To have and to hold the said whole prte portion purchase or share of land both upland and meddow; Together with all and singulare the Timbers woods underwoods swamps and all other privilidges & appurtenances and emunities, in upon or any way, belonging unto the said whole prte or share of upland and meddow or any prte or prcell therof unto the said captaine Willett and Willam Paddy theire heires and assignes forever; The said p^r^mises with all and singulare the privilidges and appurtenances belonging therunto; To appertaine unto the onely proper use and behoofe of them the said capt: Willett and Willam Paddy theire and every of theire heires and assignes forever;

The Day and yeare abovewritten m^is^ Mary Cushman the wife of the said m^r^ Thomas Cushman gave her free and full consent unto the sale of the land abovewritten with all and singulare the appurtenances belonging therunto;

(*To be continued.*)

ELDER THOMAS CUSHMAN'S WILL AND INVENTORY, AND THE RECORDS OF HIS DEATH.

Literally Transcribed from the Original Records,

BY GEORGE ERNEST BOWMAN.

ELDER THOMAS CUSHMAN died at Plymouth on 10/20 or 11/21 December, 1691. The town records give the earlier date. This is also given on his gravestone, which was erected by the church about twenty-four years after his death. I have been unable to determine which date is correct. His will and inventory are found in the Plymouth County Probate Records, Volume I, pages 129–132.

Thomas Cushman's widow, Mary (Allerton) Cushman, daughter of Isaac and Mary (Norris) Allerton, was the last female passenger to die, and the record of her death is here printed in full.

---

on the 10th day of december 1691 That precious and Eminant servant of god deceased The Elder Thomas Cushman being Entered into the 84 yeare of his age [Plym. T. R., I: 202]

The Aged Widow Mary Cushman deceassed November The 28th day 1699. [Plym. T. R., I: 203]

It pleased God to seize upon our good Elder, Mr Thomas Cushman by sicknesse & in this yeare to take him from us, He was chosen & ordained Elder of this chh, April, 6: 1649: he was neere 43 yeares in his office, his sicknesse lasted about 11 weekes; he had bin a rich blessing to this chh scores of yeares. he was grave,' sober, holy & temperate very studious & sollicitous for the peace & prosperity of the chh & to prevent & heale all breaches; He dyed, December, 11: neere the end of the 84th yeare of his life; December, 16: was kept as a day of Humiliation for his death, the Pastor prayed & preached, Mr Arnold & the Pastors 2 sons asisted in prayer; much of Gods prescence went away from this chh when this blessed Pillar was removed. [Plym. Ch. Rcds., I: II: 17, under year 1691]

Elder Thomas Cushman dyed, December, 11: having within two moneths finished the 84th yeare of his life; He was ordained Ruling Elder of this church, April, 6: 1649: he was neere 43 yeares in his office. [Plym. Ch. Rcds., I: V: 22]

[Plymouth County Probate Records, I: 129–132]
[p. 129] To all People to whome these presents shall Come etc. Know ye that I Thomas Cushman senr of the Town of Plimouth in New England being through Gods mercy and Goodness unto me at this present in some measure of Good health of Body and of sound understanding and strength of memory yet considering my frailty and uncertainty of my abiding in this vale of tears Do make this to be my last will and Testament And by these presents I do make this to be my last will and Testament to Remain firme and Inviolable for ever as followeth. Imprimis I Give and bequeath my Soul to God that Gave it and my Body to ye dust & to be decently Buried in hopes of ye Grace of God through Jesus Christ to Enter into a joyfull Resurrection — And for my outward Estate I dispose of as followeth vizt I will and bequeath unto my Dear and loving wife Mary Cushman All my house and housing together with all my uplands and meadow lands I am now possessed of in the Township of New Plimouth to be for her use and support during ye time of her naturall life Excepting such parcels as I do in this my will Give to my children: Item I Give unto my Son Thomas Cushman two twenty acre lots lying upon the Southerly side of mr Joseph Bradfords land as also ye enlargements at ye head of those lots And also twenty acres of upland more or less lying upon the Easterly Side of Jones River by the Bridge with a skirt of meadow lying by said River And also one third of my meadow

at Winnatuxet And also a parcell of salt marsh meadow from our spring unto a Creek westerly of a salt hole and so down to ye River which said parcel of meadow is to be his after our decease. All ye abovesaid Parcels of upland and meadows I do by these presents Give and Bequeath unto my son Tho: Cushman to him and his heirs for Ever. Item I Give unto my son Isaac Cushman one twenty acre lot with ye addition at ye head lying on the northerly side of Samuel ffullers land in ye Township of Plimouth and also the one half of my land lying at Namasket Pond in ye Township of Middleborough as Also ye one half of my Right in the Sixteen shilling Purchase so Called in the Township abovesaid and also one third part of my meadow at Winnatuxet in Plimouth All which parcels of uplands and meadows last above expressed I do by these presents Give & bequeath unto my Son Isaac Cushman and to him & his heirs for ever together with all the priviledges thereunto belonging. Item I do Give unto my son Elkanah Cushman one twenty acre lot with the addition at the head lying on the Northerly side of ye land I now Improve But in Case my Son Thomas's now dwelling house be upon part of this lot my will is my Son Thomas Enjoy ye land his house now Standeth on without molestation. As also I Give to my Son Elkanah Cushman the one half of my land lying at Namasket Pond as also ye one half of the Sixteen shilling Purchase above Expressed as also one third of my meadow at Winnatuxet All the abovesaid Parcels of lands and meadows last above Expressed with all the priveledges thereunto belonging I do by these presents Give unto my Son Elkanah Cushman and to his heires for Ever Item I do Give unto my Son Eleazer Cushman The Rest of my lands both uplands and meadow lands not above disposed of in Plimouth and duxborough as also my now dwelling house and outhousing which house and lands I do by these [p. 130] Presents Give and bequeath unto my Son Eleazer Cushman to him and his heires for ever to enjoy after I and my wife are deceased And my will is that my four Sons Thomas Isaac Elkanah & Eleazer Shall Each of them allow twenty shillings to their Sisters that is to say Sarah Hoaks and Lidiah Harlow As also my will is that if any of my Sons Se cause to make sale of their land I have Given them in Plimouth that they do let their Brothers that do Reside in Plimouth have the said lands as they shall be valued by Indifferent men as also my will is and I do by these presents Give and bequeath unto my three Grandchildren in Lin the Children of my daughter Mary Hutchinson deceased to each of them twenty shillings to be paid unto them out of my Estate

Soone after my decease And I do Constitute and appoint my Dear and loving wife Mary Cushman to be the sole Executrix of this my last will and Testament my debts legacies and funerall charges being first paid my will is that what ever other Estate is found of mine in Goods Chattels or debts Either in Plimouth or Else where shall be for ye support of my wife During her naturall life And my will is that what Remains of my sd estate at my wifes decease the one half I do Give to my Son Eliaz Cushman and the other half unto my two daughters to Sarah Hoaks and Lidiah Harlow to be equally divided between them And my will is And I do by these presents appoint my two sons Thomas Cushman & Isaac Cushman and Thomas ffaunce to be ye Supervisors of this my last will and Testament much confiding in their love and faithfullness to be helpfull to my Sd Executrix in the acting and disposing of Particulars according to the tenour thereof thus hoping that this my last will and Testament will be performed and Kept Revoaking all other wills either written or verball I have in Witness thereof Set to my hand and Seal on the 22^d of October 1690

Signed Sealed and declared	Thomas Cushman sen^r
to be his last will and	and a (seal)
Testament In presence	
of us Witnesses	

James Warren
Thomas ffaunce.

James Warren and Thomas ffaunce the witnesses here named made oath before the County Court at Plimouth March y^e 16th: $169\frac{1}{2}$ that they were present and saw the above named m^r Thomas Cushman Signe and Seal and heard him declare the above written to be his last will and Testament And that to y^e best of their judgment he was of sound mind and memory when he so did.

Attest Saml Sprague Clerk

[p. 131] An addition to y^e last will of Thomas Cushman sen^r which is as followeth Whereas in my last will which was in sixteene hundred & ninety That I then left out a certain peece of land undisposed of which was one hundred acres of land lying in the Township of Plimouth upon a Brooke comonly called Colchester Brooke on both sides of ye Sd Brooke which I Reserved to sell for my Support or my wifes after my decease My will is therefore That my Son Thomas Cushman and my Son Isaac Cushman shall have the abovesd hundred acres of land to be divided equally between them to them and their heires and Assigns for ever Provided that they equally shall pay or cause to be paid ten pounds in currant Silver money to me abovesaid Thomas Cushman sen^{r} or my wife Mary Cushman after my decease or after decease to be paid equally to my to daughters Sarah Hauks and Lidia Harlow Also I the abovesaid Thomas Cushman do will and bequeath to my four sons Thomas Cushman and Isaac Cushman and Elkanah Cushman and Eleazer Cushman all my Books equally to be divided among them onely two small Books to my Daughter Lidiah Harlow And my best Bible to my loving wife Mary Cushman likewise also I do Give and bequeath unto my Son Elkanah Cushman one acre of meadow which was Granted unto me lying at Doteis meadows.

This Addition is to the last will of me Elder Thomas Cushman of Plimouth being now in perfect understanding: Aprill: 1: 1691

Signed Sealed and delivered in presence of us witnesses
Jonathan Shaw sen^{r}
Persis Shaw
her P mark

Thomas Cushman sen^{r} (seal)

Jonathan Shaw one of y^{e} witnesses here named made oath before y^{e} County Court at Plimouth March 16th $169\frac{1}{2}$ that he was Present and saw Elder Thomas Cushman above named Signe seal & heard him declare the above written Codicil to be his will. and an addition to his former will And that he y^{e} Sd Shaw Subscribed to it as a witness and that he saw Persis his Wife Subscribe with him as a witness alsoe.

Attest Saml Sprague Clerk

March 16th $169\frac{1}{2}$ Mrs Mary Cushman Relict widdow of Elder Thomas Cushman late of Plimouth deceased Coming personally before y^{e} County Court then held at Plimouth did freely acknowledge y^{t} she hath Received fifty two shillings and Six pence of Isaac Cushman her Son in part of y^{e} five pounds which y^{e} Sd Isaac is to pay for his part of ye 100 acres of land at Colchester abovesaid:

Attest Saml Sprague Clerk:

Memorandum that
Persis Shaw ye other witness made oath Before Wm Bradford Esqr Judge of Probate that She also was present and saw and

heard ye within named Elder Cushman Sign Seal & declare this within written Codicill as an Addition to his Will And that he was of Sound mind and memory when he did ye Same to the best of her judgment.

Sep^t^ 25th 1701. Attest Saml Sprague Register

[p. 132] An Inventory of the Estate of Mr Thomas Cushman Senr late of Plimouth deceased taken and apprized by us whose names are here unto Subscribed on ye 17th day of Decemb^r^ 1691:

	£	s	d
Imprimis his wearing Apparell both linnen and woollen	04	02	00
Item in Books at	04	00	00
Item in Cash	01	02	00
Item in two Beds and Bedding to them	10	00	00
Item in Pewter and Brass	02	15	00
Item in Iron pots & Kettles hakes & other jron vessels	01	12	00
Item in Tables and Chests and chaires	01	16	00
Item In Cotton & Sheeps wooll & linnen yarn & flax	01	03	00
Item in Saddle Bridle and Pillion	01	05	00
Item in Linnen wheel and old lumber	00	15	00
Item in Iron wedges and Glass Bottels	00	05	00
Item in Cart tacklen	00	10	00
Item in Indian and English Corne	04	01	00
Item in Neat Cattell	13	10	00
Item in sheep	01	00	00
Item in Swine	00	18	00
Item in a Loome	01	05	00
Item in Debts due from ye Estate	00	08	00

Thomas Cushman
Isaac Cushman
Thomas ffaunce.

Mrs Mary Cushman Relict widdow of Elder Thomas Cushman late of Plimouth deceased Made oath before ye County Court at Plimouth March 16th 169½ that ye above written is a true Inventory of the Goods and Chattels of her Sd late husband So far as she yet Knoweth and that if more shall be discovered to her she will make it Known.

Attest Saml Sprague Clericus

SIXTH ANNUAL REPORT OF GEORGE ERNEST BOWMAN, SECRETARY OF THE SOCIETY OF MAYFLOWER DESCENDANTS IN THE COMMONWEALTH OF MASSACHUSETTS.

READ AT THE SIXTH ANNUAL MEETING, AT BOSTON, MASS., 21 NOVEMBER, 1901, AND PRINTED BY ORDER OF THE SOCIETY.

IN presenting my sixth annual report as Secretary of the Society of Mayflower Descendants in the Commonwealth of Massachusetts, I have thought that a brief review of the Society's work since it was organized would be of interest and value, showing what important results can be obtained by doing thoroughly systematic work in accordance with a carefully developed plan. We can say without fear of contradiction that the work which this Massachusetts Society of Mayflower Descendants has begun is not only the most ambitious, but the most important genealogical work ever attempted.

Before describing the special work which we have undertaken in connection with the publication of The Mayflower Descendant and the compilation of The Mayflower Genealogies, I will briefly outline the general history of the Society.

On Saturday afternoon, 28 March, 1896, sixteen of the thirty ladies and gentlemen whose signatures to the articles of association I had secured met at the Hotel Vendome in this city and organized a Society of Mayflower Descendants. We were able to fill every one of the fifteen offices, something which no other State Society has been able to do at the date of its organization.

Our Membership Committee has approved seven hundred and sixty-nine preliminary applications, and at a meeting of the Board of Assistants held this afternoon our six hundred and ninety-third member was elected. There have been twenty-five deaths, twenty-seven resignations (the greater number resigning because they had become charter members of new State Societies), and four members have been dropped from the roll (one because his line of descent was found to be incorrect, three for non-payment of annual dues). Our present membership is, therefore, six hundred and thirty-seven, distributed as follows: in Massachusetts, 457; New York, 33; Maine, 21; Rhode Island, 15; Iowa, 12; Michigan, 11; Ohio, 11; California, 9; Wisconsin, 8; Illinois, 7; New Hampshire, 7; Pennsylvania,

7; Connecticut, 5; Colorado, 4; Minnesota, 4; Maryland, 3; New Jersey, 3; District of Columbia, 2; Kentucky, 2; Missouri, 2; Vermont, 2; Florida, 1; Indiana, 1; North Carolina, 1; Oregon, 1; Texas, 1; Virginia, 1; Hawaii, 1; British Columbia, 1; Nova Scotia, 1; Russia, 1; Switzerland, 2.

We have elected eleven members who were over ninety years of age. Four of them still survive, Mrs. Nathaniel B. Hall of Hyannis, Mass., aged ninety-six years, two months, twenty-two days; Mrs. Isaac Curtis of Lynn, Mass., aged ninety-two years, three months, ten days; Mr. Joshua Delano of Kingston, Mass., aged ninety-one years, five months, fifteen days; Mr. Daniel Cushman of Kingston, Mass., aged ninety-one years, three months, eleven days.

Mrs. Mary Russell (Winslow) Bradford of Cambridge, Mass., sixth in descent from James Chilton and fifth in descent from Mary (Chilton) Winslow, was born 9 June, 1793, was elected on her one hundred and fifth birthday, 9 June, 1898, and deceased 27 August, 1899, at the age of one hundred and six years, two months and eighteen days.

Mr. Joseph Davis Jones of Boston, seventh in descent from John Howland, was born 31 December, 1797, was elected 29 August, 1898, and passed away 12 January, 1899, aged one hundred and one years and twelve days.

The most interesting case of longevity on our records is that of Mrs. Nathaniel B. Hall and her twin sister Mrs. James Smith, of Barnstable, seventh in descent from John Howland. They were born 30 August, 1805, signed their pedigree papers on their ninety-third birthday, 30 August, 1898, and were elected three days later. Mrs. Smith died 24 March, 1899, aged ninety-three years, six months and twenty-five days. Mrs. Hall, as before stated, is now living at Hyannis.

The ages at death of the other four were as follows: Mr. David Thomas, ninety-three years, eleven months, six days; Mr. Freeman Foster, ninety-three years, nine months, twenty-six days; Mrs. Thomas E. Keely, ninety-three years, one month, fifteen days; Miss Zeruah Soule, ninety-two years, four months, sixteen days.

From the earliest days of the Society your Secretary has urged the members who are descended from more than one Mayflower ancestor to file supplemental papers showing such descent. No fee is required when supplemental lines of descent are filed, as it is the policy of this Society to encourage in every possible way search for Mayflower lines.

Every line of descent accepted by this Society, whether

original or supplemental, is recorded in The Mayflower Descendant, and those who have supplemental claims not yet filed are again requested to present them as early as possible.

The 693 members elected have filed 1547 different lines of descent. Mr. Frederick Alonzo Turner, Jr. is descended from twenty-two Mayflower passengers. Mrs. Alonzo B. Bray has twenty different lines of Mayflower descent. She has eight different lines from Governor Bradford. Mr. Edwin S. Crandon has proved descent from ten different Mayflower families.

The first column of figures in the following table shows the number of members of the Massachusetts Society descended from each Mayflower passenger. The second column shows the number of different lines of descent from each passenger already filed by our members. Every passenger from whom descent can be proved is represented in the Massachusetts Society.

John Alden	181	230	Dr. Samuel Fuller	23	23
Isaac Allerton	45	45	Stephen Hopkins	81	94
John Billington	14	17	John Howland	133	179
William Bradford	81	93	Degory Priest	18	21
William Brewster	172	217	Thomas Rogers	33	37
Peter Brown	23	27	Henry Samson	13	13
James Chilton	52	57	George Soule	40	42
Francis Cooke	89	111	Myles Standish	35	37
Edward Doty	22	24	Richard Warren	158	208
Francis Eaton	31	31	William White	9	11
Edward Fuller	25	25	Edward Winslow	5	5

The Society has held twenty-six meetings, including excursions to Plymouth, Duxbury, Kingston and Squantum. It also gave a dinner at the Samoset House at Plymouth, to the delegates and their friends who attended the first General Congress in 1897, and a reception at the same place to those present at the extra session held in 1898.

On 19 October, 1896, when the Society was less than seven months old, and had but eighty-four members, the office No. 623 Tremont Building, Boston, was leased for the Society's headquarters. If our work continues to expand as rapidly as it has done in the past we shall very soon need more room.

Soon after the organization of the Society your Secretary called attention to the importance of collecting a library, which should eventually include everything in print relating to the Pilgrims and their descendants and to the towns comprising the "Old Colony," also original documents and relics. He at the same time began to solicit donations for this purpose. As a result we now own 579 bound volumes and pamphlets, of which 161 are gifts; 177 old documents, such as deeds, inventories, bills of sale, letters etc., of which 150 are gifts; 142 photographs, of which 69 are gifts; a high chest of drawers about 150 years old, our first legacy; 4 framed engravings and photographs, all gifts; and other miscellaneous articles.

In addition to the property just mentioned it was my good fortune to secure the deposit, in March, 1897, of the Brewster Book * and, later, of the Fitch Diary † with the Society, for preservation and publication. The Brewster Book has been repaired at the expense of the Society and can now be handled without danger of farther damage.

In June, 1897, a prize of fifty dollars was offered for a design for a book-plate, and in January, 1898, this was awarded to Mr. Charles E. Heil of Boston.

Many of our books need rebinding, and the pamphlets should be bound at once or they will wear out rapidly. A card catalogue of the library and cabinet is also greatly needed, and we especially need funds available at short notice for the purchase of rare volumes which are seldom offered for sale.

There are many books and pamphlets which we should own, and which can be purchased at prices ranging from fifty cents upward. Your Secretary will be pleased to give their titles to any one who wishes to present books to our library. All gifts for any of the purposes mentioned will be acknowledged in The Mayflower Descendant.

Allow me at this point to call your particular attention to the chest of drawers already mentioned. This was bequeathed to the Society by Miss Harriet Lawrence Adams of Boston, seventh in descent from John Alden, who was elected a member 31 December, 1897, and passed away 4 November, 1900. The chest once belonged to the great grand-parents of Miss Adams, but not in her line of descent from John Alden. It was delivered to the Society 12 March, 1901.

Are there not others who would like to remember the Society when planning the future distribution of their estate, or who would like to deposit with us for preservation old documents or relics? It may be well to remind our members and friends that the Society's office is located in a modern, fire-proof building, and that as an additional protection we have, since February, 1899, owned a very large safe in which there is still room for many valuable gifts and loans.

On 30 September, 1897, at a special meeting of the Society

* Mfr. Desc., I: 1. † Ibid, I: 36.

held on the spot, Dr. Thomas Bradford Drew of Plymouth, since deceased, in behalf of descendants of Governor William Bradford, delivered to your Secretary, for the Massachusetts Society, a deed of a portion of the estate formerly owned by the Governor in that part of Plymouth which is now the town of Kingston. Our Committee on Marking Historic Sites has since collected from Bradford descendants the necessary funds, and has placed on the plot, to which has been given the name "Bradford Meerstead," a handsome bronze tablet suitably inscribed and attached to a massive boulder.

On Friday afternoon, 21 November, 1900, at the Central Church in this city, was held our first Forefathers' Day service in commemoration of the Landing of the Pilgrims. It has been decided to make such a memorial service an important feature of our annual programme.

Before the Society was a year old your Secretary began to urge the importance of doing something towards preserving and making readily accessible the vast amount of genealogical and historical data buried in the ancient Plymouth Colony records and in the various town and county records, and in June, 1897, it was decided to make a beginning by printing a literal transcript of the vital records of one of the smaller towns. Before your Secretary was able to prepare these records for the printer it occurred to him that a quarterly magazine, published by this Society and devoted exclusively to Pilgrim genealogy and history, would meet the needs of a wider range of searchers, since it would allow of the publication of more varied matter and enable us to print in installments many different records. After a careful study of this project he laid the matter before the Board of Assistants, who considered it for several months and finally voted to publish such a magazine, choosing your Secretary as its Editor.

After a long period of careful preparatory work the first number of "The Mayflower Descendant" was issued on 1 July, 1899, and was dated January, 1899, as it seemed best to have the volumes begin with the calendar year. Owing to the Editor's continued efforts to supply the demand for genealogies as well as transcripts of records, he has been unable to bring the issue up to date, but the amount of material already accumulated warrants the promise that he will do so during the coming year.

We have already begun in The Mayflower Descendant the publication of "Francis Cooke and His Descendants" and "Richard Warren and His Descendants"; of literal transcripts of the Plymouth Colony Wills and Inventories, the Plymouth Colony Deeds, and the vital records of the towns of Barnstable, Bridgewater, Dartmouth, Eastham and Orleans, Halifax, Harwich, Marshfield, Middleborough, Plymouth, Plympton, Scituate and Yarmouth; and have begun abstracts of the Barnstable County Wills and Inventories.

We have published a literal transcript of every known will and inventory of a Mayflower passenger, except Governor Edward Winslow's (which will appear in the fourth volume), and have begun to publish those of the second generation.

Before "The Mayflower Descendant" was thought of, your Secretary had begun the compilation, as a personal undertaking, of "The Mayflower Genealogies," intended to include every descendant, *in all male and female lines*, of every Mayflower passenger, and the data already collected by him was turned over to the Society when it was decided to publish the magazine.

In the compilation of The Mayflower Genealogies, it is intended to exhaust every available source of information. The installments already printed show with what thoroughness the records are being searched for every item about each person named. Since each one of the twenty-two Mayflower families settled first at Plymouth, it is evident that, in order to avoid a great waste of time and money, the compilations of the genealogies of all these families should be carried on by, or under the control of, one organization. If each family is taken up independently, thousands of pages of original records, already in many cases very badly worn, must receive an immense amount of totally unnecessary handling, and the waste of time and money will be enormous.

In order to avoid going over the same ground many times, we have begun the indexing of every name found in the Plymouth Colony Wills, the Plymouth Colony Deeds and the Probate and Land Records of Plymouth, Barnstable and Bristol Counties. We have also been obliged to re-index the twelve printed volumes of Plymouth Colony Records (adding over 2000 references), the two printed volumes of Plymouth Town Records (adding over 1100 references) and the printed volume of Duxbury Town Records (adding 1600 references).

The compilation of the Mayflower Genealogies in the thorough way in which we are carrying on the work will take a long time and will be very expensive, but it will never have to be done over again. The progress of this most important work will be determined by the amount of the receipts for the Colonial Research Fund. This fund is made up of the fees for genealogical searches made, and gifts from those interested in the work. The Committee on Historical Research hopes to receive in gifts at least $2000 to expend on the genealogies during the coming year. Unconditional gifts for the general work are especially desired, but contributions for particular lines of work will be gratefully received.*

In addition to the indexes mentioned we have collected a great amount of data about the first four or five generations of the different families, including hundreds of vital records and abstracts of wills and deeds not yet published. The use of this large and constantly increasing accumulation of data in supplying information to those who are trying to prove Pilgrim descent has added somewhat to the Colonial Research Fund during the past year. Those who are thinking of having any search made in the records of any part of the "Old Colony" are reminded that every such search made by this Society adds to our material for future use, while the fees received all go to the Colonial Research Fund. The Society's work will thus be helped in two ways at the same time.

One year ago, at the suggestion of your Secretary, it was voted to set apart each year, from the funds of the Society, the sum of twenty-five cents for each member at the date of the annual meeting, to form a Tri-Centennial Publication Fund. This fund will be allowed to accumulate until 1920, the tri-centennial anniversary of the Landing of the Pilgrims, and will then be used to defray the expense of a memorial volume or volumes. This Society should at that time be in a position to publish a series of volumes of Pilgrim genealogy and history which will be of incalculable value, and it is none too early to begin to make plans for such a work.

In conclusion I would say that in publishing The Mayflower Descendant, the first historical magazine to pay for itself from the start; and in undertaking the compilation of The Mayflower Genealogies, the most comprehensive and the most important genealogical work ever attempted, the Society of Mayflower Descendants in the Commonwealth of Massachusetts has made a record unequalled by any other patriotic-hereditary society, a record in which it may justly take the greatest pride; and it has accomplished this entirely unaided by any other Society, the contributions received from persons not members of the Massachusetts Society having amounted to less than eighty dollars.

* **For a list of the special Funds see Pilgrim Notes and Queries in this issue.**

In order that we may continue this great work on which we have entered and keep it up to the high standard we have set, the Committee on Historical Research, the Committee on Publication and the Editor all need your hearty co-operation and encouragement. Having that, you may rest assured that they will spare no effort to add to the prestige already acquired.

THE TRIENNIAL CONGRESS HELD SEPTEMBER 15, 1900.

[Explanatory Note. Justice to the Publication Committee and the Editor demands a statement of the reasons for the long delay in printing this account.

At the Congress held at Plymouth on Saturday, September 15, 1900, it was voted that the proceedings of the Congress should be published in full in the Mayflower Descendant, and sent to every member of the General Society. At the meeting of the General Board of Assistants, held at New York on February 8, 1901, "It was announced that the Congress had ordered that the minutes of the Congress be printed in full in the Mayflower Descendant . . . The Secretary was ordered to furnish the minutes of Congress and this meeting for that purpose."* On July 24, 1901, more than ten months after the Congress had ordered the minutes printed, and more than five months after the General Board had again ordered them furnished, the Secretary General mailed to the Editor the minutes of the Board meeting, prefacing them as follows: "Print account of Congress in full, as it appears in the General Book." Said account of the General Congress is not a complete record of the acts of the Congress, as witness the omission of any reference to the vote ordering the publication of the minutes; the omission of the names of donors of historic sites, and of other important matters. Since it has proved impossible to obtain the *minutes* of the Congress of 1900 for publication, we have finally decided to reprint (with a number of corrections) the incomplete account in the General Society's book, together with a verbatim copy of the Secretary General's report of the meeting of the General Board of Assistants.]

The Second Triennial Congress was held at Plymouth, Massachusetts, September 15, 1900. Deputy Governor General Lombard, having been designated to act in the absence of the Governor General, presided, and the Congress elected the Historian General as its secretary *pro tempore*, in the absence of the Secretary General.

The Rev. Dr. Daniel F. Warren invoked the divine blessing.

The following were appointed a committee on credentials: Frederick W. Parker, Edwin A. Hill and Howland Davis. They reported eighty-one delegates present, as follows — New York: Richard Henry Greene, John Taylor Terry, Howland Davis, William Milne Grinnell, James LeBaron Willard, Walter Steuben Carter, John Newel Tilden, John Whittlesey Walton,

* Minutes of the Board meeting near the end of this article.

Warren C. Crane, Edward S. Atwood, Linus E. Fuller, Marshall W. Greene, Mrs. Sylvanus Reed, Cyrus F. Paine, Mrs. Stephen V. C. White, Marguerite T. Doane, Frederick N. LeBaron, Mrs. Emma B. Chamberlin, Hamilton B. Tompkins, Mrs. R. H. Greene, H. K. Bush-Brown, Cassius M. Wicker, Mrs. Albert H. Pitkin, Mrs. Charles H. Terry, Charles Henry Wight, Mrs. H. C. Manning, Lewis Deitz, Mrs. F. W. Hopkins, and Mrs. James M. McKinlay — twenty-nine.

Connecticut: William Waldo Hyde, Charles Dudley Warner, Rev. James Gibson Johnson, Percy Coe Eggleston, Nathan Holt Smith, Edwin A. Hill, Sylvester C. Dunham, Mrs. Catherine A. D. Bramble, Mrs. Frances W. B. Downes and Lucy Palmer Butler — ten.

Massachusetts: Myles Standish, M.D., Frederick W. Parker, William T. Davis, Frederick S. Vaill, George C. Nightingale, Charles A. Burditt, Edward T. Barker, L. Emery Holden, Horace H. Soule, Jr., J. Weston Allen, Alfred S. Johnson, Mrs. Edward T. Barker, Susan Barker Willard, Abby Louise Allen, Mrs. Nelson V. Titus, Mrs. Charles H. Fisher, Mrs. Samuel G. Webber, Mrs. John A. Remick, Maria G. Webber, Sarah S. Webber, Mrs. John F. Gaylord, Mrs. Frederick N. Knapp, Mrs. William S. Kyle, Caroline B. Warren, Mrs. James E. Sherman and Mary Russell Hodge — twenty-six.

Pennsylvania: Josiah Granville Leach, Ashbel Welch, Mrs. William H. McCartney, Eben Francis Barker, Lucretia C. Lennig, Anne Law Hubbell and A. R. Welch — seven.

Illinois: Josiah Lewis Lombard, Mrs. E. W. Blatchford and Edward Milton Adams — three.

District of Columbia: William Lowrey Marsh, Algernon A. Aspinwall, Mrs. Preston H. Bailhache, Mrs. William H. Chany — four.

Ohio: Herbert Jenney, William Howard Doane and Ida F. Doane — three.

New Jersey: Rev. Daniel F. Warren, D.D., and Mrs. J. H. Oglesby — two.

The following officers were elected: Governor General, Henry E. Howland; Deputy Governors General, Charles Dudley Warner *, Connecticut; Winslow Warren, Massachusetts; Francis Olcott Allen, Pennsylvania; Josiah Lewis Lombard, Illinois; William Lowrey Marsh, District of Columbia; Herbert Jenny, Ohio; Rev. Daniel F. Warren, D.D., New Jersey; Captain General, Myles Standish, M.D.; Elder General, Rev.

* Deceased October 20, 1900. Lyman Denison Brewster elected by the General Board of Assistants February 8, 1901.

Edward Lord Clark, D.D.; Secretary General, Richard Henry Greene; Treasurer General, James Mauran Rhodes; Historian General, Rodney Macdonough *; Surgeon General, Orlando Brown, M.D.; Assistants, Howland Davis, New York; Rev. Roderick Terry, D.D., New York; William Waldo Hyde, Connecticut; George Ernest Bowman, Massachusetts; Josiah Granville Leach, Pennsylvania; Victor Clifton Alderson, Illinois; Harry Weston Van Dyke, District of Columbia.

A committee on constitutional revision was named, consisting of Winslow Warren, William Waldo Hyde, Walter S. Carter, L. Emery Holden and Walter M. Howland.

The committee to publish the book was discharged, and R. H. Greene was made chairman of a new committee, with J. Granville Leach, Prof. Victor C. Alderson, Jeremiah Richards and Dr. Myles Standish.

Thanks were voted to the donors of historic sites, and Lorenzo D. Baker, John B. Perry, Warren W. Small and Mary J. Perry were appointed committee for Corn Hill, and Lorenzo D. Baker, William Thomas Davis and Frederick Wesley Parker for Truro sites.

A committee for the reception Saturday evening at the Samoset was named, consisting of Marshall W. Greene, Ashbel Welch, Mrs. Edward T. Barker, Mrs. S. V. White and Mrs. E. G. Chamberlin.

Announcements were made of Brewster and Howland meetings, and the dedication of Bradford boulder and tablet at Kingston on Monday, the presentation to the Massachusetts Society to be made by William T. Davis of Plymouth, and to be received by Richard Henry Greene of New York.

Two services were arranged for the Sabbath: in the afternoon at Clark's Island, which, on account of the storm, was held at the Samoset; in the evening at the Church of the Pilgrimage, where the principal address was made by Rev. Dr. James Gibson Johnson — subject: "The Nation's Debt to the Pilgrims." The pastor, Rev. D. Melancthon James, Dr. Warren and Mr. Greene also took part in the service. The choir was reinforced by delegates under the lead of W. Howard Doane, composer of the music of the Mayflower Song, which, with Mrs. Hemans' Hymn and other appropriate selections, was well rendered.

Pilgrimages were made on the different days of the week to the Winslow Burying-ground and Webster House, Marshfield; the Alden and Standish houses, cemetery and monument, Dux-

* Elected by the General Board of Assistants, February 8, 1901.

bury; the Howland site at Kingston; and the many points of interest in Plymouth.

Minutes of the Board Meeting.

The General Board met at the office Hon. Henry E. Howland, pursuant to call dated January 7, 1901 on February 8th, 1901 at 3 o'clock P. M.

The Governor General in the chair and the following members present: Deputy Governors General Hyde, Lombard, Marsh and Warren of New Jersey; Treasurer General Rhodes; Captain Gen. Standish; Assistants Leach and Terry; and Sec. Gen. Greene.

The minutes were read and approved.

The Treasurer General made his report which was received and placed on file.

Mr. Marsh moved that the Secretary General notify each society which had not paid a charter fee that the same is due. Seconded and carried.

The form of Charter was exhibited and adopted.

Mr. Leach moved that the form of charter as shown be approved and adopted, and the Secretary General be directed to have enough prepared to meet the needs of the society. Seconded and carried.

Mr. Lombard moved that whenever doubt is thrown upon the eligibility of any member that the society of which he or she is a member be advised to require proof to be furnished, and in default thereof that such member be dropped from the roll. Seconded and carried.

Rodney Macdonough a member of the Massachusetts Society was nominated by Dr. Standish, and seconded by Mr. Greene, for the office of Historian General. He was elected.

Lyman D. Brewster, a member of the Connecticut Society, was nominated by Mr. Hyde, for Deputy Gov. General in place of Charles Dudley Warner deceased. Dr. Terry seconded the nomination, and he was elected.

The matter of assessments for 1899, 1900 and 1901 referred to the board by the congress; and the cost of publication of General Book, ordered by the congress and placed in the hands of a committee by it, was taken up.

Mr. Marsh moved that the Treasurer General be instructed to credit to the publication fund one dollar per capita for each society which had paid the assessment levied for 1898 being one half of said assessment. Seconded and carried.

Mr. Marsh moved that the committee for publication be authorized to proceed with the work at a cost not to exceed the sum of four thousand dollars. Seconded and carried.

Mr. Marsh moved that an assessment be levied on each state society on its full membership as of this day at two dollars per capita. Seconded and carried.

Mr. Lombard moved that the Congress be called together next September and a committee be appointed to arrange for the meeting and select the place. Seconded and carried.

The chair appointed as such committee Messrs. Lombard and Marsh. On motion the Governor General was added and made chairman.

It was announced that the Congress had ordered that the minutes of the congress be printed in full in the Mayflower Descendant and sent to every member of the society, and that the General Society should pay to the Massachusetts Society one hundred dollars therefor. The Secretary was ordered to furnish the minutes of congress and of this meeting for that purpose.

An application was read from residents of the State of Wisconsin filed with the Secretary General Dec. 20, 1900, and a charter was granted.

An application was read from residents of the State of Rhode Island, filed with the Secretary General Jan. 14, 1901, and charter was granted.

An application was read from residents of the State of Michigan, filed with the Secretary General Feb. 4, 1901, and charter was granted.

An application was read from residents of the State of Minnesota, filed with the Secretary General, but some of the names, though approved by the State Historians were either awaiting the action of the Historian General or the report of the membership committees.

On motion duly seconded the matter of granting a charter to members in the State of Minnesota was left to the Secretary General with power to issue a charter whenever the application bears the requisite twenty signatures.

On motion adjourned.

RICHD. H. GREENE, *Sec. Gen.*

REPORTS FROM STATE SOCIETIES.

MASSACHUSETTS SOCIETY.

THE Sixth Annual Meeting and Dinner of the Massachusetts Society were held at the Hotel Brunswick, Boston, on Thursday afternoon and evening, November 21, 1901. The Secretary's report was ordered printed in full in The Mayflower Descendant.

After the dinner addresses were made by Governor Standish, who presided, by Hon. James M. W. Hall, Professor Wilfred H. Munro, Professor Albert Bushnell Hart and Mr. J. Henry Sears, and parts of the Secretary's report were again read in accordance with a vote of the Society at the afternoon meeting. Congratulatory telegrams were sent to and received from the New York, Illinois, Ohio and District of Columbia Societies.

The following officers were elected for the year 1901-1902:

Governor,	Myles Standish, M.D.
Deputy Governor,	Winslow Warren.
Captain,	Charles Augustus Hopkins.
Elder,	Rev. George Hodges, D.D.
Secretary,	George Ernest Bowman.
Treasurer,	Marcus Morton.
Historian,	Frederick Wesley Parker.
Surgeon,	Samuel Jason Mixter, M.D.
Assistants,	Morton Dexter, Mrs. Burr Porter, Mrs. William Lawrie, Henry Southworth Shaw, Sumner Bass Pearmain, Horace Homer Soule, Jr., Mrs. C. Peter Clark.

On Saturday afternoon, December 21, 1901, the Massachusetts Society held its Second Annual Forefathers' Day Service, at King's Chapel, Boston. The Rev. George Hodges, D.D., the Elder of the Society, conducted the devotional services, and the Rev. Frederick Baylies Allen delivered the address, which is printed in full in this number.

The following Standing Committees for the year 1901-1902 have been appointed by the Board of Assistants:

Marking Historic Sites: Charles Francis Adams, Gamaliel Bradford, Rev. Edward L. Clark, D.D., Myles Standish, M.D., Winslow Warren.

Historical Research: John Mason Little, F. Apthorp Foster, Boylston A. Beal, Rodney Macdonough, George Ernest Bowman.

Publication: Morton Dexter, Winslow Warren, John F. Hill, Frederick W. Parker, George Ernest Bowman.

Library: Theodore S. Lazell, Benjamin F. Stevens, Miss Ellen Chase, Mrs. J. Payson Bradley, Rev. Edward H. Rudd.

Membership: Mrs. John Holmes Morison, Miss Sarah H. Crocker, Mrs. Walter M. Farwell, Mrs. Frederic A. Turner, Mrs. Edward T. Barker.

Finance: L. Loring Brooks, George H. Leonard, Henry D. Forbes, Joseph H. Goodspeed, Fisher Ames.

Entertainment: J. Weston Allen, Miss Harriet A. Shaw, Horace H. Soule, Jr., Mrs. John A. Remick, Ray Greene Huling.

Donations to the Library and Cabinet.

"Richard Warren of the Mayflower and Some of His Descendants," from the compiler, Mrs. Washington A. Roebling.

"Records of the Court of Assistants, Colony of Massachusetts Bay, 1630–1692, Vol. I, 1673–1692," from John Noble, Esq.

"A Finding List of Genealogies and Local History in the Syracuse Public Library, Syracuse, N. Y.," from the Library.

"Sprague Family Items," from the compiler, Dwight H. Kelton, LL.D.

Framed Engraving. "The Departure of the Pilgrims," from Mrs. George Agry, Jr.

"Supplement to Members and Ascendants of the Massachusetts Society of the Colonial Dames of America, 1898–99," from Mrs. Francis P. Sprague.

"History and Genealogy of the Bangs Family in America," from Mr. J. Henry Sears.

"An Index to Taintor's Colchester (Conn.) Records," from the compiler, Mr. James Knox Blish.

"An Address by Rev. Frank T. Bayley, D.D., to the Society of Colonial Wars in Colorado, October 30, 1901," from the Society.

"Fourteenth Report on Public Records," from Hon. Robert T. Swan.

Members Elected.

October 25, 1901.

682. Mrs. George Herbert Crocker, Fitchburg, eighth from John Alden.
683. Mrs. Alphonso Livingston Gilkey, Portland, Me., seventh from William Bradford.
684. Mrs. Adams Crocker, Fitchburg, eighth from John Alden.
685. Mrs. Ira Bliss Keith, Lynn, eighth from Stephen Hopkins, seventh from Gyles Hopkins.
686. Mrs. Frank Melville Breed, Lynn, eighth from John Alden.
687. Mrs. Frank Albert Higgins, Boston, eighth from John Alden.
688. George Edward Barnard, Lynn, eighth from Stephen Hopkins, seventh from Gyles Hopkins.

November 21, 1901.

689. William Burdick Stevens, Boston, eighth from Richard Warren.
690. Mrs. Theodore Studley Lazell, Boston, ninth from William Bradford.
691. Mrs. Monroe Ayer, Boston, sixth from John Howland.
692. Mrs. John Henry Ball, Bridgewater, sixth from John Howland.
693. Rev. Edward Huntting Rudd, Dedham, ninth from William Brewster, eighth from Love Brewster.

Supplemental Lines Filed.

October, 1901.

111. Miss Amy W. Alden, tenth from John Billington, ninth from Francis Billington; ninth from Francis Cooke; tenth from Francis Cooke; ninth from Francis Eaton, eighth from Samuel Eaton; ninth from Dr. Samuel Fuller; ninth from George Soule.
208. James M. W. Hall, eighth from Richard Warren.

679. Daniel Cushman, seventh from John Alden: seventh from Francis Cooke: seventh from Stephen Hopkins; seventh from Myles Standish.

November, 1901.

571. Mrs. Albert Sauveur, ninth from John Billington, eighth from Francis Billington; eighth from Francis Eaton, seventh from Samuel Eaton; eighth from Dr. Samuel Fuller; eighth from Stephen Hopkins.

576. Miss Maria S. Daniels, eighth from John Howland; ninth from John Howland.

591. John A. Daniels, eighth from John Howland.

638. Fisher Ames, sixth from John Alden; seventh from John Alden: eighth from William Brewster, seventh from Love Brewster; eighth from James Chilton, seventh from Mary Chilton; eighth from Thomas Rogers; eighth from Richard Warren.

674. Mrs. Henry T. Coe, ninth from John Alden: ninth from Peter Brown; ninth from Francis Cooke; ninth from Francis Eaton.

December, 1901.

690. Mrs. Theodore S. Lazell, ninth from John Alden; tenth from John Alden; tenth (two lines) from William Brewster; ninth from Love Brewster; ninth from Stephen Hopkins: tenth from Thomas Rogers; ninth from Henry Samson; ninth from Richard Warren.

NEW YORK SOCIETY.

The Seventh Annual Meeting and Dinner were held at Delmonico's, New York City, on Thursday evening, November 21, 1901. Addresses were made by Hon. James M. Beck, Rev. James M. Buckley, D.D., LL.D., Rev. Henry Elliott Mott, D.D., Hon. John L. McLaurin, John Foord and Hon. Lyman D. Brewster. Congratulatory telegrams were sent to the Massachusetts, Maine and Illinois Societies: and were received from the Massachusetts, Ohio, Illinois and District of Columbia Societies.

The following officers were elected:

Governor,	William Winton Goodrich.
Deputy Governor,	Rev. Roderick Terry, D.D.
Captain,	J. Bayard Backus.
Elder,	Rev. Daniel Frederick Warren, D.D.
Secretary,	Charles Waldo Haskins.
Treasurer,	William Lanman Bull.
Historian,	Richard Henry Greene.
Surgeon,	Gorham Bacon, M.D.

Members Elected.

October 2, 1901.

667. Josephine Ward Swann, Princeton, N. J., seventh from Edward Winslow.

November 6, 1901.

668. Miss Marie E. Ives, New York, eighth from John Howland.

669. Joseph Baker Bourne. New York. tenth from John Alden.
670. Franklin Whetstone Hopkins. New York, ninth from Stephen Hopkins, eighth from Constance Hopkins.

December 4, 1901.
671. William Stowell Mills, Brooklyn, eighth from Edward Fuller, seventh from Samuel² Fuller.
672. Mrs. Loyd Wheaton, Manila, P. I., seventh from William Bradford.
673. Mrs. Herbert Turrell, New York, ninth from John Howland.

CONNECTICUT SOCIETY.

Mr. William M. Stark of New London was elected Secretary, December 16, 1901, to succeed Mr. Nathan H. Smith, resigned.

PENNSYLVANIA SOCIETY.

The Annual Meeting was held at the Hotel Stratford, Philadelphia, on Friday, November 22, 1901. The following officers were elected:

Governor,	Charlemagne Tower, Jr.
Deputy Governor,	Francis Olcott Allen.
Captain,	Charles A. Brinley.
Secretary,	George Champlin Mason.
Historian,	J. Granville Leach.
Surgeon,	Charles Peaslee Turner, M.D.
Assistants,	Ashbel Welch, James Crosby Brown, Craige Lippincott, Eben Francis Barker, George E. Bartol, William H. Castle, Edward Clinton Lee.

Member Elected.

October 2, 1901.
136. Louis Barcroft Runk, Philadelphia, eleventh from Thomas Rogers.

ILLINOIS SOCIETY.

The Annual Banquet was held at Chicago on Thursday evening, November 21, 1901. Rev. William M. Lawrence delivered an address on "The Contribution of the Mayflower Society to the Historic Spirit." Rt. Rev. Charles E. Cheney then presented to the retiring Governor, Mr. Walter Morton Howland, a silver loving cup, appropriately engraved, as a token of esteem and friendship, from the members of the Society.

The Annual Meeting was held at Chicago, on Friday, November 22, 1901, and the following officers were elected:

Governor,	Dr. James Nevins Hyde.
Deputy Governor,	Professor Victor Clifton Alderson.
Elder,	Rt. Rev. Charles Edward Cheney.
Secretary,	Mrs. Walter Morton Howland.
Treasurer,	Paul Blatchford.
Historian,	Theron Royal Woodward.
Captain,	Isaac Burrows Snow.
Surgeon,	Dr. Harry Cushman Worthington.

Assistants, Miss Cornelia Gray Lunt, Mrs. Nelson C. Gridley, Mrs. Henry C. Purmort, Mrs. Albert Antisdel, Mrs. Seymour Morris, John Smith Sargent, Solon Tenney French.

Members Elected.

November 13, 1901.

86. Louis Brackett Bishop, Chicago, ninth from William Brewster.
87. Isaac Gross Lombard, Chicago, eighth from Stephen Hopkins, seventh from Constance Hopkins.
88. George McMurtry Ludlow, Chicago, eighth from Edward Doty.
89. Mrs. Charles Albert Ward, Evanston, ninth from John Alden.

OHIO SOCIETY.

The Fourth Annual Meeting was held at Cincinnati, November 21, 1901, and the following officers were elected:

Governor,	Herbert Jenney.
Deputy Governor,	Mrs. Frank J. Jones.
Captain,	William H. Doane.
Elder,	Rev. John Hugh Ely.
Secretary,	Miss Clara Chipman Newton.
Treasurer,	Henry C. Yergason.
Historian,	William H. Pabodie.
Surgeon,	Dr. Herman J. Groesbeck.
Assistants,	Mrs. Frank R. Ellis, Mrs. Henry M. Curtis, Mrs. George Hoadly, Jr., Mrs. Albert H. Chatfield, Charles D. Jones, Charles H. Newton.

The following committees have been appointed:

Membership: Mrs. Frank J. Jones, Mrs. Henry M. Curtis, Miss Ida F. Doane.

Finance: Dr. Herman J. Groesbeck, William H. Doane, Charles Bartlett.

Entertainment and Property: Mrs. Albert H. Chatfield, Miss Frances L' H. Jones, Mrs. George Hoadly, Jr.

Publication: Charles D. Jones, Edward Wyllys Buell, Mrs. Frank R. Ellis.

DISTRICT OF COLUMBIA SOCIETY.

Members Elected.

October 8, 1901.

119. William Sherman Washburn, Washington, tenth from Francis Cooke.
120. Harry Stimson Howard, Burlington, Vt., ninth from Francis Cooke.

November 12, 1901.

121. Henry Myron Kendall. Washington, eighth from William Brewster.
122. James Fitch Millard, Cleveland, O., seventh from William Bradford.

November 21, 1901.

123. Samuel Mitchell Rainey, Hudson, N. Y., ninth from John Howland.

WISCONSIN SOCIETY.

Members Elected.

November 2, 1901.
32. Mrs. Edward M. Fuller, Madison, eighth from William Bradford.
33. Shirley Fuller, Madison, ninth from William Bradford.

November 29, 1901.
34. Mrs. Robert A. Williams, Milwaukee, eighth from William Bradford.

December 6, 1901.
35. William J. H. Strong, Beloit, eighth from Henry Samson.
December 16, 1901.
36. Mrs. Corwin Dewey Harper, Oshkosh, eighth from Richard Warren.

MICHIGAN SOCIETY.

The First Annual Meeting and Banquet were held at the Russell House, Detroit, Thursday, November 21, 1901. Addresses were made by Mrs. Alfred Russell, Mrs. J. E. Emerson, Mrs. W. J. Chittenden, Mrs. R. H. Fyfe, Mrs. E. B. Gibbs, Rev. L. S. McCollester, Mr. Alfred Russell and Rev. Charles W. Woodcock.

The following officers were elected:

Governor,	James Dudley Hawks.
Deputy Governor,	Paul A. L. Doty.
Secretary,	Mrs. Lyman Hayden Baldwin.
Treasurer,	Mrs. Austin Yates Ladue.
Assistants,	Mrs. H. H. H. Crapo-Smith, Mrs. David D. Cady, Ralph Stone, Charles Dana Standish.

MAINE SOCIETY.

A charter for a Society of Mayflower Descendants in the State of Maine was granted September 6, 1901, to the following named members: Archie Lee Talbot, John F. Hill, Hiram L. Pichon, Mrs. Emma Huntington Nason, Charles Livingston Cushman, Mrs. Charles Livingston Cushman, Philip Foster Turner, Frederick Sturdivant Vaill, Mrs. Charlotte F. S. Vaill, Henry Nathaniel Fairbanks, Mrs. Henry Nathaniel Fairbanks, Miss Nora Lucy Fairbanks, Augustus Hatch Babcock, Joseph Parker Bass, Willis Ellis Parsons, William Cushing Donnell, Miss Martha Cobb Wight, Miss Annabel Stetson, Miss Julia Cornelia Vaill, Edward Griswold Vaill.

The Society was organized at the Lithgow Library, Augusta, November 21, 1901, and the following officers were elected:

Governor,	John Fremont Hill.
Deputy Governor,	Archie Lee Talbot.
Captain,	Henry Nathaniel Fairbanks.
Secretary,	Frederick Sturdivant Vaill.
Treasurer,	Hiram Leander Pishon.
Historian,	Philip Foster Turner.
Assistants,	Joseph Parker Bass, Willis Ellis Parsons, Mrs. Emma Huntington Nason, Charles Livingston Cushman, Miss Annabel Stetson.

PILGRIM NOTES AND QUERIES.

NOTES.

THE COLONIAL RESEARCH WORK. The attention of our readers is called to the report of the Secretary of the Massachusetts Society, on pages 43–50 of this number. Since that report was made much has been accomplished. The work of abstracting the four volumes of Plymouth Colony Wills and Inventories is nearly completed; and four of the five unpublished volumes of Plymouth Colony Deeds have been abstracted. The indexing of all the names in these abstracts of both Wills and Deeds is nearly finished, so that we are now able to turn quickly to nearly every reference to any name in these records.

In 1685 Plymouth Colony was divided into three counties, Plymouth, Barnstable and Bristol, each with its separate Probate and Land Registry. We have begun to abstract and index the records of these three counties, but the progress of the work is very slow owing to lack of funds to pay for necessary assistance.

In addition to the re-indexing of printed records and the indexing of probate and land records, plans have been made for the preparation of a card catalogue of all persons, *in every generation*, whose descent from a Mayflower passenger we have verified by original records. Each card will contain a person's name and residence, the date and place of his or her birth, marriage and death, with the names of parents, husband, or wife, and children; also references to the records which prove the facts stated. We have already proved thousands of descents, many of them heretofore unknown, and are constantly adding to the number. With such a card catalogue, when a query as to the possible Mayflower ancestry of a person is received, it will take but a moment to see if that name appears in the catalogue. If it is found there, the line (or lines) of Mayflower descent, with the necessary proofs, can be transcribed very quickly.

The rapid accumulation of data by the Society makes such a catalogue an immediate necessity, and it will be of incalculable value in the future, not only in the work of compiling the Mayflower Genealogies, but in our work of assisting those in search of Mayflower ancestry and in the preparation of supplemental lines.

We have also begun a card catalogue of names and addresses of all persons now living who claim Mayflower descent. This will be of value in many ways, and we shall be glad to receive lists of such names from our readers.

The work which the Massachusetts Society is carrying on benefits not only its own members, but the members of every other State Society, and in fact *every* person having Mayflower ancestry. Several thousands of dollars have already been expended on this work, and only about four hundred dollars have been contributed by persons not members of the Massachusetts Society.

It is to be hoped that others will come forward and assist us to carry on this great undertaking. In order that contributors may have a more definite idea of the use to which their gifts are put, sub-divisions of the

Colonial Research Fund will be established, the name in each case indicating clearly the purpose of the fund.

The Committee on Historical Research particularly desires unrestricted gifts for the general research work. but gifts for any one or more of the special funds can be used to good advantage.

The special sub-divisions of the Colonial Research Fund will be as follows:

ALDEN RESEARCH FUND.
ALLERTON RESEARCH FUND.
BILLINGTON RESEARCH FUND,
BRADFORD RESEARCH FUND,
BREWSTER RESEARCH FUND,
BROWN RESEARCH FUND,
CHILTON RESEARCH FUND,
COOKE RESEARCH FUND,

and so on through the list of families: Doty, Eaton, E. Fuller, S. Fuller, Hopkins, Howland, Priest, Rogers, Samson, Soule, Standish, Warren, White, Winslow.

PLYMOUTH COLONY INDEX FUND (To complete Plymouth Colony Wills and Deeds),
PLYMOUTH COUNTY INDEX FUND (County Probate and Land Records),
BARNSTABLE COUNTY INDEX FUND (County Probate Records),
BRISTOL COUNTY INDEX FUND (County Probate and Land Records).

All contributions should be sent to the Editor, who will return receipts and acknowledge the gifts in this department, crediting each to the special fund designated by the donor.

At least $2000 will be needed for the year's work, and a generous and prompt response to this appeal for funds is greatly to be desired if the work is to continue as heretofore. *Bis dat qui cito dat.*

COLONIAL RESEARCH FUND. Contributions to the $2000.00 fund not heretofore acknowledged: Edwin S. Crandon, $35.00; Amos R. Little, $25.00; Mrs. Abby H. Bartlett, $5.00; James K. Blish, $5.00; Mrs. Charles R. Brayton, $4.00: James D. Hawks, $2.00; Edward C. Hawks, $2.00; Mrs. George F. Arnold, $2.00; Mrs. J. Bolton Winpenny, $2.00; Mrs. George R. Stetson, $2.00; George F. Baker, M.D., $2.00; Charles A. Clark, $2.00; Frederick C. Seabury, $2.00; Julius E. Soule, $2.00; Charles J. North, $2.00; Mrs. Samuel Lapham, $2.00; George E. Bartol, $2.00; Mrs. William W. Karr. $2.00; Mrs. A. T. Freedley, $2.00; Miss Ann M. Sears, $2.00: Lyman D. Brewster, $2.00; Previously ackowledged $439.00; Total, $545.00. The Editor has also presented five hundred sets of Bowman's Ancestral Charts and ten copies of the Freeman Genealogy, to be sold for the benefit of this fund, in accordance with the extremely liberal offers in our advertising pages.

CO-OPERATION IN GENEALOGICAL RESEARCH. An illustration of the way in which both time and money are wasted because of lack of co-operation and system in genealogical research has recently come to our notice. A gentleman who was anxious to find the names of some unidentified wives in his ancestral lines paid for the examination of *every page* of certain voluminous records. This Society must eventually have these records examined again, in the same exhaustive manner. In order to avoid the necessity of frequent repetitions of such examinations, *every name* in these thousands of pages will be indexed as the work progresses.

If we had known in advance that the examination mentioned was to be made, we could doubtless have arranged to co-operate and by dividing the total cost equitably make the expense to each much less. The saving in wear and tear of the records themselves would also have been considerable.

TRANSCRIPTS AND ABSTRACTS OF WILLS OF SECOND AND LATER GENERATIONS. We have printed a literal transcript of every known will and inventory of a Mayflower passenger, and have begun to do the same for the second generation wills.

Governor Winslow's will completed the series of known wills of Mayflower passengers.

The series of wills and inventories of the second generation, begun in volume two, will be continued until all have been printed in full, but their number is so great it will take several years to complete the series. The order in which they will be printed will, therefore, be determined by the wishes of contributors to the Colonial Research Fund.

The wills of the third and succeeding generations are far too numerous to think of publishing them in full unless descendants are willing to pay the additional expense involved.

We shall begin in this volume a series of careful abstracts of third generation wills and inventories, the order in which they will appear to be determined as in the case of the second generation series.

Contributors to the Colonial Research Fund are invited to indicate to the Editor, when making remittances, which wills of the second and third generations they desire to see printed first.

GEORGE SOULE'S AUTOGRAPH. The Editor has discovered an autograph of George Soule of the Mayflower, written in 1668. He has never heard of the existence of any other specimen of Soule's handwriting, and will be very grateful for information concerning others that may be found. A half-tone reproduction and a literal transcript of the document to which this and other interesting signatures are attached will be given in the April number.

THE SUPPLY OF BACK NUMBERS. We can no longer supply single copies of July, 1899, (Vol. I, No. 3); July, 1900, (Vol. II, No. 3); October, 1900, (Vol. II, No. 4). The few remaining copies of these numbers will be reserved to make up sets and bound volumes. Less than fifty complete sets remain unsold.

UNIDENTIFIED WIVES AND MARRIAGEABLE WOMEN. Every one interested in genealogical research knows of many instances in which nothing is known of an ancestor's wife except her given name. On the other hand many cases can be pointed out where there is evidence that a daughter has been married, but the name of her husband is not mentioned, or where there are daughters of proper age, but no record of their marriage. It is evident that if the records of all unidentified wives named Hannah, for example, and of all marriageable women of that name, could be brought together, a careful comparison of the known facts about each would in many cases result in the identification of many of these wives and husbands.

In order to facilitate this work of identification the Editor has begun a card catalogue of Unidentified Wives and Marriageable Women. This catalogue will be strictly limited to families of Plymouth, Barnstable and Bristol Counties.

Queries.

[*Queries are inserted for Subscribers only, and are strictly limited to Pilgrim lines. Those which can be answered by study of printed records, genealogies, &c., cannot be inserted. Answers should be sent to the Editor, for publication in later issues.*]

44. Bradford–Arthur. In the "Descendants of Nathaniel Ely" it is stated that Rheumah Ely married Bradford Arthur, son of Richard and Hannah (Bradford) Arthur, that Bradford Arthur was born at Groton, Conn., 20 September, 1773, and that his mother, Hannah Bradford, was a great grand-daughter of Governor Bradford. Who were her parents? When and where was she born and married? * * *

45. Bradford–Brewster. In the Norwich, Conn., records is the following record: "Mr. Seabury Brewster of Norwich and Miss Sally Bradford of Montville were Married Together on the 25th Day of December A. D. 1785." Wanted: The ancestry, with all dates, of Sally Bradford. * * *

46. Bradford. Who was the wife of Thomas[3] Bradford (*William,*[2] *Gov. William*[1]) and when were they married? * * *

47. Soule. Wanted: The names, with dates of birth, of the children of Nathan Soule, whose marriage, 27 October, 1762, to Sarah Birdsall is recorded in the Oblong and Nine Partners, N. Y., Friends records. * * *

Book Note.

The Macdonough-Hackstaff Ancestry. By Rodney Macdonough. Boston, 1901. Limited edition of 300 copies, printed from type on high grade paper, wide margins and uncut. Square 8vo. pp. xii + 526. Bound in linen. Price $7.50. For sale by the author at 205 Washington St., Boston, Mass.

One can hardly say too much in praise of the careful work done by Mr. Macdonough in the preparation of this valuable contribution to the history of the Macdonough, Hackstaff, Hawxhurst, Pratt, Priest, Shaler and allied families. Imbued with the true spirit of critical historical research, he has not been content to accept the statements of others, but has himself consulted the original records, and printed literal transcripts of them in many cases, giving also full-page reproductions of the documents, or facsimiles of the signatures.

Mr. Macdonough's researches have brought to light much valuable material which will be of especial interest to our readers. His identification of John Pratt of Oyster Bay, Long Island, as the son of Phineas Pratt of Plymouth and Charlestown, Mass., by his wife Mary the daughter of Degory Priest of the Mayflower, adds hundreds to the number of those who can claim Mayflower descent. The numerous descendants of Phineas Pratt will be particularly interested in the half-tone reproduction of his will, and in the facsimile of his signature.

A portion of the book which will be of especial value to the general public is the article on the author's grandfather, Commodore Thomas Macdonough, the hero of Lake Champlain. This article includes a large part of an autobiography left by the Commodore which has never been made public.

In addition to the reproductions of documents and autographs the volume contains numerous other illustrations, many of them full-page; and its value is greatly enhanced by a carefully prepared full-name index.

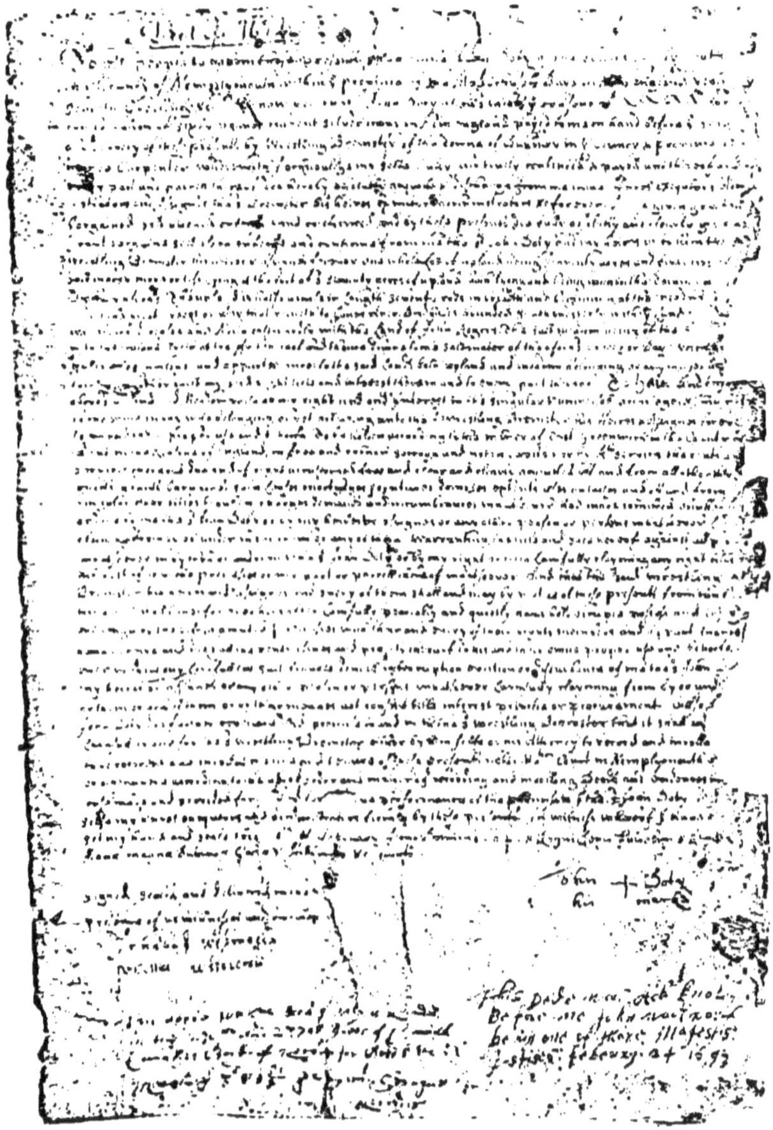

JOHN DOTY'S DEED TO WRESTLING BREWSTER

THE MAYFLOWER DESCENDANT

Vol. IV. APRIL, 1902. No. 2.

JOHN[2] DOTY'S DEED TO WRESTLING BREWSTER.

THE following deed from John[2] Doty (*Edward*[1]) to Wrestling[3] Brewster (*Love*[2], *William*[1]) is copied from the original document presented to the Massachusetts Society of Mayflower Descendants by Miss Flora L. Brewster of Kingston, Mass. This deed is in the handwriting of Rev. Ichabod Wiswall of Duxbury, and he with his wife Priscilla[3] Pabodie (*Elizabeth*[2] *Alden, John*[1]) signed it as witnesses. It is probable that when he began to write the deed he forgot that John Doty's wife had died three months earlier. This would account for the blank shown in the illustration where the wife's name would ordinarily have been inserted.

To all people to whom these presents shall come John Doty of the Towne of plymouth i(n) the County of New plymouth within ye province of the Massachusets Baye in New england yeom(an) Sendeth Greeting &c. Know yee that I John Doty afore s^d^ with ye consent of (*) for (and) in consideration of sixty pounds current silver mony in New england payed to me in hand before ye seali(ng) and delivery of these presents by Wrestling Brewster of the Towne of Duxbury in ye County & province above named Carpenter wherewith I acknouledge my selfe fully and truely contented & payed and thereof and of every part and parcell thereof doe hereby absolutly acquitte & discharge from me mine Heires exiqutors Adm(ini)strators and Assignes the s^d^ Brewster his heires executors administrators &c for ever. I (hav)e given granted bargained sold aliened enfeoffed and confirmed and by these presents doe fully absolutly and clearly give grant bargaine sell alien enfeoffe and confirme from me the s^d^ John Doty and my heires unto him the

* The name was omitted.

s(d) Wrestling Brewster his heires & assignes forever. one whole Lott of upland being Seaventy acres and five acres of salt marsh more or less Lying at the foot of s^d^ seaventy acres of upland both lying and being within the Towneshi(p of) Duxbury afore s^d^. The upland is halfe a mile in Length seventy rods in breadth and beginning at the meadow (*worn*) it and the great Creeke or Bay that runeth to Jones river Bridge is bounded Southwesterly with ye Land (*worn*) Wadsworth deceased and North eastwardly with the Land of John Rogers. The salt meadow being of the s(*worn*) with the upland lyeth at the ffoot thereof and thence downe to the salt water of the aforesd Creeke or Bay. with (*worn*)gular the privileges and appurtenances to the said Lands both upland and meadow belonging or anywayes ap(per)taining (toge)ther with my said right title and interest therein and to every part there of. To have and t(o hold) above sd upland and Meadow with all my right title and Interest in the singular & universall privileges & Imun(ities) to the same in any wise belonging or yet accrueing unto the sd Wrestling Brewster his Heires & Assignes for ev(er) to his and their proper use and behoofe: To be holden according to the maner of East Greenwich in the County of Kent in the Realme of England, in free and comon soccage and not in Capite nor by Kts service: the rents and services thereout due and of right accustomed free and clear and clearly acquitted off and from all other & fo(rmer) guifts grants bargaines sales Leases mortgadges Joyntures dowries extents uses entailes and off and from (*worn*) singular other titles troubles charges demands and incumbrances whatsoever had made comitted omitte(d) or done by me the sd John Doty or by my heires or assignes or any other person or persons whatsoever L(awfully) claiming from by or under me or them or any of them. Warranting the title and sale hereof against all per-(sons) whatsoever in by thro or under me the sd John Doty or by my right or title Lawfully clayming any right title o(r) interest of or in the premisses or any part or parcell thereof whatsoever: And that the said Wrestling Brewster his heires and assignes and every of them shall and may by virtue of these presents from time (to) time and at all times for ever hereafter Lawfully peaceably and quietly have hold occupie possess and injoy (all) and singular the before granted premisses with their and every of their rights members and appurteinance(s) have receive and take all the rents issues and profits there of to his and their owne proper use and behoofe, (for) ever without any Lawfull lett suit trouble deniall interruption eviction or disturbance of me the s[d] John D(oty) my heires or assignes or any other person or persons whatsoever Lawfully clayming from by or und(er) (him) or them or any of them or by their meanes act consent title interest privitie or procurement. Allso (*worn*) John Doty doe further covenant and promise to and with the s[d] Wrestling Brewster that it shall an(d may be) Lawfull to and for the s[d] Wrestling Brewster either by himselfe or his Attorney to record and inrolle (or cause) to be recorded and inrolled the title and tenure of these presents in his Ma[ties] Court in New plymouth (*worn*) or otherwhere according to the usuall order and maner of recording and inrolling Deeds and evidences in (such) case made and provided for. And for (the tr)ue performance of the premisses I the s[d] John Doty (*worn*) selfe my heires exequtors and administrators firmly by these presents. In witness whereof I have h(erunt)o set my hand and seale this 24th of ffebruary Anno Domini 169$\frac{2}{3}$: & Regni Regis Gulielmi & Regina Maria magna Britania Galia & Hibernia &c. quinto.

Signed Sealed and delivered in the presence of us wittnesses underwritten
Ichabod Wisewalle
Priscilla Wisewall

John + Doty
his marke
(seal)

This Dede was Ackknoleg(ed) Before me John wadsworth being one of thare Majestis Justises: feberry. 24 169$\frac{2}{3}$

This above written Deed of sale is Recorded. in the 236th and 237th pages of Plimouth Counties Book of Records for Deeds &c.

March y[e] 3[d] 169$\frac{3}{4}$ pr Sam[l] Sprague Recorder

MIDDLEBOROUGH, MASS., VITAL RECORDS.

(*Continued from Vol. III, p. 236.*)

[Vol. I, p. 45] Jacob Hayford the son of John hayford: and of Lydia his wife was born: october: 24 1715

Samuel Hayford the son of John Hayford and of Lydia his wife was born: September: 17 1719

John Tayler the son of John Tayler and of Elisabeth his wife was born june the 14 1719

Robert Tayler the son of John Tayler and of Elisabeth his wife was born *

* The date was not filled in.

James Labaron the son of James Labaron and of Martha his Wife : was born : decem^r^ : 22 1721
Jonathan Pierce the son of Thomas Pierce : & of Naomi his Wife was born March the : 23. 1721/2
Joanna Bate the daughter of Joseph Bate and of Joanna his Wife was born : May. 28 1718
Mercy Bate the daughter of Joseph Bate : and of Joanna his Wife was born august 8 1719
Joseph Bate the son of Joseph Bate and of Joanna his Wife was born March : 18 1721/2
Nathan Vaughan the son of Georg Vaughan & of Faithfull his wife was born Octo : 4 1721
Amasa Tomson the son of Thomas Tomson. & of Mary his wife : was born april : 18 1722
Jemima Wood the daughter of Elnathan Wood and of Mary his Wife : was born July 21 1712
Jedidah Wood the daughter of Elnathan Wood and of Mary his Wife was born March 27 1715
Ephraim Wood the son of Elnathan Wood ; and of Mary his wife was born May the : 8 1716
Mary Wood the daughter of Elnathan Wood and of Mary his wife was born : October 5 1719
Lydia Wood the daughter of Elnathan Wood and of Mary his Wife was born July the 1 1722
Sarah Warren the daughter : of Samuel Warren and of Elinor his wife was born : February : 9 1721/2
Jabez Vaughan : & : } sons of Jabez Vaughan : and of Deborah his
Ebenezer Vaughan } Wife were born Twins : September : the 7 1722
Jerusha Connant the daughter of Josiah Connant : and of Elisabeth his Wife was born : January : 8 1701 : 2
Mary Connant the daughter of Josiah Connant : & of Elisabeth his wife : was born December 20 1703
Prudence Connant ye daughter of Josiah Connant : & of Elisabeth his wife was born : March : the 3 1707
Joseph Connant the son of Josiah Connant & of Elisabeth his wife was born : August the 30 1709
Susanna Connant the daughter of Josiah Connant & of Elisabeth his wife was born : august the : 7 1711
Josiah Connant the son of Josiah Connant : & of Elisabeth his wife was born January 20 1717 : 18
Timothy Fuller the son of Jonathan Fuller : & of Elinor his Wife was born June 29 1721
Noah Tinkham the son of Isaac Tinkham & of Abijah his Wife was born July 25 1722
Thankfull King the daughter of Ichabod King : and of Judith his Wife Was born November : 4 1718
Caleb King the son of Ichabod King : and of Judith his Wife was born october : 3 1720

Georg King the son of Ichabod King: and of Judith his Wife was born: May. 18 1722
Martha Tinkham the daughter of Samuel Tinkham Junior & of Mary his wife was born august 23 1720
Peter Tinkham the son of Samuel Tinkham Junr. & of Mary his wife Was born May. 16: 1722
Thankfull Cob the daughter of James Cob: and of Thankfull his wife was born June: 4 1722
John Richmond the son of John Richmond and of Sarah his wife was born April 28 1720
Dorothy Renolds * the daughter of Isaac Renolds and of Dorothy his wife was born: October 29 1708
Elisabeth Renolds * the daughter of Isaac Renolds & of Dorothy his wife was born: January. 28 1709 : 10
Mary Renolds * the daughter of Isaac Renolds: & of Dorothy his wife was born July: 17 : 1712
Benjamin Renolds * the son of Isaac Renolds & of Dorothy his wife was born June the 4 1715
Isaac Renolds * the son of Isaac Renolds and of Dorothy his wife was born July the: 17 1721
Israel Thomas the son of William Thomas sen^{r} and of Sarah his Wife was born January 27 1712 : 13
Betty Thomas the daughter of William Thomas sen^{r}: & of Sarah his wife was born February 20 1715 : 16
Ephraim Thomas the son of William Thomas senr: & of Sarah his Wife: was born Novem^{r}: 8 1718
Elisha Thomas the son of William Thomas sen^{r}: and of Sarah his wife was born May the: 11 1721
Mary Standish the daughter of Ichabod Standish: & of Phebe his Wife was born January 14 1722 : 3
Hannah Tinkham the daughter of John Tinkham: & of Hannah his wife was born April: 10 1723
Daniel Taylor the son of John Taylor by Elisabeth his wife was born December: 17 1720

[p. 47] Cornelius Wescoat ye son of James and Mary Wescoat his Wife was Born ye 4th Day of February Anno Dom. 1729–30
Joannah Wescoat ye Daughter of James and Mary Wescoat his Wife was Born The 29th: Day of Augst Anno domi 1731
Richard Wescoat y^{e} son of James and Mary Wescoat his Wife was Born Augst y^{e} 14th Anno Domini 1732
James Wescoat y^{e} son of James and Mary Wescoat his Wife was Born y^{e} 4th Day of February Anno domini 173$\frac{4}{5}$
Joseph Cobb The son of Gershom and Meletiah Cob his Wife was born y^{e} 23^{d} Day of January Anno Domi 1735/6
Ebenezer Donham the son of Lemuel Donham by Elizabeth his wife was born January y^{e}: 4th: 1737/8

* Compare the record of this family printed in Vol. III, p. 236.

Sarah Miller the Daughter of Elias Miller by Sarah his wife was born December the: 23rd: 1734:
Elias Miller the son of Elias Miller by Sarah his wife was born January the: 7th: 1737/8
Mary Samson and } Daughters of Obadiah Samson by Mary his wife
Martha Samson } were born Twins November: 18th: 1737
Zephaniah Wood the son of Thomas Wood by Hannah his wife was born April the: 12th: 1737
Jacob Tomson the son of Jacob Tomson by Elizabeth his wife was born March: 28th: 1738:
Joshua Raymond the son of James Raymond by Elizabeth his wife was born March the: 19th: 1735/6
Ithamar Raymond the son of James Raymond by Elizabeth his wife was born June the 21st 1737
Joshua Waterman the son of Joseph Waterman by Patience his wife was born March the: 16th: 1737/8
James Hayford the son of Ebenezer Hayford by Mary his wife was born March the: 10th: 1734/5
Mary Hayford the Daughter of Ebenezer Hayford by Mary his wife was born May the: 4th: 1737
Samuel Barrows the son of Ebenezer Barrows by Sarah his wife was born April the: 4th: 1738
Francis Gayward the son of Francis Gayward by Anna his wife was born August the 23rd 1738
William Barlow the son of William Barlow by Joanna his wife was born July 12th: 1738
William Barrows the son of Samuel Barrows Jun[r] by Susanna his wife was born June the: 16: 1738:
Benjamin Tucker the son of Benjamin Tucker by Sarah his wife was born July the: 7th: 1738

[p. 53] Middleboro: after lawfull publication
John Tinkham and Hannah Howland both of Middleboro were married december the 11 1716
James Rayment and mercy Tinkham both of Middleboro were married december 27: 1716
Nehemiah Washburn of Bridgwater and Mary Elmes of Middleboro were Married december the 27: 1716
Moses Seekens of Middleboro: & Damaris Thrasher of Taunton were married November 7 1717
Isaac Tinkham and Abijah Wood both of Middleborough: were married: Decem: 12: 1717
Henry Wood and Mary Tinkham both of Middleboro were married December: 24 1717
John Vaughan and Jerusha Wood both of Middleboro were Married February 19 $17\frac{17}{18}$
Samuel Tinkham and Patience Cob both of Middleboro were married February 20 $17\frac{17}{18}$

Abiel Wood Junr: & Mercy Hacket both of Middleboro: were Married February 25 $17\frac{18}{17}$

Edward Bumpas of Rochester: & Martha Rayment of Middleboro: were married Febryary 28 $17\frac{18}{17}$

James Cob and Thankfull Thomas both of Middleboro were married March 6 $17\frac{18}{17}$

Josiah Hascol & Sarah Kanady: both of Middleboro were Married March: 26: 1718

Isaac Thayer & Deliverance Parlour: both of Middleboro: were married March 27 1718

Richard Everson of Plimton: & Penelepe Bumpas of middleboro were married: March 31 1718

Joseph Williams of Rochester & Margaret Darling of Middleboro were married May 6 1718

David Thomas of Middleboro & Elisabeth Kannady of Plimton were married June 25 1718 pr me Peter Thacher

December the: 11: 1718 Then Nathanael Smith of Rehoboth and Susanna Wood of Middleboro after due publication: were married by me Peter Thacher

December: 12: 1718: Then marryed Jeremiah Thomas Junr: and Miriam Thomas both of the town of middleboro: after their being Lawfully published by me Peter Thacher

March: 26: 1719: Then Marryed John Fuller and Hannah Thomas both of the town of Middleboro: After lawfull publication: Peter Thacher

Samuel Tinkham Junior and Mary Staples both of the town of middleboro were married December the first: 1719: by me Peter Thacher

Eleazer Carver and Katherine Elmes both of middleboro. were married Decem: 2: 1719 by me Peter Thacher

January: $17\frac{20}{19}$: Then Marryed Jabez Wood and Hannah Nelson both of the Town of Middleborough: after Lawfull publication and consent of parents by Peter Thacher

January: 1: $17\frac{20}{19}$: Then married Ebenezer Donham of Plimouth: and Abigail Smith of Middleborough: after lawfull publication and consent of parents by me Peter Thacher

January: (*): $17\frac{20}{19}$: Then married John Darling and Jemima Lewes both of the town of Middleboro: after lawfull publication and consent of parents by me Peter Thacher

[p. 54] February: 4th: $17\frac{19}{20}$: Then Married Richard Whitaker of Rehoboth and Ann Wood of Middleborough after lawfull publication attested from each town by me Peter Thacher

April: 29: 1720 then Married Mr Jeremiah Thomas of Middleboro: and Mary Durfe of Freetown: after lawfull publication well attested from each town by me Peter Thacher

* The day of the month was not filled in.

July : 11 : 1720 : then : married Edward Thomas Junr : and Abigail Parlour both of the town of Middleborough after lawfull publication and consent of parents by me Peter Thacher

July : 20 : 1720 : Peter Norton Pedlar : and Rozilla Randal of Middleborough were married by me the subscriber after lawfull publication Peter Thacher

Capt Joseph Vaughan and Mrs Mercy Fuller both of Middleborough : were married December the : 2nd : 1720 by me Peter Thacher

December the 23^{d} : 1720 then Robert Mackfun and Joanna Tinkham both of Middleborough after lawfull publication : were married by me Peter Thacher

May the 4th : 1721 Then Nehemiah Bennet & Mercy Tomson both of the town of Middleborough : after Lawfull publication were married by me Peter Thacher

June 22 : 1721 : William Thomas Junr : & Hannah Turner : both of Middleborough after lawfull publication : were married by me Peter Thacher

October : 5th : 1721 : Cornelius Holmes of Plimton and Lydia Bennet of Middleborough : were Married : after Lawfull publication : by me : Peter Thacher

October : 12 : 1721 : John Cox and Hannah Smith both of Middleborough : after Lawfull publication were married by me Peter Thacher

October : 17 : 1721. John Darling and Elisabeth Bennet both of Middleborough after lawfull publication were married by me Peter Thacher

Samuel Packard Junr : and Anne Leach : both of the town of Bridgwater : were Married July the third : 1722 : by me Jacob Tomson Justice of the peace

Sept : 6 : 1722 Thomas Parlour and Hannah King both of Middleborough after legal publication and with consent of Parents were married by Peter Thacher

Joseph Faunce and Martha Soul both of Middleborough : were married February the 14th 172$\frac{3}{4}$: by me Jacob Tomson Justice of the peace

James Barret and Mary Wormall both of the town of Bridgwater : were marryed September the : 5 : 1723 : by me Jacob Tomson Justice of the peace

Josiah Wormall and Grace Sprague both of the town of Duxborough Were Married : December the Twenty Fifth 1723 : by me Jacob Tomson Justice of the peace

October : 24 : 1723 John Tomson and Elisabeth Thomas both of Middleborough after lawfull publication and consent of parents : were married : by me Peter Thacher

[p. 55] October 29 1723 Thomas Wastcoat of Dighton : and Hannah Renolds of Middleborough were married by me Peter Thacher

November 23d : 1723 Moses Standish of plymton : and Rachel Cob of middleborough after Lawfull publication and consent of parents : were married : by me Peter Thacher

November 27 1723 : Jonathan Packard of Bridgwater : and Abigail Tomson of middleborough : after Lawfull publication : and consent of parents : were married by me Peter Thacher

November 30 : 1723 Frances Moro : and Mary Morse both of Middleborough after lawfull publication were married by me Peter Thacher

January 13 $172\frac{4}{3}$ George Hacket and Lydia Thomas both of Middleborough after lawfull publication : and consent of parents were married by me Peter Thacher

March : 12 $172\frac{4}{3}$ Jedidiah Thomas and Lois Nelson both of Middleborough after lawfull publication and consent of parents : were married : by me Peter Thacher

Jonathan Inglee and Deborah Morton of Middleborough were Married upon the 27th day of February : 1723/4 : by me Samuel Prince Justice of the peace

Aaron Seekins and Lydia Hayford : both of the town of Middleborough Were Marryed January the 12 1724 : 5 by me Jacob Tomson Justice of the peace

John Pratt and Hannah Turner both of the town of Middleborough were Married February the : 18th $172\frac{5}{4}$: by me : Jacob Tomson Justice of the peace

November 18 1724 : Joseph Bennet Junr and Thankfull Sprout : both of middleborough after lawfull publication and consent of parents were married Pr Peter Thacher

January 17 $172\frac{5}{4}$ Japheth Turner and Elisabeth Morse both of middleborough after lawfull publication and Consent of parents : were married : Pr Peter Thacher

March 26 : 1725 Samuel Leach of Bridgwater and Content Barden of middleborough after lawfull publication were married by Peter Thacher

June 8 : 1725 : Jonathan Smith and Sarah Churchill both of Middleborough were then married Pr Peter Thacher

John Cob Junior and Mary Connant : both of the town of Middleborough were married August the : 26 1725 : by me : Jacob Tomson Justice of the peace

Timothy Mitchell and Deborah Packard both of the town of Bridgwater : were married : December the second : 1725 : by me Jacob Tomson Justice of the peace

William Ripley and Hannah Bosworth both of the town of plimton Were Married February the : 24th : 1725 : by me Jacob Tomson Justice of the peace

[p. 56] Deacon Ebenezer Tinkham Deceased april the : 8th : 1718 : In the 70 year of his age

Elisabeth Tinkham the wife of Deacon Ebenezer Tinkham Deceased april the : 8th : 1718 In the (*) year of her age

Elisabeth Tinkham the Daughter of Deacon Ebenezer Tinkham decesed March 27th : 1715 In the (*) year of her age

Jeremiah Tinkham the son of Deacon Ebenezer Tinkham Deceased april the : 5th : 1715 In the : 34th : year of his age

priscilla Tinkham the daughter of Deacon Ebenezer Tinkham Deceased April the : 16 : 1715 In the (*) year of her age

Patience Tinkham the Wife of Ebenezer Tinkham Junior Deceased March the : 29 : 1718 In the 37th year of her age

Hannah Hacket the Wife of Edward Hacket deceased May the ninth 1715

Samuel Wood senior Deceased : February the third $17\frac{18}{17}$: In the 70th year of his age

Rebeckah Wood Widdow of Samuel Wood Senior Deceased February the : 10 $17\frac{18}{17}$ In the 67th year of her age

Rebekah Vaughan the wife of Georg Vaughan deceased February the : 1 : $17\frac{19}{18}$

Frances Barrows the son of Samuel Barrows deceased : March : 17 : $17\frac{18}{17}$ in the 5th year of his ag(e)

Mercy Barrows the wife of Samuel Barrows deceased : March 25 : 1718 in the 44th year of her age

Thomas Palmer : Eldest son of Doctour Thomas Palmer and of Elisabeth his Wife Deceased July the 18th 1719 : In the 20th year of his age

Sarah Palmer Daughter of Doctor Thomas Palmer and of Elisabeth his Wife Deceased Sept : the first 1719 : In the second year of her age

Zurishaddai Palmer the son of Doctor Thomas Palmer and of Elisabeth his wife Deceased October the 18th 1719 : In the 18th year of his age

Anna Lovel the Daughter of James Lovel Deceased Sept the Sixth : 1719

Desire Howland the daughter of Nathan Howland : and of Frances his wife Deceased March the. (†) : $17\frac{19}{18}$: in the fifth year of her age

Esther Wood the daughter of Henry Wood and of Mary his wife Deceased May the : 9th : 1721 : aged three months and nine dayes

Peter Lovel the son of John Lovel and of Mary his Wife : Deceased April the 4th : 1724 In the ninteenth year of his age

Samuel Eaton Deceased : March the 8th : 1723 : 4 : In the sixty first year of his age

Susanna Smith the wife of Jonathan Smith : Deceased May the : 11 : 1724 In the thirtieth year of her age

Mary Reed the daughter of James Reed . Deceased July the 17th : 1724 : In the twenty seventh year of her age

* The age was not filled in. † The day of the month was not filled in.

John Hacket the son of John Hacket Deceased: May the 31st 1712: aged 44 dayes

Joanna Cob the Wife of John Cob Junior Deceased November the Eleventh 1724 In the thirty second year of her age

Elisha Vaughan Deceased: May the: 23d: 1724: In the 44th year of his age

Thomas Vaughan the son of Elisha Vaughan Deceased March 20th 17$\frac{20}{19}$ In the sixth year of his age

Joseph Vaughan the son of Capt Joseph Vaughan Deceased april the 5th 1718 In the 28th year of his age

Thankfull Hacket the daughter of John Hacket: deceased Febr: 5: 172$\frac{5}{4}$: aged Ten days

(*To be continued.*)

PLYMOUTH COLONY WILLS AND INVENTORIES.

(*Continued from Vol. III, page 225.*)

[Vol. I, fol. 40] Mr Willm Kempe 1641

Lres of Administracon are graunted to mris Elizabeth Kempe the second of November in the xviith yeare of the Raigne of our Sovraigne Lord Charles King of England &c. to administer upon all the goods cattells and Debts wch Willm Kemp her husband Dyed possessed of or were Due & apprtaineing unto him at the tyme of his Decease prvided she exhibite a true Inventory thereof wth all convenyent speede.

A true Inventory of all the goods and Chattells moveable of mr Willm Kemp of Duxborrow late Deceased taken by us whose names are hereunto sett at the request of mrs Elizabeth Kemp this 23th Septembr in the yeare of or Lord God 1641.

In the Inner Chamber	*li s d*
Inpris i feather bed and two pillowes	03 . 00 . 00
It 3 white blanketts	01 . 00 . 00
It i blew Rugg	01 . 00 . 00
It 4 yerds of white fusteon	00 . 05 . 00
It i pillow case	00 . 01 . 06
It 2 remnants of Canvas	00 . 02 . 00
It i remnant of white fusteon	00 . 00 . 06
It i remnant of girth web & 4 buckles	00 . 02 . 00
It 3 paire of traces & a new Rope wth some small ropes ·	00 . 10 . 00

It 4 Iron boxes for cart wheeles & 4 new Iron hoopes for wheels	00 . 12 . 00
It i latin water pot for a garden	00 . 00 . 08
It i paire of garden sheares	00 . 01 . 06
It 2 iron washers & 5 iron clouts new & 2 new plow slips	00 . 01 . 06
It 2 horse locks & keeyes	00 . 01 . 00
It 2 nibbs and i ring for a sythe	00 . 00 . 06
It 2 paire of hinges	00 . 01 . 06
It 12 harrow teeth	00 . 01 . 06
It 20 Iron staples & 3 iron bolts	00 . 04 . 00
It i bill hooke and 5 old sickles	00 . 03 . 00
It i iron acar staff	00 . 00 . 06
It 2 padlocks & i stock lock	00 . 02 . 06
It i iron baile for a kettle	00 . 00 . 08
It certaine peecs of old iron	00 . 04 . 00
It i pitch fork pronges	00 . 00 . 08
It i red basill	00 . 00 . 08
It 3 q^r^ of a yard of buckrome	00 . 00 . 08
It i smale curtaine & a prcell of fring	00 . 01 . 00
It Curtaine Ringes & sadlers nayles	00 . 01 . 00
	07 . 19 . 10
It a prcell of Twine	00 . 02 . 00
It i new shooe	00 . 01 . 00
It quarries of glasse	00 . 02 . 00
It i spitt	00 . 00 . 08
It i horse bitt a crupper & i bridle Reane	00 . 00 . 08
It 2 joyned stooles	00 . 02 . 00
It 3 smale Remnants of new cloth	00 . 01 . 06
It i bushell of wheate brann	00 . 00 . 04
It 3 barrells 2 firkins 2 hogsheads & a half barrell	00 . 05 . 00
It 2 earthern potts	00 . 00 . 04
It 2 sheets of leade	00 . 02 . 00
It 3 cases for guns of list wth other lumber	00 . 01 . 06
	00 . 19 00

In the Kitchen Chamber.

It i flock bedd and two boulsters	00 . 12 . 00
It 2 white blanketts & i old greene Rugg	00 . 15 . 00
It 5 smale peecs of bend leather & 2 shoomaker knives	00 . 03 . 04
It i small pursnett & 2 lines	00 . 02 . 00
It i red basill	00 . 00 . 08
It a prcell of 6^d^ nayles	00 . 03 . 00
It i weyer sieve	00 . 01 . 06
It i smale bagg of feathers	00 . 01 . 00
It i sieve	00 . 00 . 03
It i prcell of unthrest beanes	00 . 00 . 06
It i paire of old sheets	00 . 02 . 00
It i hogshead & a shelfe	00 . 00 . 08

It i thwart sawe	00 . 03 . 00
It i old tapstry carpett	00 . 04 . 00
It 2 eathern old oyle potts	00 . 00 . 04
It i paire of new hempen sheets	00 . 12 . 00
It vi paire of couse thinn sheets	02 . 00 . 00
It certaine lumber	00 . 00 . 08
It i great boxe	00 . 01 . 00
	05 . 01 11

In the parlor

It i paire of bras brandirons	00 . 12 . 00
It i belt and hangers	00 . 12 . 00
It i Dagger	00 . 01 . 00
It i rapier staffe	00 . 01 . 00
It i girdle wth silv^r^ buckles	00 . 02 . 00
It 10 silver spoones	02 . 10 . 00
It i jugg pott tipt wth silv^r^	00 . 10 . 00
It i cup tipt wth silver	00 . 04 . 00
It i gould ringe	00 . 18 . 00
It 6 thrum queshions	00 . 12 . 00
It 2 old Darnix queshions	00 . 00 . 08
	06 . 02 08

[fol. 41] It i framed table	00 . 10 . 00
It 4 joyned stooles and 2 joyned chaires	00 . 10 . 00
It i old brodred stoole	00 . 01 . 00
It i great chest	00 . 08 . 00
It i smale chest	00 . 01 . 06
It i trunck covered wth seale skins	01 . 00 . 00
It 2 smale old Truncks	00 . 05 . 00
It i Cabbanett	00 . 04 . 00
It 2 old boxes	00 . 00 . 04
It i case of bottles	00 . 03 . 00
It 2 brushes	00 . 00 . 08
It i new hatt	00 . 10 . 00
It 4 hattbands	00 . 01 . 04
It 4 old hatts	00 . 01 . 04
It a remnant silk bone lace	00 . 02 . 00
It glew and an old black boxe	00 . 00 . 06
It 5 paire of flaxen sheets i paire of new hempen	04 . 00 . 00
It 2 duzzen of fine napkins & 2 table cloathes	02 . 00 . 00
It i sheete	00 . 06 . 00
It 5 holland pillow coats	01 . 00 . 00
It 2 duzzen of Course napkins	00 . 10 . 00
It 3 paire of old pillow coates	00 . 03 . 00
It 7 course towells	00 . 03 . 00
It 3 course table cloathes	00 . 07 . 00
It i hand towell	00 . 02 . 00
It i remnant of holland	00 . 04 . 00
It 2 short table cloaths	00 . 06 . 00

It 2 yerds of white fusteon	00 . 01 . 04
It i wrought holland cubberd cloth	00 . 08 . 00
It i leather hat case	00 . 03 . 00
It i half holland shirt & i holland shirt	00 . 12 . 00
It 6 shirts	00 . 12 . 00
It 7 holland handkerchiefs	00 . 07 . 00
It 10 capps	00 . 05 . 00
It 13 bands	00 . 08 . 00
It 3 handkercheiffs	00 . 02 . 00
It 3 smale pillowes	00 . 02 . 00
It i paire of linnen bootehose i fusteon wascoate & a remnant canvas	00 . 04 . 00
It i rubbing brush	00 . 00 . 02
It nutmeggs	00 . 03 . 00
It ginger	00 . 01 . 00
It cloves	00 . 00 . 08
It a remnant of fine holland i yerd of bone lace	00 . 04 . 00
It i spining wheele	00 . 03 . 00
It 3 irish stockings	00 . 02 . 00
	16 . 17 . 10
It 3 paire of wollen stockings	00 . 06 . 00
It 5 blew curtaines and vallence	01 . 16 . 00
It i^li^ of gray threed	00 . 02 . 00
It i buffe coate	01 . 10 . 00
It i cloake	00 . 13 . 06
It i greene Curtaine	00 . 01 . 00
It i leather Dublet wth silv^r^ buttons	01 . 00 . 00
It i paire of gloves	00 . 01 . 00
It i paire of breeches and a Dublett	01 . 00 . 00
It i frize jerkine	00 . 08 . 00
It i black suite and gerdle	01 . 05 . 00
It i black cloake	01 . 10 . 00
It 3 horsmans coats	02 . 00 . 00
It i boulster tick	00 . 04 . 00
It 116 bunches of threed buttons	00 . 18 . 00
It i darnix carpett	00 . 03 . 00
It i remnant of broad cloth	00 . 02 . 00
It i long coate	00 . 10 . 00
It i dublet & i Casock	00 . 03 . 00
It 2 yerds of saye	00 . 05 . 00
It 6 yerds ½ tammey	00 . 18 . 00
It 2 remnants of stuff	00 . 04 . 00
It i feather pillow	00 . 02 . 00
It 2 greene vallens	00 . 02 . 00
It i paire of linnen drawers	00 . 01 . 00
It bookes and paper	08 . 00 . 00
	23 04 . 06

In the outlett Inner Roome

It 3 blanketts	00 . 15 . 00
It i flockbed & boulster	00 . 10 . 00
It i chaire & i tubb	00 . 06 . 00
It 5 earthen panns i butter pott	00 . 02 . 00
	01 . 13 . 00

In the Cellor

It i hogshead & 3 firkins	00 . 05 06

In the wash house.

It 3 cheese fatt i soyle dish	00 . 02 . 06
It 2 latten pans & 2 earthen potts	00 . 01 . 06
It i stone pott i earthen pott	00 . 00 . 08
It 2 dossen trenchers	00 . 00 . 08
It 2 payles i wodden platter i traye	00 . 03 . 00
It i melting ladle	00 . 01 . 06
It i iron pott 2 paire of pott hookes	00 . 06 . 00
It i iron dripping pann	00 . 04 . 00
It i iron kettle	00 . 10 . 00
	01 . 10 . 04

[fol. 42] In the kitchen

It i Corslett and headpeece	01 . 00 . 00
It 2 paire of bandiliers	00 . 02 . 06
It i case of pistolls	00 . 10 . 00
It i paire of Wollen sheares	00 . 01 . 00
It 2 swordes	00 . 06 . 00
It 2 Carbines	01 . 00 . 00
It i fowling piece	00 . 15 . 00
It i half pike & a rest	00 . 03 00
It i jack and 3 spitts	00 . 16 . 00
It 2 paire of bootes	00 . 03 . 00
It i trowell	00 . 00 . 06
It i bread grater	00 . 01 . 06
It 2 leaden waights	00 . 06 . 00
It i lanthorne	00 . 00 . 08
It i halbert	00 . 03 . 00
It i warmeing pann & i gally pott	00 . 05 . 06
It 9 platters and a voyder	01 . 10 . 00
It 8 pewter dishes 2 basons i Cullender	00 . 17 . 00
It 6 great porringes	00 . 07 . 00
It 2 pye plates 2 smale plates	00 . 04 . 00
It 3 chamber potts	00 . 03 . 00
It 4 candlesticks	00 . 04 . 00
It i bason	00 . 01 . 00
It i pint pott & a peuter pottle	00 . 01 . 06
It i ewer	00 . 01 . 06
It 4 sawcers 3 salts 4 porringers i tinn copper	00 . 02 . 06
It 2 smale plattes i quart pott	00 . 02 . 00
It 2 plate covrings i stewpan 2 tinn candlesticks	00 . 02 . 06

It i flaggon	00 . 02 . 00
It 2 bras candlesticks & i bras ladle	00 . 04 . 00
It chaffeing dish i scummer i little morter	00 . 09 . 00
It i bras skellet & i posnett	00 . 05 . 06
It 3 bras panns	01 . 00 . 00
It i great bras kettle	01 . 00 . 00
It i little kettle	00 . 05 . 00
It i old bras pott	00 . 12 . 00
It stone jugg i leather bottle ½ a pike	00 . 02 . 06
It 12 trenchers	00 . 00 . 06
It i salt	00 . 05 . 00
It i smothing iron	00 . 01 . 06
It i slick stone 2 mackrell lines i melting ladle	00 . 02 . 00
It i frying pann	00 . 02 . 00
It i paire of towe cards	00 . 01 . 00
	14 . 01 . 08
It 3 mattocks	00 . 06 . 00
It 6 hoes 3 axes	00 . 10 . 00
It 4 wedges	00 . 03 . 00
It i iron shovell	00 . 03 . 00
It i lampe	00 . 00 . 06
It fire pan tonges and Andiron	00 . 04 . 00
It i paire of bellowes	00 . 01 . 00
It 2 paire of pott hangers	00 . 06 . 00
It an adze 2 frowes i hammer	00 . 05 . 00
It i gouge 2 chissells i drawing kniffe	00 . 03 . 00
It i handsaw i hatchett a little grafting saw i pr shott moulds and i paire pinchers	00 . 06 . 00
It 2 augors i perser	00 . 01 . 06
It i bagg wth bulletts pouder horne & moulds	00 . 02 . 00
It i shott bagg	00 . 00 . 02
	02 . 11 02
Without Doores.	
It i grindlestone	00 . 04 . 00
It hempe and seede undressed.	00 . 10 . 00
It garden stuffe	00 . 05 . 00
It 2 Cocks of hey	02 . 00 . 00
It 2 ladders	00 . 04 . 00
It 2 chest of glasse	00 . 15 . 00
	03 . 18 00
In the Cow house	
It 5 goate skins	00 . 01 . 00
It i seane nett	00 . 05 . 00
In the barne	
It i steele Mill	00 . 10 . 00
It sampe morter	00 . 02 . 00
It i bushell	00 . 03 . 00

It i sack cloth and 2 sacks	00 . 06 . 00
It a copper wth a wodden Curbe	01 . 00 . 00
It 2 hogsheads 2 barrells	00 . 05 . 00
It 4 pitchforks & 2 rakes	00 . 05 . 00
It glasse leade	00 . 12 . 00
It 12½ thrane of Rye	03 . 00 . 00
It 12 .thrane of sumer wheate	03 . 00 . 00
It peas	00 . 12 . 00
It 4 bushell Indian Corne	00 . 10 . 00
It 2 steare Calves	02 . 00 . 00
It 2 yeareling heiffers	06 . 00 . 00
It i yeareling heiffer	02 . 10 . 00
It 2 yearling steers	03 . 00 . 00
It i sow shoate & a barrow shoate	00 . 13 . 00
It 2 oxen 4 yers old	14 . 00 . 00
	38 . 14 . 00
[fol. 43] It 6 ewe goates	02 . 00 . 00
It 4 ewe lambes	00 . 12 . 00
It i weather 2 yeres old	00 . 08 . 00
It 4 yereling weathers	00 . 13 . 04
It 2 yoakes & two cheanes	00 . 15 . 00
	04 . 8 . 04

At m[r] Partich house

It i fowling peece	01 . 00 . 00
It i smale old fowleing peece	00 . 05 . 00
It i sieve	00 . 00 . 04
It i boxe	00 . 01 . 06
It i boxe	00 . 04 . 00
It i cradle	00 . 04 . 00
It i hanging bedstead	00 . 02 . 06
It 2 cowes & i diseased	07 . 00 . 00
It i heiffer 2 yere old	03 . 00 . 00
It i steare 2 yere old	03 . 00 . 00
It i Coult	06 . 00 . 00
It 6 hoggs	04 . 00 . 00
It i hogg	01 . 00 . 00
It i Cannow	00 . 05 . 00
It i fann	00 . 03 . 00
It i weane rope	00 . 03 . 00
It i peck wth pitch in it	00 . 01 . 00
It Indian Corne 1000 hills old & new esteemed 50 bushell	06 . 00 . 00
It i stillyerd	00 . 02 . 00
It i still	00 . 16 . 00
It i Hutchell	00 . 05 . 00
It i bell	00 . 00 . 08
It i shallop	10 . 00 . 00

It i ewe lambe	00 . 10 . 00
It 8 foules	00 . 04 . 00
It a rake head	00 . 00 . 02
	44 . 07 . 02

This Inventory was subscribed by Wm Collyer
his was but, 169 15. 5 : Jonathan Brewster
tot. 172. 9. 5. Christopher Waddesworth
Comfort Starr.

more debts oweing to him and what he owed verte

In debts oweing to Mr Willm Kemp at his death

	li s d
It by mr William Collier	00 . 17 . 08
It by Captaine Standish	00 . 12 . 00
It by mr Alden	00 . 18 . 00
It by Christopher Waddesworth 12 bushells of Indian Corne & i bushell of Rye	
It by Nicholas Robins	00 . 09 . 00
It by Willm Brett	02 . 05 . 00
It by John Willis	01 . 02 . 00
It by Joseph Biddle	00 . 08 . 00

Debts oweing by mr Kemp at his Death

It to mr Atwood 5 bushell of Indian corne i bushell of wheate
It to mr Hanberry 16 bushell of Indian Corne
It to mr Partrich 4 bushell of Indian Corne & 2 bush wheate & i bushell of Rye & 3s 2d in money
It to John Hill of Boston x bushell of Indian Corne

This Inventory was exhibited upon the Oath of mris Elizabeth Kemp at the Court held the fift of Aprill in the xviiith yeare of the now Raigne of or Sovraigne Lord Charles King of England &c before Willm Bradford gent Govr Edward Winslow Thomas Prence Willm Collyer & Miles Standish gent Assistants &c

(*To be continued.*)

PLYMOUTH COLONY DEEDS.

(*Continued from p. 37.*)

[Vol. II, Pt. I, p. 84]

The 4th of October 1653

Memorand : That Edward Tilson of the Towne of Plymouth

Doth acknowlidge that for and in consideracon of the summe of ten shillings pr annum to bee paied unto him in currant comoditie of the Countrey to bee paied att his house att Plymouth aforsaid by Thomas Byrd of Scittuate hee hath sett and to farme lett unto the said Thomas Byrd forty acres of upland ground lying att the North river in the liberties of Scittuate aforsaid; lying next the land of the said Thomas Byrd and Thomas Rawlins which said land the said Thomas Byrd is to have on the tearmes aforsaid the tearme of seaven yeare unles the said Edward Tilson either himselfe or any from by or under him shall make use of it at any time within the said tearme of seaven yeares if soe then the said Thomas Byrd is to surrender it againe; And alsoe the said Edward Tilson reserveth unto himselfe the mersh land belonging unto the said upland (*worn*)ly The said Thomas Byrd is to have the after pasture therof and whatsoever charge the said Thomas Byrd shalbee att in Breaking up of the said land incase hee shall not bee satisfyed by the use of the land it shalbee put to reference of two Indifferent men; and what they shall Determine in the p^r^mises shalbee prformed

[p. 85. The first deed on this page, Myles Standish to Thomas Willett, we printed in Vol. II, p. 127.]

The 3^d^ of November 1653

Memorand; That capt: Thomas Willett of the towne of Plymouth in the Jurisdiction of new Plymouth in new England in america Doth acknowlidge that for and in consideration of the full summe of twenty eight pounds to him alreddy paied by m^r^ John Browne of the Towne of Rehoboth in the Jurisdiction aforsaid Jent: hee hath freely and absolutely barganed allianated and sold enfeofed and confeirmed; and by these p^r^sents Doth bargane sell enfeofe and confeirme unto the said m^r^ John Browne all that his prte and proprietie of land which hee lately bought of Experience Michell which Did before the said sale belonge unto him as purchaser att Sowamsett Mattapoisett & places adiacent both upland and meddow with all and singulare the appurtenances privilidges and emunities belonging therunto or to any prte or prcell therof; To have and to hold the said prte and portion and proprietie of land both upland and meddow att Sowamsett Mattapoisett and places adiacent with all and singulare the appurtenances privilidges and emunities belonging therunto or to any prte or prcell therof; To the said m^r^ John Browne his heires and assignes for ever; the said p^r^mises with all and singulare the appurtenances belonging therunto to appertaine unto the onely proper use and behoofe of him the said m^r John Browne his heires and assignes for ever

Thomas Willett ;

The 3^d of November 1653

Memorand : That I John Browne abovemencioned Doe assigne give and bequeath unto my two sonnes viz John Browne and James Browne all my right title and enterest which I have into a prcell or tracts of land which this p^rsent Day I have bought of my sonneinlaw capt : Thomas Willett lying att Sowamsett Mattapoisett and places adiacent both upland and meddow with all and singulare the appurtenances privilidges and emunities belonging therunto or unto any prte or prcell therof ; To have and to hold the said land bought of my soninlaw aforsaid both upland and meddow att Sowamsett Mattapoisett and places adiacent ; which was formerly the propriety and portion belonging to Experience Michell as purchaser in the said places unto my said two sonnes videlecet John Browne and James Browne theire heires and assignes for ever ; the said p^rmises with all and singulare the appurtenances privilidges and emunities belonging therunto or unto any prte or prcell therof with all and singulare my right title and enterest into the same I Doe heerby freely and absolutly give and make over unto my said two sonnes John Browne and James Browne unto them and theire heires and assignes for ever ;

John Browne

[p. 87] 1653 Bradford Govr

A Comission appointed to bee recorded

To all her Maties of Swedens Governors captaines and subiectes of what ranke and sort whatsoever ;

fforasmuch as Lawrance Cornelius one of her Maties of Swedens subiects, in New Sweden is Desirus with himselfe and companie and barque or sloope upon this coast of america to trad and traffacke peacably with such as are in alliance with the Crowne of Sweden ; this his Desire I found to bee reasonable and have given him therfore Comission under my hand and seale ; I Doe therfore Desire and entreat all Comaunders governors or prsons of what quallitie soever they may bee that are in alliance with the Crowne of Sweden aforsaid that they will carry respectively and frindly to him and his companie and suffer him quietly to pase and repase and to Doe his busines quietly without molestacon and to shew him all the favor and frindshipp they may; And wee Doe engage ourselves to Doe the like unto theires as occation shall p^r^sent;

Dated in New Sweden
in the fortt Christina
the first of october 1653

John Prince
Govr
his (seale)

Wheras by an order of court wee were appointed to view certaine Lands lyinge over against Road Iland and to lay them forth by such bounds as wee saw meet, if wee found them not to bee p^r^judiciall to any And wee haveing Dilligently viewed the same Doe Determine the bounds to bee from the valley att the uttermost south point of the mersh of Punkatest neare the Indian fortt eight miles up into the countrey; Easterly from the end of the eight mile to range northerly unto the great river that cometh from Taunton unto Road Iland; the salt water betwixt Road Iland and the mayne to bee the westerly bounds And if any of the lands formerly graunted unto the old comers or purchasers shall extend so fare as to fall within any prte of these lines then soe much to bee added or made good uppon the Northerly prte of the bounds upon the river that cometh from Taunton; soe as the whole quantitie of these bounds shalbee to the vallue and quantity of eight mile Square and these lands to belonge unto such as are now the Inhabitants of the towne of Plymouth;

Dated the 26th of June 1653

Myles Standish
John Browne

[p. 89] 1653 Bradford Govr

Wheras Divers yeares sence there was a greivance that our Pastor Mr Charles Chauncy was troubled withall which hee expressed to our church and bretheren of Scittuate; the occation wherof was this that our Pastor prceived that contrary to his expectation som prsons amongst us questioned his enterest and proprietie in his now Dwelling house att Scittuate with the outhouses and grounds belonging to it; These are to Testify to all men whom these p^r^sents may conserne that wee Richard Sillis and Thomas Ensigne being then Deacons of the said church of Scittuate were sent with the consent of M^r^ hatherley and all the rest of the bretheren assembled then together to consult about the said greivance of our Pastor and the redresse of it; with this message; to our Pastor m^r^ Charles Chauncy; to this effect that the said church of Scittuate Did emediately and freely bestow upon him the said m^r^ Charles Chauncy the said Dwelling house outhouses and lands appertaining therunto bought by m^r Timothy hatherley of m^r Willam Varssall with the addition of another building made att the churches cost; And this wee Tistify of our owne best knowlidge and remembrance;

This above written was Testifyed upon oath by Richard Sillis and Thomas Ensigne the third Day of October 1653

before us Thomas Prence
Myles Standish
John Browne

The sixt of December 1653

Memorand; That Leiftenant Perigrine White of the towne of marshfeild in the Jurisdiction of new Plymouth in New England in america Doth acknowlidge that for and in consideration of the full summe of forty pounds to him in hand payed by capt: Thomas Willett of the Towne of Plymouth in the Jurisdiction aforsaid wherwith hee Doth acknowlidge himselfe Satisfyed contented and fully payed; hee hath freely and absolutly barganed allianated and sold enfeofed and confeirmed and by these Doeth bargane sell enfeofe and confeirme unto the said capt: Willett all that his prte and proprietie of land which as Purchaser or old comer; belongeth unto him att Sowamsett Mattapoisett and places adiacent both upland and meddow with all and singulare the appurtenances privilidges and emunities belonging unto the same; as alsoe the said Leiftenant White is to Defray all charges ariseing by the Indian purchase of the said p^rmises; To have and to hold his said prte portion and proprietie of land both upland and meddow which as purchaser or old comer belongeth unto him att Sowamsett Mattapoisett and places adiacent with all and singulare the appurtenances privilidges and emunities belonging therunto or to any prte or prcell therof unto the said captaine Thomas Willett his heires and assignes forever; The said p^rmises with all and singulare the appurtenances therunto belonging to appertaine unto the onely proper use and behoofe of him the said capt: Willett his heires and assignes for ever; and alsoe the said Leiftenant White heerby covenanteth that his brother Resolved White shall give his (*worn*) and full consent unto the sale of the abovesaid premi(ses)

This sale was acknowlidged before capt: Standish asistant; the Day and yeare above written;

(*To be continued.*)

PHINEAS PRATT OF PLYMOUTH AND CHARLESTOWN.

(*Reprinted, with additions, from "The Macdonough–Hackstaff Ancestry.*")

BY RODNEY MACDONOUGH.

THE opening up of a new country and the planting of settlements therein are usually due to commercial enterprise and activity; occasionally to political or religious expediency.

New England furnishes no exception to the general rule, and these influences will supply a raison d'etre for each of the early settlements within her borders. Commercial enterprise, the foundation of the colonization idea, was the strongest of the three forces and naturally found expression in the establishment of numerous plantations dedicated to trade and barter. Among the earliest of these was Wessagusset, a neighbor of Plymouth. It is not the purpose of the writer to enter into the details of the settlement and subsequent history of Wessagusset, but to give what facts are known concerning one who was intimately connected with that plantation and later with Plymouth and Charlestown, Phineas Pratt.

The following brief account of the coming of Phineas and his early experiences here shows the hardships, the dangers and the sufferings undergone by those who sought new homes in a new country, and a recital of these happenings, in whatever form presented, can hardly fail to interest his descendants both because of a feeling of kinship and because of the attendant circumstances of time and place. Phineas himself has left us, in his "Declaration," a most interesting account of the affairs of the early settlers and his own experiences. The writer has quoted freely from this invaluable document, printed in the Massachusetts Historical Society Collections (Fourth Series, IV, 476), and the quotations will be readily recognized.

Phineas was one of a small party sent by Thomas Weston, a London merchant, and a Mr. Beachamp, in the Sparrow to prepare the way for the settlement of a new colony.* This party consisted of but six or seven persons. Bradford says seven.† Winslow says six or seven.‡ Phineas says "we being but 10 men," referring to the initial trip of the Sparrow's

* Bradford's History (London, 1896), 72. † Ibid., 72, 78.

‡ Winslow's "Good Newes from New England" (London, 1624), 11.

boat to Plymouth, but this number no doubt included the Master's Mate and two or three seamen of the Sparrow, thus leaving six or seven in Weston's party. It is certain that others of the Sparrow's crew besides the Master's Mate accompanied the settlers on this trip to take back the boat, for Winslow says the party "brought no more prouision for the present than serued the Boats gang for their returne to the ship."* Some sixty more men were to follow this party later.

The Sparrow sailed for Massachusetts Bay, "but wanting a pilote," writes Phineas, "we Ariued att Damoralls Cove. The men y[t] belong to y[e] ship, ther fishing, had newly set up a may pole & weare very mery. We maed hast to prepare a boat fit for costing. Then said Mr. Rodgers, Master of our ship, 'heare ar Many ships & at Munhigin, but no man y[t] does vndertake to be yo[r] pilate; for they say y[t] an Indian Caled Rumhigin vndertook to pilot a boat to Plimoth, but thay all lost tha[r] Lives.' Then said Mr. Gibbs, Mast[rs] Mate of our ship, 'I will venter my Liue wth y[m].' At this Time of our discouery, we first Ariued att Smithe's Ilands, first soe Caled by Capt. Smith, att the Time of his discouery of New Eingland, ... fterwards Caled Ilands of Sholes; ffrom thence to Cape Ann . . . . so Caled by Capt Mason; from thence to y[e] Mathechusits Bay. Ther we continued 4 or 5 days. Then we pseaued, y[t] on the south part of the Bay, weare fewest of the natives of the Cuntry Dwelling ther. We thought best to begine our plantation, but fearing A great Company of Salvages, we being but 10 men, thought it best to see if our friends weare Living at Plimoth. Then sayling Along the Cost, not knowing the harber, thay shot of a peece of Ardinance, and at our coming Ashore, they entertaned vs wth 3 vally of shotts."

Phineas and his party reached Plymouth the last of May, 1622. The month is given by Bradford and the context shows the year. He says:—"But about y[e] *later end of may*, they spied *a boat* at sea (which at first they thought had beene some french-man) but it proued a shalop which came from a ship which M[r] Weston, & an other, had set out a fishing, at a place called Damarins-coue .40. leagues to y[e] eastward of them; wher were y[t] year many more ships come a fishing. This boat brought .7. passengers; and some letters, but no uitails, nor any hope of any."† Bradford does not mention the name of the vessel to which the shallop belonged, but this omission is supplied by Winslow, who writes:—"This Boat proued to be a

* Winslow's "Good Newes from New England" (London, 1624), 11.

† Bradford's History (London, 1856), 72.

shallop that belonged to a fishing ship, called the Sparrow, set forth by Master *Thomas Weston*, late Merchant and Citizen of London, which brought six or seuen passengers at his charge, that should before haue beene landed at our Plantation, who also brought no more prouision for the present than serued the Boats gang for their returne to the ship."*

The Plymouth colonists being greatly in need of provisions at this time, the men of the Sparrow accompanied some of them to the fishing fleet at the Damariscove Islands to procure what food the ships could spare. Their friends "did what they could freely" and the party returned to Plymouth with such necessaries as the fleet could spare from its scanty store.

It has been thought that after this expedition Phineas and his companions returned from Plymouth to the Sparrow and there awaited the coming of the rest of Weston's company.† The writer does not agree with this view. Phineas himself is silent on this point, merely saying, "At this Time, on or two of them went wth vs in our vesill to ye place of ffishing to bye vicktuals." Weston plainly expected them to stay at Plymouth until the rest of the party came, for in a letter to Governor Carver delivered by the Sparrow party on their arrival he says:—" . . . we haue sent *this ship*, and these pasengers on our owne accounte. Whom we desire you will frendly entertaine, & supply with shuch necesaries as you cane spare, and they wante &c. . . . To ye end our desire may be effected, which I assure my selfe will be also for your good we pray you giue them entertainmente in your houses ye time they shall be with you. That they may lose no time, but may presently goe in hand to fell trees, & cleaue them, to ye end lading may be ready and our ship stay not."‡ Bradford says:—". . . they tooke compassion of those .7. men. Which *this ship* (*which fished to ye eastward*) *had kept till planting time was ouer*, and so could set no corne. And allso wanting vitals, (for yey turned them off wthout any) and indeed wanted for them selues) neither was their salt-pan come, so as yey could not performe any of those things which Mr. Weston. had appointed; and might haue starued if ye plantation had not succoured them, who in their wants, gaue them as good as any of their owne."§ The expression "yey turned them off," used by Bradford in connection with their leaving the Sparrow, contains the implication that they were not expected to return.

* Winslow's "Good Newes," 11.

† Phineas Pratt and Some of His Descendants, 19.

‡ Bradford's History, 72, 73. § Ibid., 75.

In a passage already quoted Winslow says the party brought no more provisions than would suffice for the return of the boat's "gang" to the ship,* thus also indicating that the boat's crew were expected to return, but not the settlers. But the most conclusive evidence we have that Phineas and his companions returned to Plymouth with the party who went to the fishing fleet for provisions and there (at Plymouth) awaited the coming of the Charity and the Swan is Bradford's statement when he writes, referring to the reception of Weston's 60 colonists by those vessels: — "So as they had receiued his former company of .7. men and vitailed them as their owne hitherto, so they also receiued these (being *aboute* .60. *lusty men*) and gaue housing for them selues, and their goods, and many being sicke they had ye best means ye place could aford them; . . ."† But one interpretation can be placed upon the words "vitailed them as their owne hitherto" and that is that Phineas and his companions had been offered, and had accepted, the hospitality of the Plymouth men after leaving the Sparrow and that they were living in Plymouth at the time of the arrival of the rest of the party in the Charity and the Swan.

"In the end of Iune, or beginning of Iuly, came into our harbour two ships of Master *Westons* aforesaid, the one called the Charitie, the other the Swan, hauing in them some fifty or sixty men sent ouer at his owne charge to plant for him."‡ There is a discrepancy of about a month between the date of the arrival of these vessels as given by Winslow and the date given by Phineas. The latter says: — "8 or 9 weeks after this, to of our ships Arived att Plimoth." By "this" he refers either to the time of the arrival of his party at Plymouth in the latter part of May, 1622, or to the subsequent trip to the fishing fleet for provisions. In either case "8 or 9 weeks after" would bring the Charity and Swan to Plymouth the end of July or the first of August, 1622.

Shortly after the arrival of these two vessels Weston's men began the settlement of Wessagusset. The leading man was Richard Greene, a brother-in-law of Weston. He died, however, on a subsequent visit to Plymouth and was succeeded by John Sanders. For a time all went well. The Wessagusset settlers, however, had never experienced the rigors of a New England winter and consequently made little or no preparation against the severe winter months. Levett says in his "Voyage into New England": — "they neither applyed themselues to planting of corne nor taking of fish, more than for their present

* "Good Newes," 11. † Bradford's History, 78, 79. ‡ "Good Newes," 13.

use, but went about to built Castles in the Aire, and making of Forts, neglecting the plentifull time of fishing. When Winter came their forts would not keepe out hunger, and they hauing no provision beforehand, and wanting both powder and shot to kill Deare and Fowle, many were starued to death, and the rest hardly escaped. There are foure of his men which escaped, now at my plantation, who haue related unto me the whole businesse."*

As the season advanced the situation of the settlers became perilous in the extreme. Provisions ran short and many of them actually died of starvation. Their loss in numbers, want of food and isolated position placed them completely in the power of the natives. Late in 1622 (old style) the Indians formed a plan to cut off the English both at Wessagusset and Plymouth on the same day. Phineas, then about 30 years old, learning of the intended massacre, resolved to warn the settlers at Plymouth and ask their assistance. No one being willing to accompany him, he determined to go alone.

Waiting for a favorable opportunity, he said good-bye to his friends and with considerable difficulty eluded the vigilance of the Indians and set out alone on his perilous undertaking. The Indians, learning of his escape, pursued him, but without success.

"I Run Southward tell 3 of ye Clock, but the snow being in many places, I was the more distresed becaus of my ffoot steps. The sonn being beclouded, I wandered, not knowing my way; but att the Goeing down of the sonn, it apeared Red; then hearing a great howling of wolfs, I came to a River; the water being depe & cold & many Rocks, I pased through wth much adoe. Then was I in great distres — ffant for want of ffood, weary with Running, ffearing to make a ffier because of ym yt pshued me. Then I came to a depe dell or hole, ther being much wood falen into it. Then I said in my thoughts, this is God's providence that heare I may make a fier. Then haveing maed a fier, the stars began to a pear and I saw Ursa Magor & the . . . . pole yet fearing . . . . beclouded. The day following I began to trafell . . . . . but being unable, I went back to the fier the day ffal . . . . sonn shined & about three of the clock I came to that part . . . Plimoth bay wher ther is a Town of Later Time . . . . Duxbery. Then passing by the water on my left hand . . . cam to a brock & ther was a path. Haveing but a short Time to Consider . . . . ffearing to goe beyond the plantation, I kept Running in the path; then passing through James Ryuer I said in my thoughts, now am I as a deare Chased . . . the wolfs. If I perish, what will be the Condish. . . . of distresed Einglish men. Then finding a peec of a . . . I took it up & Caried it in my hand. Then finding a . . of a Jurkin, I Caried them under my arme. Then said I in my . . . . God hath giuen me these two tookens for my Comfort; yt now he will giue me my live for a pray. Then Running down a hill J . . . an English man Coming in the

* Baxter's "Christopher Levett, of York," 125, 126.

path before me. Then I sat down on a tree & Rising up to salute him said, 'Mr. Hamdin, I am Glad to see you aliue.' He said 'I am Glad & full of wonder to see you aliue: lett us sitt downe, I see you are weary.'"

Bradford says, referring to Phineas' dangerous undertaking:—"In ye meane time, came one of them from ye Massachucts with a small pack at his back, and though he knew not a foote of ye way yet he got safe hither, but lost his way, which was well for him for he was pursued, and so was mist. He tould them hear, how all things stood amongst them, and that he durst stay no longer, he apprehended they (by what he obserued) would be all knokt in ye head shortly."* "*This mans name*," writes Nathaniel Morton, "*was* Phinehas Pratt, *who hath penned the particular of his perilous Journey, and some other things relating to this Tragedy*."†

Phineas reached Plymouth on March 24, 1622/3. The minor dates are given by Winslow and the context gives the year. He writes:—"The three and twentith of March being now come, which is a yeerely Court-day, . . . we came to this conclusion, That Captaine *Standish* should take so many men as he thought sufficient to make his party good against all the *Indians* in the *Massachuset-bay*; . . . but on the next day before hee could goe, came one of M^r^. *Westons* Company by land vnto vs, with his packe at his backe, who made a pitifull narration of their lamentable and weake estate."‡

Two or three days after his coming, according to Phineas, and the next day (March 25, 1623),§ according to Winslow, Captain Myles Standish and his party started on the expedition which resulted in inflicting on the Indians the doom they had in store for the English and in saving the remnant of the Wessagusset colony.

It was evidently not Phineas' intention to part from his own company entirely, for when he arrived at Plymouth after his difficult and dangerous journey, he only asked that "hee might there remaine till things were better settled at the other plantation."§ After Myles Standish rescued the Wessagusset party from their perilous position and relieved their immediate necessities, a majority of them decided to abandon the settlement and make their way home, while some of them chose to return with Standish and join the Plymouth colony. "Now were M^r^. *Westons* people resolued to leaue their Plantation and goe for *Munhiggen*, hoping to get passage and returne with

* Bradford's History, 94.

† "New England's Memorial" (Boston, 1721), 57.

‡ "Good Newes," 37, 38. § Ibid., 39.

the fishing ships. . . . Some of them disliked the choyce of the body to goe to *Munhiggen*, and therfore desiring to goe with him to *Plimouth*, he tooke them into the shallop: and seeing them set sayle and cleere of the *Massachuset bay*, he tooke leaue and returned to *Plimouth*, . . ."*

As soon as he was physically able, Phineas rejoined his company at Piscataqua. Those of the Wessagusset colony who returned to Plymouth with Standish had no doubt told Phineas of the plan of the majority of the party to return to England, if they could, by way of Monhegan Island, and it is quite possible that he, too, went to Piscataqua in the hope of securing passage home in one of the fishing fleet. But whatever his plan may have been, he did not return to England and we find him a little later engaged in skirmishes with the Indians at Dorchester and at Agawam (Ipswich), but he does not tell us what took him to those places. "Three times we fought with them" he says in his petition to the General Court in 1668, referring to the encounters with the Indians at Wessagusset, Dorchester and Agawam.

"In the latter end of Iuly and the beginning of August,"† 1623, according to Winslow, the Anne and the Little James arrived at Plymouth. Some time between their arrival and the beginning of 1624 (old style) there was a division of land at Plymouth among the passengers of the Mayflower, Fortune and Anne on the basis of one acre to each person for seven years' continual use.‡ This division must have been after August 14, 1623, for William Bradford's wife, Alice Bradford, shared therein, and they were married on that date. It was probably made late in 1623 (old style), very likely in March, just before the April planting of 1624. Phineas is put down among the Anne's passengers and was assigned one acre. He must, therefore, have returned to Plymouth prior to the division and settled there.

As to why he shared in the division at all, not being a passenger by either the Mayflower, Fortune or Anne — it is very likely that when he returned to Plymouth and expressed a desire to remain there he was received as an inhabitant and permitted to share in the subsequent allotment of land. Joshua Pratt, with whom he is associated in the list of the Anne's passengers, is not known to have been related to him.

As an inhabitant of Plymouth Phineas' name occurs frequently in the colony records during his residence there and

* "Good Newes," 44, 45. † Ibid., 51.

‡ Mayflower Descendant, I: 227–230.

after he went to Charlestown. The following extracts are from the original records except in one or two cases which are indicated. It appears that he was a joiner, and he so calls himself in various deeds and in his will.

1623. Mentioned in a list which follows "The fales of their grounds which came over in the shipe called the Anne according as their were cast. 1623." *

This was the division of land among the passengers of the Mayflower, Fortune and Anne made probably in March, 1623 (old style). The probable reason why Phineas was included in this division has already been mentioned.

1627, May 22. Assigned to Francis Cooke's company in the division of cattle.

"To this lot fell the least of the 4 black Heyfers Came in the Jacob and two shee goats." †

1627. Appears on a list of "The Names of the Purchasers" of Plymouth. [Court Orders, II: 244]

1633. Mentioned in a list of "The Names of the ffreemen of the Incorporacon of Plymoth in New England An: 1633." [Court Orders, I: 1]

1633, March 25. Taxed nine shillings. [Court Orders, I: 9]

1633, October 28. "Phineas Pratt referred to further hearing at the same time about the goods of Godbert Godbertson & Zara his wife." [Court Orders, I: 35]

1633, November 11. "At this Court Phineas Prat appointed to take into his possession all the goods & chattels of Godbert Godbertson & Zarah his wife & safely to preserue them according to an Inventory presented upon oath to be true & just by m^r^ Joh Done & m^r^ Steph. Hopkins." [Court Orders, I: 37]

Godbert Godbertson was the stepfather of Mary Priest (daughter of Degory Priest) whom Phineas married.

1633/4, January 2. Taxed nine shillings. [Court Orders, I: 61]

1633/4, March 10. "Whereas Phineas Prat joyner in the behalfe of Marah his wife is possessed of thirty Acres of land neer unto the high Cliffe the said Phineas & Marah haue exchanged the fee simple thereof wth m^r^ Thomas Prence for other thirty Acres of land at Wynslows stand and next adjoyning to an other portion of land belonging to the said Phineas: But whereas there is a brooke w^th^in the said thirty acres thus

* Mayflower Descendant, I: 230. † Ibid., I: 149.

exchanged & acknowledged by mutuall consent whereat John Come Gent may freely make use of, It is granted to him his heires or assignes provided he so make use of the said water as the said phineas be not annoyed thereby. but either by convenient inclosure at the Cost of the said Joh. or otherwise shall saue harmeles the said phin. & his heires from any detri^t^ or annoyance that shall or may befall them the said Phines & Marah their heires & assigne[s]" [Court Orders, I: 57]

1635/6, March 2. "At the same Court, A Jury of twelue being impaniled and charged in the moneth of ffebr foregoing to enquire after the death of John Deacon in the behalfe of our Soveraigne Lord the king. gaue in their verdict as followeth in their owne words and under their hands, vizt

"Having searched the dead body we finde not any blowes or wounds or any other bodily hurt. We finde that bodily weakenes caused by long fasting & wearines by going to & fro wth extream cold of the season were the causes of his death.

"Their names were John Jenny John Cooke Will Basset Joseph Rogers William Hoskins, Thomas Cushman George Partridge Stephen Tracy Abraham Peirce Richard Cluffe Tho. Clarke Phineas Pratt." [Court Orders, I: 87]

1635/6, March 14. "At a generall meeting the 14th of March concerning the hey grownds for Plymoth & Duxbarrough" it was ordered "That Phineas Pratt haue between ffr Billington and his owne howse." [Court Orders, I: 88, 89]

1636, November 7. "At the same time Tristram Clarke appointed to haue eight Acres of land fowr in breadth & two in length on the south side a porcon allotted formerly to m^r^ John Coombe between Phineas Pratt & widow Billington." [Court Orders, I: 96]

1636/7, January 14. "Januar 14th 1636 There is graunted this day by the Court of Assistants to James Skiffe Tenn acres of lands lying next vnto the lands graunted to Thirston Clarke (five in length & two in breadth) betweene the lands of Phineas Pratt & widdow Billington five acres whereof are part of those lands due vnto him for his service Donn to m^r^ Isaack Olerton and thother fiue acres are in the right of Peter Talbott for service by Indenture prformed to Edward Doty." [Court Orders, I: 98]

1636/7, March 7. His name appears in a list of Plymouth freemen. [Court Orders, I: 104]

1636/7, March 20. There is assigned "To Phineas Pratt and m^r^ Coomes the hey ground they had the last yeare." [Court Orders, I: 110]

1637, July 12. Edward Dotey sells to Richard Derby his property at the "high Cliffe" purchased of Joshua Pratt, Phineas Pratt and John Shaw. [Plym. Col. Deeds, XII: 20]

1637, October 2. Is a juryman at the meeting of the General Court. [Plym. Col. Judicial Acts, 3]

1640, June 1. Granted five acres of land.* [Court Orders, I: 236]

1640, August 3. "fforasmuch as it appeareth by the testymony of Josuah Pratt & otherwise that The two acrees of vpland lying at Wellingsly brook on the north side of the lotts giuen Godbert Godbertson, were giuen by the said Godbert Godbertson to John Combe gent & Phineas Pratt in marriage wth their wiues his Daughters The Court Doth confirme the said two acrees vnto the said John Combe & Phineas Pratt their heires and assignes for eu^r^." [Court Orders, I: 241]

1640, August 5. "Memorand the fift day of August 1640 That John Combe gent and Phineas Pratt joyner Do acknowledg that for and in consideracon of the sum of three pounds sterl to them in hand payd by John Barnes of new Plymouth haue freely and absolutely bargained and sould vnto the said John Barnes his heires & Assignes all those two acrees of vpland wch they had of Goodbert Godbertson in marryage wth their wiues lyinge on the North side next to the Towneward of that parcell of vpland at Wellingsley brooke wch fell to him by lott in the first Diuisions, and all their right title and interrest of and into the said two acrees of vpland wth all and singuler thapp^r^tences thereto belonging To haue & to hold the said two acrees of vpland wth all and singuler their app^r^tences vnto the said John Barnes his heires Assignes foreuer To the onely p^r^per vse & behoofe of him the said John Barnes his heires & Assignes for euer." [Plym. Col. Deeds, I: 101]

1640, November 2. Granted six acres of "meddowing in the North meddow by Joanes Riuer." [Court Orders, I: 249]

1642, April 5. John Combe sells to Thomas Prence "all those his two acrees of Marsh meddow lying before the house of the said Thom Prence at Joanes Riuer next to the Marsh meddow of Phineas Pratt . . ." [Plym. Col. Deeds, I: 138]

1642, May 7. Joshua Pratt sells to Edward Dotey "one acre of vpland lying at the heigh Cliff betwixt the lands of Phineas Pratt & John Shawe . . ." [Plym. Col. Deeds, I: 142]

1642, December 31. John Barnes sells to Edward Edwards

* This entry is crossed out in the original records.

certain property purchased from Thomas Hill and "the two acrees of vpland lying at wellingsly brooke lately purchased of Mr John Combe & Phineas Pratt . . ." [Plym. Col. Deeds, I: 154]

1643, August. Appears on a list of Plymouth men able to bear arms. The same year (no minor dates given) his name, crossed out and with interlinear notation "gon," appears on a list of Plymouth freemen. [Plym. Col. Records, VIII: 174, 187] His name was crossed out and the note made, of course, after he left Plymouth.

1644, June 22. "At a Townes meeting the xxiith June 1644

"In case of Alarume in tyme of warr or Danger these Divisions of the Towneship are to be observed. & these companys to repaire together

At Joanes river	mr Bradfords famyly one mr Princes one mr Hanbury one mr Howland one ffrancis Cooke one Phineas Pratt Gregory Armestrong John Winslow mr Lee"

Of the other two companies the first was ordered to assemble "At the Ele river" and the second at Wellingsly. [Plym. Town Reds., I: 27]

1644, October 30. Edward Edwards sells to Thomas Whitney the property which was formerly Thomas Hill's and "the two acrees bought of phineas Pratt" by John Barnes and sold to him (Edwards) December 31, 1642. [Plym. Col. Deeds, I: 154]

1644, November 5. "The fift of Novemb^{r} 1644 Memorand That Thomas Bunting dwelling wth Phineas Pratt hath wth and by the consent of the said Phineas put himself as a servant to Dwell wth John Cooke Junio^{r} from the fifteenth Day of this instant Novemb^{r} for and During the terme of eight yeares now next ensuing and fully to be compleate and ended the said John Cooke fynding vnto his said servant meate drink and apparell During the said terme and in thend thereof Double to apparell him throughout and to pay him twelue bushells of Indian Corne. The said John Cooke haueing payd the said Phineas for him one melch cowe valued at v^{li} and fourty shillings in money and is to to lead the said Phineas two loades of hey yearely During the terme of seauen yeares now next ensuinge." [Court Orders, II: 106]

(*To be continued.*)

GEORGE SOULE'S AUTOGRAPH.

BY GEORGE ERNEST BOWMAN.

THE only autograph of George Soule of the Mayflower of which I have yet learned is his signature as a witness to the will of John Barnes of Plymouth, and was written 6/16 March, 1667/8. Soule was the first witness to sign, and fortunately "Senr" was written after his name. This proves conclusively that the witness was George Soule of the Mayflower and not his son, George².

An examination of the half-tone reproduction of the will, facing this page, shows that Soule wrote a very good hand, but there are evident signs of trembling, which may have been due to age.

The will is preserved in the "Scrap Book" in the Registry of Deeds at Plymouth. It is written on the first page of a four-page folio, and is in fair condition. The pages are twelve and one-fourth inches tall by seven and seven-eighths inches wide. The top of the first page has evidently been used in place of a copy book.

The second witness, Samuel Seabury, married for his second wife Martha³ Pabodie (*Elizabeth² Alden, John¹*).

In this will John Barnes calls Henry Samson's wife (Ann Plummer) his cousin. This connection will probably be helpful in finding her ancestry.

The will was recorded in the Plymouth Colony Wills and Inventories, Volume III, Part I, page 31, from which the record of the probate is taken. The transcript of the will is made from the original document.

The last Will and Testament of Mr John Barnes of Plymouth in New England late Deceased; exhibited to the court

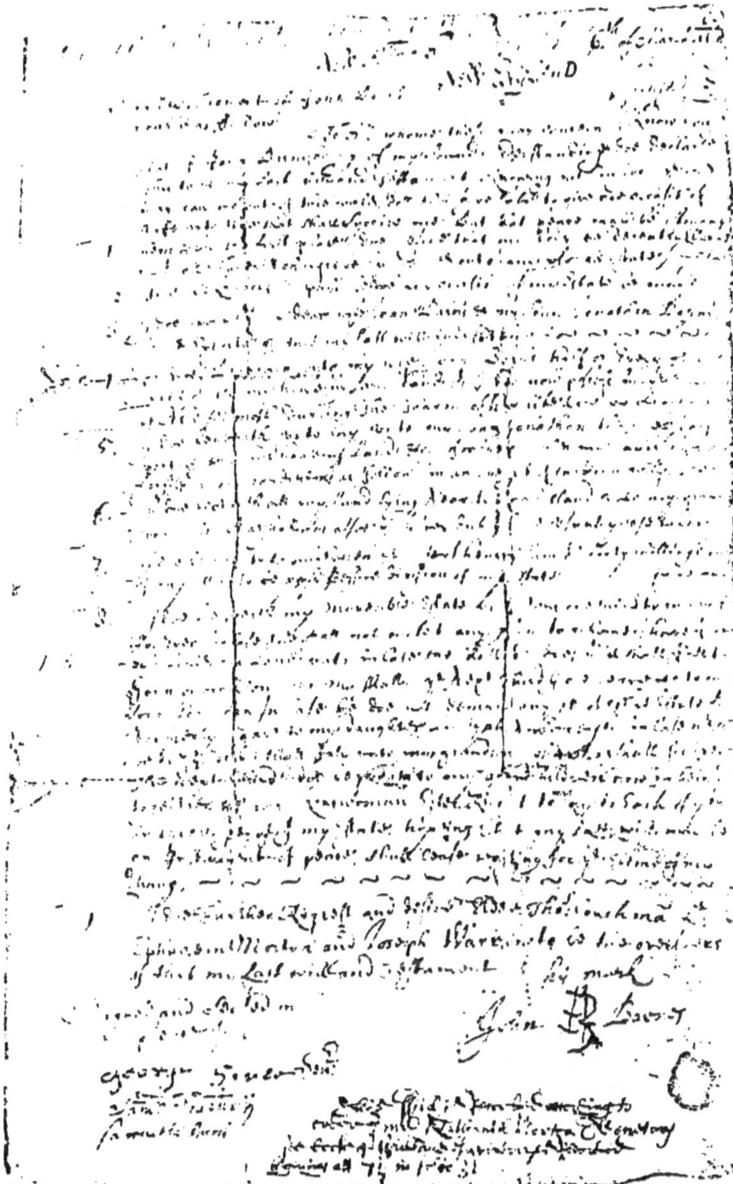

GEORGE SOULE'S AUTOGRAPH

held att Plymouth the 29th of October anno Dom 1671 on the oathes of Mr Samuell Saberry and Samuell hunt as followeth;

New Plimoth. New England. 6th. of March. 16^{67}_{68}

The Last will & Testament of John Barn's which is as follow's.

To All whome these may concern. Know you That I John Barn's being of my Sound understanding &c: doe declaire This to be my last will and Testament. Knowing not how soon ye lord may call me out of this world. doe theirfore labor to give noe occasio' of striffe unto those that shall Survive me: But that peace may be Among them:

1. In the first place I doe desire that my body be decently buryed all yt all Funerall charges be Exspended out of my psonall Estate

2. That all Legacys be pay'd, before any division of my Estate be may'd

3. I doe apoynt yt my dear wife Joan Barn's & my Sonn Jonathan Barn's be ye Executors of this my last will and Testament

4. I doe Bequeath unto my wife Joan Barn's half of Every pt and pcell of all my houseing and lands yt I doe now possess in ye Township of New Plimoth dureing The Tearm of her life.

5. I doe bequeath unto my unto my Sonn Jonathan the other half part of my sayd houseing land's &c: fforEver unles my say'd Sonn shall forfitt it on condittion's as ffollow's in an oyr* pt of this my will.

6. I doe bequeath all my land lying Near to Road Island unto my grandsonn John Marshall. as alsoe ye silver dish yt I doe usually use to Eate in

7. I doe bequeath to my Cozen ye wife of henery Samso. forty shillings out of my Estate to be pay'd Beffore division of my Estate.

8. I doe Bequeath my moveable Estate as follow's one third to my wife for Ever in Case she shall not molest any pson to whome I have fformerly sould any Land's unto in Case she shall soe doe, yn it shall ffall to Sonn, or grandson John Marshall. ye Next Third I doe bequeath to my sonn Jonathan In Case he doe not demand any pt of That Estate yt fformerly I gave to my daughter Lyddyah. Now deceased. in Case he

* This is evidently a mistake for "other." The copy in the Colony Records reads: "in any one."

shall Soe doe y^n third shall ffall unto my grandson John Marshall ffor Ever The Next (t)hird I doe bequeath to my gr(an)dchildren now in being togeither wth my Kinswoman Ester Ricket to say to Each of y^m an Equall pt of y^t my Estate: hopeing That my last will may be an Instrument of peace; shall cease waiting for ye Time of my chang,

9. I doe Further Request and desire Elder Thos: Couchma L^t: Ephraem Morton and Joseph Warren to be the overseers of this my Last will and Testament

Signed and sealed In
ye p^rsence of
George Soule Senr:
Saml: Seabury
samuell hunt

his mark
John Ɪ B Barnes
(seal)

This Will is recorded according to order p^r me Nathaniel Morton Secretary see book of Wills and Inventorys recorded begining att 71; in folio 31

WILLIAM BREWSTER.

His True Position in Our Colonial History.

[*An Address Delivered before the Massachusetts Society of Mayflower Descendants, 13 February, 1902, at Boston.*]

By Hon. Lyman Denison Brewster.

The story of the Mayflower and Plymouth Rock is the story of the formation of a little Separatist or Congregational Church at Scrooby, England, its escape to Holland, its migration from thence to Plymouth, and its establishment there as the first embodiment in America of freedom in the Church and equality in the State.

William Brewster cradled the church at Scrooby, in his own home. He devoted his means to the support of its ministers and the succor of its members. After suffering fine and imprisonment and risking his life for this heresy, he helped the little flock to Holland, where his duty as elder intrusted him especially with the discipline and building up of the Church and the preservation therein of soundness of doctrine. This duty he successfully performed with great gentleness and equal firmness. While in Leyden his arrest was sought for publishing Protestant books for circulation in England and Scotland.

He was in every respect the co-equal and colleague with Robinson in all the measures for preparing the voyage to America, and shares with Carver and Cushman the honor of procuring the requisite London assistance.

That he drafted the Compact of November 21, 1620, in the cabin of the Mayflower seems almost certain. That he was the moral, religious and spiritual leader of the Colony during its first years of peril and struggle and its chief civil adviser and trusted guide until the time of his death is quite certain. But for his ecclesiastical position he would have been Governor of the Colony.

So that, while it was perhaps unfortunate, as a matter of good taste, that Rev. Ashbel Steele entitled his valuable biography "Chief of the Pilgrims: or The Life and Time of William Brewster"—unfortunate, since the modest Elder of Plymouth was the last man in the world to institute comparisons with his brethren, it is nevertheless true as a matter of history that he was indeed in the fullest sense "The Chief of the Pilgrims." And it is also true that having the rare felicity to be both the founder of the first free Church in America and also the founder of the first free colony in America, he was in a sense in which no other man, not even Roger Williams (as I shall show) can claim the honor—the first Apostle of both civil and religious liberty on this continent.

In the light of recent research he stands out more clearly than ever, the leading figure of the Mayflower and of Plymouth. In the prime of his intellectual vigor, in the 54th year of his age, the only reason why the Elder was not chosen the first Governor of the Plymouth Colony, says Hutchinson in his History, was that "He was their ruling elder, which seems to have been the bar to his being their Governor—civil and ecclesiastical office, in the same person, being then deemed incompatible." Perhaps an equally cogent reason was that an outlawed exile would hardly be "persona grata" to the officers of the Crown.

Some subsequent historians, not realizing that, as Judge Baylies says, "the power of the church was then superior to the civil power," or the true reason of the apparent but not real subordination of the Elder to the Governors (Carver and Bradford), have failed to give to the heroic Elder the supremacy he deserves over each and all, as the heart, brain and soul of the new Plymouth enterprise, without whom it could hardly have been attempted, with whom it became the most memorable and successful pioneer colonization on the American continent after its discovery by Columbus.

Let me mention some of the admirable qualities of his leadership. Not intending in the least to suggest a word in derogation or depreciation of the good qualities, nay the grand qualities of those superb fellow Pilgrims, Bradford, Winslow, Carver and Standish, I will state briefly what he was, what he accomplished.

Of gentle birth, educated at Cambridge, a courtier before he was twenty years of age, in high esteem with Her Majesty's Secretary of State, treated by him more like a son than a servant, soon a member of the English Embassy to Holland, after loyally and faithfully serving his patron Davidson who was deposed from his high position by the perfidy of the Queen, he, after suffering years of persecution in building up the Mayflower church at Scrooby, left his native land, his position and his fortune, to be an exile in Holland and a pilgrim in America.

A word each on his scholarship, his statesmanship, his saintliness and his standing among the Founders of States.

First, as to his scholarship and ability as a lay preacher. It was always known that he was a trained scholar of the greatest of English Universities, but it remained for the late Dr. Dexter to show the depth and breadth, the fulness and ripeness of his learning and wisdom. Dr. Dexter wrote to me that he regarded him as the ablest man of the first generation of New England colonists, and no man was better qualified to give that judgment. While a persecuted refugee in Leyden he published and in some instances himself printed and edited both popular and erudite theological treatises in Latin and English. While living in his log house in Plymouth, built by his own hands, he yearly received supplies of newly published books in Latin and English, and his library was inventoried at his death in 1644 at four hundred volumes.

Dr. Dexter took the brief headings of the inventory deciphered by Mr. Winsor and tracing out the books through the leading libraries of England and Europe, restored the full titles. Sixty-two were in Latin and ninety-eight commentaries on or translations of the Bible. Dr. Dexter says:

"It is my strong impression that it is very doubtful whether, for its first quarter-century, New England anywhere else had so rich a collection of exegetical literature as this."

With such a scholar to explain the Scriptures, which was the chief function of the pulpit in those days, it is no wonder that when a minister who came over in 1629 was chosen to be the Plymouth pastor, the people "finding him to be a man of low gifts and parts, they, as providence gave opportunity, improved others as his assistants." And this scholar worked with his own hands to build his house in Plymouth, and afterwards in Duxbury, and up to the age of nearly eighty helped to cultivate his own farm. And there is nothing to show, says one biographer, in the records that he ever asked for or received any salary.

But the crowning glory of this wealth of learning and knowledge was this. For thirty years it was devoted constantly, utterly and superbly to the people with whom he had cast his hazardous lot. All he could learn he freely imparted to those he taught.

He was a scholar and preacher from the people, with the people, for the people and to the people, and in their close companionship of toil and danger the people did indeed hear him gladly. Of their place of worship and order of assembling De Rasiere, a wise observer from Holland in 1627 gives this often repeated but always interesting sketch:

He says: "Upon the hill they had a large square house, with a flat roof, made of thick sawn planks, stayed with oak beams, upon the top of which they have six cannons, which shoot iron balls of four and five pounds, and command the surrounding country. The lower part they use for their church, where they preach on Sundays and the usual holidays. They assemble by beat of drum, each with his musket or firelock, in front of the captain's door; they have their cloaks on, and place themselves in order, three abreast, and are led by a sergeant without beat of drum. Behind comes the Governor, in a long robe; beside him on the right hand comes the preacher with his cloak on, and on the left hand the captain with his side-arms and cloak on, and with a small cane in his hand; and so they march in good order, and each sets his arms down near him. Thus they enter their place of worship, constantly on their guard night and day."

How much Governor Bradford, the excellent governor of the colony for over thirty years, owed not only to the guidance, but to the training, teaching and companionship of his old neighbor, comrade and life-long friend, his grateful words bear full witness. He says of Brewster that "he was foremost in our adventure in England and in Holland and here." John Brown of Bedford calls him "The Great Heart of their pilgrimage." Dr. Griffis says "from the first Brewster was the soul of the Plymouth colony."

The devout Elder was regarded with the utmost veneration and reverence in his later years by the colonists of the eight towns into which the little settlement of 1620 had grown. Hence I think the popular impression of the old patriarch pictures him with the austere severity and rigid narrowness of an old iron-sides, rather than with the "sweetness and light" of Hampden and Milton. Nothing could be further from the truth. Humblest and gentlest of men, his flock almost worshipped him because they loved him and had reason to love him, while that love was returned in full measure, and the chronicle says of his death in which he "so sweetly departed this life unto a better": "We did all grievously mourn his loss as that of a dear and loving friend."

Of his personal qualities Bradford says: "He was wise and discreet and well spoken, having a grave and deliberate utterance, of a very cheerful spirit, very sociable and pleasant amongst his friends, of an humble and modest mind, of a peaceable disposition, undervaluing himself and his own abilities, and sometimes overvaluing others; inoffensive and innocent in his life and conversation, which gained him the love of those without, as well as those within. . . . . He was tender-hearted, and compassionate of such as were in misery, but especially of such as had been of good estate and rank, and were fallen unto want and poverty, either for goodness and religion's sake, or by the injury and oppression of others. . . . . In teaching, he was moving and stirring of affections, also very plain and distinct in what he taught. . . . . He had a singular good gift in prayer, both public and private. . . . . He always thought it were better for ministers to pray oftener, and divide their prayers, than be long and tedious in the same."

"He taught twice every Sabbath, and that both powerfully and profitably, to the great contentment of his hearers, and their comfortable edification; yea, many were brought to God by his ministrie. He did more in this behalf in a year, than many that have their hundreds a year do in all their lives." Bradford's whole eulogy of his beloved friend and pastor is the most pathetic and beautiful passage in his History of New Plymouth so lately restored to the State of Massachusetts.

Next as a statesman. If the acorn is judged by the oak it produces, he had no superior in that age of great statesmen. How far-reaching the policy that foresaw that the refugees must leave Holland, if they would preserve their English morals with their English freedom! How tersely in the short Social Compact which we believe he penned, impromptu apparently, in the cabin of the Mayflower is the whole genius of "Liberty, Equality and Fraternity" put in a few lines! Well has it been called the "germ of all our American Constitutions and Declarations of Right" — "Magna Charta reinforced by the spirit of the Dutch Common-wealth."

Professor Goldwin Smith in his brilliant little book called "The United States Political History 1492–1871" tells us that the recital, in the Compact signed on the Mayflower, of the colonists' allegiance and fealty to King James was a great and serious mistake and "created a relation false from the beginning," that in it "lay the fatal seeds of misunderstanding" etc. On the contrary the mistake is all on the side of the Professor. Not to have acknowledged that fealty and allegiance would have been false and if interpreted as seriously intended would have been suicidal. It was because they intended to be English colonists and English freemen that they left Holland. In all the business of procuring their charter that fealty is assumed and this allegiance and fealty is reiterated and reaffirmed in the Plymouth Code of 1636, of whose drafters the Elder was one.

How superior the wise, peaceful, just and courageous policy of the Plymouth Colony in its treatment of the Indians and its fellow colonies! And the man who always had the last word in these important matters — the Joshua and Nestor of the plantation was Elder William Brewster. Here again see the crowning glory of his success as a political philosopher. He put his glorious theory of Equality and Fraternity into practice, and Liberty could not help being the result. The first Plymouth town meeting of equal citizens with equal rights had in it the seeds of Yorktown and Gettysburg. It was the first clear prophecy of the Republic which was to extend from ocean to ocean.

Dr. Gregory of Edinburgh in his recent work on Puritanism, cool and judicial Scotchman as he is, sums up the consensus of historians when he says "It is not too much to say that in a very real and profound sense the Mayflower carried with her the destinies of the world. Her crew (evidently the doctor means her passengers) were not only the pioneers of civil and religious liberty, they were the heralds of a faith which tested by the heroic men it has formed and heroic actions it has produced may indeed challenge comparison with any faith by which men have been moulded and inspired. The struggle they were called upon to wage was a struggle for liberty not only in the New World but in the old, and but for the planting of Puritanism in New England the victory of Puritanism in the

Mother Country would have been short lived, and shorn of its most characteristic features and products." And in spite of all criticism Bancroft states but a fact when he says that "in the cabin of the Mayflower humanity recovered its rights and instituted government on the basis of equal laws for the general good."

Dr. Gregory in summing up the influence of the Mayflower and Plymouth Rock, wisely and justly, it seems to me, merges and blends the Pilgrim Separatist and the Massachusetts colony Puritans as exerting essentially the same influence after 1630 on subsequent history, since all the Puritans of New England soon became Separatists.

Better than all, he was a saint in a church where saint worship was abolished. Of his own sincere, devout, spiritual, religious faith and practice every day of his exiled life bore witness. But what especially distinguished him as a religious leader in those days was his breadth, toleration and charity. When that sturdy and heroic heretic Roger Williams in Plymouth denounced the Mother Church in England as Anti-Christ, pronouncing it sinful to attend its worship or to fellowship with it, the more charitable Leader of the Pilgrims refused to go with him or to hold to any such nonsense. In fact the spiritual descendants of William Brewster and John Robinson were not more Jonathan Edwards and the New England Calvinists than Phillips Brooks, Horace Bushnell, Henry Ward Beecher and Charles Briggs. "The Pilgrims were neither Puritans nor Persecutors" was the motto I saw some years ago written over the spot across the street from which Elder William built his house. But in reality the Pilgrim was, as Dr. Dexter says, "The Puritan in the superlative degree."

John Robinson and Roger Williams are justly praised as the fathers and apostles of religious toleration in their age. But William Brewster was more Catholic and tolerant than either, at an earlier date.

"Paget" according to Powicke in his recent Life of Henry Barrows "says that Robinson had 'tolerated' his fellow elder 'for this long time' in this practice" and "this practice" was the custom of hearing ministers of the Church of England, and it is a touching evidence of the Elder's influence on the life and belief of his beloved pastor that there was found in the study of John Robinson after his decease a treatise on "The Lawfulness of Hearing of the Ministers of the Church of England." We have already seen how on this very point the Elder of Plymouth was more tolerant than Roger Williams in the new colony. The sturdy leader who surpassed both John Robinson and Roger Williams in true catholicity and toleration before 1620 may well stand for the Pioneer of Religious Liberty in New England and America.

The claim that the Elder was in the slightest degree blameworthy in advising the Plymouth Church to accept Roger Williams' petition for a dismissal from that church to the church in Salem will hardly pass muster with any student of history thoroughly conversant with the "chip on the shoulder" characteristics of the great Founder of Rhode Island, or who has thoughtfully read Bradford's words of tender regret at the parting — words which undoubtedly echoed the sentiments of the Elder.

It seems to me that Dr. Gregory's criticism of the unstinted laudation of the intrepid Baptist by Mr. Strauss when he puts him on a level with Luther and Cromwell is fully justified. There seems to be a lack of historical perspective.

Easily first among the Pilgrims (for Robinson the master mind of all was not a Pilgrim as he stayed on the other side of the seas and is out of the comparison), how does the scholar, teacher and sainted father of the first colony of New England stand among the founders of states? Lord Bacon puts the founders of States in the first rank of the Great Men of the world. It seems to me that depends on the motive, and method of their achievements. Where conquest and greed are the motives and treachery and bloodshed the methods, I see nothing to admire or respect. But what colony was ever founded on loftier aims, with more devoted sacrifice and by more honorable methods than that which was started in possession at Plymouth two hundred and eighty two years ago. Its free spirit has taken possession of the continent. The man whose thought originated, whose spirit pervaded, whose presence stimulated, whose counsels preserved that colony in its infancy can well bear comparison with any of the famous colonizers of the continent.

It was no accident that made William Brewster the planter of a great church, and pioneer of a great state. The long schooling in Holland after the sharp persecution in England seems to have educated the Pilgrims and their great leader to a more gracious spirit, a more Christian sense of the relations of man to man than was possessed by the subsequent New England colonists. There was less bigotry, no persecution and little of the superstition and narrowness that darkened the history of most of the other New England colonies. The bond that kept together that immortal band through flood and famine, pestilence and peril, was not commercial or primarily political. It was religious and spiritual. It was faith in God and the Gospel of the Christ. And their spiritual leader full of that faith himself, inspired his flock with his own zeal and moulded the colony not only during his own life but for a whole generation after. The very symmetry and perfection of William Brewster's character, have in a sense prevented a full and just recognition of his services to church and state.

But to my mind the entire sanity, moderation, self-restraint, the grand common-sense of the founder of Plymouth constitutes one of his most attractive characteristics. Too often, alas, have the reformers of the world, the founders of states and systems had the one-sided vehemence of a John the Baptist instead of sharing something in the serene dignity and repose of the Master. Patience, humility, indomitable fortitude, unquenchable hope, purity of life and purpose, kindliness of heart, sympathy for the weak and poor, fidelity to the death for all that is right, absolute abhorrence for all that is wrong, are they not worthy human qualities although their possessors forsooth be termed Puritans? But these pilgrims although puritans of the puritans in their moral steadfastness, were also free in a large degree from the narrowness, intolerance and vulgarity that have elsewhere sometimes characterized those who held the name. How much of this freedom must we fairly attribute to their leader and teacher? See the effectiveness as well as the quality of his work! In England he not only made of his home a Meeting house, but he provided its pastors and devoted his means and his life to his brethren who sought to reform what he and they believed the unscriptural practices of the Church established by law. When the little flock had gathered again after their hazardous flight to Holland, not only did his printing press at Leyden furnish to Scotland and England exactly the English Protestant literature which the Reformation most needed, but his wise eldership contributed no less than the genius of Robinson to preserve and shape a church worthy of being the pioneer church of New England.

In Plymouth — elder, advisor, Nestor of the little band, Dr. Dexter tells us there is every reason to believe the English books of his library were openly accessible to all and formed in reality the first Public Library of New England. A preacher who never had been a priest, a pastor who had never been an ordained clergyman, he was the fitting leader of a band of Independents who were to found a Church without a Bishop as well as a State without a King. Opposed to all ritualism and formalism, to any ceremonials not in their opinion plainly enjoined by the word of God, the Plymouth Colony, under the Elder's wise and able guidance preserved a moderation, sanity and freedom from extravagance and superstition not always prevalent in the other Puritan Colonies.

There have been many saints in Old England and in New England well beloved we may believe of God and man, but how many of his energy and of such influence on the future, who were so free from asceticism, fanaticism, ignorance and superstition? How many unembittered by such persecution, unnarrowed by such isolation? This "Chief of the Pilgrims" was a Puritan of the Puritans in all that makes puritanism a power for good, for purity, for piety, for valor, and a terror to evil doers, but in nothing else. The sourness, the barrenness, the vulgarities of puritanism seemed left out of Elder Brewster's composition.

And it is a pleasant thought, I am sure, for every member of our society to realize that the more the records are searched, the more clearly it appears that the spiritual leader of our Pilgrim Ancestors — the transplanter of the first New England Meeting House, the suggester of the first New England town-meeting, was in everything throughout his life, in everything we know of his thought and action, a noble Christian gentleman.

ISAAC ALLERTON'S DEPOSITION.

Isaacke Allerton of New Plimmouth in New England merchant aged about 53 yeares sworne saith that the ship White Angell was heretofore in the yeare of our Lord 1631 bought at Bristoll of Alderman Aldworth by this deponent to the use of M^r^. James Sherley M^r^. Richard Andrewes M^r^. John Beauchamp of London merchants M^r^. Timothy Hatherley then of London feltmaker & this deponent, but this deponent saith that the said Timothy Hatherley did afterwards refuse to accept of the said bargaine. And this deponent saith that the ship Frendship was heretofore hired & victualled by this deponent in the yeare aforesaid for the use of the said M^r^. Sherley M^r^. Andrews M^r^. Beauchampe M^r^. Hatherley and all the partners & purchasers of the plantation of Plimmouth aforesaid. And further this deponent saith that afterwards divers losses falling out upon the said ship Friendship the said M^{r}. Hatherley and this deponent did in the behalf of themselves & the said M^{r}. Sherley M^{r}. Andrews & M^{r}. Beauchampe agree & undertake to discharge & save harmlesse all the rest of the said partners & purchasers of & from the said losses for two hundred pounds.

From this deposition, made on 26 September, 1639, we learn that Isaac Allerton was born about 1586, and that he resided in 1639 at Plymouth.

The deposition was made before Thomas Lechford, and is reprinted from the American Antiquarian Society's edition of his "Note Book," page 189.

PLYMOUTH, MASS., VITAL RECORDS.

(*Continued from Vol. III, page 124.*)

[Vol. I, p. 52] The Children of Elisha Holmes & sarah holmes his Wife
1 Marcy born June ye 26th 1696
2 Elisha born January 19th 1698
3 Joseph born July 11th 1700
4 Elizabeth born March 13th 1702
5 Jabiz born January 28 1704
6 Elnathan born January 19 1705
7 John born March 27th 1707
8 Sarah born in March 1709
The Children of Elisha holme & Suanna his Wife
1 Rebecka born Agust 18th 1720
2 Nathaniel born Agust 18 1722
The Children of Micajah Dunham & Elizabeth Dunham his wife
1 Joshua born on y^{e} 30th of June 1701
2 Joseph born on y^{e} 12th of March 170$\frac{4}{5}$
3 Abigaiel born on y^{e} 19th of July. 1707
The Children of John Curtice
1 ffrances born on y^{e} 20th of May 1696
2 hannah born on y^{e} 20th of Aprill 1698
3 John born on y^{e} 31 of March 1702
4 Elizabeth born on y^{e} 20th of May 1704
The Children of Jacob Tinkcom & Lydia his Wife
1 Hannah Tinkcom Born Octr. 31. 1747.
2 Lydia Tinkcom Born Novr 15. 1749.
3 Mary Tinkcom Born. Novr 28. 1751
4 Jacob Tinkcom Born, Sep^{t} 10. 1754

[p. 53] The Children of helkiah Tincom & Ruth Tincom his Wife

1 helkiah born August 15th 1685
2 Mary born August 13th 1687
3 John born March 27th 1689
4 Jacob born June 15th 1691
5 Caleb born october 12th 1693
6 Sarah born on the 30th of January 1696 Deceased on ye 22d of February 17$\frac{13}{14}$
7 Ebenazar born on ye. 3d of May 1698
8 Ruth born on ye 13th of ffebruary 1701
9 Peter Tinkcom born April 1st. 1706.

The Children of Solomon Bartlett & Joanna his Wife
1 Solomon Bartlett Born July 18th. 1751.
2 James Bartlett Born Janry. 2. 1754
3 Benjamin Bartlett Born, Novr. 14th 1755.
4 Abigail Bartlett Borne

The Children of Caleb Cook & Jane his Wife
1 John born on ye 5th of ffebruary 168$\frac{2}{3}$
2 Marcy born on ye 21 of ffebruary 168$\frac{3}{4}$: Deseased ffebruary 11th 170$\frac{3}{4}$
3 Ann Cooke born on the 21 of August 1686
4 Jane born on ye 16th of March 168$\frac{8}{9}$
5 Elizabeth born on ye 30th of November 1691
6 Mary born on ye 20th: of August 1694
7 Caleb born on ye 17th of Aprill 1697
8 James born on ye 19th of August 1700
9 Joseph born on ye 28 of November 1703

The Children of James howland & Mary his Wife
1 hannah born on ye 16th of october 1699
2 Abigaiel born ye 29th of october 1702
3 Elizabeth born on ye 2d of december 1704
4 Thankfull born September 25th 1709
5 John Born March 14th 1711
6 James born August first 1713

[p. 54] The Children of Robert Cushman & Perses his Wife
1 Robert born on ye 2d of July 1698
2 Ruth born on ye 25 of March 1700
3 Abigaiell born on ye 3d of July 1701
4 Hannah born Desember 25th 1705
5 Thomas born ffebruary 14 1706
6 Joshua born october 14 1707
7 Jonathan born ye 28 July 1712

The Children of peter Tomson & Sarah Tomson his Wife
1 Sarah born october 30th 1699
2 Peter born on ye 30th of June 1701
3 James born on the second of ffebruary 170$\frac{2}{3}$
4 Joseph born on the 3 of June 1706

The Children: of Elish Cobb & Lidiah Cobb his Wife
1 Elisha born on the 11th of June 1704

2 Lemuel born on yᵉ 10 of agust 1706
3 silvanos born on yᵉ 18 of March 1709
4 Hust born June 20 1711 Deceased March 20th $17\frac{12}{13}$
5 Lidiah born Apriel 17 1713
6 hanna born November 11th 1716
7 John born July 13 1719
8 Jabiz born on September: 6 1721
The Children of James Cobb & patience Cobb his Wife
1 Mallatiah born on the 22d of June 1706 Deseasd augst 20 1719
2 James born on yᵉ 13 of June 1708
3 Girshom born August 1711 Deceased in agust 1714
4 Joanna born yᵉ 9th of february 1715 Deceased february 16th $170\frac{17}{18}$
5 Girshom born March 16th $170\frac{16}{17}$
6 Martha born on yᵉ 9th of ffebruary $170\frac{18}{19}$

[p. 55] The Child of Jabiz Dunkin & Bethyah his Wife
1 Samuel born on the 22d of August 1705
The Children of: Benoney Lucos & of Repentance Lucos his Wife
1 Marey born on yᵉ 4th of May 1684
2 Samuel born on yᵉ 24 of July 1689
3 Joannah born on yᵉ 9th of ffebruary 1691
4 Sarah born on yᵉ 14 of Desember 1692
5 Elisha born on yᵉ 7th of ffebruary 1699
6 Bethyah born on yᵉ 29th of May 1704
The Children of John Barrows & Sarah his Wife
1 hannah born on yᵉ 19th of ffebruary 1700
2 Samuel born on yᵉ 11 of March $170\frac{2}{3}$
3 Ruth born on yᵉ 13th of June 1705
The Children of William Torrey & Mary his Wife
1 Mary Torrey Born, October 26th. 1749.
2. William Torrey Born, Octʳ. 30. 1751.
3. Anna Torrey. Born. Decʳ 6th. 1753
4. Joseph. Torrey. Born. Novʳ. 21st 1755 Deceased Ap: 25. 1757

[p. 56] The Children of Thomas howland & Joanna howland his wife
1 Consider born on yᵉ 28th of august 1700
2 Joannah born on yᵉ(*) June 1702 She Deceased June 5th 1715
3 Experiance born on yᵉ last of November 1705
4 Thomas born November 23 1707
5 Elizabeth born May 23d 1710
6 hannah Born on yᵉ: 19: Day of Desember 1712
7 Joanna born on yᵉ 7th of May 1716 Deced 1810
8 Joseph born on yᵉ 24 of July 1718
The Child of Thomas Dotey & Elizabeth his Wife
Thomas born on the 26 Day of January: 1704

* The day was omitted.

The Child of Edward Stephens Junr. & Phebe his Wife
Edward Stephens born Febry. 6th 1747/8.
The Children of Jobe Gibbs & Juduth Gibbs his Wife
Elizabeth born on the 15th of August 1706
The Child of Benjamin Bartlett Junr. & Jean his Wife
Benjamin Bartlett Born Augst. 18. 1752

[p. 57] The Children of John Faunce and of Abigaill Faunce His Wife
1 : Nathaniell Born August ye. 27th 1706.
2 : John Born May ye 2d 1709
3 : Marsey Borne. octtober ye 31 : 1711
4 : Abigaill Borne May ye 22 : 1715
5 Jane Borne. May ye 21 : 1717 :
6. Patience Born: July. ye. 13th : 1721
The Children of Beniamin Soule. and of. Sarah his Wife
1 Zachariah Born March ye 21 1694
2 Hanah Born March ye. 18 : 1696
3 Sarah Born May ye. 9 1699
4 Deborah Born Aprill ye 23 1702
5. Beniamin Born June. ye 5th 1704.
The Child of Joseph Church & of Juduth Church his wife
1 Sarah born on ye 4th of August 1706
The Children of Nathl Warren & Sarah his Wife
1 Hannah Warren born Janry. 27th. 1735/6. Deceased March 28th 1736
2 (*) born Sept. 6. 1737. Deceased Sept 12. 1737
3 Nathaniel Warren born May 2. 1740. Deceased Sept. 4 1740
4 Sarah Warren born Janry. 8th 17†
5 Hannah Warren born, Mar: 14. 17†
6. Susannah Warren born, June 8. 1746
7 John Warren born, Novr. 18. 1748. Deceased. Augst. 30 1749
8. Abigail Warren born May 25. 1753
9 Ruth Warren born Augst: 30t. 1758

[p. 58] The Children of John Carver & Mary Carver his Wife
1 John born september : 7 1692
2 Robert born september 30th 1694
3 Mary born october 4th 1696
4 hannah born March 8 1700
The Children of James Drew, & Mary Drew his Wife
1 Hannah Drew born Novr. 25. 1751.
2 James Drew born April 16. 1754.
3 William Drew. Born Decr. 29. 1755. Deceasd. Octr. ye. 6th. 1757
4 Mary Drew. Born. Octr. 8th. 1757.
5 William Drew Born Sept. 29th. 1760
6 Sarah Drew Born Novr. 3. 1762

* Name omitted. † The years were not completed.

7 Priscilla Drew Born Aug^{t}: 11th. 1765 Carry^{d}. Down
The Children of John Andros
1 Sarah born March: 16: 169$\frac{5}{6}$
2 Joannah born December 26. 1697
3 John born october 22^{d} 1699
4 Mary born January 8th 1701
5 Ebenazar born May: 5: 1704
The Children of James Clark Junr. & Susannah his Wife
Abigail Clark Born Decr y^{e}. 22. 1752
John Clark Borne Jan^{ry}. 5. 1754
The Children of James Drew & Mary his wife
8 Lydia Drew born June 8th. 1767
9 Betsey Drew born Sep^{t} 12th. 1769 Deceas^{d} July 24th 1772
The Children of John Rickard Junior & sarah Rickard his Wife
1 James born November 15th 1706
The Children of Joell Ellice and Elizabeth Ellice his Wife
1 Joell born on y^{e} 21st of ffebruary 170: $\frac{1}{2}$
2 John born on y^{e} 18th of September 1714
The Chidren of Dennis Sturmey & Elizabeth his Wife
1 Rebeckah Sturmey Born Augst 25 1751. Deceas^{d}. Octr. 1751
2 Thomas Sturmey Born 13th of Jan^{ry}. 1753 New Stile

(*To be continued.*)

THE PORTIONS OF STEPHEN HOPKINS' DAUGHTERS, AND THE ESTATE OF ELIZABETH[2] HOPKINS.

Transcribed from the Original Records,

BY GEORGE ERNEST BOWMAN.

STEPHEN HOPKINS bequeathed all his movable estate, not specifically mentioned, to his four daughters, Deborah, Damaris, Ruth and Elizabeth, to be equally divided between them.* The division of this property, made by Caleb[2] Hopkins and Myles Standish, is recorded in Plymouth Colony Wills and Inventories, Volume I, folios 65 and 66.

Caleb[2] Hopkins died before 1651,† but no record of the settlement of his estate can be found on the Plymouth records. It is possible that the land sold by Elizabeth[2] Hopkins to Jacob[2] Cooke (*Francis*[1]) was a part of Caleb's estate.

The agreement concerning Elizabeth's estate shows that

* Mfr. Desc., II: 12. † Ibid., I: 13.

she had disappeared and that her relatives thought that she was probably dead.

[fol. 65] The sev'all porcons of the children of mr Steven Hopkins Deceased as they were Devided equally by Capt Myles Standish Caleb Hopkins their brother

To Deborah Damaris Ruth and Elizabeth.

Debrahs porcon

	l	*s*	*d*
Inpris i bed boulster pillowe & a phillip & cheney pettycoate	04	10	00
It i silver spoone	00	08	00
It i wrought cov'ing and an old blankett	00	16	00
It 3 sheets	00	08	00
It i pillow beere	00	03	00
It i Diapr napkine	00	02	06
It i great Chest	00	08	00
It i alkemy spoone	00	00	02
It i Iron pott i bras pott i bras skellet & a Kettle	01	02	00
It 5 trenchers 2 peuter platters i bason i quart pott 2 poringers i tinnen candlestick half a pint pot	0	12	00
It i paire of scales and waights	00	05	00
It Due for hempe	00	02	00
It more for part of a cloake	00	10	00

Damaris porcon

Inpris i feather bed boulster pillow a stray bed a suite of cloathes another pettycote and a beaver muffe	04	10	00
It i silver spoone	00	08	00
It ii checker coverings	00	16	00
It i peere of linnen sheets	00	08	00
It i pillow beere	00	03	00
It 2 napkins & 2 table cloths	00	02	06
It i chest box and a Case	00	08	00
It an Alkemy spoone	00	00	02
It i great Cittell	01	02	00
It 5 trenchers 2 pewter platters 1 quart pot i pynt pott i salt 2 porringers i chamber pott i tin candlestick i earthen judg i linke & i sive	00	12	00
It i stoole	00	05	00
It Due for hemp	00	02	00
It for part of a cloake	00	10	00

Ruth Hopkins part

	l s d
Inpris i feather bed pillow & a cloth growne	04 . 10 . 00
It i silvr spoone	00 . 06 . 00
It i greene rugg & bastable blankett	00 . 16 . 00
It i paire of sheets	00 . 08 . 00
It i pillow beere	00 . 03 . 00
It a table cloth	00 . 02 . 06
It linnen wheele i wollen wheele i joyned stoole	00 . 08 . 00
It i spoone	00 . 00 . 02
It i Kettle a Churne bellowe tonges fire shovell spitt pot hookes gridiron & an Iron to lay before the fyre	01 . 02 . 00
It 5 trenchers two platters two porringers a pewter candlestick i puter cup a chamber pot a beaker i cullender & a tinn funell	00 . 12 . 00
It i half bushell i half peck ii hand sawes 3 Iron hoopes	00 . 05 . 00
It for hemp	00 . 02 . 00
It for prt of a cloake	00 . 10 . 00

ffor Elizabeth Hopkins as followeth.

The agreement betweene Richard Sparrow on thone prt and Captaine Myles Standish and Caleb Hopkins on thother prt concrning Eliz: Hopkins

Inpris That the said Richard shall have the said Elizabeth Hopkins as his owne child untill the tyme of her marryage or untill shee be nineteene yeares of age.

2ly. In consideracon of the weaknes of the Child and her inabillytie to prforme such service as may acquite their charges in bringing of her up and that shee bee not too much oppressed now in her childhood wth hard labour It is agreed that Richard Sparrow shall have putt into his hands her whole estate and to have the use of yt for the tyme of her continuance wth him. Onely one heiffer reserved wch is now in the hands of Gyles Hopkins of Yarmouth

[the tearmes of this agreement are fully prformed by Richard Sparrow *]

3 It is agreed that if it should so fall out by the prvidence of God that Goodwyfe Sparrow should be taken away by Death Then Elizabeth Hopkins shalbe free to be Disposed off as Captaine Standish & Caleb Hopkins shall think meete & likewise her estate.

4 That if the wyfe of Richard Sparrow be taken away

* This note is on the margin of the page.

by Death wth in three yeares then he is to be allowed twelve months tyme to pay the estate back againe: if after three yeares till the expiracon of the terme then he is to be allowed nine months.

5 It is agreed that if it should please God to take away the said Elizabeth Hopkins by Death then her estate to returne to Captaine Standish and Caleb Hopkins to be Disposed of amongst the rest of her Sisters according to the Will of m^r Hopkins provided Richard Sparrow be allowed convenyent tyme for the payment of the same namely if in three years then twelve months if after then nine months

6. That whensoev^r this estate is to be returned Richard Sparrow is to pay it in a Melch Cowe a feather bed and things belonging thereto and the remayndcr thone half in wheate and thother in Indian Corne wee meane by the featherbed and things belonging to the same valued and worth as now they are deliv^red. witnes our hands this xxx^th of the ix^th month 1644.

The estate to be returned is fifteene pounds one shilling & two pence in manner & forme abovesaid

Witnes our hands — Myles Standish
Willm Paddy — Caleb Hopkins
Thomas Willet — Rich. Sparrow.

[fol. 66] The coppy of note or writing under the hand of the said Richard Sparrow for the payment of a part of Ruth hopkins porcon This witnesseth That I Richard Sparrow of Plymouth have received the half of a Cow from Capt Miles Standish wch is Ruth Hopkins In consideracon of wch I the said Richard Sparrow am to pay to the said Capt Miles Standish in the behalf of Ruth Hopkins and for her use: two yeare old heiffers or two yeare old Steeres at the expiracon of three yeares or sooner, such as shalbe m^rchantable witnes my hand this xv^th of the 8th 1644

Witnes — Rich Sparrow
Willm Paddy.

May the 19th 1647

These witnesseth that I have received two young steers in full Satisfaction for halfe a Cow which was Ruth hopkins which Richard Sparrow bought of mee upon such tearmes; for which I had a bill of him but this shalbee for a full Discharge, I say received two steers;

Myles Standish

Elizabeth Hopkins to Jacob Cooke.

[Plym. Col. Deeds, II : I : 196]
1657 Prence Govr:

The 10th of October 1657

Memorandum That Elizabeth hopkins Doth acknowlige that for and in Consideration of a valluable sume to her alreddy satisfyed and fully paied by Jacob Cooke of the towne of Plymouth planter shee hath fully freely and absolutly bargained allianated and sold enfeofed and Confeirmed and by these p^r^sents Doth bargaine sell enfeofe and Confeirme unto the said Jacob Cooke all that her portion or prcell of meddow that shee hath in the great meddow att Joanses river viz ten acres of ffresh meddow bee it more or lesse lying betwixt the meddow of Capt: Thomas Willett and m^r^ John Done runing from woodside to woodside To have and to hold the said ten acres of meddow bee it more or lesse lying in the meddow Comonly Called the great meddow att Joanses river runing and being bounded as above expressed with all and singulare the appurtenances and privilidges belonging therunto; unto the said Jacob Cooke his heires and assignes for ever The said p^r^mises with all and singulare the privilidges belonging therunto with all the said Elizabeth hopkins her right title and Interest of and into the same or any prte or prcell therof to belong and appertaine unto the onely proper use and behoofe of him the said Jacob Cooke his heires and Assignes for ever;

Elizabeth Hopkins' Estate Settled.

[Plym. Col. Wills, II : I : 90, 91]

[fol. 90] An Inventory of the estate of Elizabeth hopkins which is in the hands of Jacob Cooke taken this 6th of october 1659 as likewise what prte of her said estate is in the hands of Andrew Ring an Inventory therof likewise taken the Day and yeare abovesaid and attested on the oathes of the said Andrew ringe and Jacob Cooke before the Court and by the Court ordered to be recorded as followeth

	ll	*s*	*d*
Imp^r^: one Cow	03	00	00
It a yeare and vantage heifer	01	10	00
It halfe a Cow Calfe of this yeare	00	07	00
It five ewe sheep	04	00	00
It one sheep weather	00	08	00
It one ewe lambe and an halfe	00	15	00
It one weather lambe and an halfe	00	14	00

It one kittle att 2 bushells of wheat	00	08	00
It a quart pot	00	01	00
It att Gorge Bonums one Cow	03	00	00
It halfe a yearling heiffer	00	15	00
It halfe a Calfe	00	07	00
It a rugge one pillow one bedd one blankett and bolster	05	10	00
It one warming pan one pestle and morter	00	10	00
It one brasse Skillett	00	01	00
It one bread grater and an Indian Tray	00	02	00
It 2 old silver spoones	00	10	00
It one garden spott	01	00	00
It one Cow killed the last yeare	03	00	00
It woole	00	16	00
summa	26	14	00

To some thinges remaining in Gyles hopkins hand with a smale matter in Mrs Standishes * hand;

Thomas Southworth John Morton;

[fol. 91] 1659 Prence Govr

A writing ordered by the Court to bee recorded as followeth;

These p^r^sents Testifyeth that wee whose Names are underwritten according to our best understanding have vallued the Cattle that goeth under the Name of Elizabeth hopkinses her Cattle and are in the Custitie of Gyles hopkins and Doe vallue the one halfe of three steers and a poor Calfe att eight pounds and five shillings and one very smale poor Cow and an old Cow being Defective att six pound;

the 29th : 7^m^ : (59) our hands John ffreeman
Edward Banges

Att the Court held att Plymouth the. 5^t^ of october 1659 It was ordered by the Court and agreed by Andrew ringe Jacob Cooke and Gyles hopkins; that incase Elizabeth hopkins Doe Come Noe more; that the prticulars of Cattle above expressed viz: the one halfe of three steers and a poore Calfe and the poor Cow and the old Cow above expressed soe vallued as abovsaid; shalbee the said Gyles hopkins his prte and portion of the estate of Elizabeth hopkins and the said Gyles hopkins accepted therof soe to bee; and therfore these p^r^sents Doth Declare that the said Gyles hopkins Doth heerby quitt Claime unto any more of the said estate of Elizabeth hopkins and that neither hee nor his heires are not to Demaund of; or molest the said Andrew Ringe or Jacob Cooke in the peacable enjoyment of that which they have of the estate of Elizabeth hopkins; neither them nor theire heires or assignes for ever;

* This is the latest known mention of Barbara Standish.

BARNSTABLE, MASS., VITAL RECORDS.

(Continued from Vol. III, p. 152.)

[Vol. I, p. 404] Eleazer Crocker and Ruth Chipman Married 7 April 1682
Their Son Benoni Born 13 of May 1682
Their Daughter Bethiah born 23 Septr 1683
Their Son Nathan born ye 27 of April 1685
Their Son Daniel born ye 23 of March 1686/7
Sarah Born March 23 1689
Theophilus born 11 of March 1691
Eleazer born 3 of August & Ruth also twins 1693
Abel born 15 June 1695
Rebekah his Daughter was born 10 Decem^{r} 1697
his Wife Ruth Dyed 8th of April 1698
his Son Benoni Dyed 3 Feb : 1701
Richard Childs & Elizabeth Crocker Married
his son Samuel born 6 of Novr 1679
his Daughter Elizabeth 23 Janr^{y} 1681 & Died 5 weeks after
his Son Thomas born Jan^{ry} 10 1682
his Daughter Hannah born 22 Janr^{y} 1684
his Son Timothy was born 22 Septr 1686
his Son Ebenezer born March Latter End 1691 as I think
his Daughter Elizabeth born 6 June 1692
his Son James born 6 Novr 1694
his Daughter Mercy born 7 May 1697
his Son Joseph born 5 March 1699 1700
Thankful 15 August 1702
Deacon Richard Childs Wife Died 1716 ye 15th Day of January
Increase Clap & Elizabeth Goodspeed ye vid : of Nath^{ll} Goodspeed Married In Octo^{r} 1675
his son John Clap born In Octo^{r} 1676
their Daughter Charity born In March 1677
Their Son Thomas Clap born In January 1681 & Died In January 1683
Their Son Thomas born In Decem^{r} 1684
Isaac Chapman & Rebecca Leonard Married 2 September 1678
their Daughter Lydia born 15 December 1679
Their Son John Born ye 12 of May 1681
their Daughter Hannah born 26 of Decem 1682
Their son James Born 5 August 1685
Their Daughter Abigail born ye 11 of July 1687
Their Daughter Hannah Died 6 of July 1689
Their Daughter Hannah born April 10th 1690

Their son Isaac born 29 Decem 1692
Their Son Ralph Born 19 January 1695
Their Daughter Rebecca born 10 June 1697
Edward Crowel & Mary Lothrop Married ye 16 of January 1673.
their Daughter Mary born of a Lords Day Morning ye 15 of March 1674
their Daughter unnamed born ye 14 of March a Tuesday 1676 & Died of a Lords Day ye 19 of March 1676
Their Son Yelverton born a Saturday Night February ye 17th
their son Joseph born March 1st on ye Lords Day *
Their Son Benjamin born a Thirsday ye 14 of April
Their Daughter Bathshua born Tuesday ye 26 of June & Dyed In ye Spring 1684
their son Edward born 6 of June 1685

[p. 405] The births of ye Children of John Chipman
his Daughter Hope born 31 of August 1652
his Daughter Lydia 25 of Decemr 1654
his Daughter Hannah ye 14 Janry 1658
his Son John ye 2nd of March 1656/7 & Dyed ye 29 May following
his Son Samuel ye 15 of April 1661
Ruth born ye Last of December 1663
Bethiah ye 1 of July 1666
Mercy born ye 6 of Feb 1668
his son John Born 3rd of March 1670
his Daughter Desire born 26 of Feb 1673
his Wife Hope Dyed ye 8 of January 1683
James Claghorn & Abia Lumbard 6 January 1654
his son James born 29 January 1654
his Daughter Mary born 26 Octor 1655
his Daughter Elizabeth born In April 1658
his Daughter Sarah 3 Jany 1659
his son Robert born ye 27 Octor 1661
Shobal not recorded †
Samuel Chipman & Sarah Cob. Married 27 Dececem 1686
Their Son Thomas born 17 Nov 1687
Their Son Samuel born 6 of August 1689
Their son John Born Feb 16 1691
his Daughter Abigail born 15 Septr 1692
his Son Joseph 10 of January 10 1694
his Son Jacob born 30 August 1695
his Son Seth born 24 of Feb 1697
his Daughter Hannah born 24 Septr 1699
Sarah Born Novr 1 1701
Barnabas born March 24 1702
Robert Claghorn his Daughter Abia born Aug 13 1702

* This is in the margin, opposite the preceding entry.
† This entry is in a different hand.

his Son Joseph born 25 August 1704
Nathaniel Born 10 of November 1707
Samuel 23 of June 1711
Shobal Claghorn his son James born In August 1689
Thomas 20 of March 1692/3
Shobal 20 of Septem^r 1696
Robert 18 of July 1699
Benjamin 14 of June 1701
his Daughter Mary born in 1707
his Daughter Jane In 1709
Their son Ebenezer born July 30 1712
his Daughter Thankful born 1690 30th January Dyed 1696 In January

(*To be continued.*)

EPHRAIM TINKHAM'S WILL AND INVENTORY.

Transcribed from the Original Records,

BY GEORGE ERNEST BOWMAN.

EPHRAIM TINKHAM died at Plymouth between 17/27 January, 1683/4, the date of his will, and 20/30 May, 1685, the day his inventory was taken. His wife Mary was the daughter of Peter Brown of the Mayflower. The record of the will and inventory are found in the Plymouth Colony Wills and Inventories, Volume IV, Part II, pages 110 and 111.

[p.110] Know all men to whome these p^r sents shall Come That I Epharim Tincom seni^r of the Towne of Plymouth in New England being at ye day of ye date hereof but weake of body, but blessed be god of sound & perfect & well disposing memory not knowing how soon it may please god to Change my Temporall life to death doe therfore make these p^r sents to be my last will & Testament to Continue for ever firme & Inviolable in manner & forme following: Imp^rmis I will & bequeath unto my dear & loveing Wife Mary Tincom my now dwelling house & housing that is in Plymouth with ye orchyard belonging there unto, and all my lands meadowes with ye appurtenances & privildges belonging unto them lying & being in ye Townships of Plymouth Middlebury Dartmouth or any other place in this

Colony whatsoever that belongs to me Excepting such lands as I shall perticulerly dispose of in this my will, I give them all as afforesd unto my wife for her support & Comfort for & during her naturall life : Item I will & bequeath unto my Eldest son Epharim Tincome that hundred acre lott he lives on in ye Township of Middlebury ioyning to ye land of Samuel Wood Item I give to my son Ebenezer Tincom ye other other hundred acre lott that ioynes to my son Epharims to them & their heirs for ever. with ye meadow lands belonging to it lying in Middleburys great meadow, Item, I give & bequeath unto my son Peter Tincome that share of land he now lives on in ye Township of Middlebury neer whetstone vynyard brooke & all ye meadows belonging to it to him & to his heirs for ever, Item : I give unto my son Elkiah one third part of a share of land lying at Dartmouth to him & his heirs for ever Item I give unto my two sons John Tincum & Isaack Tincom that my now dwelling place housing orchards lands meadows & all ye priviledges belonging to it after their mothers decease to be equally devided between them, I say to them & their heirs for ever Item I give & bequeath unto my daughter Mary Tomson fifty acres of upland which was given me by ye Towne of Plimouth & lyes in ye Township of Plimouth neer ye place that is comonly caled Momponsett, my will is also what my wife shall leave at her decease be it good or Chattels that it shall be devided amongst my seaven Children my eldest son to have a double portion, my six guns they are already disposed of unto my six sons who have them for their proper use. Item I will & bequeath unto my dear & loveing Wife Mary Tincome my debts being first paid all my goods cattle or Chattles & debts whatsoever are due & belonging unto me & to pay all debts that they lawfully appear that I doe owe, And I doe by these presents appoint & make & ordaine my dear & loveing wife Mary Tincome to be my sole Executrix of this my last will & Testament to administer upon my said estate to pay such debts I owe & receive such debts as are due to me. & to make choyce of my son Epharim Tincome to be helpfull to her in ye same, As also to see my body be decently buried & to defray ye Charge thereof, Thus hopeing that this my last will & Testament will be performed according to ye Tenure thereof. I Comitt my body to ye dust, & my soul to god that gave it By these p^r^sents ratifiing & Confirming my said wife Mary Tincome to be my sole & lawfull Executrix revoking & makeing void all other my former wills written or verball : In witness where of I ye aforesaid Epharim Tincom seni^r^ have here unto sett my hand & seal this seventeen day of January one thousand six hundred eightie three :

Signed sealed & declared to be my last will & Testament. in presence of
William Hoskins senr
Jonathan Shaw senr :

Ephriam Tincome senior
his mark : **E T** & (seal)

This will was proved in ye Court held at Plymouth ye fifth of June 1685 on ye oaths of William Hoskins & Jonathan Shaw who testified upon oath that they saw Sericant Tincome sign seal & declare this to be his last will & Testament & that he was of disposing mind & memory so to doe :

[p. 111] An Inventory of ye estate of Epharim Tincome senir taken & apprised ye 20 day of may 1685 by us whose names ar under written

	li	*s*	*d*
Inprmis his wearing Clothes & hatt	03	17	0
Item one bible & other smale books	00	17	0
It in ye inner roome one bed & bolster 1 rug 1 pair blankets one pair sheets	06	00	0
It one bed bolster 1 pair of sheets one pair of blanketts one rug	05	00	0
It 14 yards of Cotton & lining Cloth	01	13	0
It 2 chests & one smale Trunk 4 meal baggs	01	04	0
It one great Wheel one little wheel one hatchell 3 pair of cards	00	17	0
It in ye Kitchen one Copper Kettle	01	00	0
It one smale Table and 4 Chairs	00	10	0
It one old warming pan and litle brass Kittle	00	03	0
It 2 Iron potts one Iron Kettle & posnett	00	17	0
It 3 Tramels & Iron spitt 2 pair pott hooks one pair of tongs & gridiron	01	00	0
It 3 pewter platters one bason & Champer pott	00	13	6
It 2 old pewter pots one little pewter bottle 7 spoons	00	0*	0
It 5 pewter poringers one salt celler	00	04	0
It one lanthorne old candlestick & frying pan	00	02	6
It one earthen pan one stone iug 2 earthen potts	00	02	0
It 2 wooden boles & Trayes & other dishes	00	09	0
It one Churne 3 pailes with other smal wooden things	00	08	0
It in ye Chamber one bed one pair of sheets one pair blanketts one rug	05	10	0
It one pillow 2 pair of pillobees	00	07	0
It one sifeten trough 2 sives one washing tub on halfe bushell & other lumber	01	00	0

* Either 05 or 07.

It also Iron tools 5 sickles 2 sythes & sneath	00	10	0
It 4 axes 2 hows one spade 3 forks with severall other iron tools	02	00	0
It one Cart & plough & tackling belonging to them	03	00	0
It as to Cattell 3 yoke of oxen and 2 steers	21	00	0
It more 8 Calves 1 steer one bull 3 yeerlings	22	00	0
It 23 sheep and 5 swine	09	05	0
It 6 guns and one rapier	04	10	0
It as to his housing & lands in plimouth & lands in middlebury & dartmouth	407	10	0
the whole sum. is	500	17	9
Debts due from yᵉ estate	04	08	4
more Debts due from yᵉ estate	01	10	0

Nathaniel Southworth
Thomas Faunce

MARSHFIELD, MASS., VITAL RECORDS.

(*Continued from Vol. III, p. 189.*)

[Vol. I, p. 14] Rebeca Snow the Daugter of Josias Snow & Rebeca his wife was Born the 16 day of June 1685

Samuel Thomas the son of Samuel Thomas & Marcy his wife was born the 7th day of Desember. 1685

Deborah The Daughter of Micael fford and bethiah his wife was Born October 24th 1686

John Holmes the son of Samuel Holmes & Mary his wife was Born the 18 day of Novembr 1686

Elizabeth the Daughter of John Sumers and Elizabeth his wife was born the. 26. day of Desember. 1686.

Mary the Daughter of Samuell Dogett & Mary his wife was born the 26 day of Aprill 1687

Samuel the son of John Sherman & Jane his wife was Born febuary. 22. 1686.

John the son of Jonathan Eames & Hanah his wife was Born the 9th day of May 1687.

Mercy the Daughter of Anthony Eames & Mercy his wife was born the first of October. 1687

Samuel Barker the Son of John Barker & Desire his wife was Born Aprill. 23. 1686

John Carver the son of William Carver & Elizabeth his Wife was born Desember the first 1683

William the son of William Carver & Elizabeth his Wife was born October 29th 1685

Josiah the son of William Carver & Elizabeth his wife was born february the 2d 1687
Abigail the Daughter of Jacob Dingley & Elizabeth his wife was born the 16th day of July 1687 .
Mercy the Daughter of Anthony Eames & Mercy his wife was Bourn. October. 1. 1687
Elenor the Daughter of Samuel Baker & Patience his wife was born April 10 1679
Josias Baker son of Samuel Baker and Patience his wife was born feb. 1. 1685
Deborah the Daughter of John Sherman & Jane his wife was born the 4th day of Sept 1689
Anthony Eames & Marcy Sawyer were Married Desember 2d. 1686.
Joseph Otis and Dorothy Thomas were Married the 20th day of November 1688. by Mr Thomas Mighell Minester
John Dogett and Mehittabell Trewant were Married on the twenty-third day of September 1691
John Croade and Deborah Thomas were Married the first day of Desember 1692 by Mr Samuel Arnold Minester
Samuel Little & Sarah Gray were Married before Mr Alden May 13th 1682
Mr Nathaniel Thomas & Mrs Mary Appleton were Maried June the 20th. 1694. by M(r) John Rogers Mines(ter)
John Sawye(r &) Rebecka Sn(ow) were Conjoyn(ed) in Marriage (*worn*) 23d 1694 b(y) Mr Weld M(inester)
Samuell Ba (*worn*) and Sarah (*worn*) were Marr (*worn*) the 27 (*worn*)

(*To be continued.*)

REPORTS FROM STATE SOCIETIES.

MASSACHUSETTS SOCIETY.

The twenty-ninth meeting of the Massachusetts Society was held at the Hotel Vendome, Boston, on Thursday afternoon, 13 February, 1902. Hon. Lyman D. Brewster, the Governor of the Connecticut Society delivered an address on "William Brewster, His True Position in our Colonial History." Hon. Henry S. Washburn read an original poem entitled "The Pilgrim Lovers, A Legend of Cape Cod." Rev. George R. W. Scott, D.D., made an appeal for contributions to help pay the debt on the John Robinson Memorial Church at Gainsborough, England. The Society, by vote, appropriated fifty dollars for this purpose, and a committee composed of Mr. Charles A. Hopkins, Rev. Frederick B. Allen and Mr. J. Weston Allen, was appointed to solicit additional contributions from the members. Several songs were given by Mr. Harry Goodhue, and the usual informal reception followed. Two hundred and fifty-eight members and guests were present.

Donations to the Library and Cabinet.

Photograph of a Portrait of Mrs. Mercy (Hinckley) Prince, from Mr. Arthur Harlow.

Four Photographs of Mr. Daniel Cushman, over ninety years of age, from Miss Mary Trow.

"Ancestors and Descendants of Joseph Wescot Tinker," from the compiler, Mr. Frederick James Libbie.

"Second Congregational Church, Manomet, Mass., Anniversary Celebration. 1738–1898," and "Dying and Behold We Live," both from the author, Rev. Haig Adadourian.

"The Litchfield Family in America, Part I, No. 1," from the compiler, Mr. Wilford J. Litchfield.

"Elder William Brewster, A Monograph," from the author, Mr. William Howell Read.

"Roger Conant in America as Governor and Citizen," from the author, Mrs. Sarah S. Bartlet.

"Cambridge Concordance" (London, 1698), from Mrs. Godfrey Ryder.

Members Elected.

February 12, 1902.

694. Thomas Sedgwick Steele, Boston, eighth from William Bradford.
695. Mrs. Chalmers Meek Williamson, Jackson, Miss., eighth from William Bradford.
696. Mrs. Donald Purple Hart, Boston, ninth from William Bradford.
697. Joseph Aldrich Bursley, Fort Wayne, Ind., ninth from John Howland.
698. Mrs. Justice H. Bowman, Toledo, O., eighth from John Alden.
699. Mrs. Leslie Clark Wead, Brookline, eighth from Henry Samson.
700. Lawrence Whitcomb, Brookline, eighth from Henry Samson.
701. William Stearns Simmons, Sharon, ninth from John Alden.

March 27, 1902.

702. Miss Ella Agnes Bush, Boston, ninth from Myles Standish.
703. Mrs. Grant Charles Madill, Ogdensburg, N. Y., ninth from William Bradford.
704. Mrs. Henry Hobart Porter, Jr., Lawrence, Long Island, N. Y., tenth from William Bradford.
705. Mrs. Edward Livingston Davis, Boston, eighth from Stephen Hopkins.
706. Miss Mary Goddard Fuller, Boston, eighth from Edward Fuller, seventh from Samuel[2] Fuller.
707. George Batcheller Perkins, Boston, ninth from William Bradford.
708. Charles Brooks Perkins, Brookline, ninth from William Bradford.
709. Mrs. Charles Brooks Perkins, Boston, ninth from William Brewster.
710. Miss Adeline Amelia Bigelow, Boston, eighth from John Alden.

Supplemental Lines Filed.

January, 1902.

579. Boylston A. Beal, ninth from John Alden: ninth from William Brewster; eighth from George Soule.
667. George A. Dary, ninth from John Billington, eighth from Francis Billington.

March, 1902.
155. Mrs. Burr Porter, seventh from George Soule.
266. Edwin S. Crandon, ninth from George Soule.
267. Mrs. Edward Y. Swift, eighth from John Howland; eighth from Richard Warren.
636. Stephen D. Salmon, ninth from John Alden.

PENNSYLVANIA SOCIETY.

The Annual Dinner of the Society was held at the Hotel Stratford, Philadelphia, on Thursday, January 23, 1902.

At a meeting held February 6, 1902, the Treasurer, Mr. James Mauran Rhodes resigned, and was then elected Second Deputy Governor. Mr. James Mauran Rhodes, Jr., was elected Treasurer, to fill the vacancy.

PILGRIM NOTES AND QUERIES.

NOTES.

THE COLONIAL RESEARCH FUND. Our readers are reminded that every copy of the "Freeman Genealogy" and "The Ancient Estate of Governor William Bradford" and every set of "Ancestral Charts" sold by the Massachusetts Society, as stated in our advertising pages. helps along the Colonial Research Work, since the entire proceeds are added to the Colonial Research Fund.

The following additional contributions to the $2000.00 Fund have been received: Charles S. Cook, $100.00; The Rhode Island Society of Mayflower Descendants, $25.00: Miss Emma C. B. Jones, $2.00; Previously acknowledged, $545.00; Total, $672.00.

THE MAYFLOWER GENEALOGIES. In order to bring the magazine up to date it has been found necessary to postpone the publication of the first installment of "Stephen Hopkins and His Descendants." We now hope to have it ready for the October number, which we expect to issue early in October.

VITAL STATISTICS OF THE MAYFLOWER PASSENGERS. Additional data from Original Records. (See Vol. II, pp. 114, 254.)

Isaac Allerton was born about 1586.

Sarah (Collier) (Brewster) Parke, double widow of Love Brewster and Richard Parke, was born about 1615, and died at Plymouth 26 April /6 May, 1691.

Mary (———) Brown, widow of Peter Brown, was living at Plymouth 2/12 January, 1633/4.

Hester (———) Cooke, widow of Francis Cooke, died before 18/28 December, 1675.

Ann (Plummer) Samson, wife of Henry Samson, was living 24 December, 1668 /3 January, 1669.

Richard More died at Salem, after 19/29 March, 1693/4. His first wife, Christian (Hunt) More, was born about 1616, and died at Salem, 18/28 March, 1676/7. He married, second, Jane[2] Hollingsworth (*Richard*[1]), who was born about 1631 and died at Salem, 8/18 October, 1686.

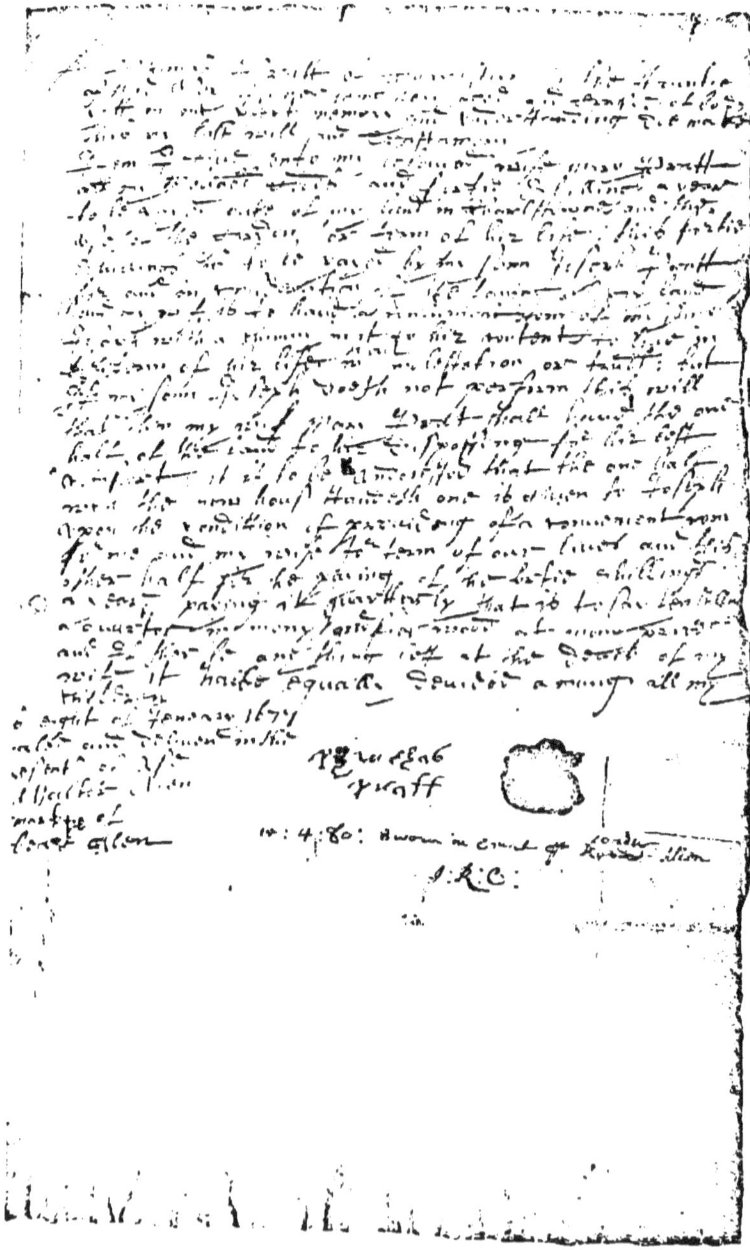

PHINEAS PRATT'S WILL.

THE MAYFLOWER DESCENDANT

Vol. IV. JULY, 1902. No. 3.

PHINEAS PRATT OF PLYMOUTH AND CHARLESTOWN.

(*Concluded from page 98.*)

1646, September 17. "The .17. of y^e^ .7. month .1646. phineas prate came before ye Goue^r^ and acknowledged the sale of his house & land, with all ye appurtenances thertoo belonging; to John Cooke, according to a deed then exhibited which they desired might be recorded Also his wife came before ye Gou^r^ and gaue her consente to ye same sale.

"Allso Samuell Cudberte did ye same day & year aboue writen, freely relinquish all ye claime, title, or Intrest, that he euer had, or might pretend to haue, to any parte, or parcell of ye lands afforsaid As also from those for which they were exchanged with m^r^ prence. And did freely giue, grante, and make ouer all ye right, and Intreste that he euer had, or hereafter, should haue, or at any time might pretend to haue, to any parte or parcell of ye lands aforesaid, and those mentioned in ye deede Insuing to Phineas Prate, & his heires, & assignes for euer; for his, & their onely proper vse & behoofe.

William Bradford Gou^r^" *

The .26. of August .1646.

These presents doe witnes that Phineas Prate of Plimoth Joyner, for & in consideration of ye sume of twenty pounds sterl: to be payed by John Cooke Jun of plimoth afforesaid planter, in maner & forme following, that is to say fiue pounds to be payed in cloathing within one month nexte after ye date hearof fiue pounds in march next, either in wheat, or comodities, fiue pounds in a milch cowe as shee shall be prised by .2. Indifferent men chosen by either party one, and ye last .5^li^. this time twelfe months. Hath freely and absolutly barganined and sould, & by these presents doth bargaine & sell vnto the said John Cooke, all y^t^ his house, & howsing, and

* The autograph of Governor Bradford is appended to the original entry.

gardine place and orchard (excepting yͤ fruite trees now growing therin, or so many of them to be deliured to the said Phineas, or his assignes when he shall demande them, so it be in due time) and fiftie acres of vpland tow acres of meadow at Joanes riuer, and all and singuler the appurtenances thervnto belonging, and all his right, title, & Interest of & into yͤ same, & euery parte, & parcell thereof; to haue & to hold the said house, housing, garden, and orchard (excepting before excepted) the fiftie Acers of vpland, and yͤ .2. Acres of meadow at Joans riuer, with the sixe Acres of vpland meadow, at the great meadow with all, & euery their appurtenances, vnto the said John Cooke, his heirs, & assignes, for euer. and to the onely proper vse, & behofe of him the said John Cooke, his heires and assignes for euer, and with warranties against all people, from by or vnder him, claiming any righte, title, or Interest of, & into the said premises or any parte or parcell therof, and espetially against Samuell Cudberte his heirs, & assignes for euer by these presents; And the said Phineas Prate doth further Couenante and grant by these presents, that it shall & may be lawfull too, & for the said John Cooke either by him selfe, or his Atturney to enrole, or recorde the title or tenure of these before the Gouernour for yͤ time being, according to yͤ vsuall order & manor of enrolling & recording deeds, & euidences in his Maties Court at plimoth in shuch case made, & prouided In witnes wherof the said Phineas Prate hath herevnto sett his hand & seale the day & year first aboue writen

In yͤ presence of Phineas Prate
Ralfe Whoory
William Pady
Thomas Willet
Nathanell Sowther

And in consideration of yͤ sume of .2s. 6d. to yͤ said Phineas Prate in hand paid hath freely, & absolutly bargained & sould vnto yͤ said John Cooke all his right title & Interest, of & into any lands lying at the head or ende, of yͤ afforesaid bargained premises before the sealing and delivery of these presents. [Plym. Col. Deeds, I: 224]

1650, October 24. Thomas Prence sells to John Cooke, Jr., "two acars of mersh meddow bee it more or lesse lying before the house and land of the Elder Cushman at Joaneses riuer next vnto a pʳcell of meddow which was samtimes Phenias Prats;" [Plym. Col. Deeds, I: 329]

The same year (no minor dates given) in recording the bounds of a grant of land in 1641 to John Cooke, Jr., at "Rockey nooke," reference is made to "the lots adioyning which the said John Cook hath bought of Phenias Prat;" [Plym. Col. Deeds, I: 350]

1658, June 5. "June the fift 1658 liberty was graunted by the Court vnto Phenias Prat or any for him to looke out a pʳcell or tract of land to accomodate him and his Posterite withall together with other ffreemen; or alone as hee shall think meet and to make reporte of the same vnto the Court; that soe a Considerable proportion thereof may bee Confeirmed vnto him;" [Court Orders, III: 139]

1664, June 8. "In reference vnto the Request of Phineas Pratte; and the Elder Bates in the behalfe of the Children of Clement Briggs; That wheras they the said Phineas Pratt and Clement Briggs haue not had theire proportions of land with others of this Jurisdiction formerly Called Purchassers or old Comers; That they might haue some Consideration of land in that respect in a p^r^cell or tract of land lying neare vnto the line betwixt the massachusetts Jurisdiction and vs neare vnto Waymouth; The Court Doth graunt vnto the said Phineas Pratt and vnto two of the said Clement Briggs his sonnes viz: Dauid Briggs and Remember Briggs three hundred and fifty acrees of the said lands with all and singulare the appurtenances thervnto belonging vnto them and theire heires and assignes for euer viz: vnto the said Phineas Pratt two p^r^tes of three of the said three hundred and fifty acrees; and the remainder therof vnto the two sonnes of the said Clement Briggs afornamed and this to bee layed forth for them by John Jacob of hingham and John Whitmarsh of Waymouth and incase any Indian or Indians shall heerafter lay claime vnto the said lands That the said Phineas Prat and the Elder Bates stand bound to the Court to answare the Charge of the Purchase therof and all other nessesary Charges about the said land;"

marginal note: —

"this land was layed out afterwards by order of the court by John Whitmarsh and John Jacob and is att the Path that leads from Waymouth to Bridgwater; as it is said a litle brooke running through the same" [Court Orders, IV: 75]

1664, October 4. James Lovell, of Weymouth, desires to take up land "neare the place where Phenias Prat and the sonnes of Clement Briggs were accomodated; between theire land and the line of the Pattent;" [Court Orders, IV: 82]

1665, June 7. "A Certaine p^r^cell of meddow or such swampy ground as tendeth towards meddow is graunted by the Court vnto Pheneas Pratt and James Louell lying on the westerly side of Phenias Pratts land that was graunted vnto him the last June Court neare vnto the line betwixt the Massachusetts and this Jurisdiction the said p^r^cell being about foure or fiue acrees bee it more or lesse to bee equally Deuided betwixt them the said Pheneas Pratt and James Louell to them and theire heires and assignes for euer" [Court Orders, IV: 102]

1668, October 29. "In Reference vnto the Request of James Lovell for to haue an addition of swampey land neare vnto his land hee hath in the right of m[r] Nathaniel Souther The Court haue ordered that m[r] Constant Southworth and Cornett Studson shall view the said land and alowe him twelue acrees therof; besides that which hee hath alreddy graunted vnto him with Phenias Pratt;" [Court Orders, V: 3]

1672/3, January 1. Phineas and Mary Pratt, of Charlestown, sell to John Shaw, Sr., of Weymouth, the land granted by the Court June 8, 1664, and June 7, 1665. [Plym. Col. Deeds, III: 271]

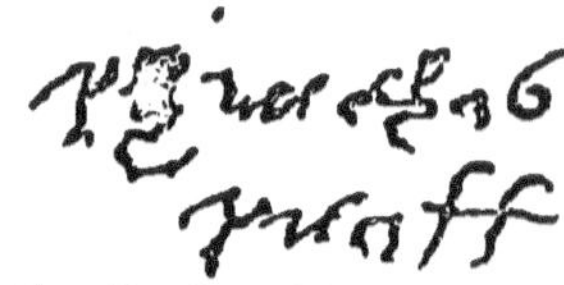

From his will dated January 8, 1677/8.

The foregoing records are interesting as determining within a comparatively brief period the time of Phineas' settling at and leaving Plymouth, as indicating the part of the town in which he lived and as showing that he was regarded as one of the "old comers" or "Purchasers" of Plymouth. But their chief interest and value is in serving to identify his wife and to fix the approximate date of his marriage. These two interesting details are dwelt upon later.

From Plymouth he removed to Charlestown, where, on May 20, 1648, he bought a house and garden from George Bunker. It is impossible to say just when he left Plymouth. He sold his home there August 26, 1646, and is described in the deed as being "of Plimoth." On September 17, three weeks later, he and his wife appeared before the Governor, he to ask to have the deed recorded and she to give her consent to the sale, so they were no doubt still living there at that time. He is described in the Charlestown deed as being an inhabitant "in the same towne" as the grantor, *i. e.*, Charlestown. He must, therefore, have left Plymouth in the interval between the recording of the Plymouth deed September 17, 1646, and the purchase of the Charlestown property May 20, 1648.

The entry made in the records by John Greene, town clerk, concerning the transfer of the Charlestown house and land is as follows:—

A sale of a House and a garden in Charltowne By George Bunker vnto Phinias Prat the 20th of the 3[d] month 1648.

Know all men by these presents That I George Bunker Inhabitant in Charltowne have sould assigned and set over, and by this declare that I doe sell assign and set over unto Phinias Prat Inhabitant in the same towne A House or Tenement with a garden to it adioyning: which house and garden stands and is scituate in Charltowne in the great through fare street which goes from the Neck of land into the market place, this hous and garden stands right over against the way that goes up to the windmill hill, and that way which goes intoo elbow lane, the house is bounded on the front by the street way, or by the west, and the hous and garden is bounded East by the back street which goes to the pitt where the Beasts drinke, and where the Creek begins wch runs on the back syde of the maiors garden into Charls River, and it is bounded Northward by samuell Howard, and south ward by Thomas Carter senio^r^: Alsoe I Georg Bunker doe acknowledg my selfe to bee fully payd and satisfied for this sayd hous and garden, And I doe heer by resigne all my Right, Titell, and interest vnto the sayd house and garden vnto the sayd Phinias Prat to be his and his heigres for ever.

John Greene.

[Charlestown Book of Possessions, 117]

This property was sold April 10, 1711, to Benjamin Lawrence by Phineas' son Joseph who inherited it. [Middlesex Co. Deeds, XV: 501]

On March 1, 1657/8, there was a division of land in accordance with "The Returne of the Committee, Apoynted by the Inhabitants of Charltowne, for the division, of the wood and Commons one Mistick syde," and Phineas drew lot No. 54 containing 2½ commons and a certain proportion of woodland. [Book of Possessions, 87].

In 1662 he presented to the General Court of the Massachusetts Bay Colony that interesting and valuable paper which he called "A Decliration of the Afaires of the Einglish People [that first] Inhabited New Eingland." Either accompanying or following this document was a petition on which the General Court took the following action May 7 of the same year (1662): —

In Ans^r^: to. ye petition of. phineas Prat. of charls Toune. who presented this Court wth a narrative of the streights & hardships that the first planters of this Colony vnderwent in their endeavors to plant themselves at plimouth. & since wherof he was. one The Court judgeth it meet to Graunt him Three. hundred acres of land where it is to be had not hindering a plantation *

A few years later, June 1, 1665, there is the following entry in the Court records: —

Layd out to Phineas Pratt of Charls Toune three hundred acres of land (more or lesse). in the wilderness. on the East of merremack Riuer neere the vpper end of Nacooke brooke on the South East of it it begins at a great sare Pjne standing anent the midle of nacooke pond & joyneth. to the ljne of fiue hundred acres of land lately granted to the Toune of Billirrikey on the south of it ninety sixe pole & so continues a streight ljne two hundred & sixe pole further vnto a white oake bounded wth P from thence it turnes vnder the side of a great hill one hundred fifty & two pole vnto another white oake marked wth P. which stands on the North side of an other great hill. & on the south Corner of a little swampe from thence

* Mass. Bay Rcds., IV: 402.

it runns neere the west & by south. two hundred pole to a great Red oake bounded as before. from thence the closing ljne to the first Pine is two hundred & ninety pole. the exact forme of it together wth the rule of finding the exact lines is fully demonstrated by this inclosed plott taken of the same 20 8mo 1664.

By Jonathan Danforth. survejor

The Court Allows & approoues of this Returne.*

In October, 1668, Phineas, then about 75 years old, presented another petition to the General Court in which, while expressing his thankfulness for the grant of land made him three years before in answer to his first petition, he refers to his physical infirmities and present lack of the actual necessities of life and entreats that he may receive some measure of support in his old age. "Yet my necessity causeth me farther to entreat you," he writes, and there is here an intimation that his first petition had not been answered quite as he expected—that he had asked for bread and had been given a stone in the shape of three hundred acres of land in the wilderness. The Court acted unfavorably on the petition now presented, not recognizing his claim to further assistance. This paper does not appear in the Court records and a careful search fails to find it among the unpublished State Archives. It is reprinted here from an article by Mr. Richard Frothingham, Jr., in the Massachusetts Historical Society Collections (Fourth Series, IV, 487), in which it was printed for the first time from the original, then evidently in Mr. Frothingham's hands, with the following prefatory note, viz:—"This Petition is printed from a manuscript of the date of 1668, as is evident from the autograph attestation of Torrey and Pyncheon, though it is so unlike the 'Declaration,' both in composition and chirography, as to make it certain that it is not in the handwriting of Pratt."

To the Honoured the Generall Court, holden at Boston, this Oct. 1668.

I acknowledg my self truly thankfull unto the Honoured Court for that they gave me at the time I presented an History called, A declaration of the affaires of the English people, that first inhabited New England. Yet my necessity causeth me farther to entreat you to consider what my service hath been unto my dread Soveraign Lord King James of famous memory. I am one of that litle number, ten men that arrived in Massachusets Bay for the setling of a Plantation, & am the remainder of the forlorn hope sixty men. We bought the south part of the Bay of Aberdecest their Sachem. Ten of our company died of famine. Then said ye Natives of the Countrey, let us kill them, whilst they are weak, or they will possesse our Countrey, & drive us away. Three times we fought with them, thirty miles I was pursued for my life, in time of frost, and snow, as a deer chased with wolves. Two of our men were kill'd in warr, one shot in the shoulder. It was not by the wit of man, nor by ye strength of the arme of flesh, that

* Ibid., IV: 471.

we prevailed against them. But God, that overrules all power, put fear in their hearts. And now seeing God hath added a New England to old Engl. and given both to our dread Soverg Lord King Charles the second, many thousand people enjoy the peace thereof; Now in times of prosperity, I beseech you consider the day of small things; for I was almost frozen in time of our weak beginnings, and now am lame. My humble request is for that may be for my subsistance the remaining time of my life. And I shall be obliged.

Your thankfull servant,

Phinehas Pratt.

The Deputyes Doe not Judge meete to graunt this petition, wth refference to the consent of or Honoed magists. hereto.

William Torrey, Cleric.

The Magistrates consent wth their bretheren the Deputys.

Jo: Pynchon, Pr Curiam.

Phineas had apparently reached a point where he required assistance. He was old and he was lame, a condition which materially impaired his ability to provide for himself. The Selectmen of Charlestown came to his relief in a most generous manner, as the following extracts from the town orders will show, and the assistance granted Phineas during his lifetime was extended to his widow.

1668/9, January 25. "Also ordered Counstable. Jno. Hayman to supply Phineas Pratt with so much as his prsent low Conditiō. may require." [Charlestown Town Orders, III: 96]

1669, March 26. "This day also mr Randll. Nicholes was desired to deliver to Phineas Pratt 200 foote of good bords fitt for his use this on the townes Accott. to be repaid him in season." [Town Orders, III: 100]

1677, October 1. "Order to Zech. Johnson Constable to pay to ye Necessity of ffather Prat forty shillings in pay as sutable as he can & place it to ye townes Accot." [Town Orders, III: 205]

1678, December 4. "Ordered Severall Bills to be graunted viz Two of 20s. Each to Tho: Smith 2d. Counts for keeping Swains Childe To Good. wf. Parker a Bill to Goodm: Clew for 20s for her prst relief To Goodm Pratt a Bill for 40s.

pr J R Recorder"*

1679, October 6. "Ordrd. yt 20s. In mony be given Phenius. Pratt for his releefe. & this to be payd by Constable. Newell

By ye ordr of ye Selectmen J: N R"†

1679, December 14. "Ordrd. yt Phenius. Pratt. hath twenty shillings In mony allowed for his Releife. payd by J N:

J: N: R:"‡

* Town Orders, IV: 2. † Ibid., IV: 16. ‡ Ibid., IV: 17.

Phineas' wife was Mary, daughter of Degory and Sarah (Allerton) (Vincent) Priest. She was born in Leyden, Holland, probably within a year or two after the marriage of her parents November 4, 1611. Neither she nor her sister nor mother came with Degory Priest in the Mayflower to Plymouth in 1620. After her husband's death there on January 1, 1620/21, the widow married Godbert Godbertson at Leyden November 13, 1621, and, with her two daughters, Mary and Sarah Priest, came with him to Plymouth in the Anne in 1623.

There Mary Priest met and married Phineas Pratt. It has been frequently stated that they were married in 1630. There is not a particle of evidence in the Plymouth records to support this statement, though it must be admitted that neither is there any evidence to disprove it. The most the records prove is that they were married *after* the division of cattle May 22, 1627, and *before* Godbert Godbertson's death, which occurred prior to October 24, 1633, the date of the inventory of his estate. [Mfr. Desc., I: 154]

The division of land in 1623 contains the names of the heads of families only, but the division of cattle May 22, 1627, contains the names of all persons in the colony at the time (except possibly some of the servants), grouped in families. Thus, in the Godbertson family, we find Godbert Godbertson, Sarah Godbertson, Samuel Godbertson, Mary Priest and Sarah Priest. The order in which the names of the sisters occur indicates that Mary was the older, for, in those cases where the relative ages of the children are known, the children are found arranged in order of birth, the males first.

Phineas died in Charlestown April 19, 1680, and a stone still marks the spot where he is buried in the Old Burying Ground. He was born about 1593, as is shown by his deposition already printed in this magazine. [II: 46]. His wife survived him, dying probably just prior to July 22, 1689, for on that date there is the following entry in the town orders:—

> Then Mr Jacob Green Senr & Mr Eleazr Phillips were & are Impowered to Apprize the goods of Widd. Pratt who lately deed at Tho Barbar. and to dispose of the same for the sattisfing her Debt to Tho. Barbars wife. & as their discretion shall direct them. And so to make returne thereof to the selectmen at their next meeting
>
> By ordr of the selectMen
>
> Jno Newell *

It is evident from this item that the provision in Phineas' will for the permanent use by his widow of a room in their

* Town Orders, IV: 93.

house had, probably by an agreement between the mother and son, either not been carried out or the arrangement had been terminated.

During his long residence in Charlestown Phineas appears only once in the land records as grantor and that is on January 21, 1662/3, when he and his wife Mary sold to John Smith a wood lot in Charlestown's further common.* On December 31, 1681, Mary Pratt, Phineas' widow, and her son Joseph sold to Solomon and Samuel Phip[p]s a cow common within the limits of the Charlestown stinted common on the south side of Mystic River.† On January 1, 1681/2, Joseph sold to John Simpson a certain piece of land in Charlestown and the deed was signed not only by Joseph but also by Mary Pratt, his mother, and Dorcas Pratt, his wife, as interested parties, although Joseph is the only grantor mentioned in the body of the deed.‡ On February 14, 1680/81, there was a division "of the Stinted Comon[s] in Charles Towne on this Side Mistick river," among the proprietors thereof and Mary and Joseph were jointly allotted one common containing an acre and a half.§

The two following items from the town orders show that the aid given Phineas was generously extended to his widow:—

1683/4, February 5. "Then orderd Twenty. Shill. vnto Widow Pratt & Twenty Shill to Wido Davie wch is for their releifes." [Town Orders, IV: 56]

1686/7, March 7. "Then Agreed y[t] M[r] Jn[o] Call Supply the Wido Pratt wth what she needs for her releife: Like wise to supply Tho Orton & Tho March wth Bread" [Town Orders, IV: 84]

Phineas' will‖ was made January 8, 1677/8, and probated June 15, 1680. An inventory‖ of his estate was made May 21, 1680, and presented in Court June 15, 1680. From it we learn that the widow had been appointed executrix. For some reason the 300 acres of land granted him by the General Court in 1662 and laid out in 1665 were not included in the inventory. Daniel Fletcher was appointed administrator of this portion of the estate December 28, 1722, and on May 6, 1723, Henry Farwell, Joseph Blanchard and Thomas Blanchard were ap-

* Middlesex Co. Deeds, X: 136. † Ibid., VIII: 499.

‡ Ibid., IX: 245. § Book of Possessions, 235, 236.

‖ Middlesex Co. Probate Files, First Series, No. 12,762.

pointed to appraise this property. They reported on November 25, 1723, that they valued it at £135. One of the most interesting and valuable papers connected with the settlement of the estate is that dated July 31, 1738, and endorsed "Phineas Pratts Children."* It is as follows: —

July 31. 1738.

The Return of the Commissrs appointed to apprize & Destribute the Real Estate of Phinehas Pratt late of Charlstown Dec'd — (Commission wanting) read — present, sundry of the Heirs.

memorandm — say To the Children severally (if Liveing) or to their Heirs (if Deceas'd)

John is Dead
& Peter Dead } Ergo — say only to their Heirs each to give Bond to refund, &c.

Each one his share to be allotted to him when he shall have given Bond to refund, &c,

Is pd 5 settlement & 6/ for 6 Bonds. pd by James Perry.

John Pratt Decd
Saml
Daniel
Peter Decd
Mary } Sureties { Saml. Pratt of Middlebury Wheelwright William Swan of Cambe. Husbandman Will: Thomas of Middleborough Gentleman James Perry of Charlestown Chairmaker.

Joseph
Aaron
Mercy } their shares bought by Danl: Fletcher

Recd. settlement, Recording, Bond &c 14. pd. by Will: Swan.

charges of settlement advanced

by Sam. Pratt	26—14—3
by Wm Thomas	10—03—0
by Wm Swan	3—14—0
by James Perry	11—15—6
	52—6—9

1/9th whereof is 5—16—3⅔.
Commission not returned.

The estate was settled in this year (1738). A remarkable feature is the unusual period, fifty-eight years, which intervened between Phineas' death and the final division.

The children of Phineas and Mary (Priest) Pratt were: —

1. John, married Ann (or Anna), daughter of John and Anna (Williams) Barker, in or before 1664. The information regarding Ann's parents was not secured until after the printing of the article on her husband, John Pratt, in the third volume of this magazine. 2. Samuel. 3. Daniel. 4. Peter. 5. Mary. 6. Joseph. 7. Aaron. 8. Mercy.

* Middlesex Co. Probate Files, First Series, No. 12,762.

WILL.*

I Phinias Pratt of Charlstown in the Countie of Midellsex Joyner being very aged and Crazye of body yett in my pfect memory and vnderstanding doe make This my last will and Teastamoen

Item I giue vnto my belouied wife Mary Pratt all my mouabl goods and fortie Shillings a year to be payed oute of my land in Charlstowne and the use of the gardon for term of hir life: this fortie Shillings is to be payed by my sonn Joseph Pratt for and in consideration of the hauing of my land and my wif is to haue a conuenient room of my sonn Joseph with a chimny in it to hir content to liue in for term of hir life. without molestation or trubl; but If my sonn Joseph doeth not perform this will that then my wif Mary Prat shall haue the one half of the land to hir Dispossing for hir best comfort: it is to be vnderstod that the one half wch the new hous standeth one is giuen to Joseph vpon the condistion of prouiding of a conuenient room for me and my wife for term of our liues and this other half for the paying of the fortie Shillings a year paying it quartterly that is to say ten shllig a quarter in mony and fier wood at mony price and If ther be any thing left at the death of my wife it shalbe equally deuided a mung all my children.

this eight of Jeneary 1677 Phinehas Pratt
Sealed and deliuerd in the
presents of Use
Walter Alen
the marke of
Rebeack Alen

15 : 4 : 80 : Sworn in Court pr Walter Allen
J : R : C :

INVENTORY.

Ann Innvytory of the Estat of Phinias Prat of Charlstown deceased

a psell of land	18	00	00
In primis in woolen clothes of his	01	10	00
It in linning shirts	00	09	00
It 8 pillober & 5 napkins	00	13	00
It 5 sheetts	01	04	00
It 4 blanckitts & 2 rugs	02	05	00
It a bed boulster & pillo	02	10	00
It a small bed	00	08	00
It 2 culbards 2 Chests one box	01	05	00
It peuter	02	02	00
It 2 bras Skillitts 5s a warmg pan 5s	00	10	00
It 2 Iorn potts on Skillit	00	09	00
It 2 Iorn keettells	01	06	00
It a tramil & fring pan	00	03	00
It a small tabell 2 chayers	00	05	00
It a pr of hose 2 bages	00	04	00
It earthen war 5 trenchers	00	02	06
It wooden ware	00	02	00
It a hachit a houldfast a froue	00	05	00

* See illustration facing page 129.

It lumber	00	16	00
It bookes	00	08	00
	16	16	06
	34	16	06

thes goods are prized by
Larenc Dowce & henery Balcom
the 21 : 3 : 1680
15 : 4 : 80 Sworn in Court by the executrix Mary Pratt
as attest, Tho : Danforth. R.
Added. 4. 12. 81. Cow comon in charlstown stinted comon. 06 00 00

EASTHAM AND ORLEANS, MASS., VITAL RECORDS.

(*Continued from page 34.*)

[p. 23] steven Merick and Mercy Bangs weare Maried the 28th of December in the yeare 1670

Steven Merick the sonn of Steven merick was borne the 26th day of March 1673

Richard Webber and Sarrah Strout were Married by mr Samll Treat march ye 4th 1707/8

Nathanll Mayo Jur and Ruth Doane were married by Mr Samll Treat July ye 13th 1710

Elisabeth Mayo the Daughter of Nathanael and Ruth Mayo was born at Eastham on the twenty ninth day of September Anno Domini 1712

Nathanael Mayo the son of Nathanael and Ruth Mayo was Born at Eastham on the twenty fourth day of august anno 1714

abigaile mayo the daughter of Nathanael and Ruth Mayo was Born at Eastham on ye twenty fourth day of September anno domini: 1716

Ruth mayo the daughter of Nathanael and Ruth Mayo was Born at Eastham on the Seventeenth Day of November anno domini: 1719

Abigail mayo the daughter of Nathanael and Ruth Mayo dyed March ye 8th 172½

Jeremiah Smith and Hannah atwood was maried the. 3d. of Jenuarie in the year : 1677

Mercy Smith the daughter of Jeremiah Smith was borne the: 17th. of feburarie : 1678

Abigaell Smith the daughter of Jeremiah Smith was borne the first day of June : 1681

Jeremiah Smith the sonne of Jeremiah Smith was borne the 18th of Agust 1685

Hannah Smith the daughter of Jeremiah and Hannah Smith was Borne at Eastham: about the middle of September in the year Sixteen hundred ninety and one:

Jeremiah Smith Senior dyed on the 29th day of April Anno Dom 1706

Hanah Smith Widdow of Jeremiah Smith Deceased dyed on the twenty ninth day of March Anno domini 1729

George luis the Son of Thomas and Jone lewis was Born at Eastham anno Dom 1691 on the sixth day of may

Nathanael lewis the son of Thomas and Jone lewis was Born at Eastham on the 31th day of march anno Dom: 1696

Rebecca Lewis the daughter of Thomas and Jone lewis was Born at Eastham on the 17th day of march anno Dom: 169$\frac{7}{8}$

Beniamin Lewis the son of Thomas and Jone lewis was at Eastham on the 8th day of october anno Domini 1700

Sarah Lewis the daughter of Thomas and Jone lewis was Born at Eastham on the 2nd day of June anno: dom: 1702

apphia Lewis the Daughter of Thomas and Jone lewis was Born at Eastham on the 9th day of may anno dom 1704

[p. 23a] Eldad attwood and anna Snow weare Maried the: 14th: of feburarie 1683

Marie attwood the daughter of Eldad attwood was borne the latter end of November in the yeare; 1684

John Atwood the Son of Eldad and Anne Atwood was born the tenth day of August 1686

Anne Atwood the Daughter of Eldad and Anne Atwood was Born in January 1687/8

Deborah atwood the Daughter of Eldad and Anne Atwood was born in March 1690

Sarah Atwood the Daughter of Eldad and Anne Atwood was Born in April 1792 *

Eldad Atwood the Son of Eldad and Anne Atwood was Born July the ninth 1695

Ebenezer Atwood the Son of Eldad and Anne Atwood was born in march 1697/8

Beniamen Atwood the Son of Eldad and Anne Atwood was born in June 1701

Ralph Smith the Son of Thomas and Mary Smith was Born at Eastham the twenty third day of october annodom 1682

Rebecca Smith the Daughter of Thomas and mary Smith was Born at Eastham the last day of march Anno dom 1685

Thomas Smith the Son of Thomas Smith was Born at Eastham the twenty ninth day of Januarie anno dom 1687/8

David Smith the Son of Thomas and mary Smith was Born at Eastham the latter end of march Anno dom 1691

* This is evidently an error for "1692."

Jonathan Smith the Son of Thomas and mary Smith was Born at Eastham the fifth day of July Anno dom 1693

Isaac Smith the son of Thomas and mary Smith was Born at Eastham the 3^d^ day of June 1695

Jesse Smith the Son of Thomas and mary Smith was Born at Eastham the 31st day of January Anno dom 1703/4

Isaac Smith the Son of Thomas and mary Smith dyed the 26th day of april Anno : 1704

Mary Smith Widdow and relict of Thomas Smith Dyed on the 22nd day of March anno domini 1726/7

John Higgins and Hannah Mayo were married by Mr Samuell Treat on the fifth day of august anno Domini : 1713

John Taylor and abigaile Hopkins were married by Mr Samuel Treat on the third day of September anno Domini : 1713 *

Abiah Harding and Rebecca young were married by Mr Samuell Treat on the twenty fourth day of September anno Domini 1713

[p. 24] John Knowles and Apphiah Bangs weare Maried the 28th of December in the yeare 1670

Eadward knowles the sonn of John knowles was borne the 7th day of November in the yeare 1671

John knowles the sonn of John knowles was borne the 10th day of July in the yeare 1673

John knowles a daughter named Rebecah borne the second day of March in the yeare 1674 ales 75

William Twining Junior and Ruth Cole wear Maried the 21th of March : 16 88/89

William Twining Junior a daughter borne Named Elizabeth agust: 25th 1690

Thankfull Twining the daughter of William and Ruth Twining was Borne the eleventh : day : of January in the year : 1696 : 7

Ruth : Twining the daugter of William and Ruth Twining was Borne at Eastham : the Seaven and twentieth day of august in the year 1699

Hannah the daughter of William and Ruth Twining was born the 2^d^ day of April 1702

William Twining the Son of William and Ruth Twining was Born at Eastham the Secund day of September in the year 1704

Barnabas Twining the Son of William and Ruth Twining was Born at Eastham the twenty ninth day of September in the year of our Lord 1705

Mercy Twining the Daughter of William and Ruth Twining was born at Eastham the 20th day of febuary anno 1707/8

(*To be continued.*)

* This entry has been crossed out.

MAJOR WILLIAM BRADFORD'S WILL AND INVENTORY.

Transcribed from the Original Records,

BY GEORGE ERNEST BOWMAN.

MAJOR WILLIAM[2] BRADFORD (*Gov. William*[1]) died at Plymouth on Saturday, 20 February /2 March, 1703/4. His will and inventory are found in the Plymouth County Probate Records, Volume II, pages 40–43.

[p. 40] The Last Will & Testament of William Bradford living in the Township of Plimouth in the Province of the Massachusets Bay in New England

I the s^d^ William Bradford being Exercised with many bodily Infirmitys which gives me cause to think the time of my dissolution to be near being of a disposeing mind & memory do make ordaine & constitute this my last will & Testament as followeth.

Imp^r^: I Commit my soul to God my Creator & my body to the dust of the Earth to be decently buried in hopes of a glorious resurection through the meritts of my dear Redeemer the Lord Jesus Christ. As to what outward Estate it hath Pleased God to bless me with I dispose of the same as followeth my debts being all first faithfully fully & truly satisfied and paid.

Imp^r^: my Will is that my Loving wife Mary Bradford have her thirds in my Lands & meadows where I now dwell in the Township of Plimouth as also in all my lands or meadow which I have Elce where not by me heretofore disposed of dureing her naturall life & that she have with David Bradford my son the house in which I live with the barn & orchard by it during her life & after her decease that my s^d^ son David Bradford shall have my s^d^ house barn & orchard to him & his heirs for ever saveing that my Will is that my sons Ephraim Bradford & Hezekiah Bradford shall have so much Interest in my s^d^ house as to have liberty to dwell therein till they can provide for themselves otherwise.

ffurther my Will is that my wife before mentioned shall have a third part of all my goods & Chattells for her own forever togather with a bed & sutable furniture to it

Item to my Eldest son John Bradford I have made over tracts of Lands and meadows as p^r deed under my hand & seal appeareth whereon he now liveth further I give & bequeath to him my fathers manuscript viz: a Narrative of the begining of New Plimouth Pareus upon the Revelations and Barriffs Military discipline.

Item To my Grandson William Bradford the son of my son William Bradford deceased I have given tracts of Land & meadow as Appear under my hand & seal further I give to him when he shall come of age one of Mr Perkins his workes.

Item To my son Thomas Bradford I have given a portion in Lands in Norwich (which were the Lands of my brother John Bradford) as p^r: deed under my hand & seal may Appear.

Item To my son Samuel Bradford I have given tracts of Land under my hand & seal as may appear;

Item to my son Joseph Bradford a portion of Lands near Norwich aforesaid (which was his Mothers & part I Purchased) as may appear under hand & seal also I give to him the history of the Netherlands, & a Rapier.

Item I give & bequeath unto my four sons John Bradford Thomas Bradford Samuel Bradford & Joseph Bradford all that my Pattent Right which I have to the head of Cape Cod.

Item I give & bequeath to my son Samuel Bradford my right of Commonage or Common Right which I have in the Township of Duxborrough.

Item It is my Will that my sons Israel Bradford Ephraim Bradford David Bradford & Hezekiah Bradford shall have all that my farm or tenement whereon I now dwell togather with all the fences orchads trees and fruittrees [p. 41] ffruittrees (Except what is above Excepted) standing or growing thereon wth all other Lands meadows swamps or right of lands that I now have within the Township of Plimouth lying on the Northerly side of the brooke Commonly called stony brooke with all & singuler the previledges thereof which s^d lands meadows farme or tenement aboves^d I do by these presents give bequeath & demise to my s^d four sons, (that is to say Each of them an Equal part or proportion) to them & their heirs for ever not to be sold given or made away either the whole or any part thereof Except to Each other or some bearing the name of the Bradfords decended from me this I give & bequeath to them hoping they will show themselves very

Carfull of dutifull & Respectfull to my Loving wife their mother dureing her life.

Item It is my will that whereas my son Israel Bradford hath been at charge in building an house upon part of the afores^{d} farm or tenement that he the s^{d} Israel shall have & Enjoy the s^{d} house for his own togather with an acre of land thereunto Adjoining to him & his heirs forever.

Item I will & bequeath to my s^{d} son Israel Bradford my belt & Rapier.

Item I Give to my son Ephraim Bradford one of my musquetts & a table with drawrs.

Item I Give to my son David Bradford my silver Bowl after his mothers decease not to be Alienated from the family of the Bradfords.

Item I Give to my son Hezekiah Bradford my gold ring & a silver spoone.

Item I Give to my Grandson John Bradford, Dr Willets works on Gensis & Exodus.

Item I Give to my Grandson William Bradford the son of John Bradford my silver wine Cup when he Comes of age.

Item I give to my daughter Mercy Steel Hannah Riply Melatiah Steel Mary Hunt to Each of them beside what portion I have already given ten shillings a peice to be paid within a year next after my decease

Item I Give & bequeath to my daughter Alce Fitch a wrought Cushion that was her Mothers.

Item I Give unto my daughter Sarah Baker two of my biggest pewter platters & also a China bason. Also a Cow to be delivered to her within a year after my decease.

Item I Give unto my son Samuel Bradford all my Lattin bookes, to Encourage him in bringing up one of his sons to Learning which said bookes it is my Will that they shall by him be given to his s^{d} son whom he shall so bring up.

Item I Give to Every one of Daughters a good booke which they may chose out of my Liberary.

Item I give to hannah the wife of my son Samuel Bradford m^{r} Borroughs upon the Eleventh of Mathew.

Item It is my will that the rest of my bookes be safely keept by my Executors & In Case my son Samuel shall bring up one of his sons to Learning to be by s^{d} Executors delivered to him when he Comes of age.

I do Constitute & Appoint my Loving sons John Bradford Samuel Bradford & Israel Bradford as Executors of this my last Will & Testament to pay such debts as I owe, to Receive my dues and to see my body decently buried, to defray the charge thereof, And to see my will (as near as they can) in all the perticulers of it performed, thus hopeing that they will faithfully perform such a trust Committed unto them I do Revoke & make void any former will by me at any time heretofore made. I the s^{d} [p. 42] I the said William Bradford have hereunto set my hand & seal this twenty ninth day of June one thousand seven hundred & three 1703

Signed Sealed & Declared to be his Last Will and Testament In presents of us
John Rogers
Thomas Loring
Ephraim Little Ju^{r}:

William Bradford (Seal)

Memorand: That on the 10th day of March Annoq: Dom: 1703 the above named Ephraim Little & Thomas Loring two of the witnesses to this Instrum^{t}: made oath that they were present with Major W^{m}: Bradford late deceased & saw him signe & seal & heard him declare this Instrument to be his last will & Testament & that he was then of a disposing mind & memory to the best of their Judgments And on the 29th day of the same month of march the above named John Rogers the other Witness above named made oath to the same before me.

Nathaniel Thomas Judge of Probates

Pli: ss: Nathaniel Thomas Esq: Appointed & Comisionated Judge of the Probate of Wills & Granting letters of administration &c: to all unto whome these presents shall Come Greeting Know yea that on the twenty ninth day of March in the year of our Lord one thousand seven hundred & four Before me at Plimouth in the County of Plimouth the Will of Major William Bradford late of Plimouth afores^{d} deceased to these presents annexed was proved approved & allowed who haveing whilst he lived & at the time of his death Goods Chattels Rights or Creditts in the County afores^{d}, And the Probate of the s^{d} will & power of Comitting administration of all & singuler the Goods Chattels Rights & Creditts of the s^{d} deceased & also the hearing Examining & allowing the accompts of the same by virtue thereof Appertaining unto me The administration of all the goods Chattels Rights & Creditts of the s^{d} deceased & his will in any manner Concerning is hereby Comitted unto John Bradford Samuel Bradford & Israel Bradford sons of the

s^d Deceased & Joynt Executors in the same Will named well & faithfully to Execute the s^d will and to administer the Estate of the s^d deceased according thereunto & to make a true & perfect Inventory of all & singuler the goods Chattels Rights & Creditts of the said deceased & to Exhibett the same into the Registry of the Court of Probate for the County afores^d at or before the twenty third day of June next Ensueing, & also to Render a plain & true accompt of their s^d administration upon oath, In testimony whereof I have hereunto set my hand & the Seal of the said Court of Probate, Dated at Plimouth afores^d the day & year first above written.
Nathaniel Thomas Register Nathaniel Thomas

Plimouth february 28 1703 The Inventory of the Estate of Major William Bradford deceased taken & apprized by us the Subscribers.

To Wearing apparrill to Cash to a Ring to arms	06 00 00
to Cattell	18 14 00
to Chares & Cushings	00 13 00
to a Chest & Cubbert & trunk	00 09 00
to mantel	00 08 00
to a Carpitt	00 03 00
to Plate	07 10 00
to pewter	01 12 00
[P. 43] To Earthen ware	00 02 06
to Iron ware	01 04 00
to table Linnen	02 00 00
to a bell	00 03 06
to a spining wheel	00 05 00
to a desk & two trunks	00 08 00
to other old Lumber	00 09 00
to bookes	15 03 00
to beds & furniture	14 08 00
to brass & bellmettle	01 08 00
	70 00 00

Thomas Loring
Elisha Wadsworth

Memorandum that on the 10th day of March 170$\frac{3}{4}$ before Nath[ll]: Thomas Esq: Judge of the Probates &c: Major John Bradford & Samuel Bradford Executors to the last will & testament of their father Major William Bradford Deceased made oath that the above written is a true Inventory of the Estate of the s^d deceased so far as they know & when they know of more that they will discover the same.

Nathaniel Thomas Register

THE DIARY OF JABEZ FITCH, JR.

(*Continued from Vol. III, p. 245.*)

SATERDAY July 2nd 1757 there was a New Piq^{t} Mounted Consisting of 192 Privats Properly officerd &c: this Day Serj^{t} Jackson & John Ashpo Came in who we Thought Had Ben Lost after Putmons Fight.

Sunday ye 3rd after I Had Made My Morning Report I went into ye Fort and Rec^{d} of Mr Ginnes 18^{s} : 6^{d} York Money for ye Days work y^{t} I Did ye 5th of June with a Party at Droy Droying Timber into ye Fort In ye Afternoon it Raind Vary Stedy Toard Night our Party Returnd from ye Lake & Brought 4 French Men that Deserted from Crown Point they Bring in News that it is Vary Short Times for Provisions there — this Night I was wornd for ye Covring Party ye Next Day.

ye 4th In ye Morning I went to work with a Party of 49 Men in ye Trench &c we were Directed By Lieu^{t} Fash of ye Royal Amaricans About 8 oClok Gen^{ll} Lyman Came in from His Scout they Brought in News that they Found Henry Shuntup in ye woods Kild & Scalpt His throat Cut & His Brest Cut open & Hart out & Gon a Larg Pies of wood Left in ye Plais of it John Kennady & Jabez Jones they Didn^{t} find But By what Signs they found they thought that they Had Carryed them off &c at Noon I Got Two Dollars Changd & Paid em Most of them away. at Night Mr Gordon Paid Me £3 : 4^{s} : For My Self 2 Corp^{ls} & 81 Men then I Paid them all off & Had S3 : 6^{d} Left for My Self &c. then Corp^{l} Thos Andrus & I went over to Mr Bests & Drinkd Some Jenava then I Came Home & Found y^{t} Most of our Company Had Listed for Ranging &c. In y^{e} Evening I was at Serj^{t} Wetss Tent where we Had Singing Hyms a Man Praid there &c

y^{e} 5th was a Stady Rainy Day we Toock an allowance Party in Fresh Provision — this Day I Sold My Indion Stockens to Joseph Kellog for 4^{s} —

y^{e} 6th In y^{e} Morning I Bought 1$\frac{1}{2}$^{lb} of Suger S1 : 6 &c. then I went to y^{e} Capt : Tent & Mad My Morning Report of y^{e} Company Carried it to y^{e} Adjutant He told Me that all those Men that Never Joind Us were Returnd Deserters this Day &c — Toard Night Mr Pummery our Setler Came Up with His Stores — I Rec^{d} A Letter from My Father Dated June 21st

another from Brother Elisha Dated ye Same Day & another from Brother Rudd Dated June 23rd

ye 7 In ye Morning I was Orderd to Wait on ye Gen^ll^ again So I Toock My Post & Had a Laisy time on it at Noon I Got a Good Dinner &c. this Day Capt : Jefferys Scouters Movd and Picht their tents By them Selves — at Night I Had Considrable Discorce with a Serj^t^ of ye Royal Amaricans who was orderly for Gen^ll^ Webb

ye 8th In ye Morning I was Relievd as Usual — Then after Breakfast I Tock a Walk over on ye Green and Wrote Some of ye forgoing Lines &c — Toard Night Mr Lothrop Came Up Here &c In ye Evening I Spent Some Time with Serj^t^ Coit — Serj^t^ Foster & Diccason were Confind By ye Regulars for Deserting their Servis Some Years Past

July ye 9th ye Annual of Bradducks Defeat &c — John Johnson of Capt Gallops Company Died & was Buried — A Number of Teems Came Up Here from Saratoge &c — Mr Pummery Got Somthing Setled at Night John Chappel was Confind By ye Gen^lls^ Orders for Geting Liquer for ye Regulars &c. Daniel Boge is Under Confinement again

Sunday July ye 10th In ye Morning I went to ye Guard Hous to Se Chappel Serj^t^ Giles was there to Visit. Boge &c : this Morning I Found out James Stephens of Canaan one of ye Carters — Chappel was taken Exceeding Poor this Day So that Doc^r^ Lord Prevaild with ye Gen^ll^ & Got Liberty for Him to Go Home to His Tent — the Stockbridg Indions Brought in a Prisoner who they Tock Near Crown Point &c — I Got Some Suger at Pummerys for Mix

ye 11th In ye Morning I Wrote a Letter to Brother Elisha — Then I Fixd to Go to ye Lake to Escort ye Kings Stores about 10 oClok we Set out I went on a Flank Guard Most of ye way to ye Half way Brook Eat Some Huccle Berrys &c at ye Brook we Refreshd our Selvs & Marchd again Near ye Round Pond we Met a Larg Scout Going over to South Bay &c A Little after Sunset we Got Up to ye Lake & Lodged In ye old Encampment this Night ye Misceters & Nats were Vary Troublesom to us — On this Command I Got Acquainted with Two of ye Boston Serj^ts^ Viz : Spaldin & Walker — This is ye First time that I Se Lake Georg this Year or Since ye 17th of Nov : last

ye 12th In ye Morning I was of in ye wood with a Party to Loock for Some Oxen we were Gon about an Hour & Found ye Oxen — About 7 oClok we Marcht Had Got about a Mile & there Came a Vary Hard Shower of Thunder & Rain which

Lasted while we Traveld three Mile then Cleard of Extreem warm we Stopd at ye Half way Brook & Refreshd as Usual there Came Down with Us one of ye Jersy Reg^t who was Going after His wife that Had Deserted from Him His Discors was Cheefly about Her on ye March &c — We Had another Shower about ye Folls then we Marchd In about 4 oClok Our Party was Commanded By Capt Waldo — After I Got in I Hered that Dan^ll Boge was Whipd 50 Lashes again — at Night Sold Pride a Knife Old Ashley was Whipd 15 Lashes

ye 13th Some Time in ye Morning we Movd our Tents Again which Tock Us Most of ye Day to Get Settled again — In ye Afternoon I went to Serj^t Comstocks Tent & Drinkd Some Grog with Him & then Discorced with Him about Home & old affairs

(*To be continued.*)

EXPERIENCE MITCHELL'S WILL AND INVENTORY.

Transcribed from the Original Records,

BY GEORGE ERNEST BOWMAN.

EXPERIENCE MITCHELL's inventory was taken 14 May, 1689, and his will was proved 4 September, 1689, therefore the date of the will, 5 December, 1689, as recorded by the clerk, Samuel Sprague, is doubtless an error. The will must have been made on 5 December in the year 1688, or possibly even earlier. The will and inventory are recorded in the Plymouth County Probate Records, Volume I, pages 44 and 45.

The wife Mary mentioned in the will was a second wife, the first one having been Jane[2] Cooke (*Francis*[1]).

[p. 44] These are to publish and declare to all whome it may Concerne that I Experience Mitchell now living in the Town of Bridgwater in the Colony of New Plimouth being through the Mercy of God of Sound judgment and memory do ordaine and make my last will and Testament in maner following vizt Into the hands of God I Comend my spirit believingly. Resigning up my soul into the everlasting Armes of Gods mercy father Son and Holy Spirit: My Body to be decently Interred at the discression of my Executor and other Christian ffriends and for my outward estate I doe will that after all my just debts and funerall expences be paid my lands and other moveables be disposed of as followeth

Imprimis I Give to my Son Edward Mitchell after my decease all my Lands both upland and meadow lying in the Town of duxbury at the place where I formerly dwelt as appeareth by deed And if it shall please God So to order that my wife Mary Mitchell Shall Survive me I Require my son Edward to take Care of her for her Comfortable Subsistance during her life provided that she will live with him at Bridgwater, but if she Rather Incline to live at duxbury I then order that half the Rent of that land at dubury shall be to my wife during her life And after my decease my Son Edward shall have the sole dispose of it as to the letting of it out for the house I acknowledge it to be his; Also the Bed and boulster two pillows one pair of sheets and two Blankets which are at my Son Edward's and we make use of I Give them to him after our decease as for my Son John I have formerly Given him his portion of land, and my will is that he Rest Sattisfied therewith, which was fourscore acres of upland and four acres of meadow lying at Namatakeesit within the Township of duxbury, this is the full of what I Intend him as to lands onely there are Severall moveables in his hand at present which are mine of which one Cowe a short gun a small Iron kettle I Give unto my Grandson Experience And the Remainder I Give unto my Son John as for my land Lying in the Town of Middlebury I Give it to my daughters Mary Shaw Sarah Haward and Hannah Haward and to my Grandson Experience Mitchell the son of my son John to be Equally divided between them. farther I Give to my daughter Mary Shaw twenty shillings to hannah Haward forty shillings in Currant pay and if my Stock Stand I Give to my Grandson Thomas Mitchell one Cowe and to my Grand daughter Mary Mitchell one Cow, I leave the dispose of my Grand daughter Mary Mitchel with my Son Edward and Joseph Bartlett as for the Rest of my moveables and Chattels I bequeath them to my son Edward Mitchell whome I appoint and ordaine sole Executor of this my last will and Testament Revoaking all other wills and Testaments whatsoever Witness my hand and Seal this fifth of december 1689:

Signed and Sealed in the Presence of Thomas Hayward
John Haward

Experience Michell & a (seal)

Leiu[t] Thomas Hayward and Ensigne John Haward the within named witnesses appeared before the Magistrates of the

County of Plimouth at Plimouth September the 4th 1689 and made oath that they were present and Saw Experience Mitchell deceased above named Signe Seal & declare this Instrument as his last will & testament & that to the best of their understandings he was of disposing mind & memory when he so did:

Attest Sam'l Sprague Cler

[p. 45] A; Inventory of the estate of Experience Mitchel of Bridgwater, taken by Ensigne John Haward and Thomas Hayward the 14 of May 1689

	ll	s	d
Imprimis In Books	00	14	00
In Iron vessels	01	16	00
It; vessels of wood and earth	00	04	00
It, in pewter	01	00	00
It, one Rundlett 2 Glass Bottles	00	03	00
It, 2 Chests one Box with Severall tooles	02	00	00
It, in Bedding boulsters pillows and Covering	06	08	00
It, in sheetes and other linnen	02	10	00
It in 2 Cows and one mare	04	10	00
It, in my Brother Johns hand one Cow one short gun & a small Iron kettle	02	12	00
	£ 21	17 *	

Edward Mitchel made oath before the magistrates of the County of Plimouth September ye 4th 1689 that the above written is a true Inventory: of the Estate vizt Goods and Chattels of the above named Experience Mitchell deceased as far as he Knows and if more shall be discovered that he will Bring it to this Inventory:

Attest Sam'l, Sprague Clerk;

THE DEPOSITION OF RICHARD CHURCH.

The Deposition of Richard Church aged about 56 yeares this Deponant saith that hee being att worke about the mill the 19th of august hearing of a Cry that the man was killed; hasted p'sently and healped to remove the earth from Thomas ffish whoe being much bruised therby was gott to bedd and in four Dayes and an halfe Dyed; and further saith not;

This deposition of Richard Church, the husband of Elizabeth[2] Warren (*Richard*[1]), was made at Sandwich on 25 August, 1664, and is recorded in the Plymouth Colony Court Orders, Volume IV, page 92.

* The summing is in a different hand.

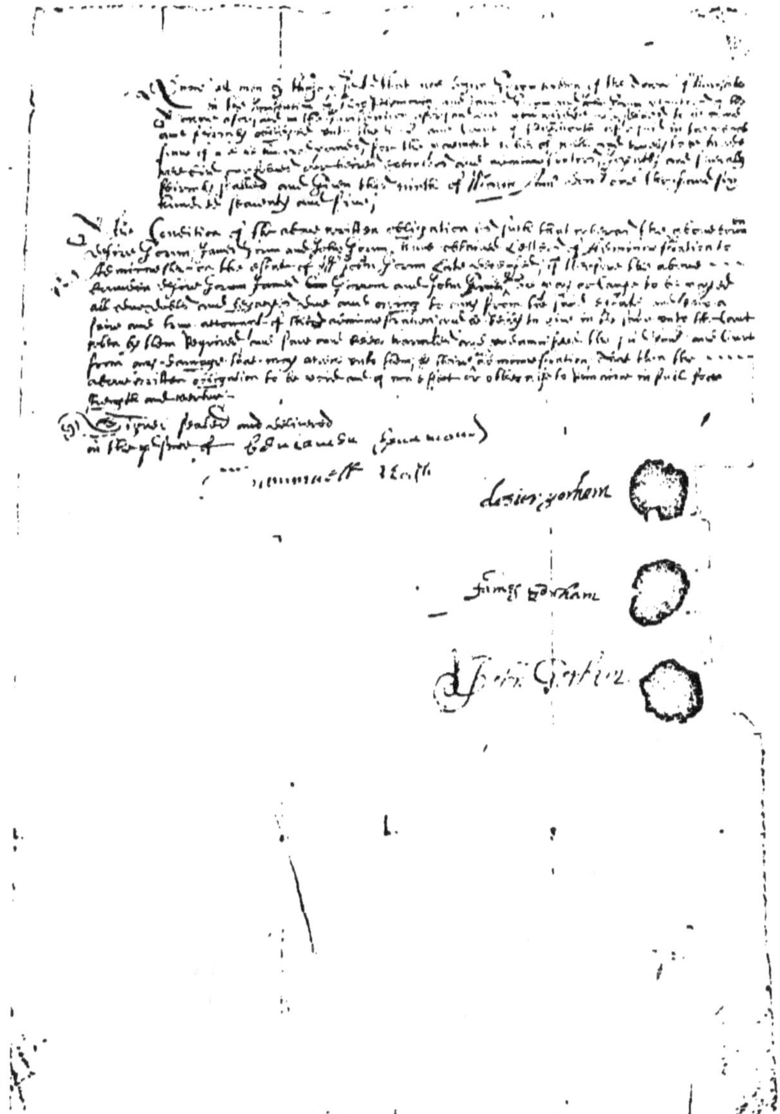

BOND OF DESIRE (HOWLAND) GORHAM

CAPTAIN JOHN GORHAM'S ESTATE.

Transcribed from the Original Records,

BY GEORGE ERNEST BOWMAN.

CAPT. JOHN GORHAM died at Swansea, but the exact date of his death is not known. The date of his burial is entered on the Swansea town records as follows: "Cap: John Goram was buryed the 5th day of february 1675" * This date in new style would be 15 February, 1676. The record of his inventory shows that he was a resident of Yarmouth at the time of his death. His widow Desire, the eldest daughter of John Howland, must have removed to Barnstable immediately, as in the bond of the administrators, dated 9 March, 1675/6, she is called "of Barnstable." On the seventh of March she and her sons James and John had been appointed administrators and their bond is the only original paper connected with the settlement of Capt. Gorham's estate of which I have learned. It is preserved in the "Scrap Book" at the Registry of Deeds at Plymouth, and the half-tone reproduction shows that it is in excellent condition. It bears the autograph signatures of Desire (Howland) Gorham and her sons James and John.

[Court Orders, V: 131]
March the 7th 1675

In reference unto the estate of Mr Gorum Deceased The Court have appointed Mr hinckley Mr Chipman and Mr huckens to take Care that such prte of the said estate which belongeth unto his youngest Children be prserved and Disposed to them as they Come to be of age; according to the agreement;

Lres of Adminnestration were Graunted by the Court unto mistris Desire Gorum, James Gorum, and John Gorum, to adminnester on the estate of Captaine John Gorum Deceased

---

BOND OF THE ADMINISTRATORS.

Know all men by these prsents that wee Desire Gorom widdow of the Towne of Barnstable in the Jurisdiction of New

* Book A, p. 147.

Plymouth; and James Gorum and John Gorum planters of the Towne aforsaid in the Jurisdiction aforsaid Doe acknowlidge our selves to be bound and feirmly oblidged unto the Govr: and Court of Plymouth aforsaid in the penall sume of a eight hundred pounds, for the payment wherof well and truely to be made wee bind our selves our heires executors and adminnestrators; Joyntly and severally feirmly sealled and Given this ninth of March Anno: Dom one thousand six hundred seaventy and five;

The Condition of the above written obligation is such that wheras the above bounen Desire Gorum; James Gorum and John Gorum; have obtained Letters of Adminnestration to Adminnester on the estate of Mr John Gorum Late Deceased; if therfore the above bounden Desire Gorum James Gorum and John Gorum Junir Doe pay or Cause to be payed all Due Debts and legacyes Due and owing to any from the said estate; and keep a faire and true accoumpt of their adminnestration; and be reddy to give in the same unto the Court when by them required; and save and keep harmles and undamnifyed the said Govr: and Court from any Damage that may acrew unto them; by theire said adminnestration; That then the above written obligation to be void and of non effect or otherwise to remaine in full force strength and vertue;

Signed sealed and Delivered	desier gorham (Seal)
in the prsence of	James Gorham (Seal)
beniamen hammond	John Gorham (Seal)
Sammuell Nash	

[Plym. Col. Wills, III : I : 162–164]
[p. 162] An Inventory of the estate of Capt: John Gorum of yarmouth late Deceased taken and apprised by Willam Crocker Barnabas Laythorpe John Thacher and John Miller the 29th of ffebruary 1675 and exhibited to the Court held att Plymouth the 7th of March 1675 on the oathes of mistris Desire Gorum widdow and James Gorum and John Gorum Junir: as followeth

Impr. 1 bed and the furniture belonging to it	07	01	00
Item 1 bed and what belonges to it	03	15	00
Item old beding	01	01	00
Item 1 bed and what belonges to it	03	19	00
Item his wearing Clothes	007	07	00
Item 1 blankett with feathers in it	00	15	00
Item 2 Chistes	00	08	00
Item 5 Cushens	00	05	00
Item to yerne ffiax and Cotton woole	05	11	00

Item to Iron tooles and Cart rope	01	00	00
Item 3 wheeles and Cardes	01	02	00
Item 13 bushells and halfe of Corne	02	00	06
Item 1 bushell of wheat	000	05	00
Item an other p^r^sell of Iron tooles in and about the mill	03	00	00
Item meate salt and the Caske the meat is in	04	00	00
Item brasse	02	10	00
Item pewter	02	00	00
Item 2 paire of stilliyards scales and waights	01	10	00
Item 4 Chaires	00	15	00
Item Iron potts kettles pothangers frying pans all Iron	02	00	00
Item 9 sheets	02	10	00
Item table Cloth and Napkins of Diaper	00	15	00
Item a smale Table Cloth and 2 Dosen of Napkins	01	16	00
Item 6 pillowbeers	00	17	00
Item linnine of his	00	15	00
Item powder and bulletts	00	05	00
Item 2 paire of sterrup Irons & Gertts	00	05	00
Item twine and paper	00	03	00
Item 2 Chestes and one box	00	18	00
Item wooden ware and seives	00	17	00
Item old barrells	00	07	00
Item in earthen ware and other smale lumber	01	05	00
Item 2 pound of fine Cotten yerne	00	04	00
Item a feirkin of sope	00	15	00
Item a brake and fflax	00	14	00
Item bolts boards square timber and Grindstone	06	06	00
sume	68	11	06
Item 3 horses 1 mare	04	05	00
Item 10 swine	03	15	00
Item 4 oxen	12	00	00
Item 8 Cowes	18	00	00
Item 2 steers 2 yeers old	03	00	00
Item 3 heiffers 3 yeer old	06	00	00
Item 5 yeerlings	02	10	00
Item 1 bull 1 heiffer three yeer old	06	00	00
Item 18 sheep	06	00	00
Item the mills and Dwelling house land and Meddow adjoyning	150	00	00
[p. 163] Item 1 Caske of Tallow	00	05	00
Item the ballences of accoumpt in the booke Due	46	08	01
Item the Tan fatts the barke mill and the 2 houses the tooles belonging to the taning	30	00	00
Item 1 Copper	02	10	00
Item 2 Gunes	03	06	00
Item the barrell of a blunderbusse	00	05	00
Item more Iron tooles	01	03	06
Item andjrons	01	00	00
Item 2 horspistoles & holsters	01	00	00

Item old Iron	00	10	00
Item more Iron tooles	01	09	00
Item 1 brasse kittle	00	16	00
Item 4 Chaires	00	18	00
Item 1 longe Table and bedsted & Curtaines	03	00	00
Item 1 bedsted	01	00	00
Item an Iron pott kettle skillett pothookes	01	07	00
Item 1 Chest	00	08	00
Item 1 paire of tonggs & pothangers	00	06	00
Item 1 Cubberd	01	00	00
Item 13 sydes of lether	06	10	00
Item 1 bedsted	00	15	00
Item a bed bolster Coverlidd & blanketts	06	05	00
Item a bed bolster rugg and blanketts	04	10	00
Item 1 settle 1 old Chaire	00	07	00
Item 1 (*) att	10	00	00
Item 1 Gould ringe	01	00	00
Item 1 Cubbert Cushen	00	15	00
Item 1 Cabbanitt	00	15	00
	337	18	07
Item a prsell of linnine	02	05	00
Item 1 Chest and a Childs blankett	00	08	00
Item 5 sheets	02	00	00
Item 1 Chest and box	00	14	00
Item old lumber	00	05	00
Item Due from John Gorum Juni[r] for hydes hee received of his father and on his accoumpt att 3[d] pr pound	52	18	06
Item a Cart takeling and plow tacklinge & old Grindstone	03	00	00
Item a hatchell	00	10	00
Item a horse in John Gorums hands	01	10	00
Item 1 smale Table	00	03	00
Item 1 Negro man			
Item more Due on the booke	01	06	09
Item Due by bill in Cash	16	00	00
Item in Cash	84	00	00
Item in plate and a watch	10	00	00
Item 2 Cards of Cloake buttons	00	05	00
Item the farme that is to say the Dwelling house barne upland and meddow and all the land in the Comon feild	450	00	00
Item Due from the Country for service Done in the warr by Capt : Gorum about			
Item a Graunt of a p[r]sell of Land att Papasquash necke			
The sume Totall : is	710	04	03

By us Willam Crocker
Barnabas Laythorpe

John Thacher
John Miller

* This item was not filled in.

[p. 164] In Reference to the settleing of the estate of Captaine John Gorume Deceased between the Mother and the Children ; The Court haveing taken into Consideration and haveing respect p^r^tely to what hath bine the Declared minde of the said Captaine Gorum in his life time and p^r^tely to the mutuall Consent of the sonnes whoe are of age as well as to what of equitie Doth, otherwise, to this Court appeer Doe order as followeth : viz :

Imp^r^ : That Desire the Relict of the said Capt : Gorum have the proffitts of one third of all the Lands housing and mill Dureing her Naturall life ; and after all Just Debts being first payed out of the moveables ; shee to have one third p^r^te of the rest of the moveables, to her owne Dispose ; and libertie to Dwell in her Now Dwelling house ; and have Improvement of the Negro Dureing her life ;

2 That James Gorum have the Dwelling house that hee now lives in, with the barne and halfe the upland belonging to the said farme

And John Gorum to have the tan vaults barke mill ; and the utinsills therunto belonging and soe much stocke as may make the said tanvaults to amount to the vallue of fifty pounds and alsoe to have the other halfe of the upland belonging to the said farme begining next to the lands of Andrew hallott, onely Deducting forty acrees out of that his halfe ; To be allowed to Joseph Gorum ; who is to have his forty acrees lye next Joseph hallotts on the upersyde of the high way, and a p^r^sell of meddow about three or four acrees ; bounded between a Creeke Comonly Called wells his Creeke and a smale Creeke Called Bacons brooke ; which with the thirty pounds hee hath alreddy received of his father, is vallued, att threescore pounds ; and to be for his p^r^te of the said estate att p^r^sent ;

And James Gorum to have the meddow lying between the said Wells his Creeke ; and the place where formerly the mill stood ; and with the house above said a longe table bedsted and two Chaires belonging therunto ; and the rest of the Marsh or meddow to be equally Devided between the said James and John Gorum ; as theire respective p^r^tes of the said estate onely that p^r^sell of land lying att stony Cove is p^r^ticularly to be equally Devided between them and it is agreed that John Gorum is to have the use of one halfe of the land that lyeth between the said Dwelling house and the tanyard, During all the time hee shall keep taning in that place, and noe longer, and if that prte of the land within the ffence falling to James his p^r^te shalbe Indifferently vallued worth more then soe much of the lands without, it shalbe made up by allowing soe much of the Greater p^rte of the lands to John without as may Countervaile the same;

3 That all the rest of the estate shalbe equally Devided between the rest of the Children viz: To Jabez Mercye Lydia hannah & Shubaall Gorum, in five equall p^rtes, excepting fifty pound in Mony first Taken out of the said estate to bringe up Shubaall to scoole, as his mother shall see fitt over and above his fift equall p^rte as aforsaid, provided that incase the p^rtes of the said five Children last Named shall amount to more then forty pounds apeece;. which the three 3 Daughters alreddy Marryed have alreddy received or are to have made up to any of them; then such overplusse of the estate to be equally Devided between those eight Children, and provided alsoe that incase any other lands belonging to the estate of Capt: Gorum by graunt from the Court or otherwise shalbe posessed, such lands shalbe equally Devided between the the sonnes that have noe lands yett assigned them, soe as incase theire respective Devissions therof together with what other portions they have received amount to more then what the other sonnes have received; then such overplusse shalbe equally Devided amongst all the sonnes to make each of theire p^rtes equall; onely the eldest son James to have a Double portion of the said overplusse of lands;

It is alsoe ordered that Care be taken in the Devision of the estate that each respectively Concerned therin shall have the sure estate Devided equally to them, and each to have his or her p^rte in the Desparate:

this following relates unto the Inventory of Capt: Gorums estate before entered;

John Gorum seni^r Disbursed for the souldery under his Comand as followeth

ffor food att Sandwich	00 07 06
ffor Syder att Captaine huchensons farme	00 08 06
my selfe with horse and furniture sixteen weekes	
a horse for my son Joseph a fortnight	
Expended upon the souldiers att severall times	01 14 00
Disbursed for three souldiers suppers att James Coles	00 01 06
John Whetston fifteen Dayes horse bridle and saddle	
Thinges omitted to be Charged in the Inventory	
Item a paire of bootes a paire of shooes 2 sackes 1 sheete 2 pitchforkes	00 18 00
for Clothes left att m^r Brownes	
Debtes omited to be substracted out of the estate of Elisha hedge	03 03 00
Debts att Boston not well knowne not haveing time but by but by Discourse with my husband	18 00 00

JOHN[2] SOULE'S INVENTORY AND THE SETTLEMENT OF HIS ESTATE.

Transcribed from the Original Records,

BY GEORGE ERNEST BOWMAN.

JOHN[2] SOULE (*George*[1]) died at Duxbury, but the date of his death is not known. He died intestate and his widow Hester was appointed administratrix, on 14 November, 1707, by Nathaniel Thomas, Judge of Probate. The record of this appointment is in the Plymouth County Probate Records, Volume II, page 87. The inventory is on the same page. The agreement between the heirs is found on page 91 of the same volume.

[p. 87] The Inventory of John Soul late of Duxbourrough Decease is as it was taken & apprized by us whose names are under written this 3[d] day of December 1707.

	ll	*s*	*d*
Viz : one Cow & heifer	2	15	0
Wareing Clothes Libery & money	5	00	0
2 swine	0	10	0
beds & beding	8	10	0
Iron Houshold stuff & tools	2	4	0
Brass & Pewter	0	12	0
two Chests with other wooden lumber	1	10	0
flax & table linen	0	10	0
to a mean Cow hide & a maire hide at y[e] Tanners in Plimouth	0	5	6
one wheel & bag with a Cannoe & spectacles	1	14	6
The Estate of Hester Soul Widdow of John Soul abovesd which she Brought with her is as follows			
Viz : 2 Iron pots with some other Lumber	1	2	0

Thomas Deleno
Abraham Samson
Ben : Deleno

Memorandum on the Ninteenth day of December 1707 before Nath[ll] Thomas Judge of the Probate of wills &c : Appeared Hester Soul & made oath y[t] the above written is a true Inventory of the Estate of her Husband John Soul late of Duxborrough Deceased so far as she knoweth & when she knoweth of more that she will Discover the same

Nath[ll] Thomas Register

[p. 91] Middleborrough December 5th 1707 Whereas we whose names are hereunto Subscribed were desired by the heirs of Mr John Soul of Duxborrough Deceased, to make apprizement of the severall percels of land which the s^{d} John Soul died seized of in the township of Middleborrough & which he had not in his life time disposed of, which we have acordingly done, according to the best of our Judgments as followeth : namely we have prized

	ll	*s*	*d*
1st The lot of Ceder Swamp in the six & twenty mens Purchase	3	0	0
2^{d} The lot of land in Assawanset neck	5	0	0
3^{d} The lot of the last division of upland in the sixteen shilling Purchase & the share of Ceder Swamp at Assonet Ceder Swamp & the undivided land in the sixteen shilling Purchase : all	7	0	0
4th The lot in the south Purchace being in Number the (*) lot	1	0	0
5th The lot in the South Purchace being in number the (*) lot	1	5	0
Joseph Vaughan total	17	5	0

Jacob Tomson

March the 5th 1707 The settlement of the Estate in lands of John Soul late of Duxborrough deceased Intestate. He haveing in his life time settled all his sons Portions in land by deed & his Daughter Sarah had only one Cow of her father in his life time & his Daughter Rachel & Rebecka haveing had nothing of their father, & he leaveing undisposed some small parcells of land at Middleborrough being apprised at 17^{ll} 5^{s} 0^{d} is by them that is to say Adam Wright in behalf of his children which he had by the said Sarah his wife Deceased & John Cob and Rachel his wife & Rebecka the wife of Edmond Weston Mutually agreed as followeth, That is to say the said Smal parcels of land as affores^{d} prized at 17^{ll} 5^{s} 0^{d} & the Cow said Sarah had of her father at 40 shillings makes 19^{ll} 5^{s} 0^{d} which being devided in three parts makes 6^{ll} 8^{s} 4^{d} to Each of them And that the Children of the said Sarah shall have the lot of the last division of upland in the sixteen shilling Purchase & the share of Ceder Swamp at Assonet Ceder Swamp & the undevidid land in the sixteen shilling Purchase all prized seven pounds to belong to the said children & their heirs the s^{d} Adam Wright haveing paid & satisfied to the s^{d} Rachel Cobb the sum of 2^{ll} 11^{s} 8^{d} & that the said Rebecka Weston shall have the lot of land in Assawamset neck prised at five pounds & the 2 lots in the south Purchace to her & her heirs both prized at fourty

*The number of the lot was omitted.

five shillings she haveing paid her sister Rachel Cobb the sum sixteen shillings & 8 pence And the said Rachel Cobb shall have the lot of Ceder Swamp in the six & twenty mens Purchace to her & her heirs prized at three pounds which with the money she has Received make Each persons share Equall & to all their satisfactions In Witness whereof they have hereunto set their hands & seals March the sixt 1707-8.

In presents of us
Nath^ll^ Thomas Ju^r^:
Joseph Soul

Adam Wright (Seal)
his marke
Rebecka weston (Seal)
her marke
John Cobb (Seal)
Rachel Cobb (Seal)
her marke

Memorand: that on the sixt day of March 1707-8. all the persons hereunto Subscribed acknowledged this Instrument to be their act & deed before me

Nathaniel Thomas J: Probates.

THOMAS LITTLE'S WILL AND INVENTORY, AND THE WILL OF HIS SON THOMAS.

Transcribed from the Original Records.

BY GEORGE ERNEST BOWMAN.

THOMAS LITTLE married Anna[2] Warren (*Richard*[1])* and lived at Plymouth and Marshfield. He died at the latter place in March, 1672. I have been unable to find the record of his death on the Marshfield town records, and it is probable that it has been lost since 1854, when a list of deaths and burials taken from the town records was printed in the New England Historical and Genealogical Register. [Vol. VIII, p. 192] The date of his burial, not his death as it has been frequently quoted, is there given as 12 March, 1671. This is old style, as is shown by the date of his will, 12 May, 1671, and the date of the inventory, 4 April, 1672.

The son Thomas (called senior after his father's death) was killed in the fight at Rehoboth, 26 March, 1676. His will is of especial interest since it gives the names of his four sisters, not named in their father's will, and shows that they and his mother were living when it was made, 19 February, 1675/6.

* Mayflower Descendant, III: 48.

[Plym. Col. Wills, III: I: 46]

[p. 46] The last Will and Testament of Thomas Little seni^r made on the 17th of May 1671, exhibited to the Court holden att Plymouth in New England the first of July 1672 on the oathes of Anthony Snow and John Carver, and ordered heer to be Recorded as followeth

I Thomas Little seni^r: being att this time in a Competent measure of health and haveing understanding and memory p^rfect; Doe make this my last will and Testament, Comitting my body to the earth and my soule to God that Gave it; and Doe Dispose of my outward estate as followeth; viz: To my loveing wife all my housing and all my land, upland and meddow on that side of the brooke; I now dwell, except, onely the meddow I purchased of Thomas Tildin and Morris Trewant; To my sonnes Isacke and Ephraim the land on the otherside of the brooke; That is to say the land I purchased of John Waterman, together with the aforsaid meddow I purchased of Thomas Tilden and Moris Trewant; which upland and meddow shalbe equally Devided between them; And all my land att Namassakett upland and meddow to my two younger sonnes Thomas and Samuell; except onely one single share of upland I purchased of Jacob Michell which I bequeath to my Grandchild John Jones except I doe better provide for him; and I doe give unto my son Ephraim one feather bedd with all meet furniture belonging therunto; That is to say a bolster and pillowes, one paire of sheets, and one paire of blanketts, one paire of pillowbears and a Rugg, to be Disposed to the said Ephraim att the time of his Marriage; and att our Decease I Doe Give to Thomas and Samuell either of them a feather bed with the like furniture belonging to them; and att the Decease of my selfe and my wife It is my will that my whole stocke of Cattle of all sorts shalbe equally Devided amongst all my Children and for the rest of my estate that is in Moveables to be left to the Despose of my wife according to her Discretion as shee shall see occation; and for my lands if any of my sonnes Die, after hee Comes to be posessed of his lands, and have noe Issue his p^rte shall then returne to the next brother; onely his wife if he have any shall enjoy the thirds of it During her life; and it is my will that my two eldest sonnes Isacke and Ephraim shall Disburse out of theire owne estates; either of them ten pounds to healp Thomas and Samuell in theire buildings att Namassakett, when they shall have occation; except by any extreordinary providence of God, it shall evidently appeer that the aforesaid Isacke or Ephraim be Disabled from p^r^forming the above said engagement; and if I should sell my single share of land att Namassakett; It is my will that my Grandchild John Jones shall have forty acrees of land out of the land of Thomas and Samuell; and att my wifes Decease Ephraim shall enjoy my housing, But the upland and meddow on that syde to be equally Devided between Isacke and Ephraim; onely the land the housing stands on and the orchyard shall belonge to Ephraim; and it is my will that Sarah Bonney shall have Convenient apparrell and a Cow att the time of her Departure out of her service;

Signed sealed and Delivered — Thomas Little
in the p^r^sence of us — And a seal
Anthony Snow
John Carver;

[p. 47] A true Inventory of the estate of Thomas Little seni^r^ exhibited to the Court held att Plymouth in New England the first of July 1672 on the oath of Anna Little widdow;

Imp^r^ his wearing Clothes	05 00 00
Item three feather beds and theire furniture belonging to them	15 00 00
Item in Table linnine	01 01 06
Item in brasse	02 01 04
Item in Iron potts and hangers and pott hookes 1 gridjron	01 10 06
Item in pewter	01 15 04
Item in earthen thinges and glasses	00 06 00
Item a Cubbord Chists Chaires boxes table and forme	03 000 00
Item for armes	02 12 04
Item for a frying pan spitt and other Iron thinges	000 07 06
Item for Cherne and pailes trayes & other wooden thinges	01 03 06
Item new Joyners worke unfinnished	10 03 00
Item for spining wheeles and Cards	00 10 00
Item for woole	01 00 00
Item for 30 bushells of Corne	04 *0 00
Item Neat Cattle	28 05 00
Item for a Mare	01 10 00
Item for sheepe	02 08 00
Item for swine	01 10 00
Item two Cart wheeles plough Irons and the Chaines	03 00 00
Item for wedges sawes hoes shovells fforkes sickles	01 04 00
Item for tooles in the shopp	01 10 00
Item for other Lumber	01 00 00

Marshfeild the 4th of Aprill 1672
Taken by us Anthony Snow
Marke Eames
ffrancis Crooker

* Blotted.

[Court Orders, V: 71, under date 14 August, 1692.]

Libertie of Adminnestration is Graunted unto Anna Little widdow the Relict of Thomas Little of Marshfeild Deceased, to adminnester on the estate of the said Thomas Little

---

[Plym. Col. Wills, III: I: 165]

The last Will and Testament of Thomas Little seni^r: made on the 19th Day of february 1675.

I Thomas Little seni^r: being att this time in a Competent measure of health haveing understanding and memory Doe make this my last Will and Testament; Comitting my Body to the earth and my soule to God that Gave it and Doe Dispose of my outward estate as followeth; viz to my loveing brother Samuell; I Doe Give all my land which is or which shall appeer to be mine; and I Doe give him all the mony I have and that which hee Can make appeer to be Due to mee; and I Doe Give him my horse which is now downe att Pokassett and my saddle and my bridle and I Doe Give him my featherbed with furniture belonging to it; and I Doe Give him all my Joyners Tooles; which is att Taunton or elsewhere and I Doe Give him all the work I have begun att Taunton; and I Doe give him my Chest and all my Clothes and I Doe Give him all my wages which is Due to mee for being a souldier and I Doe Give him all the Debts; which hee can Make appeer to be Due to mee; And for all the Rest of my estate, which is not mensioned which hee Can make appeer to be mine, I Doe Give it unto him; and I Doe bind the said Samuell, to pay all Debts which I Doe owe unto any prson or prsons which they can prove or make to appeer to be Due, and it is my will that Samuell shall Give each of my sisters; That is to say Ruth hannah Patience and Mercye each of them ten shillings in Mony and hee shall Give My loveing mother forty shillings in Mony; and for the ten pounds which Isack and Ephraim were to pay unto mee by my father will; I Doe freely Give it unto them signed sealed and delivered in the p^rsence of the witnesses

Witnes John Waterman Thomas Little and a seale
Joseph Waterman

Joseph Waterman made oath to this Will May the 31 1676 before Josiah Winslow Govr

John Waterman made oath to this Will June the 1 1676 before Josiah Winslow Govr:

RICHARD WRIGHT'S WILL AND INVENTORY.

Transcribed from the Original Records,

BY GEORGE ERNEST BOWMAN.

RICHARD WRIGHT died at Plymouth, 9 June, 1691. His wife was Hester[2] Cooke (*Francis*[1]). His will and inventory are found in the Plymouth County Probate Records, Volume I, pages 101–103.

[p. 101] I Richard Wright of ye Town of Plimouth in ye County and Colony of New Plimouth in New England being at Present of Sound and disposing mind and memory under bodily weaknesses not knowing when the hour of my death shall Come do make this my last Will and Testament in maner and forme following hereby Revoaking all former Wils First I comitt my soul to God that made it Resting on ye onely merrits of Christ my Redeemer for Eternall Salvation and my body to ye earth to be buried in a decent maner. My worldly Estate that God hath lent me I thus dispose: my will is that all my Estate Real and Personall House lands money or any moveables & Chattels in what kind soever be equally and faithfully divided betwixt my three Children Adam Esther and Mary Also my Will is that my daughter Mary have her living in my house During her Widowhoode and in as much as my son Adam hath heretofore had a full double portion in lands my will & desire is that my sd Son deal kindly in Carefull providing what in him lies for my daughter Mary price Also I Make my son and two daughters Executors of this my last Will & Testament Also I do hereby appoint & desire my loving friends John Nelson & Isaac Cushman to be Overseers of this my Will and I Intreate their care to se it faithfully prformed in a just distribution of my estate to my Children as is above Expressed In Attestation y^t^ this is my last Will and Testament I Set to my hand & seal This Eigth day of june 1691 I desire also & Impower John Sturtevant to be on of ye overseers of this my will.

Signed Sealed & declared by Richard Wright to be his last will and Testament In presence of — The mark of Richard Wright

John Cotton

Nath^ll^ Southworth

ye mark M of Martha Cobb :

june 24th 1691 Mr John Cotton and Nathll Southworth two of ye witnesses here named made oath in Plimouth before ye Magistrates of ye County of Plimouth that they were present and Saw ye above named Richard Wright Sign & Seal & heard him declare this above written to be his last will & Testament & yt to ye best of yr judgment he was of a disposing mind & memory when he so did

Attest Sam Sprague Clerk

[p. 102] June ye 19th day 1691 An Inventory of ye Estate of Richard Wright late dececcsed taken by us whose names are under written.

	li	*s*	*d*
Iten one Bed and Boulster	03	00	00
One Rugg and one Blanket	00	05	00
One Pillow	00	02	00
One Silkgrass Bed and Boulster	00	08	00
One Curtaine & two Cushions	00	01	06
One Trammill	00	03	00
One pair of Tongs	00	02	00
4 hooks	00	02	00
One Spade	00	02	00
One Ax	00	01	00
More : Old Iron	00	02	00
4 hinges	00	01	00
2 Iron Kittles	00	06	00
One Iron Skillet	00	02	06
One Iron Pot and Pott hookes	00	04	00
One ffrying Pan	00	00	06
One Warming Pan	00	08	00
One Brass Kettle	00	10	00
One Gun	00	18	00
One Sword	00	03	00
More Wooden Dishes	00	01	00
two Earthen Potts	00	00	04
One Barbours Bason	00	00	09
One Glass Bottle	00	00	04
One Book	00	01	06
One pair of sheers	00	00	06
One pair of Pillowbeers	00	03	00
3 sheetes	00	10	00
One Pewter	00	03	06
One Boul	00	02	00
One Pewter Bottle	00	01	06
One Pewter Pot	00	01	06
1 Pewter Bason and Sawcer	00	01	00
One chamber Pott	00	02	00

One Candlestick	00	00	04
One Pail	00	00	06
One chest	00	07	00
One chest	00	02	06
More old Cask	00	03	00
One Box	00	00	04
One Chaire	00	01	00
More Cloathing	00	04	00
One shirt	00	06	09
One shirt	00	04	06
[p. 103] One pair of Drawers	0	01	0
More in Small linnen	0	02	6
More in woollen Cloathing shoose & stockings & hat	0	14	0
One pewter platter	0	04	6
One Pewter Platter	0	02	6
One Pewter Platter	0	03	0
3 Porrengers	0	03	0
one Pewter Bason and Sawcer	0	04	0
one Bagg	0	06	0
one yearling in ye hand of Adam Wright	0	15	0
one ox & one Cow in ye hand of Ephraim Tinkam	4	10	0
More in ye hand of Ephraim Tinkam	0	04	6
one Blanket a Box & a Band	0	12	6
More in ye hand of Caleb Cooke	4	00	0
More in ye hand Mr Jno Cotton senr	1	01	11
More in Silver Money	5	18	04
More in ye hand of Joseph Sturtevant	0	02	6
More in ye hand of John Gray	0	07	11
One Table	0	01	0
More in ye hand of Ephraim Tinkam	1	10	0
Item the land both of upland and meadow	21	00	0
Item Charge for ye ffunerall	1	0	0
More due to William Shirtliff	0	1	4
More due to John Sturtevant	0	2	0
More due to Adam Wright	0	3	0

Isaac Cushman
John Sturtevant

June 24th 1691 Adam Wright made Oath in Plimouth before ye Magistrates of ye County of Plimouth That the before written is a True Inventory of ye estate of his ffather Richard Wright late of Plimouth deceased So far as he knoweth & that if more shall come to his knowledge he will discover it

Attest Sam'l Sprague Clerk

PLYMOUTH COLONY WILLS AND INVENTORIES.

(*Continued from page 82.*)

[Vol. I, fol. 44] William Swyft 1642
Lres of Administracon graunted unto Joane the wyfe of Willm Swyft of Sandwich lately Deceased.

An Inventory of all the goods and Cattells of the said Willm Swyft exhibited the xxix[th] of January Anno Dm 1642

	ll s d
Inpris one feather bed two boulsters 2 pillowes 2 blanketts and one rugg	04 . 00 . 00
Itm five curtaines & valence & bedstead	01 . 00 . 00
Itm one flock bed & boulster 2 blanketts & a rugg	01 . 00 . 00
Itm five cusheons	01 . 00 . 00
Itm 12 napkins & a diaper cloth	01 . 06 . 00
Itm a table cloth	00 . 07 . 00
Itm 3 paire of sheets at 13 ss pr paire	01 . 19 . 00
Itm 3 sheets at 5^s a peece	00 . 15 . 00
Itm 3 old sheets at	00 . 05 . 00
Itm 2 hand towells	00 . 02 . 00
Itm one cloake	02 . 00 . 00
Itm one shuite of apparell	00 . 13 . 00
Itm one other shuite of apparell	01 . 00 . 00
Itm one Coate	00 . 05 . 00
Itm two ruff bands & 4 playne bands	00 . 06 . 00
Itm a chest of Drawers	01 . 00 . 00
Itm one chest	00 . 08 . 00
Itm a	00 . 12 . 06
Itm a prcell of bookes	01 . 00 . 00
Itm two swordes	00 . 10 . 00
Itm two musketts at 10^s	01 . 00 . 00
Itm two paire of bandeliers	00 . 04 . 00
Itm one feather bed & boulster & one pillow & a blankett	02 . 10 . 00
Itm a cupboard	00 . 16 . 00
Itm 3 blew potts & a bason	00 . 03 . 00
Itm 2 bras kettles	01 . 05 . 00
Itm a little bras pott	00 . 03 . 04
Itm 2 skelletts a chaffing dish a ladle & 2 scimmers	00 . 08 . 00
Itm one iron pott & an iron kettle	00 . 12 . 00
Itm two paire of hangers	00 . 02 . 00
Itm 2 paire of pott hookes	00 . 01 . 00
Itm 2 paire of tongues & a firefork	00 . 02 . 00

Itm one spitt	00 . 01 . 06
Itm a short table & two chaires	00 . 06 . 06
Itm 2 stooles 2 cupboard clothes	00 . 02 . 00
Itm 2 graters	00 01 . 06
Itm a paire of littlescales i^{ll} & a ii^{ll} waight	00 . 01 . 06
Itm a warmeing pann	00 . 05 . 00
	27 . 12 10
Itm 4 seives	00 . 01 . 08
Itm 7 platters	00 . 14 . 00
Itm 3 plates	00 . 03 . 00
Itm 6 sawcers 3 porringers	00 . 03 . 00
Itm a salt seller	00 . 01 . 00
Itm 2 candlesticks	00 . 02 . 00
Itm a top for a still	00 . 02 . 00
Itm the latten	00 . 01 . 00
Itm a cross cutt sawe	00 . 02 . 00
Itm a long sawe	00 . 08 . 00
Itm a halbeard	00 . 02 . 00
Itm a french bill & a cosett	00 . 16 . 00
Itm a bedstead	00 . 02 . 00
Itm 4 augours 4 chessells	00 . 02 . 08
Itm i judg	00 . 00 . 04
Itm two chests	00 . 03 . 00
Itm an iron beame	00 . 02 . 00
Itm 2 old sythes	00 . 02 . 00
Itm a trunck	00 . 00 . 06
Itm sechell	00 . 00 . 09
Itm 5 bushells of Indian Corne	00 . 15 . 00
Itm 2 bushells of winter wheate	00 . 09 . 00
Itm 3 pecks of bins	00 . 03 . 00
Itm a bushell of peas	00 . 04 . 00
Itm 5 Indian basketts	00 . 01 . 04
Itm a sack	00 . 01 . 06
Itm two chamber potts	00 . 03 . 00
Itm a spout & a half pint pott	00 . 01 . 06
Itm 3 milk (*) at 18^{d} a peec	00 . 04 . 06
Itm a churne	00 . 03 . 00
It a bucking tub 4^{s} a milk payle 12	00 . 05 . 00
Itm a pickaxe i axe i hatchett	00 . 03 . 00
Itm trevett	00 . 01 . 06
Itm 12^{l} of butter	00 . 06 . 00
Itm a beere barrell	00 . 03 . 00
Itm 2 firkins & a buckett	00 . 02 . 06
Itm a spade 12^{d} a spining wheele 4^{s}	00 . 05 . 00
Itm a prcell of pumpkins	00 . 03 . 00
Itm a prcell of turneps	00 . 04 . 00

* Left blank.

Itm a prcell of cabedges	00 . 01 . 06
Itm a grindle stone	00 . 04 . 00
Itm a prcell of earthen potts	00 . 02 . 00
Itm an iron fatt	00 . 01 . 00
Itm for all old lumber	00 . 05 . 00
Itm for porke	05 . 00 . 00
Itm two cowes	09 . 00 . 00
	22 01 . 03
[fol. 45] Itm 4 yeong cattell at 40ˢ a peec	08 . 00 . 00
Itm a heiffer	03 . 00 . 00
Itm three calves	02 . 05 . 00
Itm 8 swyne	05 . 00 . 00
Itm a rick of hey at hoame	01 . 10 . 00
Itm another rick at Munus casset 4 loads	01 . 00 . 00
Itm 2 parts of a hide	00 . 16 . 00
Itm a cheese presse	00 . 02 . 00
Itm 10 pound of yarne	00 . 10 . 00
Itm 7 pound of cotton woll at 9½	00 . 05 . 06
Itm i hoe	00 . 03 . 00
Itm ii little barrells 18 an old cart wᵗʰ broken wheels & a calve rack 5ˢ all	00 . 06 . 06
	22 . 17 . 00
	22 . 01 . 03
	27 . 12 . 10
Sum tot.	72 . 11 . 01
Itm the house land & meddow ground	10 . 00 . 00
Itm a house & land at Sudbury in Massachusets bay mortgaged to one mʳ Burton to secure at debt of 20ˡ 10ˢ.	

Debts oweing by the said Willm Swyft at his death

	l s d
To mʳ Thomas Wallis	90 . 00 . 00
To mʳ John Buckley	89 . 00 . 00
To mʳ John Casteele	21 . 00 . 00
To mʳ Blackwell	06 . 00 . 00
To a hatmaker	02 . 00 . 00
To John Barnes	17 .
To Thom Dexter	01 . 10 . 00
To John Derby	00 . 14 . 00
To Daniell Wing	00 . 19 . 00
To Joseph Winsor	00 . 04 . 00
To Thom Butler	00 . 03 . 00
To Robte Allen	00 . 03 . 00
To Thomas Gibbs	00 . 14 . 00
To Thoms Johnson	00 . 05 . 00
To Miles Blacke	00 . 07 . 00

To m^r^ Waterhouse	04 . 18 . 00
To Goodman Armitage	05 . 00 . 00
To Hugh (*) m^r^ Noyce servant	03 . 00 . 00
ffor fun'all charges	02 . 00 . 00
ffor levyes at Sudburry	02 . 00 . 00
To m^r^ (*)	01 . 04 . 00

(*To be continued.*)

THE ESTATES OF WILLIAM SHERMAN, JUNIOR, AND ISRAEL HOLMES.

Transcribed from the Original Records,

BY GEORGE ERNEST BOWMAN.

WILLIAM SHERMAN, Jr., of Marshfield married Desire[2] Doty (*Edward*[1]) on 25 December, 1667 (4 January, 1668, New Style); † and the fact that his inventory was taken 30 December, 1680 (9 January, 1681, N. S.), makes it probable that the following entry on the Marshfield records refers to his burial: "(*worn*) Sherman Junior (*worn*) ye 17 of november 1680." ‡

Desire (Doty) Sherman married, second, on 24 November/4 December, 1681, Israel Holmes of Marshfield,§ who was drowned 24 February/6 March, 1684/5.¶ After his death she married Alexander[2] Standish (*Myles*[1]), whom she survived many years.

WILLIAM SHERMAN'S INVENTORY

[Plym. Col. Wills, IV: I: 80, 81]

[p. 80] An Inventory of all and singulare the Goods and Chattles of Willam Sherman Late of Marshfeild Deceased apprised the 30th of December 1680 by us whoe names are under subscribed;

Imp^r^: his wearing apparrell	06	00	0
Item his purse and Cash	21	12	**
Item Guns 1 sword and Amunition	02	00	0
Item 1 old horse saddle pillian and other furniture	02	12	0

* Left blank. † Mfr. Desc., II: 182; III: 90, 91. ‡ Ibid., II: 181. § Ibid., III: 42. ¶ Ibid., III: 188. ** Blotted.

Item 3 Cowes att forty five shillinges pr Cow and 2 Calves 10s Calf	07	15	0
Item 10 sheep and lambes att 45	02	05	0
Item 7 smale swine	02	03	0
Item 2 Chests 2 boxes 1 Deske	00	18	6
Item Cotton and sheeps woole fflax teer tow and yarne	01	18	6
Item Divers smale Remnants of Cloth	00	16	0
Item an old featherbed three payer of sheets and other beding	04	15	0
Item brasse pewter and earthen ware or vessell	02	09	0
Item a lookeing Glasse and Glasse bottles	00	03	0
Item a Cradle and smale Table	00	12	0
Item a meale seive wooden Dishes spoones and trenchers	00	05	0
Item 2 old baggs smale basketts salt and white Starch	00	06	0
Item 3 Iron Potts tonges Potthangers frying pan and other Iron	02	01	0
Item Divers working tooles	01	00	0
Item 7 barrells of Syder	02	16	0
Item 2 spining wheeles	00	08	0
Item Chaires payles old Caske and houshold lumber	00	14	0
Item a smale prsell of Cooper stuffe	00	08	0
Item his bookes prised att	00	16	0
Item a Syder presse	00	05	0
Item about eight bushells of Indian Corne and one bushell of Rye	01	03	0
Item porke beife and hoggs fatt	02	13	0
Item butter and Cheese	01	10	0
Item Sugar fruite and spice 6s and Tobacco 8s	00	14	0
Item fflax and ffodder	01	10	0
Item Debts Due to the estate from severall prsons; some wherof are Desparate Debts	29	12	01

The estate is Indebted about 14s

Ephraim Little
Samuell Sprague

[p. 81] Debts Due to the estate of Willam Sherman Deceased

Phillip Leanard is Debter	7	06	00
John Peterson	00	10	0
John Trowbridge	01	17	03
Samuell hatch	00	10	0
Isack Little	00	01	0
Edward Stevens	00	08	07
Walter Joyce	00	05	06
Samuell Sherman	00	04	6
John Phillips	00	15	09
John Doten	04	00	0
A Desparett Debt in the hands of Samuell Sherman	*	00	00

and in the hands of Robert Stanford about forty shillings;

* Blotted.

The Estate is endebted as followeth

To Benjamine Phillipps	00	03	00
To Timothy Willamson	00	03	06
To hopestill Besbey	00	01	06
To Ephraim Little	00	06	08
	02	14	00

Settlement of William Sherman's Estate.

[Court Orders, VI : I : 65, under date 7 March, 1681/2.]

Att this Court John Sherman of Marshfeild and Israell holmes appeered in reference unto the Disposall of the estate of Willam Sherman Juni^r^ Deceased, The said Israell holmes haveing married Desire Sherman, somtimes the wife of the aforsaid Willam Sherman The Court haveing heard the please and Discourses Concerning, the same, have settled the p^r^sonall estate unto the said Israell holmes, his heires executors and Adminnestrators, provided hee his heires executors or adminnestrators, Doe bringe up the Children of the said Willam Sherman well; untill they Come of age; and that hee his heires executors or adminnestrators Doe pay or cause to be payed the sume of fifteen pounds in specue when they Come of age, as is expressed in an obligation; under hand and seale, of the said Israell holmes, bearing Date with these p^r^sents

Israel Holmes' Inventory.

[Plym. Col. Wills IV : II : 108]

Inventory of ye estate of Israel Holmes late of Marshfield deceased taken & apprised May ye 9th 1685. p^r^ us who have under subscribed

	li	*s*	*d*
Imp^r^mis To four steers	11	00	0
To five Cowes	11	10	0
To one bull 35 shillings & one two year old steer 25 shillings	03	00	0
to 13 sheep & four lambs	04	10	0
to one horse 4^li^ & one mare 25 shillings	05	05	0
to one halfe of a yearling Colt	00	12	0
to seven smale swine & four sucking piggs	02	10	0
to 27 shilling and 5^d^ in Cash	01	07	5
to his wearing Apparell a staffe & A tobacco box	08	09	6
to severall smal books	00	16	0
to three musquets one sword powder & shott	03	00	0
to a saddle pillion & horse furniture	01	05	0
to chests boxes & a desk	01	05	6

to Cotton & sheeps wool tow & yarne	01	04	6
to severall remnants of linnen & woolen cloth	00	19	6
to 2 meal sives flax teer & other smal things	00	15	0
to several smal basketts	00	03	0
to two feather beds & beding pertaining to them	10	08	6
to brass & pewter vessels	02	05	0
to a looking glass & glass bottles	00	03	0
to earthen vessels	00	03	0
to a Table forme & table linnen	01	14	0
to a smale table & a cradle	00	10	0
to seven Chaires	00	13	0
to trenchers spoones & dishes	00	04	0
to Tubbs & pails & sundry old cask	01	19	0
to a box smoothing iron & heaters	00	03	0
to a pair of Andirons tongs fire slice & Tramels	01	09	0
to three Iron potts A frying pan & skillet	01	10	0
to two spining wheels & two pair of Cards	00	11	0
to about ten bushels of Corne not thrashed	01	05	0
to about three bushels of rye & a bushel of wheat	00	13	0
to two meal sacks & a smal quantity of salt	00	05	0
to a Cart wheels plough & yoke	01	06	0
to tools & Iron ware belonging to husbandry	01	17	0
more to sythes sickles hamers & other smal things of iron	00	07	0
to two weavers beames sleas & tackling	03	12	0
to a ladder a sider press & trough 10ˢ & to a pair of stockings	00	12	6
to a Cow hide 10ˢ & two deer skins 3ˢ	00	13	00
to Cord wood cutt in yᵉ woods	00	12	0
to tanned leather & hemp	01	06	0
Debts due to yᵉ estate	3	12	0
the estate is indebted	9	11	8

besides a house & lands in marshfield & yᵉ widdows bed not prised

Epharim Little
Samuel Sprague

Desire holmes came into this court & swore that this is a true Inventory of yᵉ estate of her husband late deceased so far as she knowes

HARWICH, MASS., VITAL RECORDS.

(*Continued from Vol. III, p. 176.*)

[p. 26] Elesabeth Snow the dafter of Thomas Snow was born the 26th of october 1693

Mary Snow the dafter of Thomas Snow was born ye 16th of may 1696

Josiah Snow the sun of Thomas Snow was born the 27 of Janeuary 1699

Ebenzer Snow the Son of Thomas Snow was born y^{e} 14th of feberary 1700

Hanah Snow the dafter of Thomas Snow was born y^{e} 21 of march 172/3

Elkenah ffreeman son to John and mercy ffreeman Junr was born october . 28th : 1702 :

Sare ffreeman the dafter of John ffreeman jun was born the the 26 of Janeuary = 1704

Marcy ffreeman daughter to s^{d} John and mercy ffreeman was born April 24th 170[*worn*]

John freeman son to John and mercy freeman was born . 13th . august 1709

Phebe freeman daughter to John and Mercy ffreeman was born novemb : 28 : 171[*worn*]

Thanckfull ffreeman daughter to John and marcy ffreeman was born october the : 6 : day 1714

Elkenah ffreeman son to John and marcy ffreeman was born febuary 8 day 171$\frac{6}{7}$

Mary freeman daughter to John and marcy freeman was born oct 13d 1719

Benjamen Rogers the Son of John Rogers was born november the 19th = 1704

Judah Rogers the Son of Judah Rogers was born the 29 of desember = 1704

Ebenezer Rogers the son of John Rogers was born was born in feberary y^{e} 17th in the yeare 169$\frac{3}{4}$

Thankfull Rogers the dafter of John rogers was born in octob[*worn*] the 24th day in the yeare 1699

John Rogers the son of John rogers was born in agust y^{e} 1[*worn*] day in the yeare 1701

Jonathan Rogers the son of John rogers was born march y^{e} 20 in the yeare 1703

Sarah Rogers daughter to John and Prissila rogers was born July 21th : 1706

Joseph rogers son to John and Priscila rogers was born septem : 20 : 1708

[p. 28] Marsy Hopkins the dafter of Judah hopkins was born the 17 day of aprell in the yeare 1703
John Hopkins the son of Judah hopkins was born the 23 of september in the yeare = 1704
Martha Hopkins the dafter of Judah hopkins was born the 25 of march in the yeare = 1705
Rebeckah Hopkins daughter to Judah and Hanah hopkins was born the tenth of october 1707 :
Judah Hopkins son to Judah and Hanah Hopkins was born october 18 170[*worn*]
Stephen Hopkins son to Judah and Hanak Hopkins was born Junuary 26th : 1711/12
desire hopkins daughter to Judah and hanah hopkins was born in November the 17 day 1714
Silvanes Hopkins son to Judah and hanah Hopkins was born febary the 14 day 1716/17
hannah hopkins Daughter to Judah and hannah hopkins was born in June 17 day 1719
Samuell hopkins son to Judah hopkins and hannah hopkins his second wife was born in march 14 : 1720/21
Thankfull Crosby the dafter of Ebenezer Corby was born november the 19th in the yeare = 1701
Marsy Crosby the dafter of Ebenezer Crosby was born november the 4th = 1703
Ebenezer Crosby son to Ebenézer Crosby was born may 5th 1706
Thomas Croby the son of John Crosby was born Aprell the 17th in the yeare = 1704
Jonathan Crosby son to John and hannah Crosby was born In November the 2 day 1705
John Crosby son to John and hannah Crosby was born in august The 14 day 1707
David Crosby son to John and hannah Crosby was born in April The 13 day 1709
Joshua Crosby son to John and hannah Crosby was born in August the 4 day 1712
Abile Crosby son to John and hanah Crosby was born in desember The 3 day 1714

[p. 29] Jabes Snow the son of princ snow was born the 11 of november the 7th day of the weck in the yeare 1699
Hanah snow the dafter of princ snow was born the 29 of november the 7th day of the weck in the yeare 1701
Samwell snow the son of princ Snow was born the 16 of desember the 5th day of the weck in the yeare 1703
mercy snow daughter to Prence and Hanah snow was born novemb 18th : 1705
Prence Snow son to Prence and hanah snow was born october 26 1707

Jonathan and David snow sons to Prence and Hanah snow were born december : 22^{d} : 1709
mary snow daughter to princ and hanah snow was born september the 10 day 1712
Joseph grifeth the son of stephen grifeth was born in march 15th in the yeare 1699/10
Stephen grifeth the son of stephen grifeth was born the 15 day of march in the yeare 1701/2
Rebekah grifith the dafter of Stephen grifeth was born the 18 day of June in the yeare 1703
Lazarus Grifith son to Stephen and Rebekah Grifith was born June . 7th . 1708
Barnabus Griffith son to stephen and Rebekah Griffith was born november 21th 1710 :
Thankfull griffith daughter to stephen and Rebekah griffith was born April the 3 day 1714
Abraham griffith son to stephen and Rebekah griffith was born in July 31 day 1716

[p. 37] Elizabeth Mayo daughter To John and Hanah Mayo was born July . 16 . 1706
stephen King son to stephen and Abegal King was Born december 22 day 1717
seth banges son to samuel and mary Bangs was born July 29 : 1705
Samuel Banges son to samuel and Mary Banges was born July 11th 1707
david Banges son to samuel and mary banges was born march 29 : 1709 :
Mary Banges daughter to samuel and mary banges was born May 2^{d} : 1711 :
Joseph Banges son to samuell and mary banges was born in January The 30 day 1712/13
mallatiah Banges daughter to samuell and mary Banges was born in march the 4 day 1714/15
sarah Banges daughter to samuell and mary Banges was Born in october the 23 day 1716
Lemuell Banges son to Samuell and mary Banges was Born in June 2 day 1719
Abijah Bangs Sone to Samuel & Mary Bangs his Wife born July 29th 1743
James and Mary Makers daughter abygaile was born march 5th 1707

[p. 38] Thomas Snow and Lidea Hamblen were maried . 30th . of septem : 1706
Elisha Hamblen son to Eliezer and Lidea hamblen was born January 26 169$\frac{8}{7}$
Lidea snow daughter . to s^{d} Thomas and Lidea snow was born July 24 : 1707 :

Thomas snow son to Thomas and Lidea snow was born June 15th 1709
Aaron snow son to Thomas and Lidea snow was born febuary 15 17$\frac{11}{10}$
Ruth Snow daughter to Thomas and lidea snow was born febuary 23 : 1712/13
hannah snow Daughter to samuell and mary snow his wife was Born in march the 9 day 1729/30
Samuel King son to John and Bathshua King was born in June 9th : day 1698 :
Ebenezer King son to sd John King was born June 15th day 1700 :
Bathshua King daughter to John and Mary King was born december 20th : 1708
marcy King daughter to John and mary King was born may 4 day 1713

[p. 40] John dillingham son to John and Lidea dillingham was born march 23d : 1702
Elizebeth daughter to sd John and Lidea dillingham was born august 2d : 1703
Lidea daughter to sd John and Lidea dillingham was born June 21th 1705
Hanah daughter to sd John and Lidea dillingham was born febuary 2d : 1706/7
Rebekah dillingham daughter to John and Lidea dillingham was born 24 June : 1709 :
Isaac dillingham son to John and Lidea dillingham was born may 4th 1711 :
Abigal dillingham daughter to John and Lidea dillingham was born June 9 day 1713
Edward dilingham son to John and Lidea dilingham was born in may The 17 day 1715
Thankfull dilingham daughter to John an Lidea dilingham was Born in April the 18 day 1718
Sarah dilingham daughter to John and Lidea dilingham was born febuary 10 day 1719/20
Nathael : Hopkins and Mercy Mayo were married may 26th 1707
David Hopkins son to Nathanael and Mercy Hopkins was born July : 13th : 1707 :
Jeremiah Hopkins son to Nathaell and Mercy hopkins was born march 14th : 1708
Elizebeth Hopkins daughter to Nathanael and Mercy Hopkins was born April 21 : 1711 :
Nathanaell hopkins son to Nathanaell and marcy hopkins was born in September the 1 day 1713
Bethyah hopkins daughter to Nathanaell and marcy hopkins was Born August the 19 day 1715
Nathanaell hopkins son to Nathanaell and marcy hopkins was Born september 15 day 1717

marcy hopkins Daughter To Nath[ll] and marcy hopkins was Born 21 day of febuary 1719/20

Ruben hopkins son to nathanaell and marcy hopkins was Born in April 4 day 1722

Samuell hopkins son to Nath[ll] and marcy hopkins was born in August the 30 day 1724

James hopkins son to Nathanaell and marcy hopkins was Born in march 20 day 1726/7

(*To be continued.*)

BARNSTABLE COUNTY, MASS., PROBATE RECORDS.

(*Continued from Vol. III, page 202.*)

THE SETTLEMENT OF JOSIAH COOK'S ESTATE.*

[Vol. I, p. 16] An Invintory of the estate of Elizabeth Cook deceased the wife [*worn*] Josiah Cook taken the third day may in the year of our Lord 1687

It to a fether Bedd	02	10	00
It to an old fether Bed	00	15	00
to 4 old pillowes	00	08	00
to a peece of a Rugg and 2 old Blankits & a peece of Cloth	00	06	00
to a Chaf Bolster	00	01	06
to two payr of pillobers	00	08	00
to 4 napkins and to towels	00	06	00
to two payer of Sheetes	00	10	00
to a course Small table Cloath and peece of an old Sheet	00	03	00
to four old Shifts	00	01	00
to a broad cloath wastcoat	00	09	00
to a searge peticoate	00	15	00
to an old home spun wastcoat	00	01	00
to 3 under wastcoats	00	02	00
to 3 peces of aprons & 3 old pathes	00	01	00
to two homespun Coats	00	11	00
to 2 old petticoats	00	04	00
to 4 Capes	00	03	00
to a small Silk hood & a silk cape and a small old Scarfe	00	02	06
to a blue apron	00	01	00

* Printed in full at the request of a liberal contributor to the Colonial Research Fund.

to 4 white Capes	00 03 00
to an old Bay apron	00 03 00
to 3 old Neck Clothes	00 01 00
to 6 dressings	00 02 00
to 4 neck hanchirchifs	00 05 00
to squares and head bands	00 01 06
to 10 small hand Clothes and old Ruges & pinns & hair-laces & a bitt or two of old cloath gloves & needls	00 01 06
to a carved Box	00 04 00
to 2 wastcoats & a pair of Bodies	00 06 00
to an old wainscot Chiest	00 04 00
to an old Chist	00 02 06
to an old Case and what was in it	0 01 00
to spice	00 01 08
to earthen pot and malasas & runlet & other old Lumber	00 03 00
to an old Cheist & stockings	00 01 06
to an hat and hatt Case	00 04 00
to Chaiers and stools	00 04 00
to a payer of shoos	00 03 00
to Brass	00 10 00
to Iron ware	00 17 00
to pewter and spoones	00 11 06
to earthen ware & a glass bottle	00 01 00
to a Jarr & oyle & whale bone	00 02 00
to an old wheel tubes & baggs and old Trayes & an old chiest to put meale in & other Loumber	00 10 00
to new Cloath & yarne and wool and Curtaines & vallance	01 17 00
to 2 old Chamber pots	00 01 00
to Books	00 04 00
to one Bushel of wheat	00 04 00
to 3 pekes of meale	00 02 03
to money	00 01 02
The Total Sum	15 07 07

[*worn*] b[y u]s Jonathan Sparrow

Meriam Deane debter to the estate 9 pence

Debtes due from the Estate	01 17 *
due from the Estate to Meriam Deane which the Court allowes her and dus app[*worn*] to be due to her	09 03 00

not praized
An old Iron pott
the frame of an old Skillet
an old payer of siszers and Som other trivial things

* Worn

Meriam Deane made oath to the truth of this Invintory in the preroga[tive] Court in Barnestable may the one and thirtith day 1687

Duely Compared with the orriganal and entred the 7th of November 168[*worn*]

Attest Joseph Lothrop Depty Regr

[p. 17] [W]here as there was great Contest varianc and strife betweene Josiah Cook Bethiah Harding and meriam deane all of Eastham in the County of Barnestable about tuching or Conserning the Estate of Josiah Cook of Eastham deaceased that was Left after the death of Elizabeth the relict of sd Josiah Cook deceased Now all whome it may conserne that the parties at variance as above sd, have agreed before the prerogative Court held in Barnestable the 31th of may 1687 Clearly fairly and plainly as followeth, that the sd Josiah first above mentioned shall pay or Cause to be paid unto Bethiah his sister the sd wife of Joseph Harding of Eastham aforesd out of his owne Estate the full Sum of fifty shillings in good merchants pay to her or her order on or before the last day of November Next Ensuing the date above mentioned : and for the estate of the sd Josiah Cook deceased left after the death of the sd Elizabeth Relict of sd Josiah Cook deceased, the sd Josiah Cook first above mentioned and the sd Bethiah his Sister to have the first Choise of fifty shillings there of at the prise as the sd estate is praised at and then the abovesd meriam deane to have the second Choise of five pounds of sd Estate as it is praized at and then the aforsaid Josiah Cook and sd Bethiah to have the 3d Choise of fifty Shillings more of sd Estate at the prise as aforesd and then the sd Meriam deane to have the Choise of four pounds and three Shillings there of at the prise aforesd, and of all that of sd Estate that is left when the said meriam deane hath her due which is nine pounds and three Shillings the rest to be Equally devided between the sd Josiah Cook and his Sister Bethiah the wife of the sd Joseph Harding

The parties above mentioned Acknowledged This above writ to be their act and deed before the Judg of the prerogative Court June the 1st 1687

Joseph Lothrop ; Clerk

(*To be continued.*)

CHATHAM, MASS., VITAL RECORDS.

Transcribed from the Original Records

BY GEORGE ERNEST BOWMAN.

[Volume I]

[p. 10] November y^e^ 10=1748 Then moses Rodgers of harwich and Elisebeth Smith of Chatham was mared in Chatham By Joseph Done Justes of Peace

Desember y^e^ 23^d^ 1748 then Edman Hall of yarmoth and Zipporah young of Chatham was mared at Chatham By Thomas winslo Justes of Pees

Desember y^e^ 23 1748 then Shubel nickrson and mary Hamelton of Chatham was mared at Chatham By Thomas winslo Justes of Pees

The above Recorded per mee Daniel Sears town Clark

[p. 11] July the 3=1747 thn Davied Ralf and Katrina twining was mared by the Reverant Joseph Lord

August the 3 1747 then mathes tayler and Desire Harding was mared by the Reverant Joseph Lord

August y^e^ 24 : 1747 then Ebneser Herd was mared to Elizebath wesen by the Revarant Joseph Lord

August the 25 1747 thn Benimon Bers was mared to Anna Nickrson by the Reverant Joseph Lord

September the 17=1747 then Joseph harding and hannah howes was mared by the Reverant Joseph Lord

october the 29=1747 then Zachriah Smalle was mared to Bethia Severanc by y^e^ Reverant Joseph Lord

July the 7=1748 then Josiah godfree and Eunis godfree both of Chatham was mared in Chatham by Joseph Done Justes of pees

September the 28=1748 then Stephen Cally* of Plymoth and Catrina flaingam of Chatham was mared In Chatham by Joseph Done Justes of peese

The above Recorded per mee Daniel Sears Town Cl[*worn*]

[p. 14] Martha Knowels the daughter of Richard and martha Knowls was born Janawery the 28 : 17$\frac{13}{14}$

Richard Knowels the sun of Richard and martha knowels was born March y^e^ 26 : 1715

Mercy knowels y^e^ daughter of Richard and martha knowels was born agust y^e^ : 9 : 1717

James knowels the sun of Richard and Martha Knowels was born november y^e^ : 11 : 1719

* "Stephen Calley" and "Catherine Flanega" in Plymouth Records, I : 235.

Cornelus Knowles : y^e^ son of Richart Knowels & Martha Knowles Was born the 10th Day of aprill : 1722 : Taken on Record : July y^e^ 2^d^ 1722 pr Me Sam^ll^ Stewart Town Clark

Rebakah Knowels y^e^ daughter of Richard and martha Knowels was born the 2 day of march 172$\frac{4}{3}$

hannah sears the daughter of paul and anne sears was born y^e^ 27 of november 1734

Thankfull Sears y^e^ daughter of Paul and ann Sears was born July y^e^ = 27 = 1736

ann Sears y^e^ daughter of Paul and ann Seares was born febwery : ye 16 = 1737/8

Ruth Sears the daughter of Paul and anna Sears was Born November y^e^ = 12 = 1740

Experans Sears y^e^ daughter of Paul and Anna Sears was Born october y^e^ = 20 = 1743

Per mee Daniel Sears town Clark

[p. 15] Mary Lumbert y^e^ Daughter of Caleb & Elizebeth Lumbert born : June : y^e^ 4th 1705 Rec^d^ : one Recor^d^ March 23 year 1722 = Recor^d^ p^r^ Me Sam^ll^ Stewart Town Cleark

Deliverance Lumbert Daughter of Caleb & Elizebeth Lumbart born the 4th day of Aprell in y^e^ Yar of Our Lord 1710 Rec^d^ one Recor^d^ March 23 & year 1722 p^r^ Me Samuel Stewart Town Clark

Elizabeth Lumbert y^e^ Daughter of Caleb & Elizabeth Lumbert born Aprill ye first 1714 Rec^d^ on Record M 23 : 1722 pr Me Sam^ll^ Stewart Town Clark

Caleb Lumbert y^e^ Son of Caleb & Eizebeth Lumbert born September y^e^ 20th 1717 Rec^d^ on Recor^d^ March 22 1722 pr Mee Sam^ll^ Stewart Town Clark

Edward Lumburt Son of Caleb Lumbert & Elizebeth Lumbert born March y^e^ 11th 172$\frac{2}{1}$ Rec^d^ on Recor^d^ M 23 & y^e^ 1722 pr Me Sam^ll^ Stewart Town Clerk

[p. 16] Judeth Nickerson Y^e^ Daughter of Jonathan & Jane Nickerson Born aprill the 9th 1720 Recor^d^ pr Me Sam^ll^ Stewart Town Cl[*worn*]

Jane Nickerso y^e^ Daughter of Jonathan & Jane Nickerson Born y^e^ 9th of Aprill 1722 Recorded p^r^ Me Samuel Stewart Town Clark

Edward Eldredg Y^e^ Son of Jehoshaphat & Elizabeth Eldredg born July : ye 17th 1702 Recor^d^ pr Mee Sam^ll^ Stewart Town Clark

Jonathan Nickerson Son of Jonathan & Jane Nickerson was born Junery ye 14 1723/4

Simeon Nickerson Son of Jonthan & Jean Nickerson was born In Aprel ye 10 anod 1727 theis Reckar Mad In Juen ye 4 anodmi 1727 pr Me Th^o^ Nickson Clark

Zipporah young ye daughter of John young and dinah young was born ye fift day of August 1730

[p. 17] Easther Smith ye Daughter of Dean : & Esther Smith Was Born y^{e} : 6 : th Day of July Anodomini 1721 Recor^{d} pr Me Sam^{ll} Stewart Town Clark

Mary hamultun the daughter of Samuel and bethiah hammeltun was born ye 4 day of march 1728

Sarah hamultun the daughter Samuell and bethiah hamultun was born ye 7 day of aprill 1730

Micheall hamulltun the son of Samuel and bethiah hamulltun was born y^{e} 30th day of aprill 1732

Mehetabel hamultun the daughter of Samuel and bethiah hamultun was born y^{e} 5 of desember 1735

Elkanah Nickerson Son of Robert & Rebekah Nickerson Was Born February y^{e} 14th 172$\frac{1}{2}$ Recorded P^{r} Me Sam^{ll} Stewart . Town Clark

[p. 18] Kezia Tucker the Daughter of Samuel & Hannah Tucker Was born November ano^{d} 1707 Recr^{d} p^{r} Me Sam^{ll} Stewart Clark

John Tuker y^{e} Son of Samuel & Hanah Tucker Born September : & Deceased September In y^{e} year 1709 Recor^{d} per Me Sam^{ll} Stewart Clark

Thankfull Tucker ye Daughter of Sam^{ll} & Hanah Tucker born September : In ye Year 1710 Recor^{d} pr Me Sam^{ll} Stewart Town Clark

Elisabeth Tucker ye Daughter 'of Samuel & Hanah Tucker Born September Anodomini 1712 Record pr Me Sam^{ll} Stewart Clark

Hannah Tucker Y^{e} Daughter of Sam^{ll} & Hanah Tucker Wass born September anodomini 1714 Recor^{d} pr Me Sam^{ll} Stewart Clark

John Tucker y^{e} Son of Sam^{ll} Hanah Tucker was Born March y^{e} 20th & year 17$\frac{16}{15}$ Recor^{d} pr Me Sam^{ll} Stewart Clark

Samuel Tucker y^{e} Son of Samuel & Hanah Tucker Was born March y^{e} 16th 17$\frac{20}{19}$ * Reord pr Me Sam^{ll} Stewart Clark

Eunice . Tucker y^{e} Daughter of Sam^{ll} & Hanah Tucke[*worn*] Born : June y^{e} 12th anodomini 1722

these taken One Recor^{d} September Y^{e} 15th 1722 by Me Samuel Stewart town Clark

[p. 19] Jeams Mitchel y^{e} Son of William & Sarah Mitchel Was Born November ye 4th Anodomini 1718 Record pr Mee Sam^{ll} Stewart Cl

Tabitha Mitchell ye Daughter of William & Sarah Mitchell Was Born July y^{e} 19th 1720 Recor^{d} pr Mee Sam^{ll} Stewart Town Clark

Marcy Mitchel Y^{e} Daughter of William & Sarah Mitchel Was Born May y^{e} 4th 1722 Recorded pr Mee Sam^{ll} Stewart Town Clark

These Taken one Record September y^{e} 22^{d} 1722 By Me Samuel Stewart Town Clark

* Apparently altered from "17$\frac{18}{17}$."

William Mitchel ye Son of William and Sarah Mitchell was Born June ye 31d 1725

Thise taken one Rakeard May ye 2 1727 pr Me Thomas Nickeson Town Clark

Jun ye 7th 1733 then Thomas godfree * and bethiah was maried by Jestice done

october 1732 then henery willson and mary harding was married by Jestice freeman

may ye 31th 1733 then benjamen barce * and elizabth godfree was maried by Jestice doane

Jun ye 19th 1733 then Shuble baker * and ledia Stuard was married by Jestice doane

[p. 20] Joseph Thorp the Son of thomas & Mehetable Thorp Was Born aprell ye the 16th Day 1720 Recorded pr Mee Samll Stewart Clark

november 1 1733 then gearg godfree and marcy knowls ware ware maried by Jestice doane

June ye 19th 1733 then Shuble backer and lediah Stuard ware maried by Jestice doane

may ye 31 1733 then benjame barce and elizabeth godfree ware maried by Jestice doan

June ye 7th 1733 then Thomas godfree and bethiah eldreadg ware marid by Jestice doan

(*To be continued.*)

THE PURCHASERS OF DARTMOUTH.

Transcribed from the Original Records,

By George Ernest Bowman.

[Plymouth Colony Deeds, Vol. II, Pt. I, pp. 106, 107]

[p. 106] 1660: Prence Govr:

A writing appointed to bee Recorded as followeth

Att a generall meeting of the Purchasers att Plymouth the seaventh of march 1652 It was ordered and fully agreed unto and Concluded by the whole that all that Tract and tracts of lands lying from the Purchassers bounds on the west side of Acoughcusse to a river called Accusshaneck and three miles to the Eastwards of the same; with all Ilands meddows woods waters rivers Creekes and all appurtenances therunto belonging

* See duplicate record on next page of original.

Should bee given to those whose names are heerunder written Containing thirty four shares and was then given alloted Assigned and sett over to them by the whole to have and to hold to them and their heires and Assignes for ever; to Devide and Dispose of the same as they should see good; and they are to Satisfy the Indians for the Purchase therof and to beare all other Due Charges that shall any way arise about the same According to their severall proportions

Willam Bradford a moyety
Captaine Standish
Mr Collyare and Sarah Brewster
mr Aldin
mistris Warren
Robert Bartlett
John ffaunce
Manasses Kemton
Gorge Morton
John Dunham
Willam Palmer
Thomas Morton
Edward holman
mistris Jeney
Joshua Pratt

Mr hickes
Tho: Southworth
James hurst
Edward Doty
John Shaw
ffrancis Cooke
John Cooke
Samuell Cutbert
John Crackston;
Stephen Tracye
ffrancis Sprague
henery Sampson
Peter Browne *
Constant Southworth
Gorge Soule

Phillip Delanoy
Moses Simons
Edward Bumpas
ffrancis Eaton;

The one halfe of John Crackstones land which was mr Willam Bradford senir: his land was pased over by the said Willam Bradford to mr John howland

Wheras these Purchasers whoe by agreement of the whole had theire proportions of Purchase land falling unto them in the places above mencioned whoe by agreement had theire severall names entered into a list (together with some other old Comers) under the hand of the honored Govr: late Deceased they Did Desire that the list of theire Names might bee recorded; but the above written originall list of Names and the agreement Could not bee found in some yeares; soe that it was Judged lost These purchasers notwithstanding still Desiring that what was theire right might bee recorded; wherupon order was given by the aforsaid Govr that it might bee Done; in which record for want of the originall list; the Names of some are entered Contrary to the originall graunt and agreement of the Purchasers. as appeers by it; and alsoe by Divers other purchasers as well as themselves; which is an occation of some Difference alreddy; and may bee of more; Therfore it is ordered by the Generall Court held att Plymouth the 8th of June 1660: that the abovesaid originall List should bee entered and the other to stand in the booke not Defaced but to bee void null and of none effect

* A careful study of the Dartmouth records and the Plymouth Colony Deeds shows that this grant was not made to a living Peter Brown, but to the heirs of "Peter Browne deceased."

[p. 107] 1654

The names of those whoe by order of the Purchasers mett att Plymouth the seaventh Day of march 1652 whoe by Joynt consent and agreement of the said purchasers are to have theire prtes shares or proportions att the place or places commonly called and knowne by the names of Acushena alias acquessent which entereth in att the westeren end of Neckatay and to Coaksett alias acoakius and places adjacent; the bounds of which Tract fully to extend 3 miles to the Eastward of the most Easterly prte of the river or Bay called Acushena aforsaid; and soe alonge the seaside to the river called Coaksett; lying on the west side of point p^r^ill and to the most westermost side of any branch of the aforsd river and to extend eight miles into the woods; The said Tract or tract[s] of Land soe bounded as abovesaid which is purchased of the Indians which were the right propriators therof; as appeers by a Deed under theire hands with all the mershes meddows rivers waters woods Timbers; and all other profitts privilidges emunities comodities and appurtenances belonging to the said Tract or Tracts above expressed or any prte or prcell therof to belonge unto the prties whose names are underwritten (whoe are in number thirty four whole prtes or shares and noe more) to them and their heires and assignes for ever;

Mr Willam Bradford one whole prte or share
capt: Standish one whole prte or share
Mr John Alden one whole prte or share
Mr Collyar and Sarah Brewster one whole prte or share
M^r^ howland and Willam Bassett one whole prte or share
Gorge Morton one whole prte or share
Mannasses Kemton one whole share
James hurst one whole share
John Dunham seni^r^ one whole share
John Shaw seni^r^ one whole share
ffrancis Cooke one whole share
John Cooke one whole share
Joshua Pratt one whole share
Gorge Soule one whole share
Constant Southworth one whole share
Thomas Southworth one whole share
Mis Jenings one whole share
Steven Tracye one whole share
John ffaunce one whole share
henery Sampson one whole share
Phillip Delanoy one whole share

Mis Warren one whole share
Robert Bartlett one whole share
Willam Palmer one whole share
Edward Dotye one whole share
Samuell hickes one whole share
Peeter Browne * one whole share
ffrancis Sprague one whole share
Moses Simons one whole share
Samuell Eaton one whole share
Thomas Morton one whole share
Samuell Cutbert one whole share
Edward holman one whole share
Edward Bumpase one whole share
In all thirty foure prtes or shares

YARMOUTH, MASS., VITAL RECORDS.

(*Continued from Vol. III, page 249.*)

[p. 16] A Regester of the Bearths and the name of [*worn*] of Zachryah and Beathiah paddock Juner : of y[*worn*]

Icobod : paddock the son of the above said za[*worn*] Beathiah : was Borne upon the fierst day of June : 16[*worn*]

Deborah paddock the daughtuer : of the above said [*worn*] and Beathiah paddock was Borne upon the second d[*worn*] Aprell 168[*worn*]

Elesabeth : paddock the daughtuer of the above said Zachryah and Beathiah was Borne upon the eleventh d[ay] of feburary : in the year of our lord 1690 :

Zachryah : paddock the son of the above said : Zachryah and Beathiah : was Borne upon the tenth daye of Novmbr : 16[*worn*]

James paddock the son of the said Zachryah and Beathi[ah] was Borne upon the : 24 : day of desember 1694

peter : paddock ye son of Zhachryah & Bethiah padd[ock] was Borne : in may ye : 27th : in ye year : 1697 :

Bethiah : paddock ye daughtur of ye said Zachryah & [*worn*] was Borne upon ye : 25th : day of may : in ye : year : 1699

Marey : paddock daugtuer of Zachryah & Bethia[h] as above, was Borne upon ye : 10th : day of July : 1701

John Paddock Son of the above Said Zacharyah and Bethyah pa[*worn*] was borne the 21st day of May in the yeare : 1703 :

* See foot-note on page 186.

daved paddock son of the above s[d] Zacharyah and Bethyah paddock was borne the 12 day of august : in the year of our lord : 170[*worn*]

Presillah paddock (daughter of the above said Zachariah and Bethyah Paddock) She was born on the : 29th day of february in the yeare : 170$\frac{8}{9}$

hanah Paddok daughter of Zachariah and Mary paddok she was born aboute the Middle of august in the year : 1709 :

anthony Paddok son of the above s[d] Zachariah & mary paddok : he was born on the fifth day of febuary : 17$\frac{10}{11}$

Charity peese the daughter of Mathew peese and hanah Marchant She was borne the 9 day of december in the yeare : 1696

tabatha leuies the daughter of hanah Marchant Shee was borne the 13 day of march in the yeare of our lord : 1703

(*To be continued.*)

REPORTS FROM STATE SOCIETIES.

MASSACHUSETTS SOCIETY.

THE thirtieth meeting of the Massachusetts Society was held at the Hotel Vendome, Boston, on Thursday afternoon, April 10, 1902.

Mr. John Howland Crandon read a paper on "Colonial and Revolutionary Social Life," and several songs were given by Mr. George Edmund Dwight. The usual informal reception followed. One hundred and eighty-nine members and guests were present.

The committee appointed to solicit contributions from the members for the John Robinson Memorial Church at Gainsborough, England, has collected the sum of one hundred and fifty-four dollars and fifty cents. This amount, with the appropriation by the Society, making a total of two hundred and four dollars and fifty cents ($204.50), has been forwarded to Rev. Samuel B. Forbes of Hartford, Conn., Treasurer of the National Council of Congregational Churches.

Contributions were received from: Mrs. Charles W. Abbott, George A. Alden, Rev. Frederick B. Allen, Mrs. Edward Anthony, Jr., L. Dow Baker, Mrs. Joshua Bates, Mrs. Alonzo B. Bray, Mrs. Charles R. Brayton, L. Loring Brooks, Charles A. Burditt, Miss Antoinette Clapp, Arthur W. Clapp, Mrs. Alexander Cochrane, Miss Sarah H. Crocker, Miss Maria S. Daniels, George A. Dary, Edwin A. DeWolf, William C. Donnell, Charles A. Dunham, Miss Edith Eliot, Miss Kate G. Field, Mrs. Charles H. Fisher, Mrs. William H. Friend, Sidney B. Gifford, Mrs. George S. Hale, Mrs. William P. Hammond, Hon. John F. Hill, Charles A. Hopkins. Harry M. Howard, Mrs. Jacob R. Huntington, Herbert Jenney, Edward King, Mrs. William S. Kyle, Mrs. William Lawrie, George H. Leonard, Miss Mary J. O. McAdoo, Mrs. James McKay, Sr., "A Member," Mrs. William Mixter, Mrs. Frank Moseley, Willard A. Nichols, David W.

Noyes, James Atkins Noyes, Edward L. Parker, Mrs. George W. Percy, Miss Frances A. Plimpton, Mrs. Henry R. Plimpton, 2d., V. C. Pond, D.M.D., "A Member," Mrs. George H. Quincy, Mrs. Henry E. Raymond, Daniel C. Remich, Mrs. John M. Rice, George E. Richardson, Mrs. George E. Richardson, Miss Mary Rivers, H. Curtis Rowley, Warren C. Rowley, Stephen D. Salmon, Henry S. Shaw, Miss Harriet A. Shaw, Mrs. James E. Shepard, Mrs. Henry M. Smith, Miss Marion A. Smith, Mrs. Samuel F. Smith, George H. Stevens, Franklin N. Thatcher, Rev. Rufus B. Tobey, Mrs. Francis E. Trafton, Edward A. Trowbridge, Mrs. Joseph H. Tyler, Mrs. Joel C. Walter, Francis A. Ware, Andrew G. Weeks, Mrs. Henry W. Wilkinson, Mrs. Horace P. Williams, Mrs. Chalmers M. Williamson.

Donations to the Library.

"Annual Report of the Registry Department of the City of Boston, 1900," from the Registrar, Mr. Edward Webster McGlenen.

"Supplement No. 2 to Members and Ascendants of the Massachusetts Society of Colonial Dames of America," from Mrs. Francis P. Sprague.

"The New Haven and Wallingford (Conn.) Johnsons," "The New Haven (Conn.) Potters" and "John Whitehead, of New Haven and Branford, Conn.," all three from the compiler, Mr. James Shepard.

"An Address by Rev. Robert F. Coyle, D.D., to the Society of Colonial Wars" (In Colorado), from the Society.

"Raymond, New Hampshire, Fifty Years Ago," from the author, Mr. David Henry Brown.

"The First Church in Plymouth, 1606–1901," from Mrs. William S. Kyle.

Thacher's "History of the Town of Plymouth," one copy each of the first edition, 1832, and the second edition, 1835, from Mr. Edwin S. Crandon.

"The Indian Sagamore Samoset" and "The Topographical Terms Interval and Intervale," both from the author, Mr. Albert Matthews.

"History of Marshfield," 1901, from the compiler, Mr. Lysander S. Richards.

"General Society, Daughters of the Revolution, Address Book, 1898," from Mrs. Leslie C. Wead.

Members Elected.

April 25, 1902.

711. Mrs. Edward Aspinwall, Sharon, ninth from John Alden.
712. Alvin A. Vinal, Norwell, tenth from William Brewster.
713. Miss Katharine Kendall Davis, Boston, eighth from William Brewster.

May 28, 1902.

714. Mrs. William Badger Lawrence, Medford, tenth from William Brewster.
715. Arthur Ellsworth Linnell, Wollaston, eleventh from William Brewster.
716. Lucian Bisbee Thompson, Boston, seventh from Francis Cooke.
717. Joseph Walter Ward, San Francisco, Cal., seventh from John Alden.

Supplemental Lines Filed.

April, 1902.

697. Joseph A. Bursley, ninth from Edward Fuller; ninth from John Howland (two lines); eighth from John Howland (four lines).

May, 1902.
635. Mrs. Edward H. Nichols, tenth from James Chilton, ninth from Mary Chilton.
705. Mrs. Edward L. Davis, eighth from Francis Cooke.
707. George B. Perkins, ninth from John Alden (three lines); tenth from John Billington, ninth from Francis Billington; tenth from William Brewster (two lines), ninth from Love Brewster; tenth from Peter Brown; tenth from Francis Cooke (two lines); tenth from Stephen Hopkins; ninth from Stephen Hopkins; ninth from George Soule (four lines); ninth from Myles Standish (three lines); tenth from Richard Warren (two lines).
709. Mrs. Charles B. Perkins, eighth from John Alden (two lines); ninth from John Billington, eighth from Francis Billington; ninth from Francis Cooke; ninth from Stephen Hopkins; eighth from Stephen Hopkins; eighth from George Soule (two lines); eighth from Myles Standish (two lines).

NEW YORK SOCIETY.

Members Elected.

January 2, 1902.
674. Mrs. Charles Henry Brown, Baltimore, Md., seventh from John Alden.
675. Mrs. Henry Oliver Ely, Binghamton, ninth from William White, eighth from Peregrine White.
676. Miss Helen Josephine Strickland, New York, eighth from Dr. Samuel Fuller.

April 2, 1902.
677. Henry A. Richmond, Buffalo, ninth from Thomas Rogers.
678. Mrs. Arthur William Austin, Buffalo, ninth from Francis Cooke, eighth from John Cooke.

May 5, 1902.
679. Edward Barnes, New York, eighth from William Bradford.
680. William Bardwell Burke, Rochester, eighth from John Howland.
681. Mrs. George W. Bowers, San Francisco, Cal., eighth from William Bradford.
682. Mrs. Charles Thompson Downes, New York, eighth from Myles Standish.

May 19, 1902.
683. Charles Miner Gorham, San Francisco, Cal., seventh from John Howland.
684. Miss Adèle Kneeland, New York, ninth from Edward Fuller.
685. Miss Marion Jane Terry, Brooklyn, ninth from Francis Cooke.

OHIO SOCIETY.

Members Elected.

April 1, 1902.
43. Mrs. Oscar William Kuhn, Cincinnati, ninth from William Bradford.

May 6, 1902.
44. Benjamin DeWolf Bartlett, Glendale, eighth from Richard Warren.

February 4, 1902.
45. Samuel Fosdick Jones, New York, N. Y., ninth from William Brewster.

DISTRICT OF COLUMBIA SOCIETY.

Member Elected.

January 14, 1902.
124. Mrs. Horace Benjamin Sarson, Omaha, Neb., eighth from William Brewster.

RHODE ISLAND SOCIETY.

Member Elected.

January 8, 1902.
29. Mrs. Walter Howland Manchester, Providence, tenth from Francis Cooke, ninth from John Cooke.

PILGRIM NOTES AND QUERIES.

Notes.

Finding New Mayflower Lines. Many of our readers are purchasing Ancestral Charts in order to get the benefit of the liberal offer made in our advertising pages. An excellent illustration of the importance of this offer to any one searching for Mayflower ancestry is furnished by the experience of the first person who sent in a chart for examination by the Editor. The sender supposed that he was a descendant of Mehitable Barrows, the second wife of Adam[3] Wright (*Hester*[2] *Cooke, Francis*[1]), and was greatly pleased when informed that his descent was from the first wife, Sarah[3] Soule (*John*[2], *George*[1]), giving him another Mayflower line.

The Editor's investigations among the original records have made him familiar with many lines of Mayflower descent hitherto unknown, and he has frequently been able to inform inquirers that they were descended from Mayflower passengers in lines which they had least suspected. Purchasers of charts on the terms stated in the advertisement will not only get the advantage of this familiarity with the original records, but will also have the satisfaction of knowing that they are helping along the work being done by the Massachusetts Society, since the entire proceeds are added to the Colonial Research Fund.

Colonial Research Fund. The following additional contributions to the $2000.00 fund have been received:

General Fund: L. Emery Holden, $100.00; Mrs. William Lawrie, $50.00; Charles J. North, $4.50; Edwin A. DeWolf, $2.00.

Bradford Fund: Mrs. Lindsay Fairfax, $100.00.

Previously acknowledged, $672.00; Total receipts to date, $928.50.

We are also informed that the New Jersey Society of Mayflower Descendants has voted to contribute $25.00 to this fund.

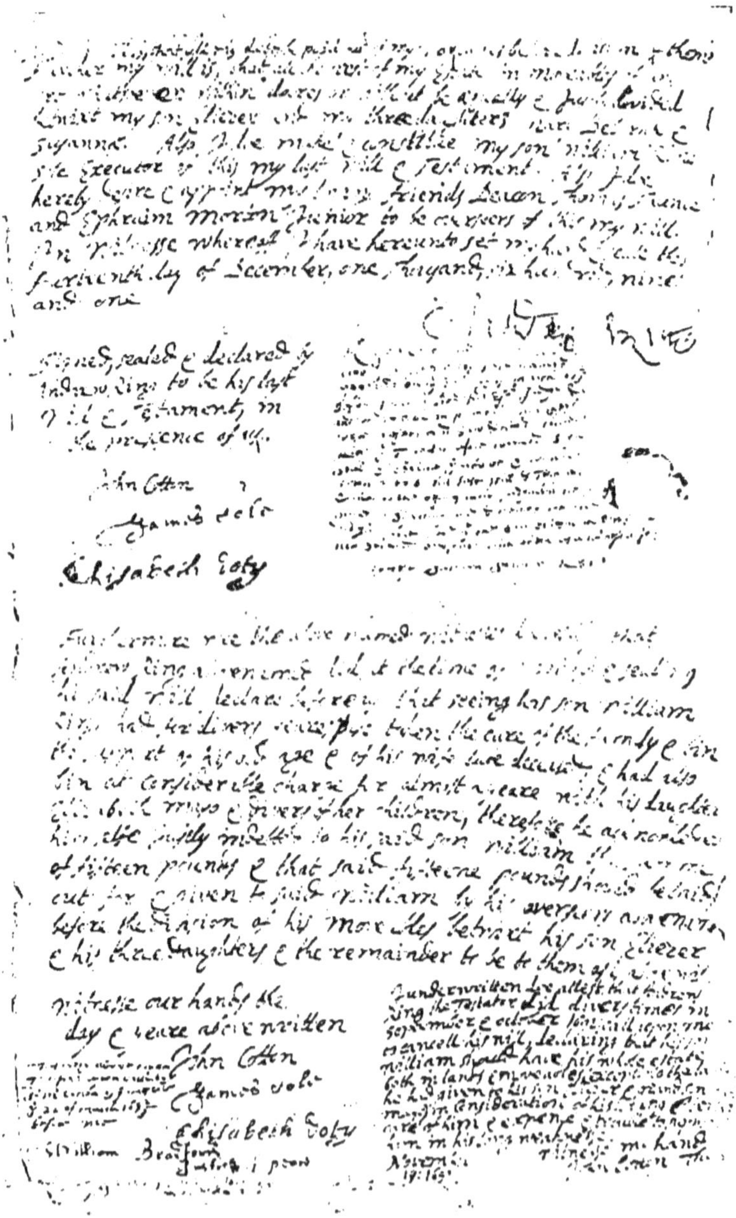

[illegible] my will is, that all the rest of my estate [illegible] shall be equally & justly divided betwixt my son Eleazer and my three daughters [illegible] Susanna. Also I the [illegible] make & ordaine my son William sole executor of this my last will & testament. Also I doe hereby desire & appoint my loving friends Deacon [illegible] and Ephraim Morton Junior to be overseers of this my will. In witnesse whereof I have hereunto set my hand & seale the [illegible] day of December, one thousand six hundred ninety and one

Signed, sealed & declared by Andrew Ringe to be his last will & testament, in the presence of us.

John Cotton
James Cole
Elizabeth Soty

Furthermore wee the above named witnesses testify that Andrew Ring [illegible] his said will declared [illegible] that seeing his son William Ring had [illegible] the care of the family [illegible] at considerable charge [illegible] with his daughter [illegible] & divers other children, therefore he [illegible] of fifteen pounds & that said fifteene pounds [illegible] given to said William by his overseers [illegible] before the division of his moveables betwixt his son Eliezer & his three daughters & the remainder to be to them as [illegible]

witnesse our hands the day & yeare above written
John Cotton
James Cole
Elizabeth Soty

William Bradford

ANDREW RING'S WILL

THE MAYFLOWER DESCENDANT

Vol. IV. OCTOBER, 1902. No. 4.

ANDREW RING'S WILL AND INVENTORY.

Literally Transcribed,

BY GEORGE ERNEST BOWMAN.

ANDREW RING's first wife was Deborah[2] Hopkins (*Stephen*[1]); his second was Lettice (——) Morton, widow of John[2] Morton (*George*[1]). He survived both wives, dying at Plymouth on Wednesday, 22 February, 1692/3. The Plymouth town records [Vol. I, p. 202] state that he died "22 of february 169¾", but this was an error of the town clerk, since the inventory was taken 18 March, 1692/3, and the will was probated 22 March, 1692/3. The Plymouth First Church records contain the following entries of the deaths of Andrew and Lettice Ring: "Andrew Ring dyed, february, 22: in his seventy fifth yeare." [Vol. I, Pt. V, p. 26, under year 1692]. "Lettice, the (second) wife of Andrew Ring, February, 22: about 66 yeares of age." [Vol. I, Pt. V, p. 20, under year 1690].

Andrew Ring's will is now in possession of the Connecticut Historical Society, at Hartford, Conn. They have had it for many years and do not know from whom they received it. Permission to photograph it was secured through the courtesy of their Librarian, Mr. Albert Carlos Bates.

The will is written on the first two pages of a four-page folio, seven and five-eighths by eleven and seven-eighths inches in size, and is very little worn. It is in the handwriting of the Rev. John Cotton of Plymouth. Our illustration shows the second page with the unusual number of ten autograph signatures, one of Andrew Ring, three of Rev. John Cotton, two of James Cole, two of Elizabeth Doty,* one of Major William Bradford and one of Samuel Sprague, the Register of Probate.

* Daughter of Jacob[2] Cooke (*Francis*[1]) and first wife of John[2] Doty (*Edward*[1]).

The third page contains two more signatures of Bradford and two more of Sprague.

The will and inventory are recorded in the Plymouth County Probate Records [Vol. I, pp. 163–165], but the record does not contain either the supplementary statement signed by the three witnesses or that signed by John Cotton alone.

The copy of the will here presented was made from the original document; the copy of the inventory was made from the probate record as the original has disappeared from the files.

The last will & Testament of Andrew Ring of Plimouth

I Andrew Ring being now stricken in yeares & weake in body, but of disposing minde & memory, not knowing how neere the day of my death may be, doe make this my last will & Testament hereby revoking all former wills.

Imprimis, I bequeath my soule into the hands of God who made it, & my body to the earth by decent buriall in hopes of a Joyfull Resurrection to eternall life by the merits of Jesus Christ my only Lord & Redeemer.

And as for the worldly estate which God hath given me, my will is, it be disposed of as followeth; I give to my Elder son william, my now dwelling house & the land & housing adjoyning thereunto, excepting that portion I have taken out of it to give to my son Eliezer as hereafter expressed; Also I give to my son william my twelve acres of upland lying in the New-feilds, & five acres lying at lout-swamp both within the township of Plimouth; Also to my son william I give foure acres of meadow lying at Southers marsh at the East end of the Cedar swamp, and three acres of meadow in the Cove, and two acres of meadow at the oake, and one acre of meadow at Dotey's meadows, all which meadows are within the township of Plimouth; Also I give to my son william one hundred acres of upland & eight acres of meadow which I have lying within the towneship of Midlebury, All the abovementioned lands, whether uplands or meadows, lying & being either in the towne of Plimouth or Midlebury, I doe hereby freely & absolutely give & bequeath to my said son william, his heires & Assignes for ever. Also to my son william, I give my plow & plowirons, all the iron worke in the cart, Horse-geares, chaine, couples, staple of the coppy-oake, working tooles, Augurs, gouges, spade, handsaw, axes, Hoe, hammer & such like. Also to my son william I give all the corne & provision laid in for the yeare.

Moreover, I give to my son Eliezer, that portion of land adjoyning to his house containing about the third part of an acre, and two acres of upland & swamp lying neere thereunto; Also I give to my son Eliezer foure acres of meadow lying at Pollapody-cove; Also I give to my son Eliezer, my twenty acre lott of upland, and my five & twenty acre lott of upland lying in the Towneship of Midlebury, This homestead now exprest & the lands, uplands & meadows in the townships either of Plimouth or Midlebury, I doe hereby freely & [a]bsolutely give & bequeath to my said son Eliezer, his heires & assignes for ever. Also I give my land at Midlebury, commonly called & knowne by the name of the sixteene-shillings purchase to my Grand-son John Mayo, son to my daughter Elizabeth Mayo late of Eastham, deceased, my will further is, that in case said John Mayo dye before he come of age or without lawfull issue, that then said land or the value of it be given to his surviving sisters, the daughters of my said daughter Elizabeth Mayo, by my Executor hereafter named. Also I give my cow, commonly called, short bob-taile cow to my Grand-son Andrew Ring son of my son Eliezer. Also I give my Heifer to my grand-daughter Mary Morton, daughter of my daughter Mary Morton. Also my will is, that all my debts be paid out of my moveables before division of them. Further my will is, that all the rest of my Estate in Moveables of any sort whatsoever within doores or without be equally & Justly divided betwixt my son Eliezer and my three daughters Mary, Deborah & Susanna. Also I doe make & constitue my son william Ring sole Executor of this my last will & Testament. Also I doe hereby desire & appoint my loving friends Deacon Thomas Faunce and Ephraim Morton Junior to be overseers of this my will.

In witnesse whereoff I have hereunto set my hand & seale this fourteenth day of December, one Thousand, six hundred, ninety and one Andrew Ring

(*seal*)

Signed, sealed & declared
by Andrew Ring to be his
last will & Testament, in
the presence of us.

John Cotton
James Cole
Elisabeth doty

Mr John Cotton and James Cole two of y^e Wittnesses here named appeared on y^e 22th day of march $169\frac{2}{3}$ Before William Bradford Esqr Judge &c and made oath in plimouth that they were present and Saw & heard Andrew Ring ye Testator afore named Sign Seal & declare ye above & within written to be his last Will & Testament & that to the best of their judgment he was of Sound & Disposing mind & memory when he did ye same And yt they saw Elizabeth Dotey now Deceased Subscribe with them as a witness also;

Attest Samuel Sprague Register

Furthermore wee the above named witnesses doe testify, that Andrew Ring abovenamed did at the time of signing & sealing his said will declare before us, that seeing his son william Ring had for divers yeares past taken the care of the family & bin the support of his old age & of his wife late deceased, & had also bin at considerable charge for almost a yeare with his daughter Elizabeth Mayo & divers of her children, therefore he acknowledged himselfe Justly indebted to his said son william the summe of fifteen pounds & that said fifteene pounds should be laid out for & given to said william by his overseers abovename[d] before the division of his moveables betwixt his son Eliezer & his three daughters, & the remainder to be to them as is above willed,

witnesse our hands the
day & yeare above written

John Cotton
James Cole
Elisabeth doty

This next above written Testified upon oath by sd mr Cotton & James Cole ye 22 of march 169$\frac{2}{3}$ before me

William Bradford
Justice of peace

I underwritten doe attest, that Andrew Ring the Testator did divers times in September & october 1692: call upon me to cancell his will, declaring that his son william should have his whole estate both in lands & moveables (excepting the lands he had given to his son Eliezer & grand son John Mayo) in Consideration of his loving & tender care of him & expence & trouble to support him in his long weaknesse:

November 19 1692: witnesse my hand
John Cotton

This Sworne to pr sd mr Cotton 22d of march 169$\frac{2}{3}$

Before me William Bradford
Justice of peace

William Bradford Esqr Commissionated By his Excellency Sr William Phips Knt Captain Generall and Governr in Chief in and over their Majesties Province of y^{e} Massachusets Bay in New England with the advice & consent of y^{e} Councill for y^{e} Granting probate of Wills & Letters of Administration within y^{e} county of plimouth &c.

To all to whome these presents shall come or may concern Greeting

Know yee that before me at plimouth on y^{e} 22th day of march 169$\frac{2}{3}$ The Will of Andrew Ring Late of plimouth aforesaid to these presents annexed Was proved approved and allowed who having while he lived and at the [tim]e of his Death Goods Chattells Rights & Credits. Y^{e} said Deceased and his Will in any maner concerning was Committed unto his Son William Ring Executor in ye Same Will named well & truly to Administer ye same And to make a true & perfect Inventory of all and Singular ye Goods Chattels Rights & Credits of ye said deceased and the same to Exhibit into ye Registers office of ye said County according to law also to Render a true and Plain account of his said Administration upon oath. In Testimony whereof I have hereunto set my hand and the seal of ye said office

(*Seal*) William Bradford

Saml Sprague Register

The Within Written Will & Probate annexed are Recorded in y^{e} 163^{d} & 164th pages of Plimouth Counties Book of Wils & Inventories:

p^{r} S : Sprague Regis^{tr}

[Plym. Co. Prob. Rcds., I: 164]

An Inventory of y^{e} estate of Andrew Ring late of Plimouth deceased Taken & apprised by us whose names are hereunto Subscribed on y^{e} 18th day of March 169$\frac{2}{3}$.

Imp^{r}: In his Wearing Apparrell both linnen and Woollen	..2	14	.
I^{t} In Books	...	.6	.
Item In Beds and Bedding & Table linnen	.11	..	.
Item In New Cloth and yarn and Hemp	...	14	.
Item In Pewter and Brass	..3	.2	6
Item In jron Pot Kettle and Pothooks & hakes & Tongs	...	10	.
Item In jron Tacklin belonging to Plow & Cart and other old jron an Iron tooles	..2	10	.
Item in Earthen vessels & Glass Bottles	...	.6	6
Item In Tables Chist Boxes Wooden vessels chairs	..1	10	.
Item in three Cows and two sucking Calves	..6	10	.
more in one heiffer one steer & two young Cattel	..5	.5	.
Item In meal Baggs	...	.6	.

Item in Debts Due to ye Estate	...	.5	.
to a Morticing ax and Spitt & some cloth and a Sythe	...	12	.
The estate Indebted			
for funerall charges & monies disbursed for Attendance	..7	.6	9
More for Dyeting Nurses	..4	12	.
More in Dyet & my attendance & wintering Cattel	..9	..	.
And I have Received of my fathers money	..5	10	.

Ephraim Morton jun^{r}
Thomas ffaunce

William Ring ye executor of ye last Will & Testament of his late father Andrew Ring deceased made oath Before William Bradford Esqr in Plimouth ye 4th day of Aprill 1693 that ye above written is a true Inventory of ye estate vizt goods & chattels of sd deceased So far as he knoweth and that if more shall Come to his knowledge he will discover it

Attest Saml Sprague Register

CHATHAM, MASS., VITAL RECORDS.

(*Continued from page 185.*)

[p. 21] Thomas : Nickerson Son of Thomas & Mary Nickerson was born December ye 24 1696 p^{r} Record^{d} Sam^{ll} Stewart Cl

Ledea : Covil ye Daughter of Joseph & Ledea Covel was born ye 12th of July 1701 Record^{d} p^{r} Me Sam^{ll} Stewart C

Thomas Nickerson : & Ledea Covel was Married ye 16th of May 1716 p^{r} Joseph Doane Just of peace. Record pr me Sam^{ll} Stewart Clark

Desiar Nickerson ye Daughter of Thomas & Ledea Nickerson was born ye fifth Day of february 1718

Thomas Nickerson y^{e} Son of Thomas & Ledea nickerson was born february y^{e} 28th 1720

Ledea : Nickerson y^{e} Daughter of thomas & Ledea Nickerson was born y^{e} 30th Day of March : 1722 & Deceased : one y^{e} 15th Day of August folowing In y^{e} s^{d} year 1722

all Taken one Record : y^{e} 18th Day of Janawary 172$\frac{2}{3}$ p^{r} Me Sam^{ll} Stewart town Clark

Ledea Nickerson y^{e} Daught of thom^{s} : Nickerson And Ledea Nickerson was born y^{e} 16 of fabary In the year of our Lord 1724 a tru Reckerd Mad by me thoms Nickerson Jur town Clark

Ansel : Nickerson Son of Th^{o} : & Ledea Nickerson was born y^{e} 2th Day of May 1727 This Rackerd Mad In Jun y^{e} 22 Day 1727 pr Me Thomas Nickerson Clark

prince Nickerson son of Th^{o} : Nickerson and Ledea Nickerson was born y^{e} 10 Day of augst anomi 1729 Reckord Made Apral y^{e} 27 = 1730 pr Me Th^{o} Nickerson Town Clark

[p. 22] Jeams Stewart : y^{e} Son of Joseph : & Mary Stewarart was born May y^{e} 9th 1722 Record p^{r} Samuel Stewart Clark
Mery Stewart y^{e} daughter of Joseph and Mery Stuart was born march y^{e} 26th 1724 Recortd p^{r} Daniel Sears Clark
Abigell Stewart ye daughter of Joseph and mary Stewar[*worn*] was born march y^{e} 15th 1726 Recorded p^{r} Daniel Sears Clar[*worn*]

[p. 23] Elisabeth Covel : y^{e} Daughter of : John & Thankfull Covill was Born July 9th 1722 Recorded pr Me Samuel Stewartt Clark

[p. 25] Ruth Collens the daughter of Joseph and Abgel Collens was born october the : 21 = 1739
Joseph Collens the Sun of Joseph and Abigel Collens was born november the = 5 = 1741
Benaiah Collens the Sun of Joseph and Abigel Collens was Borne october the : 29 = 1743
Stephen Collens the Sun of Joseph and Abigell Collens was Born october : the : 31 = 1745
This Record was mede June y^{e} 2 = 1746 Daniel Sears town Clark
Jerusha Nickson y^{e} daughter of willam and hannah nickrson was born november the 21 = 1739
Barzillai : Nickrson y^{e} Sune of willam and hannah nickrson was born march y^{e} 8 = 1743
Jonathan Nickrson y^{e} Sun of willam and hannah nickrson was Born aprel y^{e} 13 — 1747

[p. 26] Jenewery y^{e} 28 : 1741 Then Elisabeth Ray and hur two Children was worned to depart y^{e} town by Ebenezer Nickrson Constubel = per mee Daniel Sears Clark
Samuel Crowel Sun of Jonathan and Anne Crowel was Born march y^{e} 16 = 174^{3}_{2} Entred by Daniel Sears Cla[*worn*]

[p. 33] Marcy Cohoon : y^{e} Daughter of William & Sarah Cohoon Was Born May : y^{e} 7th : 1757
Sarah Cohoone : y^{e} Daughter of William & Sarah Cohoon Was Born : March 4th 1719/20
Jeams Cohoon : y^{e} Son of William & Sarah Cohoon Was Born : May y^{e} 8th : 1721
this taken one Recor^{d} : March 20th 1722/3 pr Me Sam^{ll} Stewart Clark
Hannah Collens y^{e} Daughter of Solomon and Eunes Collens was Born June y^{e} 5 = 1728

Ruben Collens ye Sun of Solomon and Eunes Collens was Born June ye 10 — 1730

Enock Collens ye Sone of Solomon and Eunes Collens was Born desember ye 2 = 1731

Asuba Collens ye daughter of Solomon and Eunes Collens was Borne June ye 10 = 1733

Cyrranas Collens ye Sone of Solomon and Eunes Collens was Born June ye 26 = 1735

Solomon Collens ye Sone of Solomon and Eunes Collens was Born march ye 23 = 1737[8]

Eunes Collens ye daughter of Solomon and Eunes Collens was Born June ye : 23 = 1742

This taken one Record febwery ye 8 : 1743 pr mee Daniel Sears town Clark

[p. 34] Rebekah Hamelton ye Daughter of Thomas : & Rebekah Hamelton was Born November ye 21.st : anodomini 1720

Nathaniel Hamelton ye Son of Thomas & Rebekah Hamelton was Born August ye 23d anodomini 1722 Put one Reccord pr me Samll Stuart Clark

Simeon rider the Son of John and mehetable rider was born aprill ye 4th 1720

Mehitable rider the daughter of John and Mehitable rider was born Jenuary ye 27—1724[5]

Zenus rider ye son of John and mehitable rider was born aprill ye 27 -- 1726

bethiah rider ye daughter of John and mehitabl rider was born september ye 11th 1728

asaph smith the son of dean and ester smith was born february the 18th 1728 -- 9

Grace Hamelton ye daughter of Thomos and Rebak Hamelton was Born July ye 24 = 1724

Lidia Hamelton ye daughter of Thomos and Rebak Hamelton was born aprel ye 24 = 1726

Jane Hamelton ye daughter of Thomos and Rebak Hamelton was born aprel ye 19 = 1728

Zeruiah Hamelton ye daughter of Thomos and Rebak Hamelton was born aprel ye 27 = 1731

Delilah Hamelton ye daughter of Thomos and Rebak Hamelton was born June ye 28 : 1734

Thomos Hamelton ye son of Thomos and Rebak Hameltone wase born september ye 14 1739

[p. 35] Meary Hopkens ye daughter of Elisha and Experans Hopkins was born March ye 12 = 1726 pr mee Daniel Sears Clark

Daved Howes The sune of Thomoes and Rebakah Howes was born may : ye : 9 = 1736

Thomos Howes the sune of Thomos and Rebakah Howes was born october : y^{e} : 31 = 1738
Richard Howes the sune of Thomos and Rebakah Howes was born april : y^{e} : 14 = 1742
Desier Atkens y^{e} daughter of Joshue and Sarah atkens was Born march y^{e} 10 — $1734^{\underline{5}}$
John Atkens y^{e} sone of Joshue and Sarah atkines was Born march y^{e} 7 : $1736^{\underline{7}}$
Susana atkens y^{e} daughter of Joshue and Sarah atkens was borne march y^{e} 6 = $1738^{\underline{9}}$
Sarah atkens y^{e} daughter of Joshue and Sarah atkens was born June y^{e} 28 = 1742
Samuel Crowel y^{e} Sun of Johnathan and ann Crowel was Born march y^{e} 16 = $1742^{\underline{3}}$
Bethia Atwod y^{e} daughter of Joseph and Deborah atwod was born febwery y^{e} 3 = $1743^{\underline{4}}$
Rebakah Crowil the daughter of Paul and Rebakah Crowel was born october the 18 = 1742
Paul Crowel y^{e} sun of Paul and Rebakh Crowel was born march the 18 = $174\frac{4}{5}$

[p. 42] Elizabeth adams the daughter of m^{r} hugh and Susanah adams was born y^{e} the 5 day of may 1713
temperence Stuard the daughter of Joseph and mary Stuard was born the 15 of march 1713

[p. 47] Darkos Done the daughter of Joseph and Darkos Done was Born : november the 2 = 1741
Joseph Done the sune of Joseph and Darkos Done was Born febwery the 10 = 1744
Hannah Done the daughter of Joseph and Darkos Done was Born october the : 29 = 1745
Ruth Done the daughter of Joseph and Darkos Done was Born march the = 25 = 1748

[p. 55] Rebekeh Sears y^{e} daughter of Daniel and Sarah Sears was born march y^{e} = 19 = 1710
Daniel Sears y^{e} sone of Daniel & Sarah Sears was born June the furst day = 1712
Sarah Sears y^{e} daughter of Daniel and Sarah Sears was born the 11 day of aprel = 1714
Marcy Sears y^{e} daughter of Daniel and Sarah Sears was born iuly the 17 = 1716
Richard Sears y^{e} son of Daniel and Sarah Sears was born aprel the 26 = 1718
Daved Sears y^{e} sone of Daniel and Sarah Sears was born aprel the 21 = 1720

Dabrah Sears ye daughter of Daniel and Sarah Sears was born october the 13 = 1722

John young the son of John and dinah young was born ye second day : of July 1733

Elisebeth Kendrick ye daughter of Soloman Kendrick and Elisibeth Kindrick was born august ye 29 = 1736

(*To be continued.*)

THE WILL AND INVENTORY OF JOHN BASS AND THE PETITION AGAINST THE APPROVAL OF THE WILL.

Transcribed from the Original Documents,

By George Ernest Bowman.

John Bass made his will 25 June, 1716, and died at Braintree, Mass., 12 September, 1716, having survived his wife Ruth[2] Alden (*John*[1]) nearly forty-two years. His will and inventory are recorded in the Suffolk County Probate Records at Boston,* and the original documents from which our copies were made, are still in the files.† With the will and inventory is preserved a petition from the testator's son, John Bass, and his son-in-law, Ephraim Thayer, praying that the will be not allowed on account of the undue influence of another son, John Bass, Jr., and his family. This petition, signed by Joseph Bass only, was presented 22 October, 1716. Since the will was allowed on that date and the petition was not entered on the probate records and no record of any appeal to a higher court can be found, it is evident that the dissatisfied heirs decided to drop the matter.

In the name of God, amen. The Twenty fifth Day of June Anno: Dom one thousand Seven Hundred & Sixteen, I, John Bass of Braintry, in the County of Suffolk, in New England, Wheel-wright, being of perfect minde and Memory, thanks be given unto God therefor; calling to mind the Mortality of my body, and knowing that it is appointed for Men once to dye, Do make and ordaine this my Last will and Testa[ment] That is to Say, Principally, and first of all, I give and recomen[d] my Soul into the Hands of God that gave it, hoping through the

* Vol. XIX, pp. 202, 203, 270. † Docket 3785.

merits, Death & Passion of my Saviour Jesus-Christ to have full and free Pardon and forgiveness of all my Sins, and to Inherit Everlasting Everlasting life; and my body I commit to the Earth to be decently buried at the Discretion of my Executor hereafter named; nothing doubting but at the General Resurrection I Shall Receive the Same againe by the mighty Power of God. And now for the Settleing the Temporal Estate wherewith It hath pleased God to bless me far above my deserts, I do order, give, and dispose the Same in manner and forme foll[ow]ing: (That is to Say) First I Will that all those Debts & duties as I owe in Right or conscience to any Person or Persons whatsoever, shall be well and truly contented, and paid, or ordained to be paid in convenient time, after my Decease, by my Executor Hereafter named.

Item, I Give and bequeath to my well beloved Son John Bass (whom I likewise constitute, make, and Ordaine my only & Sole Executor of this my last Will and Testament) that Piece of Land called the Calf-Pasture being about an acre, to him, his Heirs and assigns forever: Further I Give to my Said Son John Bass all other, my Pasture-Land, Plough-Land, Meadow, Salt & Fresh, Wood Land and other Estate whatsoever, not hereafter in this my Last Will particularly mentioned, and disposed of, to be Improved by him duri[ng] his Natural life, and after his Decease to his Son John Bass his Heirs and assigns forever, Excepting that the Said John Bass Junr Should Dye without Legal Isue, in which case my will is that it pass to the next Heir; also my Will is that the Said John Bass Junr. should Improve Some part of the abovementioned Lands during his Father's life, at his Father's pleasure. And Further my will is that whatsoever I have heretofore given to my Said Son John Bass, which hath been in his Improvement, Shall be after his Decease Decease, for his Son Samuel & which I do herby confirm to the Said Samuel Bass, his Heirs and Assigns forever, Only Reserving a Liberty to my Son John Bass aforesaid to Will any part of what I have thus given him & his Sons, unto his Wife (in Case she outlives him) during her Natural life, not Exceeding a Fourth part thereof.

Item I Give and bequeath to my Son Samuel Bass all my Lands at Stand-brook, in Salters-Farme being part of the foure-Score Acres (so called) be it more or less: also half my Lands at Rye-Island, (the whole being Ten Acres) his part to be on the Northern Side thereof: also a Strap of Land in the House Lot, in Salters Farme near Two Acres, lying between what he bought of his brother Joseph, and Coll: Quincey's Land, on the East Side of the Cart-way. Also part of the Plain-Lot (so called) so far as he hath fenced, being the Eastermost End of the Said Lott, all which I give to him his Heirs and Assigns forever.

As to my Son Joseph Bass, I have already given him, his full part or portion out of my Estate, to which I here add five Shillings, to be paid by my Executor &c

I[te]m I give and bequeath to my Two Daughters, Mary Copeland, and Sarah Thayer, each of 'em, an acre (be it more or less) of Salt Meadow (which is already in their Improvement) during their Natural life, and after their Decease to my Son John Bass if Surviving, (otherwise to his Son John) He, (and in case of his Decease, his Son John) paying five Pounds money, to the Children of each of my Said Daughters, that is in all Ten Pounds, to be distributed among them equally, Immediately after their Mother's Decease or as they come of age; also I give to my Daughters aforesaid, Each of 'em, Ten Pounds, to be paid by my Executor, in convenient time after my Decease, also all my House-hold moveables to be equally divided between them.

Item I Give to all my Grand-Daughters, that are the Children of my Two Deceased Daughters, viz Ruth, and Hannah, Ten Shillings, A-piece, to be paid to Each of them by my Executor; in convenient Time after my Decease, to Such as are of age, and the Rest as they come to age.

Item I Give to my Grandson John Bass, that Spott of Ground on which he hath Erected his Dwelling-House: And further, one half of my Barn, and Yard thereto belonging; and the other half of the Barn & yard afores^d^, I Give to his Brother Samuel Bass; these to be enjoyed by them, their Heirs & Assigns forever. and And I do hereby utterly disallow, Revoake and disannul all, and every other former Testaments, Wills, and Legacies, Bequests and Execut^rs^ by me in any ways before this Time named Willed & bequeathed, Ratifying and confirming this and no other to be my Last Will and Testament, In Wittness whereof I have hereunto Set my Hand & Seal, the Day & year abovewritten

Signed, Sealed, Published,
Pronounced and Declared — John Bass (Seal)
by the Said John Bass, as
his last Will and Testament
In the Presence of us the
Subscribers,
Susanna Webb
Jonathan Webb
Benjamin Webb

Suffolk Ss By the Honble Samuel Sewall Esqr Judge of Probate &c

The aforegoing will being presented for probate by John Bass the Executo^r^ therein named.

Susanna Webb Jonathan Webb and Benjamin Webb personally appearing made Oath that they Saw John Bass the Subscriber to the within Instrument Signe Seal and heard him publish and Declare the Same to be his last Will and Testament and that when he so did he was of sound disposeing mind and Memory According to their best discerning and that they Set to their names as wittnesses of the Execution thereof in the Said Testators presence

Boston Octob^r^: 22^d^ 1716 Samuel Sewall

Braintry November 21 : 1716

an Inventorey of the Esteate of John Bass sener Late of Braintry decst

	ll	*s*	*d*
to a Silver Cupp	3	01	00
to a hetchell wheele adds two chees fatts	00	06	06
two brass kittles & skilett	01	05	00
one Iron pott spitt tramill tongues & fire shovell & other small Iron things	00	15	00
to Severall Smale thing as hammer ax & saw	00	06	00
old Putter two platers two bassons & old puter pott	00	16	00
Earthen ware one platter two muggs	00	02	06
a long table form Cubberd box & needing trough: chorn	01	10	00
for old Lumber cheirs tubbs & pails Little table	01	04	00
for 3 old barrels . 4 . wooden dishes & . 9 . trenchers	00	06	00
three old cheests	00	06	00
a grate bible	00	06	00
a feather bead & bolster three coverleads beadstead & cord	07	15	00
his wearing cloaths	04	00	00
three shirts 3 napkins and a piiibear	01	06	00
two old baggs	00	03	00
an old Sword	00	05	00
two Cows	08	00	00
To Cash in the house	00	10	10
The land in the Pasture aboute 10 acres & half in the stoney field	55	00	00
14 acres of land in the Capt plaine	35	00	00
one Lott in the . 600 . acres	03	00	00
10 acres of upland in the farm at Ry Island	50	00	00
4 acres of land in the farm on the Island	10	00	00
2 acres & half of upland In the house lott	17	10	00
Seven acres of Salt marsh	70	00	00

one Share in the pine swamp 02 00 00

Solomon vezey
John Cleverly
Peter Adams

A Bill dated Janr 24 . 1696 . obliging Joseph Bass to pay Three pounds } £3 0 0

Febr. 11th. 1716. John Bass the executor made oath that the foregoing is a true & perfect Inventory of the estate of his Father John Bass lately deceased and that if more hereafter apear he will cause it to be added

Coram Samuel Sewall J. probate.

PETITION OF THE HEIRS.

Suffolk Ss: To the Honourable Samuel Sewall Esqr Judge of probate &ra:

Joseph Bass and Ephraim Thayer and other the Children of John Bass late of Braintry deced Humbly pray that the Will of their said late ffather may not be proved. For the following reasons

1 First because he was under great insanity of mind at makeing the Sd Will and Benjamin Webb one of the Witnesses to ye sd Will has declared that ye Testator acted Childish when he Executed the same.

2ly For that he was perswaded by his Son John Bass & wife to cutt off his Son Joseph by making this new will and being Stricken in years was much awed by his grandson John Bass.

3 For that the Testator in his life time Setled some part of his Estate by Deed upon his Son John And by his present will has given it to his Grandson Samuel Bass which Evidences that he was non Compos Mentis at the time of making ye said Will

4ly For that he has given his Wife but one forth part of his Estate when the Law of this province Sets forth one third to the widow.

5 For that there is a Legacy in the Said Will uncertain which is given to his Grandson John Basse's Son John when at the same time there is no Such person in being nor any probability that there will be at present

6 For that the Testator has given Legacys to the Daughters of his Children Ruth Webb and Hannah Adams both deced and has totally Excluded their Sons.

Boston Octor 22d 1716 Joseph Basse

HARWICH, MASS., VITAL RECORDS.

(*Continued from page 179.*)

[p. 41] Nicolas Snow and Lidea Shaw was Meryed April 4th : 1689

Jonathan son to sd Nicolas and Lidea snow was born January : 30th : 1691/2

Mark son to sd Nicolas and Lidea snow was born : April 30th 1695

Nathanael son to sd Nicolas and Lidea snow was born october : 16th : 1697

Joshua son to sd Nicolas and Lidea snow was born August 18th : 1700

Thankfull daughter to Nicolas and Lidea snow was born febuary . 7 . 1701/2

Sarah daughter to Nicolas and Lidea snow was born march . 20 . 1703/4

phebe daughter to Nicolas and Lidea snow was born November : 17 : 1705

Prence son to Nicolas and Lidea snow was born december . 26 . 1707

Richard Hopkins son to samuel and Lidea Hopkins was born November . 26 . 1707 :

Reliance Hopkins daughter to samuel and Lidea Hopkins was born November 17th : 1709

Lidea hopkins daughter to Samuell and Lidea hopkins was born In June The 1 day 1713

sarah hopkins daughter to samuell and Lidea hopkins was Born july 25 day 1717

susanna Hopkins daughter to Samuell and Lidea Hopkins was Born in July the 7 day 1719

moses hopkins hopkins son to samuell and lidea hopkins was Born in march 1721/2

Theodosius son to samuell and lidea hopkins was Born in ninth day of november 1726

Nathan hopkins son to samuell and Lidea hopkins was born in June the 16 day 1729

samuel Cole son to James and Hanah Cole was born decemb : 22 : 1695

Ruth Cole daughter to sd James and Hanah Cole was born : novemb 16 : 1698

Martha Cole daughter to sd James and hanah Cole was born July 1 : 1700

[p. 42] Stephen Merrick and Deborah Snow were Married on November 21th : 1706 :

Joshua Merrick son to stephen and Deborah merrick was born in April . 17th : 1708 :

snow myrick son to stephen and deborah myrick was born January the 15 day 1709/10

deborah myrick daughter to stephen and deborah myrick was born in June 20 day 1712

samuell myrick son to stephen and deborah myrick was born in January the 5 day 1714/15

Olever myrick son to stephen and Deborah myrick was born in december the 14 day 1716

Thomas myrick son to stephen and Deborah myrick was born in december the 12 day 1718

simmeon myrick son to stephen and Deborah myrick was born in April 1721

Jabez myrick son to stephen and Deborah myrick was born in february 1722/3

Jethro myrick son to stephen and Debroah myrick was born in Augst 1725

Relianc Hinckely daughter to Samuell and mary hinckely was born November 21 day 1714

seth Hinkly son to samuel and mary Hinkly was born decemb : 25 1707

shubel hinckley son to Samuell and mary hinckley was born march 15 : $170\frac{8}{9}$

samuell hinckley son to Samuell and mary hinckley was born In febuary 12 day 1710/11

mary hinckley daughter to Samuell and mary hinckley was born In febuary the 12 day 1710/11

mary hinckley daughter to Samuell and mary hinckley died in march : 1710/11

Edmond hinckley son to Samuell and mary hinckley was born November 20 day 1712

Judah Rogers son to Judah and Patience Rogers was born december 29th : 1704

mary rogers daughter to Judah and Patience rogers was born october : 1 : 1706

Patiance Rogers daughter to Judah and Patience Rogers was born November 9th : 1710

[p. 45] Keziah daughter to Eliezer and Patience Crosby was born may 15th : 1708

Rebekah daughter to Eliezer and Patience Crosby was born may : 12th : 1709 :

Elezer Crosby son to Elezer and Patience Crosby was born January 5th 1710/11

Silvanes Crosby son to Elezer and Patience Crosby was born November The 15 day 1712 :

Phebe Crosby daughter to Elezer and Patience Crosby was born in december the 18 day 1714

Sarah Crosby daughter to Elezer and Patience Crosby was Born in december the 8 day 1716

Isaac Crosby son to Elezer and Patance Crosby was Born in october 18 day 1719

Mary Crosby daughter to Elezer and patence Crosby was Born in November 28 day 1722

Sarah Crosby daughter to Elezer and patence Crosby was Born in in march the 18 day 1725/6

patence crosby daughter to Elezer and patence crosby was Born october the 29 day 1728

mehitabel Gray daughter to John and susana Gray was born The 7th day of April in the year 1706

Andrew Gray son to John and susana Gray was born 29th day of september : 1707 :

Anna Gray daughter to John and susana Gray was born in August . 31 . day in the year 1709

Elisha gray son John and susanah gray was born in november the 29 day 1711

Joshua gray son to John and susanah gray was born in october the 19 day 1713

Anna gray daughter to John and susanah gray was born in novembr the 30 day 1714

Ebenezer Nickerson son to william and Mary Nickerson was born : 13th : day of June : 1697

Jane Nickerson daughter to William and mary Nickerson was born . 6 . day Aprile : 1699 :

Mary Nickerson daughter to William and mary Nickerson was born august 13th : 1701 :

Thankfull Nickerson daughter to William and mary Nickerson was born July. 26th : 1705

[p. 49] Joseph Paine and Patience Sparrow were Married togather : May 27th 1691 :

Ebenezer Paine son to sd Joseph and Patience was born April The eighth : 1692 :

Hanah Paine daughter to the above sd Paine was born July fift . 1694.

Joseph Paine son to the above sd Paine was born March . 29th . 1697 :

Richard Paine son to The above sd Paine was born March 25th : 1699 :

dorcus Paine daughter to sd Paine was born may . 27th . 1701 :

Phebe Paine daughter to sd Paine was born July 30th 1703 :

Reliance Paine daughter to sd Joseph Paine was born January 27th : 1705/6

Thomas and mary paine son and daughter to Joseph and Patience Paine were born . december . 1th . 1708 :

Jonathan son to Joseph and Patience Paine was born december 10th 1710

Experan paine daughter to Joseph and patience paine was born in may 27 day 1713
John vincent and hanah seirs were married novemb 2^{d} : 1710 :
samuel seirs and Ruth mirrick were married Novemb : 2^{d} 1710 :
Abigail seirs daughter to samuel and Ruth seirs was born november 23^{d} 1711
marcy sears daughter to Samuell and Ruth seirs was born october 21^{d} : 1713
Ruth sears daughter to Samuell and Ruth sers was born july 4 : 1715
desire sears daughter to Samuell and Ruth sears was Born march 9 $171\frac{6}{7}$
Mary sears . daughter to samuell and Ruth sears was born in August the 9 day 1718

(*To be continued.*)

TWO BILLS OF SALE OF A NEGRO SLAVE.

THE following bills of sale of the negro slave London have been transcribed from the original document loaned by Mr. Everett I. Nye.

To all people to whome these presents Shall Come Greeting Know ye that I Ralph Smith of Eastham In the County of Barnstable in the province of the Massachusets Bay in New England yeoman Gardian to the orphins of John Mulford of Sd Eastham Deceased for and in Consideration of the Sum of fifty pounds passable money on Sd province to me In hand paid by Nath^{ll} ffreeman of Sd Eastham in the County and province above Sd Esqr. where of I Do here by acknowledge the receipt and my self there with fully and Intirely Satisfied and in the Capacity as above Sd Have borgained Sold Set over and Delivered and by these presents in plain and open Market acording to the Due form of law in that Case made and provided Do Bargain Set over and Deliver unto the Sd Nath^{ll} ffreeman London a Negro Man belonging to the Estate of the Sd mulford Deceased to gather with his wearing Cloaths the Sd London Negro man with his apparill to Have and to hold to the proper use and behoof to him the Sd Nath^{ll} ffreeman His Heirs Exec^{trs} Admi^{trs} and asigns for Ever. and I the

Sd Ralph Smith for my Self my heirs Execurs Admirs the Said Bergained premises unto the Sd Nathll ffreeman his Heirs Execrs Admirs and asigns against all and all manner of persons Shall warrant and for Ever Defend by these presents in witness where of I have here unto set to my hand and Seal this Second Day of Jenuary and In the year of our Lord one thousand Seven houndreud and thirty Six alies Seven

Note the words Interlined between the third and fourth line from the top which words (viz) of Sd Eastham and the words Interlined between the fourteenth and fifteenth Lines from the top (viz) belonging to the Estate of the Sd mulford Deceased were before the signing and scalling here of

Signed Sealed and Delivered Ralph. Smith (Seal)
In presence of:
Phebe Higgins
Abigail myrick

[*On the other side of the paper.*]

These presents witnesseth that I the within named Nathanll ffreeman For & In consideration of the Sum of twenty & five pounds passable money to me In hand paid by Thomas Molford Junior of the Town of Trurow in the county & province within mentioned yeoman : have therefore : Bargained Solde Sett over & Confirmed : & by these presents do for my self my heirs executors & administrators : Bargaine Sell Sett over confirm & deliver unto him the Sd Thomas Molford the negro Slave with In named called Lonon together with all the Right property & Interest which I have or of Right ought to have to the person & Service of the within named Lonon neegro by vertue of the with In written Instrument together with his wearing cloathes & other appurtenances to him any ways belonging or appertaining : To have and To hold to him the Said Thomas molford Junior his heirs & assigns forever by these presents : In witness where off I the Said Nathll ffreeman do here unto Sett my hand & Seall the day of march In the fourteenth year of his majesties = Reign anno Domini : 17$\frac{40}{41}$

Signed Sealled & delivered Nathanll ffreeman (seal)
In presence of =
Zacheus Rich
Mulfford Eldredg

PLYMOUTH FIRST CHURCH RECORDS.

Transcribed from the Original,

BY GEORGE ERNEST BOWMAN.

THE First Book of the Plymouth First Church Records consists of five parts, paged independently. The first part is an Ecclesiastical History of the Plymouth Church in the handwriting of Nathaniel Morton, for many years Secretary of the Colony. Much of it was taken bodily from Bradford's History, consequently it seems best to begin this transcript with the second part, in order that the important genealogical data scattered through this and the remaining parts may become accessible as early as possible.

In the second part there are thirty-six pages, twenty-nine in the handwriting of Rev. John Cotton, covering the thirty years, 1667 to 1697, during which he was pastor of the church. Of the remaining seven pages five are in a hand which I have not yet identified and cover the period from the departure of Mr. Cotton to the arrival of the Rev. Ephraim Little; the other two pages are blank.

[PART II.]

[p. 1] A further account of matters in & relating to the church at Plymouth from the yeare 1667: untill 1697, inclusively.

It being desired in page 59 *: in the conclusion of the Eclesiasticall History of this church, by that Godly Brother, Mr Nathaniel Morton, that Elders & Bretheren succeeding would be carefull to commit to writing what might occurre in their day for the Glory of God & good of aftertimes, these following Pages shall truly & faithfully upon certaine knowledge declare what was transacted in this chh for the space of about Thirty yeares soe far as may be Judged meet for edification.

Mr Morton in his foregoing Narrative truly declares, that after the departure of that blessed Man of God Mr Reyner from them whom he had faithfully served for the space of about eighteen yeares in the office of a Teacher, & the chh remaining sundry yeares destitute of a Teaching Elder looking up to God constantly in ordinary & extraordinary prayer to send in a suta-

* Of Part I.

ble supply for their soules, in which time sundry desireable ministers spent some time successively in preaching the word of God to them, but divine providence favoured not the settlement of any one of them, It pleased God soe to dispose in September 1666, that the church gave a call to Mr John Cotton to come & preach to them, who by reason of his then engagement to another people, could not at present accept of that call, but the chh continuing destitute of setled ministry, they did in the yeare following in July, renew their former call to him, to which He gave his consent & accordingly removed himselfe & family to Plymouth, where they arrived on November, 30 : 1667 :

1667 : There were then resident in the Place forty seven chh-membe[rs] in full communion, besides divers that were removed to other places, who upon the setlement of the ministry were called upon by the Elders to take their dismissions respectively to the severall ches where their setled abode was, this chh declaring it to be the duty of christians to be under the watch of those ches where they live, this motion was readily complyed with by all concerned.

Now inasmuch as the death of saints is pretious in the eyes of God, & God hath said, the Righteous shall be had in everlasting remembrance an account shall be given of the deaths of such espetially who were of good esteem in the chh of God :

The first breach God made in the chh within the time abovesaid was the death of Gabriel Fallowell, aged above 80 yeares, a very pretious, lively christian, one who maintained much communion with God day & night, he dyed, December, 28 : 1667 :

In 1668 : two members were admitted into the chh : & all that was transacted in the chh in this yeare was their discourse & conclusion to renew their call of Mr Cotton & to declare to him their purpose to establish him in office in the spring, the Lord disposing all our hearts to unite therein.

on the first of March dyed, John Dunham, the godly & well esteemed Deacon of the chh, one of 80 yeares old.

1669 The chh appointed, April,* 7 : 1669 : & kept it as a day of Fasting & Prayer, wherein to beg Gods prescence to be with them in directing to & in the choice of their Teaching officer. Immediately after which the church voted to set apart a day to elect & ordaine Mr Cotton to be their Pastor, & agreed that June, 30 : should be the day, which was attended, He being dismissed from Boston old church & Joyned to this chh some weekes before; The ches present at this ordination (by the

* On the margin is written : "In this April dyed blessed Mr Reyner, then Pastor of the chh at Dover."

desire of this chh) by the Elders & messengers were Barnstable, Marshfeild, Weymouth & Duxbu[ry;] Elder Thomas Cushman gave the charge & the aged Mr [p. 2] John Howland was appointed by the chh to Joyne in imposition of hands; the Reverend Mr Walley made a solemne Prayer before ordination & the Revd Mr Torrey gave the right hand of fellowship in the Name of the ches, after.

The Ruling Elder with the Pastor made it their first spetiall worke together to passe through the whole towne from family to family to enquire into the state of soules & according as they found the frames either of the children of the chh or others, soe they applyed counsells, admonitions, exhortations & incouragements, which service was attended with a blessing, for in divers with whom God had begun his work, it prevailed to stirre them up to lay hold of the Covenant, & others were awakened more seriously to attend upon the meanes of grace & to minde the concernments of their soules, & practice family-prayer more constantly, the worke of God seemed in those dayes to have a considerable reviving. The chh having not then a Deacon, the Elders called upon them to choose some to that office; Accordingly, after a chh-meeting in Private some being Nominated, every brother speaking his minde man by man, on August, 1: Robert Finney & Ephraim Morton were chosen Deacons in the publick Assembly on the Sabbath, & then ordained by the Elders. In January, the chh agreed to begin monethly church-meetings for conference, which were constantly attended for many yeares, & much good attended that exersise; Also in November, began the Catechizing of the children by the Pastor, (the Elder also accompanying him therein constantly) once a fortnight, the Males at one time & the females at the other: the catechisme then used was Mr: Perkins. The members admitted to full Communion in this yeare were twenty & seven; the practice was for men orally to make confession of faith & a declaration of their experiences of a worke of grace in the prescence of the whole congregation, having bin examined & heard before by the Elders in private & then stood propounded in publick for 2 or 3 weekes ordinarily; & the relations of the woemen being written in private from their mouths, were read in publick by the Pastor & the Elders gave Testimony that their knowledge was competent, this was the ordinary way of Admission of members at their first entrance, but if any members came from other places & had letters of Dismission they were accepted by us upon that Testimoniall & nothing further required of them.

The Lords Supper was administred 4 times in this yeare, the first of which was on August, 29:

The children Baptized this yeare, 48:

It pleased God heavily to afflict this chh & people by the Death of Capt Thomas Southworth, of whom Honourable mention is made in the foregoing Narrative, & that most deservedly; He was a great Pillar in this chh, & in the dayes of blessed M[r] Reyner, after the death of Elder Brewster (whose Name is here very pretious & ever will be soe) [p. 3] when the chh had agitations about the choice of a Ruling Elder, this M[r] Southworth was Judged by many of the chh a very sutable man for that place, yet it was wisely foresoon by Govr Bradford that the necessity of the Commonwealth would doubtlesse call for the improovment of his Talent in the Magistracy, & soe it prooved, for immediately upon the death of that Honourable Govr, he was chosen a magistrate & soe continued to his death, There were other Bretheren that did exersise their gifts for edification of the chh in the vacancy of the ministry, yet such was the desireablenesse & excelling of his Gifts & graces that for divers yeares together he was espetially singled out by the chh to carry on the publick worship, one part of the Sabbath, Elder Cushman ordinarily spending the forenoone & M[r] Southworth the afternoone; His Death was on December, 8: (about 53 yeares old) after a moneths sicknesse; His death was much lamented & is to this day, he was loved & feared & of such a conversation as commanded both. The chh kept a day of prayer for his life, Dec: 1: but his time was come to dye.

In 1670 fourteen members were admitted into the chh, 39 children were baptized, & the Lords supper was 8 times In the spring the chh set apart & observed a day of Thanksgiving for the setlement of Gods ordinances after soe long a vacancy, & the good successe of the Gospel amongst the[m.] A child of this chh who had bin here baptized, removing to Swanzey was rebaptized by the Pastor there, which the chh being informed of, did unanimously declare it to be matter of offence, & sent letters to those concerned in that action to signify that such a practice would be a barre to our Eclesiasticall communion, & desired they would doe soe noe more.

Some persons, a brother & 2 sisters that had formerly walked with this chh being now removed & not owning their chh-relation, the chh agreed & it was openly declared by the Elder in the name of the chh, that wee esteemed them noe longer to be members of us

In this yeare, 70: M[r] Richard Bourne of Sandwich sent to

the chh for messengers to take notice of the fittnesse of sundry Indians to gather into a chh, at Mashpau, the Pastor, Elder & Secretary Morton were sent thither, Elders & messengers of many other ches were there also, the Indians after confessions &c were gathered into a chh, Mr Bourne chosen & ordained their Pastor, all the ches present approoving thereoff. old Mr Eliot & our Pastor laid on hands.*

In 1671 seventeen members were admitted, 25 children baptized, the Lords supper was 10 times. Some viz, a brother & sister having sold liquors to the Indians were Admonished, & also a child of the chh for morall scandall, this chh ever practising discipline to the chh-seed when adult.

in 1672, six members were admitted, 13 children Baptized, the Lords supper was 8 times.

on February, 24: dyed Mr John Howland in his eightieth yeare, he was a good old disciple & had bin sometime a Magistrate here, a plaine-hearted christian

In 1673: was a very awfull frowne of God upon this chh & colony in the death of Mr Thomas Prince the Governour in the 73d yeare of his Age; when this Colony was in a hazardous condition upon the death of Govr Bradford, the lott was cast upon Mr Princ[e] [p. 4] to be his successour, God made him a repairer of breaches & a meanes to setle those shakings that were then threatning, he was excellently qualifyed for the office of a Governour, he had a countenance full of majesty & therein as well as otherwise was a Terrour to evill doers, he was very amiable & pleasant in his whole conversation & highly esteemed of the saints & acknowledged by all; In the time of his sicknesse the chh sought God by Fasting & Prayer, but God would not be intreated any longer to spare him, but he dyed on March, 29: & was honourably interred, April, 8:

Six more chh-members dyed in this yeare.†

The Lords supper in this yeare was seven times, but one member admitted, 14 children baptized.

In 1674: the Lords supper was 11 times, one member admitted, 17 children baptized:

Discipline viz Admonition was administred to a chh-child for sin & two in full communion upon confession of what was offensive were forgiven without any censure.

In March, 1675: the church of Eastham sent to our chh for messengers to be with them at their ordination of Mr Samuel

* This paragraph is on the margin of the page.

† On the margin of the page.

Treat to be their Pastor, the chh sent the Pastor, Elder & Deacon Finney, who attended that service, March, 17:

Lords supper was six times; 8 children were baptized.

Warr with the Indians breaking forth, the chh set apart July, 21: to be kept as a day of Humiliation, Another on January, 5: Another, February, 2: because of war & sicknesse.

(*To be continued.*)

DESIRE (HOWLAND) GORHAM'S ESTATE.

Transcribed from the Original Records,

BY GEORGE ERNEST BOWMAN.

DESIRE (Howland) GORHAM, eldest daughter of John and Elizabeth (Tilley) Howland, died at Barnstable and her death is entered on the town records [Volume I, page 414] as follows: "Mrs Desire Gorham Relict of Cap John Gorham Senr Late of Barnstable Deceas^d^ Departed this Life ye 13 Day of Octo^r^ 1683." According to the probate records her inventory was taken 3 August, 1683, more than two months earlier, and it is evident that one of these entries is incorrect. The probate record was copied from the original inventory and the town record was copied, in 1736, from the original volume now lost.*

[Plym. Col. Wills, IV: II: 63]

An Inventory of the estate of Desire Gorum taken the 3 of August 1683 and exhibited to the Court of his Mat^ie^: held att Plymouth the sixt Day of March $16\frac{8}{3}\frac{3}{4}$ on the oathes of James Gorum and John Gorum as followeth;

Imp^r^: 1 third of the Mill & lands meddowes and tooles belonging to the said Mill	35	00	0
Item 1 yoak of oxen	07	00	0
Item 5 Cowes	10	00	0
Item 2 steers of two yeers old and vantage	03	00	0
Item 1 yeerling	01	00	0
Item 3 Calves	01	00	0
Item 1 horse	01	10	0
Item 7 growne swine	03	00	0
Item 5 piggs	00	12	6

* Mayflower Descendant, II: 212.

Item in turkes & other foules	00	15	0
Item Cart wheeles and yoakes and Copes 10^{s} plow takings & Copes 4^{s}	00	14	0
Item 1 Chaine and horse gear : 2 hoes & one axe	00	08	0
Item 1 pitchforke 1^{s} and one spitt 3^{s} 6^{d}; 2 pothangers one five^{s} & one 3 shillings	00	12	0
Item 1 Iron pot and pot hookes 7^{s} one frying pan 3^{s} 6^{d} and 1 2^{s} 6^{d}	00	13	0
Item 1 Iron pot 3^{s} 1 Iron skillett 3^{s} one Iron kettle 7^{s}	00	13	0
Item 1 morter & pestle 4^{s} 2 brasse skilletts 2^{s} brasse kettle 1^{s}	00	07	0
Item Scales & waights 6^{s} a paire of stilliyards 6^{s} a warming pan 5^{s}	00	17	0
Item a skimer 2^{s} 6^{d} 1 rundelett 1^{s} 1 rundelett 6^{d}	00	04	0
Item 2 milke pailes 1^{s} 6^{d} one beer Caske 1 Copper 2^{ll} 15^{s}	02	17	6
Item 1 hogshed a barrell a butter tubb 5^{s} a washing tubb 4^{s} a round measure 9	00	09	9
Item 1 Chern 1 old paile	00	01	0
Item 1 Gun 1^{ll}: 1 smoothing Iron 1 heater 1^{s} 6^{d} one Linnin wheel and reel 5^{s}	01	06	6
Item in wooden trayes 7^{s} 2 Chaire one six shill; one 4^{s} 1 Chaire 2^{s}	00	19	00
Item a sifting trough 4^{s}; 1 Chest with a rope att the end 4^{s}	00	08	00
Item pewter 12^{s} shillings 1 Chist 2^{s} and old bible and Tillinhasts book 2^{s}	00	16	00
Item 2 glasse bottles 1^{s} 3^{d} stone Juggs 6^{d} 2 gally potts 1 brush & a viall	00	02	3
Item an Iron Candle stick 9^{d} 1 wicker baskett & other basketts 1^{s}	00	02	9
Item 1 bed bolster and 2 smale pillowes, in the Chamber 3^{ll}	03	00	0
Item 1 bed bolster 1 pillow bedsted and Cord	03	10	0
Item 1 Coverlid 1^{ll} 2 white blanketts home made, 1^{ll} 2^{s}	02	02	0
Item 1 speckled blankett 9^{s} 1 Coverlid 1^{ll} 1 green rugg 8^{s}	01	17	0
Item 1 sale blankett 6^{s} & 7 pound of fflax 7	00	13	0
Item 2 old blanketts 3^{s} 1 new sheet 12^{s} 6^{d} & 1 Course 5^{s}	01	01	6
2 silver spoones and a Dram Cup 1^{ll} 1 silver beaker 3^{ll}	04	00	0
Item 1 Cokernutt 6^{d} some smale thinges in a Capp 1^{s}	00	01	6
Item 1 whiske 4^{s} 1 hood 6^{s} a black Cape and an old hood 1^{s}	00	11	0
Item 1 green apron 1^{s} 6^{d} a paire of Sleves 1^{s} 6^{d} a silke lase 3^{d} 3^{d}	00	03	5
Item 1 paire of red stockens 6^{s} 1 white apron 5^{s} 6^{d} 1 apron 3^{s} 6^{d}	00	09	6
Item 1 paire of white Gloves 3^{s} twisted yarne 9^{d}	00	03	9
Item a p^{r}sell of white linnine that is marked;	01	02	5
	0128	16	11

Item to a womans black Cloake and Claspes	01	00	00
Item 1 old Cloth hood 4^s 1 old sarge Samar 18^s 1 serge Coat 18^s	02	00	00
Item 1 New Samar 1^{ll} 18^s : 1 Moheare Coate 12^s	02	10	00
Item Curtaines and vallence 15^s an under wastcoate 1 shilling 1^s	00	16	00
Item Indian Corn 31 bushells att 2^s 6^d pr bushell & two towells 1^s	03	18	06
Item a paire of shooes 2^s 1 hat Case 2^s some Indian Basketts 5^s	00	09	00
Item to beding & sheets that tota makes use of	02	00	00
Item to a paire of wast silver buttons 3^s in mony 13^s 10^d	00	16	10
Item 5 bushells of Rye att 3^s a bushell 15^s : the wheat Not threshed 6^s	01	01	00
Item rye not threshed 18^s one shovell & peel 1^s 3^d earthen ware & trenchers 6^d	00	19	09
Item seaming pillow Coate 3^s 6^d, one 1^s 6^d, one 2 6^d a small table Cloth	00	11	00
Item 1 sheet 5^s 6^d, 1 sheet 10, 2 twowells 1 6^d one towell 6^d	00	17	09
Item 2 pillow Coates 6^s 1 sheet 10 1 sheet 5^s 1 sheet 10^s	01	11	00
Item 1 sheet 5–6 1 sheet 10 tow towells 1^s 6^d 1 towell 9^d	00	17	09
Item 1 twowell 10^d a single Neckcloth 2^s : 3 Capps	00	04	07
[p. 64] Item one small bundle of old thinges 1^s 1 handker Chiffe one & sixpence & 1 twowell 6^d	00	03	0
Item 1 Diaper Napkin 1^s one striped neckcloth 9^d a blew Apron 1^s 6^d	00	03	3
Item 1 shift 6^s one 2^s 1 paire of stockens 1^s 6^d	00	09	6
Item 1 bundle of old aprones 1^s 1 bedstead 15^s	00	16	0
Item 1 barrill att mill 1^s 6^d one straw hatt 3^s	00	04	6
Item 1 woolen wheel and Iron spindle 3^s 6^d and bridle & Crooper 1^s 6^d	00	05	0
Item 2 yards of Lutestringe in a scraff	00	10	0
Item 1 wiker Baskett 3^s; 4 Napkins six shillings 1 smale pillow Coate; 6^d	00	10	6
Item 1 shooing horn 3^d 1 powder bar 6^d six shift 6^d one thing I Can not read *	00	02	09
Item 2 Cushens 1^s 6^d 1 sheet 6^s; one sheet 8 shilling 1 sheet 6^s	01	02	06
Item 1 sheet 6^s; and 1 sheet 7^s 1 Towell two and 6^d a Diaper table Cloth 8^s	1	03	6
Item 1 Diaper table Cloth 12^s 1 paire of holland sheets 2^{ll}	02	12	0
Item 1 pillow Coate 8^s, 2 more att 12^s one Napkin Diaper 9^d	01	00	09
Item 1 winestcott Chist 10^s shilling 3 plates a porringer and sawser 4	00	14	00
Item 6 trenchers 6^d 1 looking Grasse 8^s : 3 earthen Dishes 1^s	00	09	09

* Interlined in original.

Item 1 trunk 1s 6d : one box 5s	00	06	06
Item 3 acrees of land bought of Sowashan	00	15	00
Item more 1 shift 3s 6d som old Clothing 8s	00	11	06
Item 1 pitcher 6d	00	00	06
Item Due upon bill 40ll	30	15	11
	123	16	11
Item Due upon bill as before	40	00	00
Debts Due to the estate;	ll		
Item silver mony lent to John hawes	05	00	00
silver mony Lent to Joseph whilden	02	00	00
Debts Due from the estate as wee Doe apprehend	05	00	00

Taken and apprised by us John Thacher
John Miller

[Court Orders, VI : II : 2, under date of 5 March, 1683/4.]

In reference unto the settlement of the Estate of Desire Gorum of Yarmouth Deceased amonge the Children; It was agreed and Determined by Govr hinckley Major Bradford Deputy Govr : mr ffreeman mr Laythorp & mr Thacher Asistants alsoe with the mutuall Consent of the Children then appeering viz: James Gorum John Gorum Joseph Gorum; with the Consent likewise of the sonnes in Law as followeth;

That James Gorum have a Dubble portion of the whole estate Debts being first payed out and all the rest of the Children both sonnes and Daughters to have an equall portion; of the aforsaid estate that is John Joseph Jabez : and Shuball; Desire Temperance Elizabeth Deseased, Marsy Lidia and hannah, as Elizabeth Deceased wee Doe agree and Consent that her Children shall have an equall prte that Did belong to theire Mother as to Shuball the youngest son wheras there was fifty pound in Mony Given to his Mother to bestow upon him in Learning, wherof wee find upon account a great prte of it bestowed on him, yet wee Doe Consent and agree that hee shall have forty pound in silver mony mad up to him when hee Cometh to age out of the aforsaid estate besides his equall prte; and alsoe five pounds of his equall prte, which, to be in silver mony; which makes his 40li to be 45 pounds in mony;

BARNSTABLE, MASS., VITAL RECORDS.

(*Continued from page 122.*)

[p. 406] James Coleman his Son Edward born y^e 25 of $Octo^r$ 1695
his Daughter Martha born y^e 4 of March 1698
his Daughter Thankful born y^e 7th of Feb : 1699
a Son born y^e 26 of Feb^{ry} & Died that Day 1702
James his Son born y^e 11 of April 1704
John y^e 26 of $Sept^r$ 1706
Patence Coleman y^e 6 of May 1709
Ebenezer y^e 15 of August 1711
Nathan Crocker his Son Jabez born 10 June 1709
& Benoni his Son 24 Feb 1711/12
John Clark and Mary Benjamin were Married 16 Aug : 1695
Their son John Born 16 of Novr 1697
Elkanah Hamlin and Abigail Hamlin Married pr Justice Gorham
13 April 1711
his Son Sylvanus Hamlin Born 20 July 1712
his Son Reuben Born 13 March 1714
his Daughter Abigail 27 October 1715
his Son John y^e 2 Novr 1717
his Daughter Rachel 7 Day of Sep 1720 She Died 1722
patience born 12 June 1721
Tabitha Hamlin Born 14 April 1723
Abigail y^e wife of Elkanah Hamlin $Decea^{sd}$ May 29 1733

[p. 407] Shobal Dimock & Joann Bursley Married in April 1653
his Son Thomas born In April 1654
John born In January 1656
Timothy born In March 1658
Shobal born In Feb 1663
Joseph born In $Sept^r$ 1665
Benjamin born In March 1670
Joanna born March 1672
Thankful born Novr 1674
These Records perhaps 10 year too old *
Cap Thomas Dimock his Daughter Mehitable born $Octo^r$ 1686
Temporance born In June 1689
his Son Edward born 5 of July 1692
Thomas 25 of Decem 1694
Desire born In Feb 1696
John Dimock & Elizabeth Lumber Married Nov. 1689

* This entry is on the margin, opposite the preceding family.

his Daughter Sarah born In Decem 1690
Anna born In July 1693
Mary June 1695
his son Theophilus In Sept 1696
his Son Timothy born In July 1698
his Son Ebenezer born In Feb 1700
Thankful 5 april 1702
Elizabeth 20 april 1704
Shobal Dimock & Tabitha Lothrop Married
his Son Samuel Dimock born ye 17* of May 1702
his Daughter Joannah 24 Decem 1708 & Deceasd about 3 weeks after
his Daughter Mehitable June 20 1711
Joseph Dimock & Lydia Fuller Married 12 of May 1699
Their Son Thomas Dimock born 26 January 1699/1700
Bethiah Born 3rd of February 1702
Mehitable Born 22 of March 1707
Ensign Dimmock born 8th Day of March 1709
Ichabod born 8th Day of March 1711
Abigail born 31 June 1714
Pharoh born Septr 2 1717
David born 22 Day Decemr 1721
Daniel North ye Son of Daniel & Hannah North born 21 of Sep 1716
his Daughter Mary born ye 25 of January 1719
James born Feb 10 1720
his Son John North born Janry 10 1722
Hannah Born Sep 3 1725
Winifred yr Daughter born Nov 7th 1727
Dorothy Dun ye Daughter of John & Experience Dun was born ye 5 of January in ye year 1726
Nathan Davis & Elizabeth Phinny were married ye 25 of Nov 1714 pr Justice Parker
his Son Jabez born 7 of Octor 1715
Sarah born August 12 1717 & Deceasd 23 of sd August
his Daughter Elizabeth born 15 Sep 1718
his Son Isaac Born [*illegible*] January 1720

[p. 408] Robert Davis his Children their Births
his Daughter Deborah Born January 1645
Mary May 1648
his Son Andrew born In May 1650
John 1 of March 1652
Robert In August 1654
Josiah Septemr 1656
Hannah Septr 1658
Sarah In Octor 1660

* Altered in different ink to "07."

Josiah Davis and Ann Tayler Married June 25 1679
Their son John born 2 Sept 1681
Their Daughter Hannah born In April 1683
Their son Josiah born In August 1687
Their Son Seth In Octo^r 1692
Ruth born In Feb 1694
Sarah born In Feb 1696
Jonathan Davis born About 1698
Stephen 12 of Decem^r 1700
Anna 5 of April 1702
Joseph Davis & Hannah Cob Married March 1695 pr Mr Thacher
his Son Robert born 7 of March 1696/7
his Son Joseph born 23 of March 1698/9
James July 30 1700
Gershom 5 Sep^t 1702
Hannah 5 of March 1705
Mary 4 of June 1707
Lydia 12 of Feb 1709
Daniel Born Sep^t 28 1713
William Dexter & Sarah Vinsen Married In July 1653
his Daghter Mary born In January 1654
Stephen Dexter Born In May 1657
his Son Phillip Dexter born In Sept 1659
James Dexter his Son born In May 1662
his Son Thomas Dexter born In July 1665
his Son John Dexter born In August 1668
his Son Benjamin born In Feb 1670
John Dunham & Mary Smith Married 1 of March 1679 80
Their Son Thomas born ye 25 of Decem^r 1680
his Son John Born ye 18 of May 1682
his Son Ebenezer born ye 17 of April 1684
his Daughter Desire born ye 10 of Decem 1685
his Son Elisha born ye 1st of Septr 1687
his Daughter Mercy born 10 of June 1689
his Son Benjamin born 20 June 1691
John Dunham Deceasd 2 January 1696 Aged In his 48th year

[p. 409] John Davis & Hannah Lynnel Married 15 of March 1648
his Son John born About ye Midst January 1649
Samuel Midst Decem^r 1651
twins Hannah & Mary 3 of January 1653
twins Joseph & Benjamin June 1656
Simon Midst July 1658
Doler beginning Octo^r 1660
Jabez
Doller Davis & Hannah Linnel Married 3 of August 1681
Shobal Born 23 of April 1685
Thomas In August 1687

Hannah In Decem^r 1689
Stephen In Sep^t 1690
Thankful In march 1696
Daniel In July 1698
Job born In July 1700
Noah Born In Sept 1702
Remember Mercy 15 of Octo^r 1704
Joseph Davis & Mary Claghorn Married March 28. 1682
their Son Simon Born 19 January 1683
Mary ye 19 of June 1685
Their Son Joseph born Last of April 1687
Robert Davis 13 June 1689
James Cahoon Son of wid Mary Davis born 25 octo^r 1696
Jabez Davis & Experience Linnel Married 20 Augus 1689
Their Son Nathan born 2 March 1690
Samuel born 25 September 1692
his Daughter Bathsheba born 16 January 1694
his Son Isaac born 23 April 1696
his Daughter Abigail 26 april 1698
his Son Jacob born Last octo^r 1699
Mercy born ye 16 of Feb : 1701
John Davis Ju^r & Ruth Goodspeed Married 2nd Feb in ye year 1674
Their son John Born ye Last of Novr 1675 & Died About ye Middle of August 1681
Their son Benjamin Born ye 8 of Septem 1679
Their son John Born ye 17 of March 1684
Their son Nathaniel born ye 17 of July 1686
John Davis Ju^r his Second Wife Mary Hamlin they were Married ye 22 of Feb 1692
his Son Shobal born 10 of July 1694
James born 24 of March 1696
Ebenezer born 13 of May 1697
his Aboves^d Wife Mary Hamlin Deceas^d About ye Last of Nov 1698
John Davis Ju^r & ye Widdow Hannah Bacon Married [*illegible*] 1699 pr Mr Russel
& their Son Nicholas Born 12 March 1699 1700

[p. 410] Stephen Dexter & Anna Sanders Married 27 of April 1696
Their Daughter Mary born 24 August 1696
Their Son Born 22 Decem 1698 & Died ye January following 1698
Their Daughter Abigail born 13 of May 1699
Their Daughter Content born 5 February 1701
Their Daughter Anna born 9 of March 1702/3
Sarah Dexter born ye 1 of June 1705
Stephen born 26 July 1707
Mercy born 5 of July 1709
his Daughter Miriam born 8 of March 1712
his Son Cornelius born 21 of March 1713/14
The Marriage of William Dier & Mary Tayler Decem^r 1686

Their Daughter Lydia born ye 30 of March 1688
his Son William born ye 30 of Octo 1690
his Son Jonathan Born Feb 1692
Henry Born 11 of April 1693
Their Daughter Isabel born In July 1695
Ebenezer born 3 of April 1697
Sam^{ll} born 30 October 1698
& Judah his Son born In April 1701
Edward Davis y^e Son of Josiah Davis & Mehitable his Wife born y^e 19 of June 1713
& their Daughter Mary born y^e 8th of August 1714
their Son Josiah Was born 2 Aug 1718

[p. 411] John Ewer and Elizabeth Lumbart Married.
Their Son Shobal born
Their Son Joseph born
Their son Benjamin Ewer Born $Sept^r$ 5 1721
Shobal Ewer his Daughter Rebekah was born y^e 27 April 1715
Shobal Ewer $Deceas^d$ y^e 6th of August 1715
Thomas Ewer y^e Son of Thomas Ewer born $Decem^r$ 1673
Thomas Ewer Married with Elizabeth Lovell Octo 1684
his Son Thomas born In January 1688
Shobal born 1690
John In Feb 1692
Mehitable born $Octo^r$ 1694 & Died Novr 1694.
$Nath^{ll}$ Born in Novr 1695
Jonathan born July 1696 & Died Novr 1696.
Hezekiah Born Sepr 1697.
thankful born Latter end of Novr 1701.
His Wife Died y^e 20 day of May 1717

[p. 412] Edward Fitts Randles Children
his Daughter Hannah born In April 1649
Mary y^e Last of May 1651
his Son John y^e 7 of $Octo^r$ 1653
Joseph y^e first of March 1656
Thos y^e 16 of August 1659
Hope y^e 2 of April 1661
$Nath^{ll}$ Fitsrandle & Mary Holley Married Novr 1662
his Son John Born y^e first of Feb 1662
his Son Isaac born about y^e 7 of $Decem^r$ 1664
Mary Daughter of Richard Foxwel born 17 August 1635
Martha y^e 24 of March 1638
Ruth y^e 25 of March 1641
Dr John Fuller his Daughter Bethiah born Decem 1687
his Son John Fuller born $Octo^r$ 1689
Reliance Fuller born Sep^t 8 1691
John Fuller and Thankful Gorham Married June 16 1710 pr Mr Russel

his Daughter Hannah born 1 of april 1711
his Son John Born 3 of August 1712
Mary & Bethia twins born 1st of Septemb . 1715
his Son Nathaniel born 10 Decem : 1716
Thankful born 19 Sep 1718
Joseph Foster his Son Joseph Born 19 of Sept 1698
his Son Benjamin 16 Novr 1699
Joseph Fuller Jur his Daughter Rebekah Born Decem 29 1709
his Daughter Bethiah Born March 2 1712

[p. 413] Thos Son of Samll Fuller Senr born 18 of May /50
his Daughter Sarah 14 of December 1654
a Child born 8th of Feb 58 & buried 15 Days after
Thomas Fuller & Elizabeth Lothrop Married 29 of Decemr 1680
Their Daughter Hannah born ye 17 of Novr 1681
Their son Joseph Born ye 12 of July 1683
Their Daughter Mary born ye 6th of Aug : 1685
Their Son Benjamin Born ye 6 of Aug 1690
Their Daughter Elizabeth born ye 3 of Sep. 1692
Their Son Samuel Born ye 12 of april 1694
Their Daughter Abigail born ye 9th of January 1695/6
Jabez Fuller his Son Samuel born 23 Feb : 1687
his Son Jonathan born 10 March 1692
his Daughter Mercy born 1 April 1696
his Daughter 23 Sept 1704 Named Lois born 1704
his Son Ebenezer born 20 Feb 1708
his Daughter Mary Born
Matthew Fuller and Patience Young Married by Justice Skiff 25 Feb 1692
Their Daughter Anne Born in Nov 1693
his Son Jonathan Octor 1696
his Daughter Content born ye 19 of Feb 1698/9
Jean born in ye year 1704 & Died 1708
his Son David born Feb 1706/7 1706/7
his Son Young Born 1708
Cornelius 1710
Barnabas Fuller & Elizabeth Young Married 25 of Feb 1680
Their son Samuel born In Novr 1681
& Isaac born August 1684
& Hannah Born In Sep. 1688
his Son Ebenezer Born Latter End of April 1699
his Son Josiah born February 1709 1709
Samll Fuller his Daughter Sarah was born 16 April 1719
Joseph Fuller his Daughter Remember born 26 of May 1701
his Son Seth Fuller born (*) of Septr 1705

* The original entry was "5." In its present condition it is doubtful whether an attempt was made to change it to "1" or it was blotted accidentally. There are two blots near it.

Thankful 4 of August 1708
Benjamin Fuller his Daugher Temperance born 7 of March 1702
& his Daughter Hannah Born 20 of May 1704
John born 25 Decem 1706
& his Son James born 1 of May 1711

(*To be continued.*)

THE RECORDS OF WELLFLEET, FORMERLY THE NORTH PRECINCT OF EASTHAM, MASS.

Literally Transcribed,

By George Ernest Bowman.

The northerly part of Eastham was originally called "Billingsgate" and in 1723 it was organized as the "North Precinct" of the town. In 1763 it was incorporated as the "District of Wellfleet" and in 1775 became an independent town.

The records of the town begin with the organization of the North Precinct in 1723, the oldest volume containing sixty pages of precinct records, ninety-six pages of births, marriages and deaths and four pages of ear-marks.

[On fly leaf.]

A Book of Records for the North Precinct of Eastham Called Billinsga[te] Begining July 29 1723

[p. 1] July ye 29 1723

Billinsgate Precinct Meeting — Wherein it is voted that ye Revrnd Josiah Oakes Shall Continue in ye work of ye Ministry as formerly in this Precinct, for ye Salery of Eighty pounds a year in order for a Setlement

Billinsgate alias North Eastham Precinct —

Pursuant to what has been proposed and voted for my Setlement in the Ministry in this Precin[ct] I made ye following answer this 31 of March in ye year 1724 viz:

1 I accept of both your former and your latter Call together with your former and latter proposals Since you were a legal Precinct

2 And accordingly Shall continue in ye work of the Minis-

try in the S^{d} Precinct in order to a Setlement among you in the Ministry agreable to your vote on july 29 1723

I vote that Such my answer be witness my hand Recorded by your Clark

March 31 1724 A precinct meeting at Billinsgate Voted that John Doane aEsqir : be moderator for this meeting : also voted that John Rich be clarke and Treasurer for this year. voted also that John Doane Eqr Isaac Baker and Ebenezer Freeman be Select men or assessors

Voted also that John Doane Eqr : Isaac Baker Ebenezer Freeman and Thomas Groose and John atwood be a Comitte to Call meetings in ye Precinct as ye Law requires as also what Else ye Law directs to be done

This March meeting is ajourned until ye first munday in june next at nine of ye Clock in ye forenoon

[p. 2] June ye 1 1724

A Precinct meeting Legally Called and mett Wherein the meeting was ajourned to ye first monday in August, Except ye Comitte order it otherwise by Setting up their warrant

At a Precinct meeting warned and mett on ye 22 of june 1724 wherein John Doane Esq : was moderator : ye following proposals being read and voted at a precinct meeting in ye hamlet of Billinsgate in Eastham on ye 11 day of March 1720 We ye Comitte nominated and Sent out by ye whole body of their assembly to consider of Sum Proposals for ye encouragement and Setlement of of Mr Josiah Oakes in ye work of ye Ministry of the word to dispence ye Same among us — Have concluded as follows :

In Prime we do propose To give him ye afores^{d} Josiah Oakes his heirs and assygns forever : provided he Shall build on s^{d} land and Setle among us 20 years or during life in the work of ye Ministry ; or bue a house in this Place : four acres of upland in ye place where it may be obtained at a reasonable rate, where He and we may judge most convenient

Item we propose to give to s^{d} oak's one hundred and 20 pounds of Such mony as Shall pass between man and man or with ye Merchant at time of Payment in ye provence : ye one half to be paid at ye end of ye year 1724 ye other half at ye end of ye year 1725.

Item that his Salary from ye first of June 1722 Shall be eighty pounds a year Yearly, So long as he ye S^{d} Oakes Shall

Continue In ye Ministry among us, and S^{d} eighty Pounds is to be understood to be in Such money or pay as is aboves^{d}: and it is to be understood That If mr Oakes does not continue in s^{d} work Then s^{d} Setlement to be returned or Such part as ye major part shall order

[p. 3] June ye 22 1724

At a precinct Meeting leagaly warned and mett for ye purpose above mentioned the above written Proposals where voted by the major part hereof asembled In order to confirm the reverend mr Josiah Oakes in The work of the ministry among us in this north precin of Eastham. and also to confirm ye proposals made to ye s^{d} mr Oakes and Setle the Same on him and also to order ye assessors to assess his Salary and Setlement according to ye proposals. and monies to defry other charges risen or rising in this precinct, and that ye Treasurer pay S^{d} monies to them it Belongs to and take reciets for what they do pay out

For ye intent above mentioned June 22 1724 At a precinct meeting duly warned and mett ye abovewritten being voted by ye major part and Israel Young was chosen to Sweep the meetinghouse for eighteen Shillings ye ensuing year

at ye precinct meeting aforementioned on june ye 22 1724 The persons hereafter named entred there denial against mr Josiah Oakes any Longer continuing in ye work of ye ministry in this precinct and also against ye assessors raising any assesment for s^{d} Oakes Salary or Setlement this year ensuing — John Treat Nathaniel Treat Elisha Eldrige Sen: Samuel Brown Elisha Cole Benjamin Sweat John Young Moses Wile Samuel Smith George Williamson Benjamin Hamblin Eleazer Hamblin James Cohoon Benjamin Young Jonathan Young Barnabas Young Daniel Mayo Ebenezer Eldrige Ebenezer Freeman Jeremiah Mayo [p. 4] William Cole Samuel Mayo Elisha Eldrige jun Thomas Brown Elisha Mayo Bryent Morton Israel Young Elisha Hamblin two men at this Meeting stood neutors Charles pain and Joseph Atkins

Entred per John Rich Clerke

Febr: 26 172$\frac{4}{5}$

The Inhabitants of y^{e} North precinct of y^{e} North Precinct of Eastham being duly warned mett Togather made Choice of Jonathan Young Moderator

Voted at S^{d} meeting that Isaac Baker be imployed To build a pound in S^{d} precinct

March y^e^ 29 1725

Then y^e^ Inhabitants of y^e^ North precinct in Eastham Being legaly warned asembled and mett together, to make choice of Precinct officers as ye Law directs and made Choice of Samuel Brown Moderator for the Meeting and made Choice of Jonathan Young Clerk and Samuel Smith Treasurer. and Samuel Smith Jonathan Young Elisha Eldrige assessors for the year ensuing. and at ye above s^d^ meeting made choice of George Williamson Eliezer Hamblin Samuel Smith Jonathan Young Elisha Eldrige jun: a Comitte to warn precinct Meetings for ye year ensuing when there Shall be occasion

May ye 19 1725

The ye Inhabitants of ye north Precinct in Eastham being Legally notified . assembled and mett togather to reconsider and reasume the votes that was Supposed to be passed on ye 22 of June 1724 in this Precinct relating to mr Josiah Oakeses entring in ye work of ye Ministry for twenty years in this precinct or during life and made choice of Samuel Brown for moderator for ye meeting [p. 5] And it was concluded and voted at S^d^ meeting that those votes that was Supposed to be passed on june 22 1724 above S^d^ Relating to mr Josiah Oakes continuing in ye work of ye ministry among us twenty years or during life as also those votes proposed Relating to ye assessors Raising S^d^ oakes Salary and Setlement Shall be void and of none Effect and at ye above s^d^ meeting made choice of George Williamson and Elisha Eldrige Jun: as agents to forbid mr Oakes any more preaching in ye meeting house in ye precinct.

and also at S^d^ meeting mad choice of Samuel Brown and Samuel Smith Agents; to advise with our neighbouring Ministers Relating to ye ill circumstances of ye ministry in this precinct and also to Seek for and procure a Minister to Suply ye precinct

and it was also agreed upon and voted at ye meeting above s^d^ that about ninety pounds Shall be assessed on ye poles and Eastates of ye Precinct for ye Support of ye Ministry and other necessary charges among us for ye year ensuing. The one half to be gathered in at or before ye first day of July next and ye other half to be gathered in at or before ye first day of March following

July ye 21 1725

Then ye jnhabitants of ye North precinct of Eastham being legally notified assembled and mett to make choice of some person or persons for agents in behalf of yᵉ precinct to make answer to a petition of Josiah Oakes Clark laid before The Honarable his majesties Justices of yᵉ Court of General Sessions of yᵉ Peace holden at Barnstable . and also Sᵈ Agents to make answer to a Petition of John Doane and fifteen others of yᵉ inhabitants laid before the Same Court Relating to yᵉ jll managing of an affair in this Precinct. Whereof they made choice of Samuel Brown and Samuel Smith agents. And sᵈ agents or either of them Impowered in Behalf of Sᵈ Precinct to make answer to yᵉ Petition above mentioned

[p. 6] August yᵉ 21 1725

The Inhabitants of yᵉ North Precinct of Eastham being leagally notified assembled and mett to consider of and do what might then be Thought proper upon the advice of yᵉ Court Relating to yᵉ petition of mr Josiah Okes against the inhabitants of Sᵈ Precinct, and made choyce of Samuel Brown for moderator for yᵉ meeting

March yᵉ 1 1726

The Inhabitants of yᵉ North Precinct of Eastham Being Leagally notified . assembled and mett To make choice of precinct officers as yᵉ Law directs and made choice of jonathan Young for precinct Clarke; and made choice of John Rich Samuel Smith and Jonathan Young for assessors for yᵉ Year ensuing. and made choice of Samuel Brown for precinct treasurer. and also made choice of Samuel Smith George Williamson Jonathan Young Samuel Brown and Eleazer Hamblin for a Comitte to Call Precinct meetings yᵉ year ensuing

April yᵉ 18 1726

The Inhabitants of yᵉ North precinct of Eastham being Leagally notified. assembled and mett and made choice of Samuel Brown Moderator for the meeting and at sᵈ meeting made choice of Samuel Brown and Samuel Smith Agents in behalf of Sᵈ precinct to make answer to a petition of mr Josiah Oakes of Eastham laid before yᵉ Judges of yᵉ Superior Court to be holden at Plimouth on yᵉ last tuesday of this instant April. Sᵈ petition brought by an appeal from yᵉ judgment of yᵉ Court of yᵉ Quarter Sessions holden at Barnstable in October. 1725 and Sᵈ agents or either of them are impowered to make answer to yᵉ petition above mentioned and also Sᵈ Agents are Impowered [p. 7] To make Some agreement with yᵉ Sᵈ mr Oakes if they See Cause. it was also agreed upon and voted at s[d] meeting that about one hundred pounds money Should be raised upon y[e] poles and Eastates of y[e] Inhabitants of S[d] precinct this year for y[e] Support of y[e] ministry and defray other necessary Charges risen or arising within S[d] precinct

June y[e] 14 1726

The inhabitants of y[e] north precinct of Eastham being Leagally notified . assembled and mett and made choice of Samuel Brown Moderator for y[e] meeting and at S[d] meeting made choice of Samuel Smith John Rich Samuel Brown Jonathan Young and Eleazer Hamblin a Comitte to discourse mr Josiah Oakes, in order for an agreement of those differences that has hapned among us in s[d] precinct . and then by the major vote of y[e] Inhabitants then assembled the meeting was ajourned to munday the twenty Seventh day of this instant june at ten of y[e] Clock in the forenoon.

June y[e] 27 1726

The Inhabitants of y[e] North precinct in Eastham assembled and mett upon an ajournment afores[d] and made choice of Isaac Baker and John Atwood to add to the comitte afores[d] in order to discourse mr Oakes relating to y[e] differences aforementioned and then by the major vote y[e] meeting was ajourned to monday y[e] Eleventh day of July next at ten of the clock in y[e] forenoon

July y[e] 11 1726

The Inhabitants of y[e] North precinct of Eastham assembled and mett upon y[e] ajournment afores[d] and agreed upon and voted that if y[e] Comitte and mr Oakes have no fair prospect of an agreement Relating to y[e] s[d] Oakeses proceeding in the ministry in this precinct Contrary to y[e] minds of y[e] major part of y[e] inhabitants . [p. 8] Then y[e] afores[d] Samuel Smith John Rich Samuel Brown Jonathan Young Eleazer Hamblin Isaac Baker and John Atwood be Agents in behalf of s[d] Precinct to Call in the help of a Councel consisting of y[e] Elders and messengers of y[e] Neighbouring Churches to consider and advise whither it will not be more for the glory of God and y[e] interest of religion for mr Oakes to desist then to continue preaching in this precinct and s[d] agents to provide for y[e] entertainments of y[e] Council at y[e] charge of y[e] precinct

(*To be continued.*)

THOMAS[2] DOTY'S WILL AND INVENTORY.

Transcribed from the Original Records,

BY GEORGE ERNEST BOWMAN.

THOMAS[2] DOTY (*Edward*[1]) died at Plymouth on the fourth or fifth of December, 1678. His nuncupative will was made on the fourth and "Comitted to writing December the 5th within 24 houres after the Death of the said Thomas Dotey." His widow, Mary, made oath to the inventory 3 March, 1678/9, the day the will was probated. The will and inventory are recorded in the Plymouth Colony Wills and Inventories, Volume IV, Part I, page 33, and a torn copy of the will, possibly the original, is on page 132 of the Scrap Book.

Thomas Dotey of Plymouth being very sicke yett haveing the use of his sences and reason Did on the fourth Day of December 1678 Declare these following words To be his last will Namly that all his estate hee Gave absolutely to his wife Mary Dotey to be wholly att her Dispose and left it all with her to Improve and make use of as shee should see best; This hee Declared to be his will as above written; In the p[r]sence of Edward Dotey and Samuell Eaton and Anne Sav[*blotted*]*; And it was Comitted to writing December the 5th within 24 houres after the Death of the said Thomas Dotey;

An Inventory of the estate of Thomas Doten Deceased taken the 28th Day of January by us whose Names are under written

Item 2 Cowes 1 Calfe 4 swine	05	12	0
Item his wearing Clothes	03	16	0
Item pewter and brasse and Iron ware	02	02	0
Item 2 Chests and a box	00	14	0
Item earthen ware trenchers and spoones & Glasses	00	07	0
Item Armes and amunition	01	13	0
Item bookes	00	04	0
Item 25 pound of sheeps woole and 19 pound and an halfe of Cotton woole	01	05	2
Item lines and ledds and hookes and spliting kniffe	00	08	0

* "Savoury" in the copy in the Scrap Book.

Item a butt & old Caske payels & tubbs	00	15	0
Item 1 shees and Napkins and blankett and other old linnine	01	01	0
Item 1 paire of boots	00	12	0
Item 1 spade 1 axe 1 paire of pitchforke tynes & other old Iron	00	06	0
Item 3 old baggs one paire of Cards 1 looking Glasse	00	03	0
Item 10 pond of feathers	00	10	0
	17	16	8

Debts Dew from the estate

Item att Boston to John Poole	01	04	0
Item To ffrancis Douce	00	12	0
Item To John Winge	00	13	06
Item To Mary ffarnum	00	16	0

Debts Due from the estate att Plymouth

To m^r^ Thomas Clarke	01	10	0
To Grge Watson	01	10	0
To John Churchill	00	10	0
To John Bryant seni^r^:	00	07	0
To Abraham Jackson	00	16	00

Ephram Morton
Willam harlow

These abovewritten Will and Inventory were exhibitted to the Court held att Plymouth the third of March 1678 : 79, the Inventory on the oath of Marey Dotey widdow;

THE DIARY OF JABEZ FITCH, JR.

(*Continued from page 150.*)

FORT EDWARD Wednsday July 13th 1757 This Day there was 24 Cannon Fired In ye Evening I was at Serj^t^ Comsticks Tent Hered Several Songs there &c To Day Capt: Fitch also Movd His Tent & Capt: Jefferys Ranging Company Movd out of ye Lines Serj^t^ Jackson Left Us &c —

ye 14th I Did Considrable Writing

ye 15th In ye Morning I Exercised with ye Serj^t^ again then went to Pummerys and was Treted By those Delinquents Some time after ye Guards were Relieved I was Warnd to Go Immediately & Relieve ye Gen^lls^ Orderly Serj^t^ accordingly I went as Soon as Possable — at Noon they Gave Me a Vary Good Dinner among other Varietyies a Fig Pudden in ye Afternoon there was Several Showers — this Day there was a Gen^ll^ Revue of y^e^

Women in ye army to Examen Whether they Had the &c or Not.

ye 16th In ye Morning I Got a Treat of Mr Pummery Vary Comacolly — then I went to ye Genlls again It Raind I Set in ye Genlls Markke & there Thought of our Way of Living Here and also at Home — I was Vary Much Pestred to Keep awake But at 9 oClok was Relieved as Usual then I went Home & Slep out My Nap &c — In ye Evening I went to a Tent & Heard A Hymn Sung and a Man went to Prayer — I also Hered Serjt Mack of Capt: Wellss Company Argu Vary Strangly Upon ye Soul of Man Saying it Slept after Death till ye Genll Resecrection — Yesterday there was a Boston Man Died Vary Suddenly Soposd to Be well & Dead in a Minit as He was Playing at Ball.

Sunday ye 17th It was Vary Showery weather a Vary warm Tolk about Peas &c: In ye Evening John Bennet of ye Regular Troops Came to our Tent again Staid Some time In ye Night Told us of ye Circumstances of His Coming away and His Business at Home &c.

ye 18th In ye Morning I Exercisd as Usual — Some time Before Noon Bennet Came & Brought ye History of Cynthia &c: this Day We Made our Selvs Much Sport with Som acts of our own in ye tent — Thos Andrus Vary Sick &c:

ye 19th In ye Morning Exercisd as Usual — Docr Clevland was Soon Confind for Some Misbehaviour &c: Toard Night Cleavland was Whipd 75 Lashes according to ye Sentence of a Cort-Mareschal — I was Warnd for ye Piqt accordingly I went Capt: Bailey was officer of ye Guard — Serjt Plumer of ye Rhod Island Regt was with Me & Corpl Enos Bartholamew of ye Boston Regt who Belongd to woodSock I Had Considrable Conversation with Each of them in ye Evening I Hered From My Relatives In Providence By Serjt Plumer ye Corpl Told Me Considrable of ye Afairs of ye People at WoodStock &c: after 10 oClok Capt: Bailey Sent Me into ye Camp For ye Parole then after I Came Back He told Me to Stay in ye Tent with Him and Keep time while ye Officers Slept then I Set Down & ye Capt: & I Discorsd about Every thing till ½ after 11 then we went ye Rounds & then Reld & I Turned In & Slept till Day —

ye 20th In ye Morning I Found out one Wm Bell of Capt Bellow Compy in ye 35 Regt who is a Recruit Lately arrivd Here — I Got Some acquaintance with Him finding His Conversation to Suit Me He tels Me He Spent 3 Years in ye University of Oxford in England But Since that He Has Bin Vary

Unfortunate Has Rovd abroad in y[e] world Ben Many Years in y[e] Kings Servis Befor He Inlisted into this Reg[t] But Has Lately Kept a Scool in Merryland about 3 years — Most of this Day I Spent in Conversation with Him Toard Night I went with a Party of 15 Men with Lieu[t] Brown to Look Some Lime Ston &c: In this Party I Got Some acquaintance with one Mackhollester of y[e] Indipendants who Came from Penselvane He Gives Me Considrable Account of affairs in His Cuntry & y[e] Caus of His Listing &c — at Night We was Relievd[d] as Usual — I found Serj[t] Comstock Confind — In y[e] Evening I went to y[e] Capt[ns] Tent & they Told Me of y[e] Contlusion of y[e] Late Gen[ll] Cortmareschal one of y[e] Ragulars was to Be Shot y[e] Next Morning — Ens[n] Lewis is Cashierd and to Depart Tomorrow they tell Me — Some other officers of y[e] Massachusetts & Rhod-Island Reg[ts] Here are Cashierd — a Number of Men to Be Whipd &c.

y[e] 21st In y[e] Morning I Made My Daily Report of y[e] Compa[y] then I went out to Se y[e] Execution Just as y[e] Guard was Marching into y[e] Fort to Aid y[e] Prisoner out af I Had Waited at y[e] Gail Near ½ an Hour they Came out with y[e] Prisoner — He was in His Proper Dress only Had on a White Cap Tied at y[e] Top with a Black Ribben His Countinance was Vary Pail as He Marchd Very Slow He was Reading in a Small Book Some Times I Observd Him to Shut Up His Book & Fold His Hands Mannifesting Great Consern of Mind when He Came to y[e] Plais of Execution there was about 1000 Men Drawn up in Two Lines then y[e] Prisoner was orderd to y[e] Spot where He was Executed and y[e] Guard Parted y[e] Grannodears Marchd Up Before y[e] Crimenal After He Had Stripd of His Coat & Kneeld Down Faising of them — then after Some Stand y[e] Grannodears Fired Upon Him He Emmediately Fell Down on His Fais Partly on one Side after Some time He Made Som Motion with one Hand then a Number of them Run Up Near Him a Fired Upon Him while He was Quite Dead — When y[e] Grannodears First Fired they were about 10 Yards Distance &c — y[e] Man Executed was a Dutchman His Name was Peck &c.

Fort Edward July 21st 1757 In y[e] Morning after y[e] Execution Before Mentioned in y[e] former Pamphlet I Se Two Men that Came In from a Scout that Had Ben atacted as they Said y[e] Scout Had Ben out 2 Days Consisting of a Lieu[t] & 30 Men But before Night we was Informd y[t] Non of y[e] Scout was Kild Except the Lieu[t] & when They all Shamefully Retreted and Ran In — y[e] Lieu[t] Belongd to y[e] Massachusets Reg[t]: Then I

Had Opportunity to Spend Some time with My New Friend Mr Bell He & I Walkd over to ye Garden & Had Som Pleasing Discors Some Time afternoon He Gave Me a Coppy of Verses &c — This Day Serj^t Comstock was Reduced to ye Ranks By ye Gen^{ll}s orders for Being Confedret with John Chappel in Supplying ye Regulars with Rhum &c: at Night Oxford Negro of Capt Wellss Comp^y I Se Whipd 75 Lashes — In ye Evening I Spent Some time with John Bennet of ye Regulars an acquaintant &c. He Told Me that He was Going off ye Next Morning — Now John Chappel is Confind & Sick this Day He was Tried By ye Cort Mareschal —

July 22nd In ye Morning a Detachment From ye Whol Line was Sent to Relieve ye Forts at Still waters & Saratoge From our Company Moses Cleavland Amasa Mix & Benjn Hopkins went off. — Thos Andrus Remains Vary Poor — This Day John Thomas of ye Rhod Island Reg^t was Whipd 300 Lashes they Tell Me For Counterfiting Dollars &c. In ye Evening I went to Lieu^t Durkees Tent Se ye News Paper &c —

July 23rd In ye Morning we Exercisd as Usual — Just as ye Troop Beet to Relieve ye Guard We Was Alarmd By A Smart Fireing in ye Woods where our Carpenters were at work — The Firing Lasted Near 1/2 an Hour as Soon as Possable Gen^{ll} Lyman Got orders to Go out with a Party But there was a Larg Number went out Before — I went with ye Gen^{ll} But Before we Got to ye Party Attacted ye Enimy were Drawn off & Carryd off their Dead if they Lost any as was Soposd they Did — We all Returnd in again about in about an Hour & Brought in our Dead & wounded Men — In ye Whol Engagement was Kild of ye 35th Reg^t Serj^t Felton Corp^l Wiley of ye Independants 2 Privats of ye Massachusetts 7 D^o of ye Connecticutts 1 D^o Totall 1^s 1^c 10^p

Lieu^t Harden & Corp^l John Ames were Wounded — one of ye Rhod Islanders was Wounded ye Connecticutt Man Kild was Amos Bibens of Capt Slapps Company He Livd till Night He was Buried ye Next Morning &c. one of Capt Jeffery Men Missing

There was Several Partys Sent after ye Enimy But None Discoverd em — in ye Afternoon I went out with Capt Gallop I was Gon about 2 Hours & Got Lost from ye Capt Party & Returnd in again at Night I was Warnd for ye Fort Guard —

Sunday ye 24th Corp^l Thos Andrus was Exceeding Poor Vary Much Shatterd This Morning He Chappel Peter Button & Toba Negro Were over to ye Hospital on ye Island &c. I Mounted ye Fort Guard It Fell to My Lot to take the Ravaleen

Guard without ye Draw Bridg— I Made a Corpl of a Dutchman of ye Indipendants — From 7 oClok to 10 I Spent Cheefly in Walking ye Draw Bridg Considering ye Conserns of Life &c.

About Midnight there Came Two Men with an Express from Fort Wm Henry to Genll Webb — after I Had Sent to ye Officer of ye Fort Guard I Opend ye Gait & Let them In & Askd them what News they Told Me yt Col Parker with 350 Men went Down ye Lake Saturday Morning Sunday In ye afternoon Col Parker Capt Ogden & 60 Men Got in in ye Morning they were attacted at ye Narrows & Most of them Distroyd — This is all ye Information we Can Get at Present &c We Had a Comfortable Night I Slep Considrable

July ye 25th In ye Morning Genll Webb Marchd off for ye Lake &c — I was Relievd at ye Usual time after I Had Made Report to ye Officer of ye Fort Guard In ye Following Form

Fort Edward July 25th 1757 A Report of ye Ravelleen Guard Parole Pembrookshire — Sentries By Day 2 Sentries By Night 2 Nothing Extraordinary Has Hapend Sence I mounted — all is Well pr Jabez Fitch Serjt

About 2 oClok I Went over to ye Hospitall to Se our Sick Men there Found Andrus Poorer than Ever Seeming to Have But Little Time To Live — ye Rest of them Not Much wors — on ye Island I Accidentally Lit of Mr Bell My New friend He was Lame in one Leg —

ye 26th I was Not well Some time this Morning there Was a Man of ye Massachusetts Regt Shot threw ye Hart and Kild in an Instant By a Gun Going off accidentally in annother Tent — About Noon I went over onto ye Green with Mr Langley Then He Treated Me with a Bool of Punch &c: Toard Night there was a Hard Shower of Rain one of Capt Jeffarys Men was Whipt 50 Lashes for Sleeping on His Post &c — About Midnight ye Night Following there was a Larrem Made By a Sentry of ye Piqts Firing a Gun But it is Soposd to Be a Fals alarrem

ye 27th About 4 oClok in ye Afternoon Samll Hoscott Died — This Day a Detachment was Sent off to Relieve ye Detachment at Half Moon — John Button & Josiah Fullar of our Company Went off &c. at Night I Could By No Means Furnish Men according to ye Details Deliverd to Me — I went to ye Adjutant and Got it olterd &c.

ye 28th ye Annuel of our March to ye Lake from this Fort This Day I was Warnd to Wait on Genll Lyman But was Excusd Because there was No Other Serjt or Corpll in ye Company of from Duty — In ye Forenoon Some time I went with Ensn Howard Down about 4 Miles Below ye Brick Kils To

Look Col Pasons Hors there we Found Him with Several other Horses — Going & Coming I Marchd in ye Rear Stopd Several times and Eat Rass Berrys & Black Berrys we Got Back about 2 oClok in ye Afternoon — at Night I Se Several of ye Independants whip^{t} among others a Man was Whipt for Loosing His Blanket & He Said y^{t} He Never Rec^{d} any However He Rec^{d} 10 Lashes & Had Rec^{d} 100 ye Night before on ye Same account they were Laid on Vary S [*blotted*] too—

(*To be continued.*)

ADAM WRIGHT'S WILL AND INVENTORY.*

TRANSCRIBED BY GEORGE ERNEST BOWMAN.

ADAM WRIGHT, the son of Richard and Hester (Cooke) Wright, and the grandson of Francis Cooke of the Mayflower, died at Plympton, Mass., 20 September, 1724.† His first wife was Sarah^{3} Soule (*John*^{2}, *George*^{1}); his second was Mehitable the daughter of Robert Barrows of Plymouth. The descendants of the first wife have, therefore, two Mayflower lines and the children of the second wife but one.

Adam Wright's will and inventory are recorded in the Plymouth County Probate Records, Volume V, pages 26–29. The copy of the will here presented was made from the records, as the original has disappeared from the files, but the inventory was copied from the original document. The will was probated on 2 November, 1724, before Isaac^{3} Winslow (*Gov. Josiah*^{2}, *Gov. Edward*^{1}), Judge of Probate.

[p. 26] Know all men by these Presents y^{t} I Adam Wright of Plympton in ye County of Plymth, in new: England: being grown to old age altho by ye Blessing of God I am in perfect health & of Sound mind & memory & being minded to Settle my Estate do make & ordain this my last Will & Testament as followeth that is to Say: Imprimis I give & Bequeath unto my Son John Wright (besides what I gave Him in ye Land whereon he now dwelleth) ye Sum of five Shillings money . as also all my Rights of Land where Ever they may be found which are

* Printed in full by request of a liberal contributor to the Colonial Research Fund.

† Mayflower Descendant, I: 178.

not otherwise disposed of in this Will or otherwise by Deeds. Item [p. 27] Item: I have already given by deeds unto my two Sons Isaac Wright & Samuel Wright ye lands whereon they & I now dwell which I Esteem to be their full Part & Portion of my Estate: Item: I have already given unto my Son Moses Wright by Deed all my Lands Lying in Winnatuxitt neck which I Esteem to be his full Part & Portion of my Estate. Item: I give & Bequeath unto my two Grand: Children: viz: Joshua Pratt & Sarah his sister children of my Daughter Esther Pratt dec^d^ ye Sum of five Shillings a Peice money which with what I gave unto their s^d^ mother in her Life time I Esteem to be their full Part & Portion of my Estate. Item. I have given by Deed bearing Date with these Presents unto my Daughter Sarah Fuller ye wife of Seth Fuller all my Lands lying upon ye neck on ye northerly side of Colchester Brook which together with what moveable Estate She hath already Had I Esteem to be Her full Part & Portion of my Estate. Item: I give & bequeath unto my two Sons viz: James Wright & Nathan Wright ye Sum of one Hundred Pounds in money a Peice to be Paid unto them by my Executrix out of my Estate when they shall arrive to ye age of twenty one years old. Item: I give & bequeath unto my daughter Mary Gifferd ye wife ye wife of Jeremiah Giffered ye Sum of twenty Pounds to be Paid by my Executrix out of my moveable Estate at my decease. Item: I give & bequeath unto my Daughter Rachel Barlow ye wife of Ebenezer Barlow ye sum of twenty Pounds to be Paid by my Executrix out of my moveable Estate at my decease Item: I give & Bequeath unto my True & Loving wife mehitable Wright (whom I Likewise Constitute make & ordain to be Sole Executrix of this my Last Will & Testament) all ye Remaining Part of my Estate (my Just Debts & Funeral Charges being first Paid) to be for Her Support & Comfort So long as She Remains my widdow & to be by Her disposed of to any of my Children which She Seeth Cause but If it Should So Happen after my decease that She Shall marry then my Will is that She Shall have ye Sum of Twenty Pounds out of my Estate & that She dispose of ye Rest to my Children as aboves^d^ In Witness whereof I have hereunto Set my Hand & Seal this ninth day of aprill one thousand seven Hundred twenty three 1723

Signed Sealed & declared to be His last Will & Testament In Presence of us
Joseph Thomas
Nathaniel Fuller
Isaac Cushman Junr

Adam Wright (seal)
His mark

[*From the Original Inventory.*]

A True Inventory of the personal Estate of Adam Wright Late of Plimpton deceased prised at Plimpton the octo^{r} ye 10th: 1724 by us ye subscribers.

Imprimis his books apparel and bonds	332	9	6
Item Neat Cattle and swine	9	15	0
Indian & English Corn flax & flax seed	3	16	0
Item to hoops boxes and old Iron	2	7	0
Item sheeps wool & Cotton wool & wheels & Cards	1	11	10
Item Lumber in ye hous	1	10	08
Item Iron ware in ye house and brass	3	2	0
Item Earthen ware spoons Glasses & & one Grindstone	0	14	6
Item peuter & Cotton & Linen yarn	3	1	0
Item to beds and beding and bedsteds	26	10	0
debts due to the Estate	00	6	0
debts due from the Estate	15	18	9

Isaac Cushman Ju
Joseph Thomas
James Soul

November the 2^{d}: 1724

The above named Jsaac Cushman Junr and Joseph Thomas made oath th[*worn*] above written is a just and equall apprisement of the personall Estate of Adam Wright of Plimpton in the County of Plimoth according to the best of their Judgment

Before Isaac Winslow Judge of Probate

November the 2: 1724

Mehetable Wright Executor named in the last Will and Testemen[t] of her husband Adam Wright of Plimpton in the County of Plimoth made oath that the above written is a tru and perfect Inventory of the Estate of her sd husband Adam Wright deceased as far as is Come to her knowledg and if more hereafter appears she will also give it in

Before Isaac Winslow Judge of Probate

January the 5: 1724

James Soul made oath that the above written is a Just and equall apprisement of the Estate of Addam Wright late of Plimpton deceased according to the best of his Judgment.

Before Isaac Winslow Judge of Probate

RECORDS OF THE FIRST PARISH IN BREWSTER, FORMERLY THE FIRST PARISH IN HARWICH, MASS.

Transcribed from the Original Records,

BY GEORGE ERNEST BOWMAN.

THE original township of Harwich, Mass., extending across Cape Cod from north to south, was incorporated in 1694. The first church gathered within its limits was organized in 1700, in the northern part of the town, and in 1747 another church was established in the southern part. In 1803 the town was divided, the southern half retaining the name Harwich and the northern half being incorporated as the town of Brewster, so named in honor of Elder William Brewster. Since the division of the town the First Parish in Harwich has become the First Parish in Brewster.

The records of this church for the forty-eight years from its organization on October 16, 1700, to and including October 23, 1748, were kept by the first pastor, Rev. Nathaniel Stone. The second pastor, Rev. Isaiah Dunster, then kept the record for forty-two years, his first entry (near the bottom of page 121) being dated October 30, 1748, and his last November 14, 1790. The record for these ninety years was kept in a little book of five and seven-eighths by three and three-fourths inches in size, bound in leather-covered boards. The book originally contained two hundred and twenty pages, and twenty pages loosely stitched together were laid in at the back by Mr. Dunster whose record covers part of them. Pages 207 to 216 inclusive have been torn out, but pages 213–216, containing the beginning of Mr. Stone's account of admissions and baptisms, are still preserved with the book. With these four pages inserted in their proper place chronologically Mr. Stone's record appears to be complete. Pages 207–212 are missing. They were torn out before December 8, 1776, or were written upon before that date, since Mr. Dunster's record for the year 1776, found on pages 204–206 and then skipping to page 217, appears to be complete. The third pastor, Rev. John Simpkins, took up the record in 1791, beginning in the middle of page 237, and doubtless wrote the remaining three and one half pages of the book, but the last two pages, 239 and 240, have been lost.

The leaves of the book are very badly water-stained, and in a few the ink has eaten through the paper, but there are very few places where the writing is not legible and the edges of the leaves are very little worn.

Permission to copy these records has been secured through the courtesy of the present pastor, the Rev. Thomas Dawes, and Mr. J. Henry Sears, a member of the parish committee.

[p. 1] On Oct 16 . 1700 . the church in Harwich consisting of eight persons, was gathered, wh[ose] Chh covenant, with their names thereunto subscribed, is as followeth.

We who are by nature children of wrath, even as others, and at best but unprofitable Servants of ye Lord [*illegible*] being Sensible of our own inability eith[er] to make or keep Covenant, di[*illegible*] all confidence in ourselves, and looking up to God in X for ye help of his holy Spirit, in this Solemn work, without which, we can doe nothing as we o[*worn*] We doe here in ye presence of y^e^ [*worn*] high God, his holy Angels and this as[sem]bly, with Solemnity, fear and rever[ence] at this time make, or renew our Covenant with the Lord our God, and with one an other, and (1) We take (y^e^) true God, Father, Son and holy Ghost one God in three persons to be our God, & promiss y^t^, through his grace we will be his people. We give up our Selves and ours unto ye Lord Jehovah to be his only, wholly and forever. (2) We promiss, Jesus X willing y^t^ while [p. 2] we live together we will be carefull to observe ye rules of distributive justice, rendering each to other y^t^ honour respect and love which ye gospell of Christ requires of us, according to ye relations in which we Stand as an Eclesiastick Society, and y^t^ we will Seek to preserve and promote ye peace and grouth of this Church of Christ, and carefully avoid whatever may tend to obstruct or hinder ye Same. (3) we also promiss, Christ assisting, y^t^ we will attend ye rule in watching over one another, exhorting and admonishing one another as ye rule requireth, and [a]s occasion Shall be. We further promiss, Still depending on ye grace and strength of X, to indeavour y^t^ there may be a faithfull and through exercise of discipline, according to w^t^ Christ has appointed to be observed in his House from time to time without respect to persons. (4) And Sumarily, we Covenant y^t^ we will in all things indeavour to walk, both toward God and one toward another in Sincerity, in love and in peace as becometh ye gospell : Seeking and indeavouring ye good each of other, ye restraint of Sin, ye furtherance of ye work and cause of X amongue us; indeavouring by our good conversations to [p. 3] allure those yt are without, to a love to, & choice of yt way of holiness which we profess to walk in.

This Covenant we make ys day wth willing minds, and we bow our knees to the God and father of our Lord Jesus X, yt by his grace inabling us we may not only make, but keep Covenant and be steadfast with him therin, unto his glory and ye good of us and ours with and after us, Amen.

Nathll Stone.	Tho: Freeman
Tho: Crosbey.	Edw: Bangs.
Wm Marick	Simon Crosbie
John Freeman.	Joseph Pain.

This following Confession of faith was at the Same time made and Subscribed.

We whose names are under-written being, by ye good and gracious providence of God So far favoured yt we are broug[ht] to ye day and time Set apart for our Solemn entring into Chh estate : And the Church of X, being a City Set upon an hill, which cannot be hid; We are desirous yt our Lights may So Shine before men, yt our heavenly Father may [p. 4] be glorified; And particularly at this time yt the Light of Gospell-doctrine may Shine forth in our Solemn profession of ye Same; We doe declare our full ascent and consent unto, and firm belief and persuasion of ye truth and certainty of ye Articles of the Christian Religion according to ye word of God, and as it is laid down in ye Shorter Chatechisme, comonly called the Assemblies Chatechisme, and as it has been professed and held in the Churches which we have been heretofore joyned unto; And, by ye grace of God inabling of us doe promiss to continue therin firm unto ye End.

Nathll Stone.	Tho: Freeman.
Thomas Crosbie.	Edw: Bangs.
Wm Marick.	Simon Crosbie
John Freeman.	Joseph Pain.

After these things, on ye Same Day, Nathanaell Stone was Ordained Pastor of this Church in Harwich.

On Novem : 28 . 1700 . the Church made choice of Mr Thomas Freeman to the office of a Deacon.

[p. 213]* An Account of the names of all y[e] persons either admited into, or baptized in y[e] Church of Harwich ever-since it was first founded.

Uxor mea Reliance Stone admissa est Decem : 15. 1700.
Lieu[t] Bangs was Admited on the 2[nd] of Febru : 1701.
Tho : Snow's Son Ebenezer, baptised on March 30. 1701.
M[rs] Sarai Crosbie, Mary Bangs, & y[e] widow jane Snow were admited on Apr : 1701.
Filia (mea†) nostra Kezia Stone bap[t]izata fuit Apr : 13. 1701.
Simon Crosbies' Son John baptized on Aprill 13. 1701.
Thomas Clark & his Wife admited June 8. 1701.
Mercy Sears Admited June 15. 1701.
Rebecca Freeman; Patience Pain; Ruth Bangs; Suzannah Grey; Mary Crosbey; & Hannah Snow, all admited on June 22. 1701.
Dorcas Pain baptized June 22. 1701.
[p. 214] The Wife of Andrew Clark admited on Aug : 3. 1701.
Martha Cole baptized Aug : 17. 1701.
John, y[e] Son of Samuel Seers baptized Aug : 24. 1701.
Elkanah y[e] Son of Stephen Hopkins junior baptized Aug 31. 1701.
The Wives of John Freeman Sen[r], of Stephen Hopkins Sen[r] and jun[r], as also of John King, all admited on Sept : 14. 1701.
Samuell y[e] Son of John & Suzanna Grey, baptized Decem : 14. 1701.
Ebenezer, y[e] Son of Edward & Ruth Bangs baptized Feb : 8. 1702.
Sarai the daughter of Thomas and Sarai Clark baptized Sept : 27. 1702.
Nath[ll], the Son of John and Bathsheba King baptized on Octo : 11. 1702.
Hannah y[e] daughter of Tho. & Hannah Snow baptised on Apr : 25 1703.
Filia nostra Reliance Stone baptisata fuit May 2. 1703.
Lydia, the Daughter of John & Susanna Grey baptised on July 4. 1703.
Seth, the Son of Samuell & Mercy Seers baptised on July 18. 1703.
[p. 215] [Ph]ebe the daughter of Joseph and Pati[e]nce Pain baptized on Aug : 1. 1703.
[H]annah y[e] daughter of Simon and Mary Crosbey baptized on Jan : 30. 1703/4
Rouland the Son of Thomas and Sarai Clar[k] baptised on Apr : 9. 1704.

* Pages 213–216 inclusive are printed here in order to preserve the chronological order of the entries. See the note at the end of original page 216 and that at the beginning of original page 5 which immediately follows in this transcript.

† Crossed out in original.

Nath[ll] the Son of John & Bathsheba King baptised on Apr : 23. 1704.

Thomas Crosbey & his Wife admited, & also their children Sarah & Hannah baptized on June 4. 1704.

Thomas, ye Son of Stephen Hopkins jun : baptized on July 9. 1704.

Lidea ye daughter of Joseph Crosbey of Yarmouth baptized (by virtue of comunion of churches) on Sept : 3. 1704.

James ye Son of Silas Seers of Yarmouth, baptised (by virtue of comunion of chhes) on Sep : 17. 1704.

Mr Winslow admited Sep : 17. 1704.

& his wife yt day fortnight after.

[R]uth, ye daughter of Edw : and Ruth Bangs baptized on Feb : 4. 1704/5.

Sarah, ye daughter of John & Susanna Grey baptised on Feb. 18. 1704/5.

Deborah ye daughter of Paul Seers of Yarmouth baptized (by virtue of comunion of Chhes) on May 6. 1705.

Thomas, ye Son of Thomas and Hannah Crosbey baptized on Aug : 19. 1705.

Filius noster, Heman Stone baptizatus fuit Sept : 9. 1705.

A Son of Zech : Paddock of Yarmouth, baptized by virtue of comunion of chhs on Nov : 4. 1705.

Daniell, the Son of Simon Crosby; & Suzanna the Daughter of Thomas Clark Baptised on Dec : 9–1705.

Reliance, ye Daughter of Ensigne Pain baptized on Feb : 3. 17[05/6]

[p. 216] Mehittabell ye daughter of John & Suzanna Gr[ey] baptized on June 2. 1706

Elizabeth Mayo baptized (by virtue of comunio[n] of chhs on July 28. 1706.

Lieut : Seers, his Son Benjamin baptized on Aug : 18. 1706.

Eodem Die Joseph Crosbies son Josiah, by virtue of comunion of churches.

Thomas Lincolns Daughter Mary baptized by virtue of comunion of chhs, Sep : 15. 1706

Thomas Clarks Daughter Thankfull baptized on Jan : 26. 1707.

Ensigne Maricks Wife admited on Feb : 9. 1707.

Paul Seers his Daughter Ann baptized, by virtue of comunion of Chhs, Feb : 16. 1707.

Stephen Hopkins's Son Ebenezer baptized on Feb : 23. 1707.

Edw : Bangs's Son, Jonathan, Baptized, Mar : 23. 1707.

Simon Crosbeys Daughter Mercy, baptized, May 4. 17[07]

Lydia, the wife of Tho Snow admited July 2[*] [1707]

Thomas Snowes Daughter Lydia baptized Aug : 17. 170[7]

Mary, ye Daughter of Canelm Winslow bap[tiz]ed (by virtue of comunion of chhs) on Sep : 21. 1707

* This must be either 20 or 27.

Edw : Snowes Wife admitted on Oct : 12. 1707. and their children Thomas, Jabez, Rebeckka, and Martha baptized on the Sabbath next following.

Rome here failing, turn back to Page 5. where the Account proceedeth.

[p. 5] Of all Persons hithertoe admited into, or baptized in this Chh, See Page 213, and forward; Oct : 12. 1707.

Edward Snow admitted on Nov : 30. 1707.

John Gray's Son Andrew baptized on Feb : 8. 1708.

Filius noster, Nathan Stone, aqua Sacramentali lavatus, Feb : 22. 1708.

The Wife of Joseph Seers of Yarmouth admited on March 21. 1708.

and on ye Same day Tho : Linckhorn with his Wife & Mrs Mayo received in from other Chhs.

Zecharia Paddocks Daughter Priscilla baptised, by virtue of comunion of Chhs, on Apr : 11. 1708

Joseph Seers's Children, Zechariah, Joseph, Priscilla and Hannah baptized on May 2. 1708.

Lieutenant Nicorsons Wife of Monomoit admited on Nov : 14. 1708.

Thomas and Mary ye Son and Daughter of Ensigne Pain baptised on Dec : 5. 1708.

John Crosbey and his Wife admited on Decem : 12. 1708.

Mr Hopkins admited on Dec : 26. 1708.

Mr Hopkins; John Crosbies children viz Thomas, John & Jonathan; as also John Kings Daughter Bathsheba, all baptised on Jan 2. 1708

[p. 6] Simon Crosbies son Ebenezer, and Tho : Lincolns Son Sam^ll^ baptized on Feb : 20. 1708/9.

Prince Snow's Wife admited, and Filia nostra Thankfull baptizata, March 6. 1708/9.

Prence Snowes children, viz Jabez, Samuell, Prence, Hannah & Mercy baptized on March 20. 1708/9.

Joseph Seers his Wife dismissed from this Chh, to that in Yarmouth on Apr : 24–1709.

And at ye Same time the Wife of John Smith admited into this Church.

Thomas Clarks Son, Seth baptized on May 15. 1709.

John Crosbies Son Daved baptized on May 22. 1709.

Chillingsworth Foster admited; his two Sons James, & Chillinsworth; with Tho Crosbies Son Edward baptized, all on May 29. 1709.

Thomas Snow's Son Thomas baptized on June 19. 1709.

Lieutenant Tho : Nicorson of Monomoit, his Nine Children, viz, Jonathan, Mercy, Thomas, William, Ebenezer, Edward Nath^ll^, Mary, Thankfull, all baptized on Oct : 9. 1709.

John Gray's Daughter Anna, baptised on Oct. 23. 1709.

[J]ohn Harskall of Rochester, his son John baptis[ed] on Nov : 20. 1709.
[p. 7] Edw : Snowes Son Nath^ll^ and Chillingsworth Fosters Daughter Mary both baptized on Jan : 8. 1709/10.
Prince Snowes two Sons Jonathan and Daved baptized on Jan : 22. 1709/10.
Edw. Bangs Rebeckkah baptised on March 12. 1709/10
Israell Coles Wife dismissed from this Chh in Aprill 1710.
Simon Crosbies Son Moses baptised on June 11. 1710.
Thomas Clarkes Son Isaac baptized on Aug : 13. 1710.
Sam^ll^ Hopkinss Wife admited, and she with her Son Richard baptised on Oct : 29. 1710.
Joseph Pains son Jonathan baptised on Dec : 10. 1710.
Thomas Lincolns Daughter Mercy baptised on Dec : 31. 1710.
John Kings Wife Admitted on Jan : 14. 1710/11
Tho : Snowes Son Aaron Baptised on March 18. 1710/11.
Tho Hinckleys Widow admited and her Sons Joshua and Thomas baptized Apr : 22. 1711.
Sam^ll^ Hopkins & Stephen Griffiths Wife admited on May 6. 1711.
Stephen Griffiths Children, Joseph, Stephen, Lazarus, Barnabas, & Rebekka baptized May 20. 1711.
Charels Clarks Wife admited on June 3. 1711.
Her children John and Frances Baptized on Jue 10–1711.
Then Also Sam^ll^ Hynckley & his Wife admited and He baptized.
[p. 8] Sam^ll^ Hyncklies children Seth, Sam^ll^ & Shubael baptized on June 17. 1711.
Unice Stone, filia nostra, Baptizata fuit June 24. 1711.
Sam^ll^ Bangs and his wife admited on July 1. & She, with their children Seth, Sam^ll^, David and Mary, baptized on July 8. 1711.
Stephen Hopkins's Daughter Phebe, baptized on Aug : 12. 1711.
Kanelm Winslow's Daughter Hannah baptized on Sept : 9–1711.
Sam^ll^ Hopkins's Son Moses baptized on Dec : 30. 1711.
Simon Crosbeys son Increase baptized on Feb : 24. 1711/12.
John Gray Son Elisha baptized on March 9. 1711/12. & Chillingsworth Fosters Son Thomas on ye 16 of ye Same moneth.
John Crosbies Son Joshua baptized on Sept : 7. 1712.
William Nicorsons Wife, admited, on her dismission from Eastham Chh on ye Sabbath imediately preceeding.
Prince Snowes Daughter Mary baptized on Oct : 19. 1712.
Thomas Crosbies Daughter Abigail baptized Nov : 16. 1712.
Sam^ll^ Hynkleys son Edmund Baptized on Jan : 18. 1712/3
Thomas Lincolnes Daughter Margaret baptized on Jan : 25. 1712/13.
Thomas Snowes Daughter Ruth; & Sam^ll^ Bangs's son Josoph baptized on March 1. 1712/13
John Kings Daughter Mercy baptized on May 17. 1713.
[p. 9] Sam^ll^ Tucker of Chatham admited on May 17. 1713.
The Widow Pains Daughter Experience baptized on June 7. 1713.
Sam^ll^ Hopkinses Daughter Lidia baptized on June 14. 1713.

John Grayes Son Joshua baptized Oct : 25. 1713.
Andrew Clarks Wife admited Nov : 8. 1713.
Andrew Clarks Daughter Mehetabell baptized on Nov : 15. 1713.
Nathan^{ll} Stone Filius Noster baptizatus fuit Nov. 29. 1713.
John Freeman jun : his wife admited Mar : 14. 1713/14
his children Sarah, Mercy, John and Phebe baptized March 28. 1713/14.
Stephen Griffith's child Baptized May 16. 1714.
Thomas Snow admited on June 13. 1714.
John Freeman jun : admited July 11. 1714.
Andrew Clarks child Elizabeth baptized July 18. 1714.
Lieutenant Clarks Elizabeth Baptized Aug : 1. 1714.
Mercy Smith admited on Aug. 29. 1714.
John Freemans Thankfull Baptised on Oct : 10. 1714.
Stephen Hopkins's Hanna baptized Nov : 7. 1714.
Sam^{ll} Hynckleys Reliance baptised on Jan : 23. 1714/15
John Grayes Anna baptized Feb : 20. 1714/15.
And Widow Crosbies Abia at ye Same time.
Sam^{ll} Bangs's Melatia baptised March 6. 1714/15.
Debora Weeks and Rachell Whing admited and baptised on May 1. 1715.
John Whings Wife admited on June 12. 1715
[p. 10] Chillingsworth Foster Son Nathan baptised June 12. 1715.
Sam^{ll} Halls Wife admited on June 19. 1715.
Sam^{ll} Tuckers children viz Kezia Elizabeth and Thankfull all baptised on July 3. 1715.
Sam^{ll} Hopkins's Daughter Reliance baptized on July 24. 1715.
Achsah Stone filia nostra baptizata Sept : 4. 1715.
Sam^{ll} Scers jun : and his Wife admited on Sept : 18. 1715.
Sam^{ll} Sers's children Abigail, Ruth and Mercy Baptized Oct : 16. 1715
And at ye same time George Weeks's Daughter Abigail.
John Whings Daughter Bethia baptised on March 11. 1715/16.
On March 25. 1716. after the Death of Deacon Freeman, Mr Thomas Crosbey and Mr Thomas Lincoln were chosen by ye Chh, with ye concurrence of their Pastor to Succeed in that office.
Deacon Lincolns Daughter Thankfull baptised on May 13. 1716.
At Deacon Freemans death was seven pounds overplus of ye contributions for ye Sacrament, the one half of which was returned to ye Chh, and the other given by them to his family.

(*To be continued.*)

CAPE COD PILGRIM MEMORIAL ASSOCIATION.

To Every Patriotic American:

IT is proposed to erect upon the highest point in Provincetown, Mass., a suitable monument to commemorate the first landing of the Pilgrim fathers upon Cape Cod soil and the adoption by them of the immortal Compact of Civil Government in the cabin of the Mayflower.

This is an object which should appeal to every patriotic citizen. In this cause the people of Cape Cod have already contributed nearly $5000.00. The Commonwealth of Massachusetts by its last Legislature endorsed by unqualified approval this effort to erect such a memorial by appropriating the sum of $25,000.00, provided the same amount should be procured by the Association within three years.

The scope of its meaning and the breadth of its support are limited only by the confines of the nation, at the basis of whose strength lie the eternal principles which the Pilgrims assisted to place there.

Never was it more necessary than today that their truth should be remembered by us and impressed on others. In an essentially commercial age, when men are too often absorbed in the eager struggle for wealth; when industrial prosperity is advancing by leaps and bounds; when combinations of the wealth so created wield unprecedented power, it cannot be too often or too strongly emphasized that true national power and stability do not consist in the mere prizes of commercial supremacy but in those great underlying principles of civil and religious liberty laid down in their hour of distress and poverty, by the Pilgrims one winter day in Provincetown harbor so many years ago.

In thus honoring the Pilgrims we honor and proclaim to the nation the value of the real elements of its great prosperity. Therefore, according to your individual ability and conscience, we trust that you will aid us in this effort.

Let us all then unite in erecting an appropriate memorial to the Pilgrims as rugged and as lofty as befits their work and character, at the place where their feet touched the land whose life and history they have so greatly moulded.

It is desirable that these contributions may be so prompt

and substantial that within the ensuing year the sum of $20,000 may be secured, which will enable the Association to take advantage of the wise generosity of the Commonwealth, which has not only cordially endorsed the undertaking but has insisted on the reasonable co-operation and self help of a powerful and grateful people.

Is it too much to expect that those of us upon whom "Dame Fortune" has smiled should and will contribute to this noble undertaking a goodly amount and those of us less fortunate the sum of one dollar which will entitle the donor to become a member?

J. HENRY SEARS, President, Brewster, Mass.
R. C. NICKERSON, Chairman, East Brewster, Mass.
THOMAS C. THACHER, Boston, Mass.
WILLIAM B. LAWRENCE, Medford, Mass.
HENRY H. BAKER, Hyannis, Mass.
MARSHALL L. ADAMS, Provincetown, Mass.
EVERETT I. NYE, Wellfleet, Mass.
HENRY H. SEARS, East Dennis, Mass.
OSBORN NICKERSON, Chathamport, Mass.
Directors of Cape Cod Pilgrim Memorial Association.

[Contributions should be sent to Howard F. Hopkins, Treasurer, Provincetown, Mass.]

REPORTS FROM STATE SOCIETIES.

MASSACHUSETTS SOCIETY.

Donations to the Library and Cabinet.

"John Allen and Phoebe Deuel of Cambridge and Peru, N. Y.," from the compiler, Mr. Charles J. North.

"History of the British Dominions in North America," (London, 1773), from Miss Elizabeth Cowing.

"Samuel E. Sewall, A Memoir," from Mr. George A. Dary.

"John Hall of Wallingford, Conn.," from the compiler, Mr. James Shepard.

"Loss of the Sparrow Hawk in 1626"; "The Wreck of the Somerset, British Man-of-War"; and a Piece of a Pear Tree said to have been planted in Eastham by Gov. Thomas Prence and blown down in 1879, all from Mr. Everett Irving Nye.

Members Elected.

June 30, 1902.

718. Mrs. Charles Francis Washburn, Worcester, seventh from John Alden.
719. Miss Miriam Washburn, Worcester, eighth from William Bradford.
720. George Ulysses Grant Holman, New York, N. Y., tenth from William Brewster.
721. Rev. George Madison Bodge, Westwood, eighth from John Howland.
722. Edward Eugene Clapp, Atlanta, Ga., seventh from John Alden.

Supplemental Lines Filed.

July, 1902.

708. Charles Brooks Perkins, ninth from John Alden (three lines); tenth from John Billington, ninth from Francis Billington; tenth from William Brewster (two lines), ninth from Love Brewster; tenth from Peter Brown; tenth from Francis Cooke (two lines); tenth from Stephen Hopkins; ninth from Stephen Hopkins; ninth from George Soule (four lines); ninth from Myles Standish (three lines); tenth from Richard Warren (two lines).

August, 1902.

635. Mrs. Edward H. Nichols, ninth from John Alden, ninth from Richard Warren.

NEW YORK SOCIETY.

Member Elected.

June 6, 1902.

686. Mrs. William Rice Donaghe, Morristown, N. J., seventh from John Howland.

CONNECTICUT SOCIETY.

Members Elected.

July 14, 1902.

227. Mrs. Robert James Johnston, Humboldt, Iowa, ninth from William Brewster.
228. Mrs. William Henry Osborn, New London, ninth from John Howland.

PENNSYLVANIA SOCIETY.

Members Elected.

June 18, 1902.

137. Mrs. Andrew Thompson, Hinesdale, eighth from Edward Fuller, seventh from Samuel[2] Fuller.
138. Mrs. George Dallas Dixon, Rosemont, ninth from John Howland.
139. Mrs. John Marshall, Philadelphia, eighth from William Bradford.
140. Robert Alexander, Philadelphia, tenth from Francis Cooke, ninth from John Cooke.

141. James Frederick Fahnestock, Jr., Philadelphia, ninth from William Brewster.
142. Lincoln Godfrey, Radnor, tenth from Thomas Rogers.

ILLINOIS SOCIETY.

Members Elected.

July 8, 1902.
90. Mrs. Marvin Ansel Dean, Evanston, ninth from John Alden.
91. Myron Day Downs, Chicago, eighth from William Bradford.
92. Frederick Gale Davis, Chicago, ninth from William Brewster.

Supplemental Lines Filed.

July, 1902.
83. Glenn Wood, M.D., eighth from John Alden; ninth from William Brewster; seventh from John Howland.

DISTRICT OF COLUMBIA SOCIETY.

Members Elected.

June 14, 1902.
125. Mrs. Edward Orr Stafford, Marquette, Mich., eighth from William Bradford.
126. Horace Albert Baker, Brooklyn, N. Y., seventh from John Alden.
127. Miss Flora Louise Priscilla Johnson, Washington, eighth from John Alden.
128. Mrs. George F. Elliott, Norfolk, Va., ninth from William Bradford.
129. Axel Hayford Reed, Glencoe, Minn., eighth from William Bradford.
130. Chauncey Otis Howard, Mt. Holly, N. J., ninth from Francis Cooke.
131. Charles Harris Hopkins, Santa Barbara, Cal., seventh from Stephen Hopkins, sixth from Gyles Hopkins.
132. Rev. George Brinckerhoff Richards, Buffalo, N. Y., eighth from John Howland.
133. Joshua Freeman Grozier, Denver, Col., eighth from Stephen Hopkins, seventh from Gyles Hopkins.
134. Charles Tufts Caldwell, M.D., Washington, eighth from Isaac Allerton, seventh from Mary Allerton.
135. Miss Maybelle Raymond, Washington, eighth from Edward Doty.
136. Mrs. Price Colby Claflin, Washington, ninth from John Alden.
137. Mrs. Amherst Willoughby Barber, Washington, eighth from John Howland.
138. Edmund Southard Parker, Washington, seventh from Edward Doty.
139. Bascom Johnson, Philadelphia, Pa., eighth from John Alden.
140. Mrs. Henry Sewall Hall, Washington, seventh from John Alden.
141. Mrs. John C. Dent, Manilla, P. I., eighth from William Bradford.
142. Mrs. John G. McMillan, Hoquiam, Wash., seventh from George Soule.
143. Mrs. Lewis Randolph Bryan, Houston, Texas, eighth from William Brewster.

144. Miss Ellen Geer, Norwich, Conn., eighth from William Bradford.
145. Mrs. Arthur Bertram Skelding, Wilmington, N. C., ninth from Richard Warren.

NEW JERSEY SOCIETY.

Members Elected.

April 11, 1902.

28. Amory Thompson Skerry, Jr., Montclair, ninth from Myles Standish.
29. William Maxson Stillman, Plainfield, eighth from William Brewster.
30. Mrs. Perry Haight Bradshaw, Orange, ninth from William Brewster.
31. William Seymour Tyler, Plainfield, ninth from William Bradford.
32. Boardman Wright, Plainfield, ninth from William Bradford.
33. William George Wright, Plainfield, ninth from William Bradford.
34. Mrs. William George Wright, Plainfield, ninth from William Bradford.

PILGRIM NOTES AND QUERIES.

Notes.

Peter Brown's Children. In the January, 1903, number the Editor will present evidence, discovered by him in the original records, which seems to prove that only one child of Peter Brown's second wife survived, and that this child was Rebecca, the wife of William Snow of Duxbury and Bridgewater.

The children by the first wife were Mary, who married Ephraim Tinkham of Plymouth, and Priscilla, who became the wife of William Allen of Sandwich.

Stephen Hopkins and His Descendants. This section of The Mayflower Genealogies will begin in the next number, January, 1903. The delay has been unavoidable, and has been caused by the necessity for devoting the time to the work of bringing the magazine up to date.

Colonial Research Fund. Additional Contributions received to September 1, 1902: George Ernest Bowman, $100.00 (Received from sales of Bowman's Ancestral Charts and Freeman Genealogies, as advertised); New Jersey Society of Mayflower Descendants, $25.00; Joseph H. Goodspeed, $2.00; Previously acknowledged, $928.50; Total, $1055.50.

Holiday Gifts. We beg to remind our readers that a subscription to "The Mayflower Descendant" for the coming year will prove an exceedingly interesting and valuable holiday present for any one descended from a Mayflower passenger, even if the recipient is not a member of the Society of Mayflower Descendants. The giver will also have the satisfaction of knowing that the money expended for the gift will help along the important work of collecting information about the Pilgrims and their descendants.

The Later Generations of the Mayflower Genealogies. We are now ready to begin collecting the data required for compiling the later generations of the Mayflower Genealogies. A great deal of this material must necessarily be secured from living descendants of the different Mayflower passengers and special blanks have been prepared for this purpose. These blanks, with complete directions for filling them out, will be sent to every living descendant whose name and address can be secured, and we beg to urge upon our readers the importance of sending to us as early as possible the address of every person claiming descent from a Mayflower passenger. There are many thousands of descendants whose names can be obtained in no other way and a prompt compliance with this request will greatly facilitate the work.

We would repeat here what has been so often stated, that the Mayflower Genealogies are intended to include every descendant, in all male and female branches, of every one of the Mayflower passengers.

The success of this immense undertaking will depend entirely upon the intelligent co-operation and support of those most vitally interested in the result — the descendants living at the present time If they neglect or refuse to furnish the facts about their own immediate families they alone will be to blame if these facts do not appear in the printed genealogies.

Correspondents in sending us addresses of descendants should be particular to specify the ancestor from whom each person is descended. This will enable us to classify the names at once and will save a great deal of unnecessary time and labor. Correspondents should also remember to give their own addresses on every letter. The Editor receives many letters during the year which do not observe this important rule, and a great deal of valuable time is wasted in trying to find the proper address, and in a number of cases the search has been in vain.

Private Family Records. Many of our readers have in their possession old family bibles, diaries, almanacs, account books or other documents containing records of births, marriages or deaths not to be found on any public record; also unrecorded deeds and agreements of heirs which contain the only known proofs of various lines of descent from Mayflower passengers. It is of the utmost importance that such documents should be preserved and the facts contained therein made available for use in compiling "The Mayflower Genealogies." Many hundreds of such documents have already been destroyed by fire or by frequent and careless handling. To prevent the loss of those still in existence they should at once be deposited in fireproof safes or vaults. The entries should also be photographed or literal copies should be made by an expert. The expense of photographing is exceedingly small compared with the importance of having an exact facsimile of the document if by any accident the original is destroyed.

Owners of old documents of any kind containing genealogical data relating to lines of descent from any of the Pilgrim families are urged to deposit them with the Massachusetts Society of Mayflower Descendants for safe keeping. This Society's office is located in a modern fireproof building and a very large fireproof safe has been provided expressly for the protection of valuable documents donated to it or deposited with it. Those who are not willing to deposit their documents are requested to allow the Editor to have copies made for use in "The Mayflower Genealogies."

A number of private records have already been printed and it is much to be desired that many more should be preserved in this way.

THE MAYFLOWER DESCENDANT IN 1903.

OUR fifth volume will unquestionably be of greater interest and value than any yet published. The present number (October, 1902) will be issued on time and important articles which have been held back because it has seemed best to devote our efforts to bringing the magazine up to date can now be taken up. The initial article on "Stephen Hopkins and His Descendants" will certainly appear in the January number and will contain important new material. The article on Peter Brown's children will prove of exceptional interest to the great number of persons claiming descent from him.

The letter written in 1631 by Gov. Bradford to Gov. Winthrop of Massachusetts Bay Colony, bearing the autograph signatures of William Bradford, Thomas Prence, Myles Standish, John Alden and Dr. Samuel Fuller, will be printed from the original document, which will also be reproduced in half-tone.

An illustrated article on the name "Mayflower" will be of especial importance since it will relieve the minds of those who have been misled by the statements of careless writers to the effect that there exists no contemporary authority for the use of the name "Mayflower" as applied to the vessel in which the Pilgrims reached Plymouth in 1620.

An article on Autographs of Mayflower Passengers will be illustrated by half-tone reproductions of the exact size of the originals.

We shall begin to reprint Gov. Bradford's "Letter Book," a document with which very few persons seem to be familiar. It will prove of great interest to every Mayflower descendant.

Some important discoveries by the Editor, opening new lines of descent from Mayflower passengers, will be published.

The "Brewster Book" contains a great deal of very interesting material not yet published and in the January number will begin a transcript of the earliest entries.

Plymouth First Church Records and Brewster First Parish Records will be continued and other church records will be started.

The Records of the following towns will be continued: Barnstable, Bridgewater, Chatham, Dartmouth, Eastham and Orleans, Halifax, Harwich, Marshfield, Middleborough, Plymouth, Plympton, Scituate, Wellfleet, Yarmouth.

The printing of the Wills and Inventories of the Second and Third Generations will be continued, the order in which they are taken up being determined by the preferences of contributors to the Colonial Research Fund, as announced in the issue for January, 1902. Among the Second Generation wills not yet printed are those of the following persons: David[2] Alden, Joseph[2] Alden, Jonathan[2] Alden, William Pabodie, Thomas Delano, Moses Maverick, Edward[2] Doty, John[2] Doty, Rev. Samuel[2] Fuller, Isaac[2] Howland, Jabez[2] Howland, John[2] Howland, Joseph[2] Howland, James Brown, John[2] Rogers, Stephen[2] Samson, Thomas Bonney, Robert Sprout, George[2] Soule, Nathaniel[2] Soule, John Haskell, Alexander[2] Standish, Richard Church, Anthony Snow, Gov. Josiah[2] Winslow.

The Plymouth Colony Wills and Inventories, the Plymouth Colony Deeds, the Barnstable County Probate Records and the Diary of Jabez Fitch, Jr., will be continued. A number of Private Family Records and important Depositions will be printed. The Pilgrim Notes and Queries and Reports from State Societies will appear as usual in each number.

INDEX OF PERSONS.

ABBOTT, mrs. Charles W., 189
ABERDECEST, indian, 134
ADADOURIAN, Haig, 127
ADAMS, Charles Francis, 55
  Edward Milton, 51
  Elizabeth, 201
  Hannah, 204, 206
  Harriet Lawrence, 46
  Hugh, 201
  Marshall L., 251
  Peter, 206
  Susanna, 201
AGRY, mrs. George, Jr., 56
ALDEN, ALDIN } ——, 52
  Amy W., 56
  David, 256
  Elizabeth, 65, 98
  George A., 189
  John, 45, 46, 56–59, 62, 65, 82, 98, 126–128, 186, 187, 190, 191, 202, 252, 253, 256
  Jonathan, 256
  Joseph, 256
  Ruth, 202
ALDERSON, Victor Clifton, 52, 58
ALDWORTH, ——, 109
ALEXANDER, Robert, 252
ALLEN, ALEN } Abby Louise, 51
  Francis Olcott, 51, 58
  Frederick Baylies, 3, 55, 126, 189
  J. Weston, 51, 55, 126
  Priscilla, 254
  Rebecca, 139
  Robert, 170
  Walter, 139
  William, 254
ALLERTON, OLERTON } Isaac, 35, 37, 45, 62, 95, 109, 110, 128, 253
  Mary, 37, 253
  Sarah, 136
AMES, see also EAMES
  Fisher, 55, 57
  John, 237
ANDREWS, ANDREWES } Richard, 109, 110
ANDROS, ANDRUS } Ebenezer, 114
  Joanna, 114
  John, 114
  Mary, 114
ANDROS, ANDRUS *cont'd* } Sarah, 114
  Thomas, 148, 235, 237, 238
ANTHONY, mrs. Edward, Jr., 189
ANTISDEL, mrs. Albert, 59
APPLETON, Mary, 126
ARMITAGE, ——, 171
ARMSTRONG, ARMESTRONG } Gregory, 97
ARNOLD, ——, 38
  mrs. George F., 62
  Samuel, 126
ARTHUR, Bradford, 64
  Hannah, 64
  John, 2
  Richard, 64
ASHLEY, ——, 150
ASHPO, John, 148
ASPINWALL, Algernon A., 51
  mrs. Edward, 190
ATKINS, ATKINES, ATKENS } Desire, 201
  John, 201
  Joseph, 229
  Joshua, 201
  Sarah, 201
  Susanna, 201
ATWOOD, ATTWOOD, ATWOD } ——, 82
  Anna, 141
  Anne, 141
  Benjamin, 141
  Bethiah, 201
  Deborah, 141, 201
  Ebenezer, 141
  Edward S., 51
  Eldad, 141
  Hannah, 140
  John, 141, 228, 232
  Joseph, 201
  Mary, 141
  Sarah, 141
AUSTIN, mrs. Arthur William, 191
AYER, mrs. Monroe, 56

BA[*worn*], Samuel, 126
BABCOCK, Augustus Hatch, 60
BACKUS, J. Bayard, 57
BACON, Francis, 107

BACON } Gorham, 57
cont'd }
Hannah, 224
BAILEY, capt., 235
BAILHACHE, mrs. Preston H., 51
BAKER } Lydia, 185
BACKER }
Eleanor, 126
George F., 62
Henry H., 251
Horace Albert, 253
Isaac, 228, 229, 232
Josiah, 126
Lorenzo D., 52, 189
Patience, 31, 126
Samuel, 31, 126
Sarah, 145
Shubael, 185
BALCOM, Henry, 140
BALDWIN, mrs. Lyman Hayden, 60
BALL, mrs. John Henry, 56
BANCROFT, George, 106
BANGS } Abijah, 177
BANGES }
Apphia, 142
David, 177, 248
Ebenezer, 245
Edward, 29, 119, 244-246, 248
Elizabeth, 30
Hannah, 29, 32
Jonathan, 29, 30, 246
Joseph, 177, 248
Joshua, 32
Lydia, 30
Lemuel, 177
lieutenant, 245
Mary, 29, 177, 245, 248
Melatiah, 177, 249
Mercy, 30, 140
Rebecca, 29, 248
Ruth, 245, 246
Samuel, 30, 177, 248, 249
Sarah, 30, 177
Seth, 177, 248
Tamsen, 29
BARBER } mrs. Amherst Willoughby, 253
BARBAR }
Thomas, 136
BARDEN, Content, 73
BARKER, Anna, 138
Desire, 125
Eben Francis, 51, 58
Edward T., 51
mrs. Edward T., 51, 52, 55
John, 125, 138
Samuel, 125
BARLOW, Ebenezer, 240
Joanna, 70
Rachel, 240
William, 70
BARNARD, George Edward, 56
BARNES } Edward, 191
BARNS }
Joan, 99
John, 96-100, 170
Jonathan, 99
Lydia, 99
BARNEY, Rufus, 20
Sarah, 20
BARRET, James, 72
Mary, 72
BARROWS } Ebenezer, 70
BARROW }
Francis, 74
Hannah, 112
Henry, 106
Jemima, 20
John, 112
Mehitable, 192, 239
Mercy, 74
Peleg, 20
Robert, 239
Ruth, 112
Samuel, 70, 74, 112
Sarah, 70, 112
Susanna, 70
William, 70
BARTHOLOMEW } Enos, 235
BARTHOLAMEW }
BARTLETT } Abby H., 62
BARTLET }
Abigail, 111
Benjamin, 111, 113
Benjamin De Wolf, 191
Charles, 59
James, 111
Jean, 113
Joanna, 111
Joseph, 151
Robert, 186, 188
Sarah S., 127
Solomon, 111
BARTOL, George E., 58, 62
BASS } Hannah, 204, 206
BASSE }
John, 202-206
Joseph, 202-204, 206
Joseph Parker, 60
Mary, 204
Ruth, 202, 204, 206
Samuel, 203, 204, 206
Sarah, 204
BASSETT } William, 95, 187
BASSET }
BATCHELDER, Lydia, 18
BATCHELLER, Joanna, 21
William, 21
BATES } Albert Carlos, 193
BATE }
elder, 131
Joanna, 68
Joseph, 68
mrs. Joshua, 189
Mercy, 68
BAYLIES, Francis, 101
BEAL, Boylston A., 55, 127

BEARCE / BERS / BARCE, Anna, 182
Benjamin, 182, 185
Elizabeth, 185
Ruth, 22
BEAUCHAMP / BEACHAMP, John, 87, 109, 110
BECK, James M., 57
BEECHER, Henry Ward, 106
BEEDELL / BIDDLE, Joseph, 2, 82
BELL, William, 235, 237, 238
BELLOW, capt., 235
BENJAMIN, Mary, 221
BENNET, Elizabeth, 72
John, 235, 237
Joseph, 73
Lydia, 72
Mercy, 72
Nehemiah, 72
Thankful, 73
BENSON, Martha, 20
BERRY / BERRIE, Patience, 31
BESBEY, Hopestill, 173
BEST, ——, 148
BIBENS, Amos, 237
BIDDLE, see BEEDELL
BIGELOW, Adeline Amelia, 127
BILLINGTON, Eleanor, 95
Francis, 56, 57, 95, 127, 191, 252
John, 45, 56, 57, 62, 127, 191, 252
BIRD / BYRD, Thomas, 83
BIRDSALL, Sarah, 64
BISHOP, Louis Brackett, 59
BLACKE, Miles, 170
BLACKWELL, ——, 170
BLANCHARD, Joseph, 137
Thomas, 137
BLATCHFORD, mrs. E. W., 51
Paul, 58
BLISH, James Knox, 56, 62
BODGE, George Madison, 252
BOGE, Daniel, 149, 150
BOLTON, Gamaliel, 20
Susanna, 20
BONNEY, Sarah, 163
Thomas, 256
BONUM, George, 119
BOSWORTH, Deborah, 20
Hannah, 73
Joseph, 20
BOURNE, Joseph Baker, 58
Richard, 215, 216
Thomas, 2
BOWERS, mrs. George W., 191
BOWMAN, George Ernest, 14, 22, 37, 43, 52, 55, 98, 114, 122, 143, 150, 153, 159, 161, 165, 171, 182, 185, 193, 202, 212, 217, 227, 233, 239, 242, 254
BOWMAN *cont'd*, mrs. Justice H., 127
BRADDOCK / BRADDUCK, Edward, 149
BRADFORD, Alice, 93, 145
David, 143-145
Ephraim, 143-145
Gamaliel, 55
Hannah, 21, 64, 145
Hezekiah, 143-145
Israel, 144-146
John, 144-147
Joseph, 38, 144
Mary, 143, 145
Mary Winslow, 44
Melatiah, 145
Mercy, 15, 145
Samuel, 144-147
Sarah, 64, 145
Thomas, 64, 144
William, 3, 7, 11-13, 16, 25, 27, 29, 35, 36, 41, 45, 47, 52, 56, 58-60, 62, 64, 82, 84, 85, 87-90, 92, 93, 97, 101-104, 107, 127, 129, 143-147, 186, 187, 191, 193-198, 215, 216, 220, 252-254, 256
BRADLEY, mrs. J. Payson, 55
BRADSHAW, mrs. Perry Haight, 254
BRAMBLE, Catherine A. D., 51
BRANCH, John, 3
BRAY, mrs. Alonzo B., 45, 189
BRAYTON, mrs. Charles R., 62, 189
BREED, mrs. Frank Melville, 56
BRETT, William, 82
BREWSTER, Flora L., 65
Jonathan, 82
Love, 56, 57, 65, 128, 191, 252
Lyman Denison, 51, 53, 57, 62, 100, 126
Mary, 18
Sarah, 64, 128, 186, 187
Seabury, 64
William, 6, 7, 18, 45, 56, 57, 59, 62, 65, 100, 101, 103, 105-109, 126, 190-192, 215, 242, 252-254
Wrestling, 65-67
BRIGGS, Charles, 106
Clement, 35, 131
David, 131
Eunice, 21
Remember, 131
BRINLEY, Charles A., 58
BROOKE, Stopford W., 1
BROOKS, L. Loring, 55, 189
Phillips, 106
BROWN / BROWNE, ——, 158
mrs. Charles Henry, 191
David Henry, 190
James, 84, 256
James Crosby, 58
John, 8, 83-86, 103
lieutenant, 236

BROWN } BROWNE } *cont'd* } Mary, 122, 128, 254
Orlando, 52
Peter, 45, 57, 62, 122, 128, 186, 188, 191, 252, 254, 256
Priscilla, 254
Rebecca, 254
Samuel, 229–232
Thomas, 229
BRYAN, mrs. Lewis Randolph, 253
BRYANT, Deborah, 20
John, 234
BUCKLEY, James M., 57
John, 170
BUELL, Edward Wyllys, 59
BULL, William Lanman, 57
BUMPUS } BUMPAS } BUMPASE } Edward, 3, 71, 186, 188
Martha, 71
Penelope, 71
BUNKER, George, 132, 133
BUNTING, Thomas, 97
BURDITT, Charles A., 51, 189
BURKE, William Bardwell, 191
BURSLEY, Joanna, 221
Joseph Aldrich, 127, 190
BURTON, ——, 170
BUSH, Ella Agnes, 127
BUSH — BROWN, H. K., 51
BUSHNELL, Horace, 106
BUTLER, Lucy Palmer, 51
Thomas, 170
BUTTON, John, 238
Peter, 237

CADMAN, Phebe, 19
CADY, mrs. David D., 60
CAHOON } COHOON } COHOONE } James, 199, 224, 229
Mercy, 199
Sarah, 199
William, 199
CALDWELL, Charles Tufts, 253
CALKINS } COLKINS } Absalom, 19
Amos, 19
Anna, 19
Asa, 19
Daniel, 19
Elijah, 19
Elisha, 19
Elizabeth, 18, 19
Eunice, 19
Hannah, 19
Jemima, 19
Jonathan, 18
Lucy 18, 19
Matthew, 19
Mercy, 19
Phebe, 19
CALKINS } COLKINS } *cont'd* } Rebecca, 19
Sarah, 18, 19
Seabury, 19
Stephen, 17–19
Turner, 19
William, 19
Zurviah, 19
CALL, John, 137
CALLY } CALLEY } Catherine, 182
Stephen, 182
CANEDY, see KANADY
CARTER, Thomas, 133
Walter Steuben, 50, 52
CARVER, Eleazer, 71
Elizabeth, 125, 126
Hannah, 113
John, 89, 101, 102, 113, 125, 162, 163
Josiah, 126
Katherine, 71
Mary, 113
Robert, 113
William, 125, 126
CASTEELE, John, 170
CASTLE, William H., 58
CHAMBERLIN, mrs. Emma B., 51, 52
CHANY, mrs. William H., 51
CHAPMAN, Abigail, 120
Hannah, 120
Isaac, 120, 121
James, 120
John, 120
Lydia, 120
Ralph, 121
Rebecca, 120, 121
CHAPPEL, John, 149, 237
CHARLES, king, 135
CHASE, Desire, 31
Ellen, 55
CHATFIELD, mrs. Albert H., 59
CHAUNCY, Charles, 85
CHENEY, Charles Edward, 58
CHILDS, Ebenezer, 120
Elizabeth, 120
Hannah, 120
James, 120
Joseph, 120
Mercy, 120
Richard, 120
Samuel, 120
Thankful, 120
Thomas, 120
Timothy, 120
CHILTON, James, 44, 45, 57, 62, 191
Mary, 1, 44, 57, 191
CHIPMAN, Abigail, 121
Barnabas, 121
Bethiah, 121
Desire, 121

CHIPMAN cont'd } Hannah, 121
Hope, 121
Jacob, 121
John, 121, 153
Joseph, 121
Lydia, 121
Mercy, 121
Ruth, 120, 121
Samuel, 121
Sarah, 121
Seth, 121
Thomas, 121
CHITTENDEN, mrs. W. J., 60
CHURCH, Benjamin, 23. 29
Elizabeth, 152
Joseph, 113
Judith, 113
Richard, 152, 256
Sarah, 113
CHURCHILL, John, 234
Sarah, 73
CLAFLIN, mrs. Price Colby, 253
CLAGHORN, Abiah, 121
Benjamin, 122
Ebenezer, 122
Elizabeth, 121
James, 121, 122
Jane, 122
Joseph, 122
Mary, 121, 122, 224
Nathaniel, 122
Robert, 121, 122
Samuel, 122
Sarah, 121
Shubael, 121, 122
Thankful, 122
Thomas, 122
CLAPP, CLAP } Antoinette, 189
Arthur W., 189
Charity, 120
Edward Eugene, 252
Elizabeth, 120
Increase, 120
John, 120
Thomas, 120
CLARK, CLARKE } Abigail, 114
Andrew, 245, 249
mrs. C. Peter, 55
Charles, 248
Charles A., 62
Edward Lord, 52, 55
Elizabeth, 249
Frances, 248
Isaac, 248
James, 114
John, 114, 221, 248
lieutenant, 249
Mary, 221
Mehitable, 249
Roland, 245
CLARK, CLARKE cont'd } Sarah, 245
Seth, 247
Susanna, 114, 246
Thankful, 246
Thurston, 95
Thomas, 95, 234, 245-248
Tristram, 95
William, 23, 28
CLEAVELAND, CLEAVLAND, CLEVLAND } doctor, 235
Moses, 237
CLEVERLY, John, 206
CLEW, ——, 135
CLUFFE, Richard, 95
COBB, COB } Elisha, 111
Gershom, 69, 112
Hannah, 112, 223
Hurst, 112
Jabez, 112
James, 69, 71, 112
Joanna, 75, 112
John, 73, 75, 112, 160, 161
Joseph, 69
Lemuel, 112
Lydia, 111, 112
Martha, 112, 165
Mary, 73
Melatiah, 69, 112
Patience, 70, 112
Rachel, 73, 160, 161
Sarah, 121
Sylvanus, 112
Thankful, 69, 71
COCHRANE, mrs. Alexander, 189
COE, mrs. Henry T., 57
COIT, sergeant, 149
COLBRON, Henry, 2
COLE, Elisha, 229
Hannah, 207
Israel, 248
James, 158, 193, 195, 196, 207
Martha, 207, 245
Ruth, 142, 207
Samuel, 207
William, 229
COLEMAN, Ebenezer, 221
Edward, 221
James, 221
John, 221
Martha, 221
Patience, 221
Thankful, 221
COLLIER, COLLYER, COLLYAR, COLLYARE } Sarah, 128
William, 82, 186, 187
COLLINS, COLLENS } Abigail, 199

COLLINS / COLLENS *cont'd* } Asuba, 200
Benajah, 199
Cyrenius, 200
Enoch, 200
Eunice, 199, 200
Hannah, 199
Joseph, 199
Reuben, 200
Ruth, 199
Solomon, 199, 200
Stephen, 199
COLUMBUS, Christopher, 102
COMSTOCK / COMSTICK } sergeant, 150, 234, 236, 237
CONANT / CONNANT } Elizabeth, 68
Jerusha, 68
Joseph, 68
Josiah, 68
Mary, 68, 73
Prudence, 68
Susanna, 68
COOKE / COOK } Ann, 111
Bethiah, 181
Caleb, 111, 167
Charles S., 128
Elizabeth, 111, 179, 181, 193
Francis, 22, 45, 47, 56, 57, 59, 62, 94, 97, 114, 128, 150, 165, 186, 187, 190-193, 239, 252, 253
Hester, 128, 165, 192, 239
Jacob, 114, 118, 119, 193
James, 111
Jane, 111, 150
John, 95, 97, 111, 129, 130, 186, 187, 191, 192, 252
Joseph, 111
Josiah, 179, 181
Mary, 22, 111
Mercy, 111
Miriam, 181
COOMBS / COOMES / COOMBE / COMBE / COME } John, 95-97
COPELAND, Mary, 204
CORNELIUS, Lawrence, 84
COTTON, John, 9, 165-167, 193-196, 212, 213
COVILL / COVIL / COVEL } Elizabeth, 199
John, 199
Joseph, 198
Lydia, 198
Thankful, 199
COWING, Elizabeth, 251
COX, Hannah, 72
John, 72
CRACKSTON, John, 186
CRANDON, Edwin S., 45, 62, 128, 190
John Howland, 189
CRANE, Warren C., 51
CRAPO-SMITH, mrs. H. H. H., 60
CROADE, Deborah, 126
John, 126
CROCKER, Abel, 120
mrs. Adams, 56
Benoni, 120, 221
Bethiah, 120
Daniel, 120
Eleazer, 120
Elizabeth, 120
mrs. George Herbert, 56
Jabez, 221
Nathan, 120, 221
Rebecca, 120
Ruth, 120
Sarah, 120
Sarah H., 55, 189
Theophilus, 120
William, 154, 156
CROMWELL, Oliver, 107
CROOKER, Francis, 163
CROSBY / CROSBEY / CROSBIE / CROSBE / CROBY / CORBY } ——, 249
Abiah, 249
Abial, 176
Abigail, 248
Anne, 31
Daniel, 246
David, 176, 247
Ebenezer, 31, 176, 247
Edward, 247
Eliezer, 31, 208, 209
Hannah, 176, 245, 246
Increase, 31, 248
Isaac, 209
John, 31, 176, 245, 247, 248
Jonathan, 176, 247
Joseph, 30, 246
Joshua, 176, 248
Josiah, 246
Keziah, 208
Lydia, 246
Mary, 209, 245
Mercy, 31, 176, 246
Moses, 248
Patience, 208, 209
Phebe, 208
Rebecca, 208
Sarah, 30, 209, 245, 246
Simon, 30, 244-248
Sylvanus, 208
Thankful, 176
Thomas, 30, 31, 176, 244, 246-249
William, 31

CROWELL, CROWEL, CROWIL } Anne, 199, 201
Bathshua, 121
Benjamin, 121
Edward, 121
Jonathan, 199, 201
Joseph, 121
Mary, 121
Paul, 201
Rebecca, 201
Samuel, 199, 201
Yelverton, 121
CURTIS, CURTICE, CORTIS } Elizabeth, 110
Frances, 110
Hannah, 110
mrs. Henry M., 59
mrs. Isaac, 44
John, 110
Jonathan, 21
Joshua, 20
Molly, 21
Phebe, 20
CUSHING, John, 16
CUSHMAN, COUCHMA } Abigail, 111
Charles Livingston, 60
mrs. Charles Livingston, 60
Daniel, 44, 57, 127
Eleazer, 39–41
Elkanah, 39, 41
Fear, 21
Hannah, 111
Isaac, 39–42, 165, 167, 240, 241
Jonathan, 111
Joshua, 111
Lydia, 39–41
Mary, 22, 37–42
Persis, 111
Robert, 111
Ruth, 111
Sarah, 39–41
Thomas, 35–42, 95, 100, 101, 111, 130, 214, 215
CUTBERT, CUDBERTE, GODBERTSON } Godbert, 94, 96, 136
Samuel, 129, 130, 136, 186, 188
Sarah, 94, 136

DANFORTH, Jonathan, 134
Thomas, 140
DANIELS, John A., 57
Maria S., 57, 189
DARLING, Jemima, 71
John, 71, 72
Margaret, 71
DARY, George A., 127, 189, 251
DAVIDSON, William, 102
DAVIE, ——, 137
DAVIS, Abigail, 224
DAVIS *cont'd* } Andrew, 222
Ann, 223
Anna, 223
Bathsheba, 224
Benjamin, 223, 224
Daniel, 223, 224
Deborah, 222
Doler, 223
Ebenezer, 224
Edward, 225
mrs. Edward Livingstone, 127, 191
Elizabeth, 222
Experience, 224
Frederick Gale, 253
Gershom, 223
Hannah, 222–224
Howland, 50, 52
Isaac, 222, 224
Jabez, 222–224
Jacob, 224
James, 223, 224
Job, 224
John, 222–224
Jonathan, 223
Joseph, 223, 224
Josiah, 222, 223, 225
Katharine Kendall, 190
Lydia, 223
Mary, 222–225
Mehitable, 225
Mercy, 224
Nathan, 222, 224
Nathaniel, 224
Nicholas, 224
Noah, 224
Remember Mercy, 224
Robert, 222–224
Ruth, 223, 224
Samuel, 223, 224
Sarah, 222, 223
Seth, 223
Shobal, 223, 224
Simon, 223, 224
Stephen, 223, 224
Thankful, 224
Thomas, 223
William T., 51, 52
DAWES, Thomas, 243
DEACON, John, 95
DEAN, DEANE } mrs. Marvin Ansel, 253
Miriam, 180, 181
DEITZ, Lewis, 51
DELANO, DELANOY, DELENO } Benjamin, 159
Joshua, 44
Philip, 186, 187
Thomas, 159, 256
DENT, mrs. John C., 253
DE RASIERE, Isaac, 103
DERBY, John, 170

DERBY cont'd } Richard, 96
DE WOLF, Almon, 18
Austin, 17, 18
Edwin A., 18, 189, 192
Elisha, 18
Elvira, 18
Frances Ophelia (Oviatt), 18
John Oviatt, 17
Lucy, 18
Lydia, 18
Simon, 18
DEXTER, Abigail, 224
Anna, 224
Benjamin, 223
Content, 224
Cornelius, 224
Henry M., 102, 106, 108
James, 223
John, 223
Mary, 223, 224
Mercy, 224
Miriam, 224
Morton, 55
Philip, 223
Sarah, 223, 224
Stephen, 223, 224
Thomas, 170, 223
William, 223
DICCASON, ——, 149
DILLINGHAM DILINGHAM } Abigail, 178
Elizabeth, 178
Edward, 178
Hannah, 178
Isaac, 178
John, 178
Lydia, 178
Rebecca, 178
Sarah, 178
Thankfull, 178
DIMMOCK DIMOCK } Abigail, 222
Anna, 222
Benjamin, 221
Bethiah, 222
David, 222
Desire, 221
Ebenezer, 222
Edward, 221
Elizabeth, 221, 222
Ensign, 222
Ichabod, 222
Joanna, 221, 222
John, 221
Joseph, 221, 222
Lydia, 222
Mary, 222
Mehitable, 221, 222
Pharaoh, 222
Samuel, 222
Sarah, 222
Shobal, 221, 222
DIMMOCK DIMOCK cont'd } Tabitha, 222
Temperance, 221
Thankful, 221, 222
Theophilus, 222
Thomas, 221, 222
Timothy, 221, 222
DINGLEY, Abigail, 126
Elizabeth, 126
Jacob, 126
DIXON, mrs. George Dallas, 252
DOANE DOAN DONE } Dorcas, 201
Hannah, 201
Ida F., 51, 59
John, 94, 118, 228, 231
Joseph, 31, 182, 198, 201
justice, 185
Marguerite T., 51
Ruth, 140, 201
William Howard, 51, 52, 59
DOGGETT DOGETT } John, 126
Mary, 125
Mehitable, 126
Samuel, 125
DONAGHE, mrs. William Rice, 252
DONNELL, William Cushing, 60, 189
DOTY DOTEY DOTYE DOTEN } Desire, 171
Edward, 45, 59, 62, 65, 95, 96, 171, 186, 188, 193, 233, 253, 256
Elizabeth, 112, 193, 195, 196
John, 65-67, 172, 193, 256
Mary, 233, 234
Paul A. L., 60
Thomas, 112, 233
DOUCE DOWCE } Francis, 234
Lawrence, 140
DOWNES DOWNS } mrs. Charles Thompson, 191
Frances W. B., 51
Myron Day, 253
DREW, Elizabeth, 20, 114
Ezra, 20
Hannah, 113
James, 113, 114
Jemima, 20
Lucy, 21
Lydia, 114
Mary, 113, 114
Priscilla, 114
Sarah, 113
Thomas, 21
Thomas Bradford, 47
William, 113
DRUILLETTE, ——, 13
DUN, Dorothy, 222

DUN *cont'd* } Experience, 222
John, 222
DUNBAR, Benjamin, 21
Hannah, 21
Joseph, 21
Ruth, 21
DUNHAM / DONHAM } Abigail, 71, 110
Benjamin, 223
Charles A., 189
Desire, 223
Ebenezer, 69, 71, 223
Elisha, 223
Elizabeth, 69, 110
John, 186, 187, 213, 223
Joseph, 110
Joshua, 110
Lemuel, 69
Mary, 223
Mercy, 223
Micajah, 110
Sylvester C., 51
Thomas, 223
DUNKIN, Bethiah, 112
Jabez, 112
Samuel, 112
DUNSTER, Isaiah, 242
DURFEE / DURFE } Mary, 71
DURKEE, lieutenant, 237
DWIGHT, George Edmund, 189
DYER / DIER } Ebenezer, 225
Hannah, 32
Henry, 225
Isabel, 225
Jonathan, 225
Judah, 225
Lydia, 225
Mary, 224
Samuel, 225
William, 32, 224, 225

EAMES, Anthony, 125, 126
Hannah, 125
John, 125
Jonathan, 125
Mark, 163
Mercy, 125, 126
EATON, Francis, 45, 56, 57, 62, 186
Samuel, 56, 57, 74, 188, 233
EDWARDS, Edward, 96, 97
Jonathan, 106
EGGLESTON, Percy Coe, 51
ELDRIDGE / ELDRIGE / ELDREDG / ELDREADG } Bethiah, 185
Ebenezer, 229
Edward, 183
Elisha, 229, 230
Elizabeth, 183
ELDRIDGE / ELDRIGE / ELDREDG / ELDREADG *cont'd* } Jehoshaphat, 183
Mulford, 211
ELIZABETH, queen, 4
ELIOT / ELLIOTT } Edith, 189
mrs. George F., 253
John, 216
ELLIS / ELLICE } Elizabeth, 114
mrs. Frank R., 59
Joel, 114
John, 114
ELMES, Katherine, 71
Mary, 70
ELY, mrs. Henry Oliver, 191
John Hugh, 59
Rheumah, 64
EMERSON, mrs. J. E., 60
ENSIGNE, Thomas, 85, 86
EVERSON, Eunice, 21
Levi, 21
Penelope, 71
Richard, 71
EWER, Benjamin, 225
Elizabeth, 225
Hezekiah, 225
John, 225
Jonathan, 225
Joseph, 225
Mehitable, 225
Nathaniel, 225
Rebecca, 225
Shobal, 225
Thankful, 225
Thomas, 225

FAHNESTOCK, James Frederick, 253
FAIRBANKS, Henry Nathaniel, 60
mrs. Henry Nathaniel, 60
Nora Lucy, 60
FAIRFAX, mrs. Lindsay, 192
FALLOWELL, Gabriel, 213
FARNUM / FFARNUM } Mary, 234
FARWELL, Henry, 137
mrs. Walter M., 55
FASH, lieutenant, 148
FAUNCE / FFAUNCE } Abigail, 113
James, 22
Jane, 113
John, 113, 186, 187
Joseph, 72
Martha, 72
Mary, 22
Mercy, 113
Nathaniel, 113
Patience, 113
Priscilla, 14

FAUNCE / FFAUNCE cont'd } Thomas, 16, 17, 29, 40, 42
125, 195, 198
FAXON, Molly, 21
FELIX / FFELIX } indian, 23, 29
FELTON, sergeant, 237
FIELD, Kate G., 189
FINNEY / PHINNEY / PHINNY } Elizabeth, 222
Robert, 214, 217
FISH / FFISH } Thomas, 152
FISHER, mrs. Charles H., 51, 189
FITCH, Alice, 145
captain, 234
Elisha, 149
Jabez, 148, 234, 238
FITTSRANDLE, Edward, 225
Hannah, 225
Hope, 225
Isaac, 225
John, 225
Joseph, 225
Mary, 225
Nathaniel, 225
Thomas, 225
FLANEGA / FLAINGAM } Catherine, 182
FLETCHER, Daniel, 137, 138
FLOYD / FFLOYDE } Richard, 2
FORBES, Henry D., 55
Samuel B., 189
FORD / FFORD / FOORD } Bethiah, 125
Deborah, 125
John, 57
Michael, 125
FOSTER, Benjamin, 226
Chillingsworth, 247–249
F. Apthorp, 55
Freeman, 44
James, 247
Joseph, 226
Mary, 248
Nathan, 249
sergeant, 149
Thomas, 248
FOXWELL, Martha, 225
Mary, 225
Richard, 225
Ruth, 225
FREEDLEY, mrs. A. T., 62
FREEMAN / FFREEMAN } ——, 251
Bathsheba, 33
Ebenezer, 228, 229
Edmund, 35
Elkanah, 175
FREEMAN / FFREEMAN cont'd } John, 119, 175, 220, 244, 245, 249
justice, 185
Mary, 175
Mercy, 175, 249
Nathaniel, 31, 33, 210, 211
Phebe, 175, 249
Rebecca, 245
Sarah, 175, 249
Thankful, 175, 249
Thomas, 33, 244, 249
FRENCH, Solon Tenney, 59
FRIEND, mrs. William H., 189
FROTHINGHAM, Richard, 134
FULLER / FFULLER } Abigail, 226
Anne, 226
Barnabas, 226
Benjamin, 226, 227
Bethiah, 225, 226
Bridget, 35
Content, 226
Cornelius, 226
David, 226
Ebenezer, 226
Edward, 45, 58, 62, 127, 190, 191, 252
mrs. Edward M., 60
Elinor, 68
Elizabeth, 226
Hannah, 71, 226, 227
Isaac, 226
Jabez, 226
Jane, 226
James, 227
John, 71, 225–227
Jonathan, 68, 226
Joseph, 226
Josiah, 226, 238
Linus E., 51
Lois, 226
Lydia, 222
Mary, 226
Mary Goddard, 127
Matthew, 226
Mercy, 72, 226
Nathaniel, 226, 240
Patience, 226
Rebecca, 226
Reliance, 225
Remember, 226
Samuel, 39, 45, 56–58, 62, 127, 191, 226, 252, 256
Sarah, 226, 240
Seth, 226, 240
Shirley, 60
Temperance, 227
Thankful, 225–227
Thomas, 226
Timothy, 68
Young, 226
FYFE, mrs. R. H., 60

GALLOP, captain, 149, 237
GAYLORD, mrs. John F., 51
GAYWARD, Anna, 70
Francis, 70
GEER, Ellen, 254
GIBBS, ——, 88
mrs. E. B., 60
Elizabeth, 113
Job, 113
Judith, 113
Thomas, 170
GIFFORD / GIFFERD / GIFFERED } Jeremiah, 240
Mary, 240
Sidney B., 189
GILES, sergeant, 149
GILKEY, mrs. Alphonso Livingston, 56
GINNES,——, 148
GODBERTSON, see CUTBERT
GODFREY / GODFREE / GODFRIE / GODFRAIE / GODFRAY } Bethiah, 185
Elizabeth, 30, 185
Eunice, 182
George, 30, 185
Hannah, 30
Jonathan, 30
Josiah, 182
Lincoln, 253
Mary, 30
Mercy, 185
Moses, 30
Richard, 30
Ruth, 30
Samuel, 30
Thomas, 185
GOODHUE, Harry, 126
GOODRICH, William Winton, 57
GOODSPEED, Elizabeth, 120
Joseph H., 55, 254
Nathaniel, 120
Ruth, 224
GORDON, ——, 148
GORHAM / GORAM / GOROM / GORUM / GORUME } Charles Miner, 191
Desire, 153, 154, 157, 217, 220
Elizabeth, 220
Hannah, 158, 220
Jabez, 158, 220
James, 153, 154, 157, 158, 217, 220
John, 153, 154, 156–158, 217, 220
Joseph, 157, 158, 220
justice, 221
Lydia, 158, 220
Mercy, 158, 220
Shubael, 158, 220
Temperance, 220
Thankful, 225
GRAY / GREY } Andrew, 209, 247
Anna, 209, 247, 249
Elisha, 209, 248
John, 167, 209, 245–249
Joshua, 209, 249
Lydia, 245
Mehitable, 209, 246
Samuel, 245
Sarah, 126, 246
Susanna, 209, 245, 246
GREEN / GREENE } Jacob, 136
John, 132, 133
John Richard, 5
Marshall W., 51, 52
Richard, 90
mrs. R. H., 51
Richard Henry, 50, 52–54, 57
GREGORY, ——, 105–107
GRIDLEY, mrs. Nelson C., 59
GRIFFIS, ——, 103
GRIFFITH / GRIFITH / GRIFFETH } Abraham, 177
Barnabas, 177, 248
Joseph, 177, 248
Lazarus, 177, 248
Rebecca, 177, 248
Stephen, 177, 248, 249
Thankful, 177
GRINNELL, William Milne, 50
GROESBECK, Herman J., 59
GROOSE, Thomas, 228
GROZIER, Joshua Freeman, 253

HACKET, Edward, 74
George, 73
Hannah, 74
John, 75
Lydia, 73
Mercy, 71
Thankful, 75
HACKSTAFF, ——, 64
HALE, mrs. George S., 189
HALL, Edmund, 182
mrs. Henry Sewall, 253
James M. W., 55, 56
mrs. Nathaniel B., 44
Samuel, 249
Zipporah, 182
HALLETT / HALLOTT } Andrew, 157
Joseph, 157
HAMDIN, ——, 92
HAMILTON / HAMELTON / HAMMELTUN / HAMULTUN / HAMULLTUN } Bethiah, 184
Daniel, 30
Delilah, 200
Grace, 200
Jane, 200

HAMILTON, HAMELTON, HAMMELTUN, HAMULTUN, HAMULLTUN, cont'd, Lydia, 200
Mary, 182, 184
Mehitable, 184
Michael, 184
Nathaniel, 200
Rebecca, 200
Samuel, 184
Sarah, 30, 184
Thomas, 200
Zeruiah, 200
HAMLIN, HAMBLIN, HAMBLEN, Abigail, 221
Benjamin, 229
Eliezer, 177, 229–232
Elisha, 177, 229
Elkanah, 221
John, 221
Lydia, 177
Mary, 224
Patience, 221
Rachel, 221
Reuben, 221
Sylvanus, 221
Tabitha, 221
HAMMOND, Benjamin, 154
mrs. William P., 189
HANBURY, HANBERRY, ——, 82, 97
HARDEN, lieutenant, 237
HARDING, Abiah, 142
Bethiah, 181
Desire, 182
Hannah, 182
Joseph, 181, 182
Mary, 185
Rebecca, 142
HARLOW, Arthur, 127
Lydia, 39–41
Submit, 20
William, 234
HARPER, mrs. Corwin Dewey, 60
HART, Albert Bushnell, 55
mrs. Donald Purple, 127
HASKELL, HASCOL, HARSKALL, John, 248, 256
Josiah, 71
Sarah, 71
HASKINS, Charles Waldo, 57
HATCH, Samuel, 172
HATHAWAY, Hannah, 21
HATHERLEY, Timothy, 85, 86, 109, 110
HAWKS, HAUKS, HOAKS, Edward C., 62
James Dudley, 60, 62
Sarah, 39–41
HAWXHURST, ——, 64
HAWES, John, 220
HAYFORD, HEAFORD, Bathsheba, 21
Ebenezer, 70
Jacob, 67
James, 70
John, 67
Lydia, 67, 73
Mary, 70
Samuel, 21, 67
HAYMAN, John, 135
HAYWARD, HAWARD, Hannah, 151
John, 151, 152
Sarah, 151
Thomas, 151, 152
HEDGE, Elisha, 158
HEIL, Charles E., 46
HERD, Ebenezer, 182
Elizabeth, 182
HICKS, HICKES, HIX, Joanna, 33
Robert, 186
Samuel, 188
HIGGINS, mrs. Frank Albert, 56
Hannah, 142
John, 142
Phebe, 211
HIGGINSON, Francis, 5
HILL, Edwin A., 50, 51
John, 82
John Fremont, 55, 60, 189
Thomas, 97
HINCKLEY, HINCKELY, HINKLY, HYNCKLEY, HYNCKLIE, HYNKLEY, Edmund, 208, 248
Joshua, 248
Mary, 208
Reliance, 208, 249
Samuel, 208, 248, 249
Seth, 208, 248
Shubael, 208, 248
Thomas, 153, 220, 248
HOADLY, mrs. George, Jr., 59
HOAR, George F., 13
HODGE, Mary Russell, 51
HODGES, George, 55
HOLDEN, L. Emery, 51, 52, 192
HOLLEY, Mary, 225
HOLLINGSWORTH, Jane, 128
Richard, 128
HOLMAN, Edward, 186, 188
George Ulysses Grant, 252
HOLMES, HOLME, Cornelius, 72
Desire, 173, 174
Elisha, 110
Elizabeth, 20, 110

HOLMES / HOLME *cont'd* Elnathan, 110
Eunice, 20
Israel, 171, 173
Jabez, 110
John, 110, 125
Joseph, 110
Lydia, 21, 72
Mary, 125
Mercy, 110
Nathaniel, 110
Oliver, 21
Peleg, 20
Rebecca, 110
Samuel, 125
Sarah, 20, 110
Susanna, 110
HOOPER, John, 2
HOPKINS / HOPKENS ——, 247
Abigail, 142
Benjamin, 237
Bethiah, 178
Caleb, 114–117
Charles Augustus, 55, 126, 189
Charles Harris, 253
Constance, 58, 59
Damaris, 114, 115
David, 178
Deborah, 114, 115, 193
Desire, 176
Ebenezer, 246
Elisha, 200
Elizabeth, 114–119, 178
Elkanah, 245
Experience, 200
Franklin Whetstone, 58
mrs. F. W., 51
Gyles, 56, 116, 119, 253
Hannah, 176, 249
Howard F., 251
James, 179
Jeremiah, 178
John, 176
Judah, 176
Lydia, 207, 248
Martha, 176
Mary, 200
Mercy, 176, 178, 179
Moses, 207, 248
Nathan, 207
Nathaniel, 178, 179
Phebe, 248
Rebecca, 176
Reliance, 207, 249
Richard, 207, 248
Reuben, 179
Ruth, 114–117
Samuel, 176, 179, 207, 248, 249
Sarah, 207
Stephen, 45, 56–59, 62, 94, 114, 115, 117, 127, 128, 176, 191, 193, 245, 246, 248, 249, 252–254, 256
HOPKINS / HOPKENS *cont'd* Susanna, 207
Sylvanus, 176
Theodosius, 207
Thomas, 246
HOSCOTT, Samuel, 238
HOSKINS, William, 95, 124
HOWARD, Chauncey Otis, 253
ensign, 238
Harry M., 189
Harry Stinson, 59
Samuel, 133
HOWES, David, 200
Hannah, 182
Rebecca, 200, 201
Richard, 201
Thomas, 200, 201
HOWLAND, Abigail, 111
Consider, 112
Desire, 74, 153, 217
Elizabeth, 111, 112, 217
Experience, 112
Frances, 74
Hannah, 70, 111, 112
Henry E., 51, 53
Isaac, 256
Jabez, 256
James, 111
Joanna, 112
John, 44, 45, 56–59, 62, 97, 111, 127, 128, 153, 186, 187, 190, 191, 214, 216, 217, 252, 253, 256
Joseph, 112, 256
Mary, 111
Nathan, 74
Thankful, 111
Thomas, 112
Walter Morton, 52, 58
mrs. Walter Morton, 58
HUBBELL, Anne Law, 51
HUCKENS, Thomas, 153
HULING, Ray Greene, 55
HUNT, Christian, 128
Mary, 145
Samuel, 99, 100
HUNTINGTON, mrs. Jacob R., 189
HURST, James, 186, 187
HUTCHINSON / HUTCHENSON captain, 101, 158
Mary, 39
HYDE, James Nevins, 58
William Waldo, 51–53

INGLEE, Deborah, 73
Jonathan, 73
IRISH, John, 23
IVES, Marie E., 57

JACKSON, Abraham, 234
Deborah, 20
sergeant, 148, 234
JACOB, John, 131

JAMES, D. Melancthon, 52
king, 4, 5, 13, 105, 134
JEFFERY / JEFFARY } captain, 149, 234, 237, 238
JENNEY / JENNY / JENEY / JENINGS } Herbert, 51, 59, 189
John, 95
Sarah, 186, 187
JOHNSON, Alfred S., 51
Bascom, 253
Flora Louise Priscilla, 253
James Gibson, 51, 52
John, 149
Thomas, 170
Zachariah, 135
JOHNSTON, mrs. Robert James, 252
JONES, Charles D., 59
Emma C. B., 128
Frances L'H., 59
mrs. Frank J., 59
Jabez, 148
John, 162, 163
Joseph Davis, 44
Samuel Fosdick, 192
JOYCE, Walter, 172

KANADY / KANNADY } Elizabeth, 71
Sarah, 71
KARR, mrs. William W., 62
KEELY, mrs. Thomas E., 44
KEITH, mrs. Ira Bliss, 56
KELLOG, Joseph, 148
KELTON, Dwight H., 56
KEMP / KEMPE } Elizabeth, 75, 82
William, 75, 82
KEMPTON / KEMTON } Manasseh, 186, 187
KENDALL, Henry Myron, 59
KENDRICK / KINDRICK } Elizabeth, 202
Solomon, 202
KENNADY, John, 148
KING, Abigail, 177
Bathsheba, 245–247
Bathshua, 178
Caleb, 68
Ebenezer, 178
Edward, 189
George, 69
Hannah, 72
Ichabod, 68, 69
John, 178, 245–248
Joseph, 24, 25, 27
Judith, 68, 69
Mary, 178
Mercy, 178, 248
Nathaniel, 245, 246
Samuel, 178
Stephen, 177
Thankful, 68

KNAPP, mrs. Frederick N., 51
KNEELAND, Adele, 191
KNOWLES / KNOWLS / KNOWELS } Apphia, 142
Cornelius, 183
Edward, 142
James, 182
John, 142
Martha, 182, 183
Mercy, 182, 185
Rebecca, 142, 183
Richard, 182, 183
KUHN, mrs. Oscar William, 191
KYLE, mrs. William S., 51, 189, 190

LADUE, mrs. Austin Yates, 60
LANGLEY, ——, 238
LAPHAM, mrs. Samuel, 62
LATHROP / LOTHROP / LAYTHORP / LAYTHORPE } ——, 149
Barnabas, 23, 28, 154, 156, 220
Elizabeth, 226
Joseph, 23, 28, 181
Mary, 121
Tabitha, 222
LAWRENCE, Benjamin, 133
William Badger, 251
mrs. William Badger, 190
William M., 58
LAWRIE, mrs. William, 55, 189, 192
LAY, lord, 9
LAZELL, Theodore S., 55
mrs. Theodore S., 56, 57
LEACH, Anne, 72
Content, 73
Deborah, 20
Giles, 20
Josiah Granville, 51–53, 58
Samuel, 73
LE BARON / LABARON } Frederick N., 51
James, 68
Martha, 68
LECHFORD, Thomas, 110
LEE, ——, 97
Edward Clinton, 58
LENNIG, Lucretia C., 51
LEONARD / LEANARD } George H., 55, 189
Philip, 172
Rebecca, 120
LEVETT, Christopher, 90
LEWIS / LEWES / LEUIES / LUIS } Apphia, 141
Benjamin, 141
ensign, 236
George, 141
Joan, 141
Jemima, 71

LEWIS / LEWES / LEUIES / LUIS *cont'd* } Nathaniel, 141
Rebecca, 141
Sarah, 141
Tabitha, 189
Thomas, 141
LIBEIE, Frederick James, 127
LINCOLN / LINCKHORN } Margaret, 248
Mary, 246
Mercy, 248
Samuel, 247
Thankful, 249
Thomas, 246–249
LINNELL / LINNEL / LYNNEL } Arthur Ellsworth, 190
Experience, 224
Hannah, 223
LIPPINCOTT, Craige, 58
LITCHFIELD, Wilford I., 127
LITTLE, Amos R., 62
Anna, 161, 163, 164
Ephraim, 146, 162–164, 172–174, 212
Hannah, 164
Isaac, 162–164, 172
John Mason, 55
Mercy, 164
Patience, 164
Ruth, 164
Samuel, 126, 162–164
Sarah, 126
Thomas, 161–164
LOMBARD / LUMBARD / LUMBART / LUMBERT / LUMBURT / LUMBER } Abiah, 121
Caleb, 183
Deliverance, 183
Edward, 183
Elizabeth, 183, 221, 225
Isaac Gross, 59
Josiah Lewis, 50, 51, 53, 54
Mary, 183
LONDON, negro, 210, 211
LORD, ——, 149
Joseph, 182
LORING, Abigail, 21
Ignatius, 21
Thomas, 146, 147
LOTHROP, see LATHROP.
LOVELL / LOUELL / LOVEL } Anna, 74
Elizabeth, 225
James, 74, 131
John, 74
Mary, 74
Peter, 74
LOWELL, James Russell, 4
LUCAS / LUCOS } Benoni, 112
Bethiah, 112
Elisha, 112
Joanna, 112
Mary, 112
Repentance, 112
Samuel, 112
Sarah, 112
LUDLOW, George McMurtry, 59
LUNT, Cornelia Gray, 59
LUTHER, Martin, 107
LYMAN, general, 148, 237, 238
LYON, Asahel, 21
Fear, 21

MACDONOUGH, Rodney, 52, 53, 55, 64, 87
Thomas, 64
MACK, sergeant, 235
MACKFUN, Joanna, 72
Robert, 72
MADILL, mrs. Charles Grant, 127
MAHUREN, David, 21
Ruth, 21
MAKER, Abigail, 177
James, 177
Mary, 177
MANCHESTER, Walter Howland, 192
MANNING, mrs. H. C., 51
MARCH, Thomas, 137
MARCHANT, Hannah, 189
MARSH, William Lowrey, 51, 53, 54
MARSHALL, John, 99, 100
mrs. John, 252
MASON, George Champlin, 58
John, 88
MATTHEWS, Albert, 190
MAVERICK, Moses, 256
MAYO, ——, 247
Abigail, 140
Alice, 32
Bathsheba, 32, 33
Daniel, 229
Ebenezer, 32, 33
Elisha, 33, 229
Elizabeth, 32, 33, 140, 177, 195, 196, 246
Hannah, 33, 142, 177
Henry, 30
James, 30
Jeremiah, 229
Joanna, 32
John, 30, 177, 195, 196
Mary, 29
Mercy, 33, 178
Nathaniel, 32, 33, 140
Robert, 33
Ruth, 140
Samuel, 229
Sarah, 30
MCADOO, Mary J. O., 189
MCCARTNEY, mrs. William H., 51

McCollester / Mackhollester } ——, 236
L. S., 60
McGlenen, Edward Webster, 190
McKay, mrs. James, 189
McKinlay, mrs. James M., 51
McLaurin, John L., 57
McMillan, mrs. John G., 253
Merrick / Merick / Mirrick / Myrick / Marick } Abigail, 211
Deborah, 207, 208
ensign, 246
Jabez, 208
Jethro, 208
Joshua, 208
Mercy, 140
Oliver, 208
Ruth, 210
Samuel, 208
Simeon, 208
Snow, 208
Stephen, 140, 207, 208
Thomas, 208
William, 244
Mighell, Thomas, 126
Millard, James Fitch, 59
Miller, Elias, 70
John, 154, 156, 220
Sarah, 70
Mills, William Stowell, 58
Mitchell / Mitchel / Michell } Deborah, 73
Edward, 151, 152
Experience, 83, 84, 150–152
Hannah, 151
Jacob, 162
James, 184
Jane, 150
John, 151, 152
Mary, 150, 151
Mercy, 184
Sarah, 151, 184, 185
Tabitha, 184
Thomas, 151
Timothy, 73
William, 184, 185
Mix, ——, 149
Amasa, 237
Mixter, Samuel Jason, 55
mrs. William, 189
More, Christian, 128
Jane, 128
Lydia, 18
Richard, 128
Morison, mrs. John Holmes, 55
Morris, mrs. Seymour, 59
Morrow / Moro } Francis, 73
Mary, 73
Morse, Elizabeth, 73
Mary, 73
Morton, Bryant, 229
Deborah, 73
Ephraim, 16, 17, 100, 195, 198, 214, 234
George, 186, 187, 193
John, 23, 28, 119, 193
Lettice, 193
Marcus, 55
Mary, 195
Nathaniel, 1, 92, 100, 212, 216
Thomas, 186, 188
Moseley, mrs. Frank, 189
Mott, Henry Elliott, 57
Mulford / Molford } John, 210, 211
Thomas, 211
Munro, Abigail, 21
Benjamin, 21
Lucy Josling, 21
Wilfred H., 55

Nash, Samuel, 154
Nason, Emma Huntington, 60
Nelson, Hannah, 71
John, 165
Lois, 73
Newell, ——, 135
John, 136
Newton, Charles H., 59
Clara Chipman, 59
Elvira, 18
Nichols / Nicholes } mrs. Edward H., 191, 252
Randall, 135
Willard A., 189
Nickerson / Nickerso / Nickrson / Nickeson / Nickson / Nicorson / Nicherson } Anna, 182
Ansel, 198
Barzillai, 199
Desire, 198
Ebenezer, 199, 209, 247
Edward, 247
Elkanah, 184
Hannah, 199
Jane, 183, 209
Jerusha, 199
Jonathan, 183, 199, 247
Judith, 183
lieutenant, 247
Lydia, 198, 199
Mary, 33, 182, 198, 209, 247
Mercy, 33, 247
Nathaniel, 247
Nicholas, 33
Osborn, 251
Prince, 199

NICKERSON / NICKERSO / NICKRSON / NICKESON / NICKSON / NICORSON / NICHERSON cont'd } Rebecca, 184
R. C., 251
Robert, 184
Shubael, 182
Simeon, 183
Thankful, 209, 247
Thomas, 183, 185, 198, 199, 247
William, 33, 199, 209, 247, 248
NIGHTINGALE, George C., 51
NOBLE, John, 56
NORRIS, Mary, 37
NORTH, Charles J., 62, 192, 251
Daniel, 222
Hannah, 222
James, 222
John, 222
Mary, 222
Winifred, 222
NORTON, Peter, 72
Rozilla, 72
NOYES / NOYCE } ——, 171
David W., 190
James Atkins, 190
NYE, Everett I., 210, 251

OAKES / OKES } Josiah, 227–232
OGDEN, captain, 238
OGLESBY, mrs. J. H., 51
ORTON, Thomas, 137
OSBORN / OSBOURN } Susanna, 20
mrs. William Henry, 252
OTIS, Dorothy, 126
Joseph, 126
OVIATT, Frances Ophelia, 18
OXFORD, negro, 237

PABODIE, Elizabeth, 65, 98
Martha, 98
Priscilla, 65
William, 236
William H., 59
PACKARD, Abigail, 73
Anne, 72
Deborah, 73
Jonathan, 73
Samuel, 72
PADDOCK / PADDOK } Anthony, 189
Bethiah, 188, 189
David, 189
Deborah, 183
Elizabeth, 188
Hannah, 189
Ichabod, 188
PADDOCK / PADDOK cont'd } James, 188
John, 188
Mary, 188, 189
Peter, 188
Priscilla, 189, 247
Zachariah, 188, 189, 246, 247
PADDY / PADY } William, 35–37, 117, 130
PAGET, ——, 106
PAINE / PAIN } ——, 248
Abigail, 31, 34
Barnabas, 32
Charles, 229
Cyrus F., 51
Dorcas, 209, 245
Ebenezer, 209
Elkanah, 31
ensign, 246, 247
Experience, 210, 248
Hannah, 31–34, 209
Hugh, 31
Jonathan, 31, 209, 248
Joseph, 209, 210, 244, 245, 248
Joshua, 32
Lois, 34
Lydia, 32
Mary, 209, 247
Moses, 32
Nicholas, 33, 34
Patience, 209, 210, 245
Phebe, 31, 32, 209, 245
Philip, 34
Priscilla, 33
Reliance, 209, 246
Richard, 209
Thankful, 33
Thomas, 31, 32, 209, 247
PALMER, Elizabeth, 74
Priscilla, 20
Sarah, 74
Thomas, 74
William, 186, 188
Zurishaddai, 74
PARKE, Richard, 128
Sarah, 128
PARKER, ——, 135
colonel, 238
Edmund Southard, 253
Edward L., 190
Frederick Wesley, 50–52, 55
justice, 222
PARLOUR, Abigail, 72
Deliverance, 71
Hannah, 72
Thomas, 72
PARRIS, Benjamin, 20
Sarah, 20
PARSONS, Willis Ellis, 60
PARTRIDGE / PARTRICH / PARTICH } ——, 81, 82
George, 95

PASON, colonel, 239
PEARMAIN, Sumner Bass, 55
PEASE / PEESE } Charity, 189
Matthew, 189
PECK, ——, 236
PEIRCE, see PIERCE
PERCY, mrs. George W., 190
PERKINS, ——, 214
Charles Brooks, 127, 252
mrs. Charles Brooks, 127, 191
George Batcheller, 127, 191
PERRY, Mary J., 52
James, 138
John B., 52
PETERSON, John, 172
PHILLIPS / PHILLIPPS } Benjamin, 173
Eleazer, 136
John, 172
PHINNEY, see FINNEY
PHIPPS / PHIPS } Samuel, 137
Solomon, 137
William, 196
PICHON, Hiram Leander, 60
PIERCE / PEIRCE } Abraham, 95
Jonathan, 68
Naomi, 68
Thomas, 68
PITKIN, mrs. Albert H., 51
PLIMPTON, Frances A., 190
mrs. Henry R., 190
PLUMMER / PLUMER } Ann, 98, 128
sergeant, 235
POND, V. C., 190
POOLE, John, 234
PORTER, mrs. Burr, 55, 128
mrs. Henry Hobart, 127
POWICKE, ——, 106
PRATT / PRAT / PRATTE / PRATE } ——, 64
Aaron, 138
Anna, 138
Daniel, 138
Dorcas, 137
Esther, 240
Hannah, 73
John, 64, 73, 138
Joseph, 133, 137–139
Joshua, 93, 96, 186, 187, 240
Mary, 64, 94, 95, 132, 136–140
Mercy, 138
Peter, 138
Phineas, 64, 87–98, 129–139
Samuel, 138
Sarah, 240
PRENCE / PRINCE } Thomas, 35, 82, 86, 94, 96, 97, 118, 119, 129, 130, 183, 216, 251, 256
PRICE, Margaret, 27
Mary, 165
PRIDE, ——, 150
PRIEST, Degory, 45, 62, 64, 94, 136
Mary, 64, 94, 136, 138
Sarah, 136
PRINCE, see also PRENCE
John, 85
Mercy (Hinckley), 127
Samuel, 73
Thomas, 1
PUMMERY, ——, 148, 149, 234, 235
PURMORT, mrs. Henry C., 59
PUTMON, ——, 148
PYNCHON / PYNCHEON } John, 134, 135

QUINCY / QUINCEY } colonel, 203
mrs. George H., 190

RAINEY, Samuel Mitchell, 59
RALF, David, 182
Katrina, 182
RANDAL, Rozilla, 72
RAWLINS, Thomas, 83
RAY, Elizabeth, 199
RAYMOND / RAYMENT } Elizabeth, 70
mrs. Henry E., 190
Ithamar, 70
James, 70
Joshua, 70
Martha, 71
Maybelle, 253
Mercy, 70
READ / REED } Axel Hayford, 253
Esther, 22, 24
James, 74
Mary, 74
mrs. Sylvanus, 51
William, 22, 27
William Howell, 127
REMICH, Daniel C., 190
REMICK, mrs. John A., 51, 55
REYNER, John, 212, 215
REYNOLDS / RENOLDS } Benjamin, 69
Dorothy, 69
Elizabeth, 69
Hannah, 72
Isaac, 69
Mary, 69
RHODES, James Mauran, 52, 53, 128
RICE, mrs. John M., 190
RICH, Anne, 34
Huldah, 34
John, 228, 229, 231, 232
Joseph, 34
Obadiah, 34
Priscilla, 34
Rebecca, 34
Richard, 34

RICH cont'd } Sarah, 34
Sylvanus, 34
Zaccheus, 34, 211
RICHARDS, George Brinckerhoff, 253
Jeremiah, 52
Lysander S., 190
RICHARDSON, George E., 190
mrs. George E., 190
RICHMOND, Henry A., 191
John, 69
Sarah, 69
RICKARD / RICKET } Esther, 100
James, 114
John, 114
Sarah, 114
RIDER, see also RYDER
Bethiah, 200
John, 200
Mehitable, 200
Simeon, 200
Zenas, 200
RIDLEY, ——, 30
Mary, 30
RING / RINGE } Andrew, 118, 119, 193–198
Deborah, 193, 195
Eliezer, 194–196
Elizabeth, 195, 196
Lettice, 193
Mary, 195
Susanna, 195
William, 194–198
RIPLEY / RIPLY } Hannah, 21, 73, 145
William, 73
RIVERS, Mary, 190
ROBBINS / ROBINS } Desire, 31
Nicholas, 82
Samuel, 31
ROBINSON, John, 6–12, 101, 106–108, 126, 139
RODGERS, see ROGERS
ROEBLING, mrs. Washington A., 56
ROGERS / RODGERS } ——, 88
Benjamin, 175
Ebenezer, 175
Elizabeth, 182
John, 66, 126, 146, 175, 256
Jonathan, 175
Joseph, 95, 175
Judah, 175, 208
Mary, 208
Moses, 182
Patience, 208
Priscilla, 175
Sarah, 175
Thankful, 175
Thomas, 45, 57, 58, 62, 191, 253
ROWLEY, H. Curtis, 190
Warren C., 190
RUDD, ——, 149
Edward Huntting, 55, 56
RUMHIGIN, indian, 88
RUNK, Louis Barcroft, 58
RUSSELL, ——, 224, 225
Alfred, 60
mrs. Alfred, 60
RYDER, see also RIDER
mrs. Godfrey, 127

SALMON, Stephen D., 128, 190
SAMSON / SAMPSON / SAMSO } Abraham, 159
Ann, 98, 99, 128
Henry, 45, 57, 60, 62, 98, 99, 127, 128, 186, 187
Martha, 70
Mary, 70
Obadiah, 70
Stephen, 256
SANDERS, Anna, 224
John, 90
SARGENT, John Smith, 59
SARSON, mrs. Horace Benjamin, 192
SAUVEUR, mrs. Albert, 57
SAVOURY, Anne, 233
SAWYER, John, 126
Mercy, 126
Rebecca, 126
SCOTT, George R. W., 126
SCUDDER / SKUDER } Hannah, 32
SEABURY / SABERRY } Frederick C., 62
Martha, 98
Samuel, 98–100
SEALIS / SILLIS } Richard, 85, 86
SEARS / SEARES / SEERS / SEIRS / SERS } Abigail, 210, 249
Ann, 183, 246
Ann M., 62
Anna, 183
Anne, 183
Benjamin, 246
Daniel, 182, 183, 199–202
David, 201
Deborah, 202, 246
Desire, 210
Experience, 183
Hannah, 183, 210, 247
Henry H., 251
James, 246
J. Henry, 55, 56, 243, 251
John, 245
Joseph, 247
lieutenant, 246
Mary, 210
Mercy, 201, 210, 245, 249
Paul, 183, 246

SEARS, SEARES, SEERS, SEIRS, SERS *cont'd* Priscilla, 247
Rebecca, 201
Richard, 201
Ruth, 183, 210, 249
Samuel, 210, 245, 249
Sarah, 201, 202
Seth, 245
Silas, 246
Thankful, 183
Zachariah, 247
SEEKENS, SEEKINS Aaron, 73
Damaris, 70
Lydia, 73
Moses, 70
SEVERANCE, SEVERANC, SEVERENCE Bethiah, 182
Ebenezer, 31
SEWALL, Samuel, 205, 206
SHALER, ——, 64
SHAW, SHAWE Hannah, 31
Harriet A., 55, 190
Henry Southworth, 55, 190
John, 96, 132, 186, 187
Jonathan, 24, 25, 41, 124
Lydia, 207
Mary, 151
Persis, 41
SHEPARD, James, 190, 251
mrs. James E., 190
SHERMAN, Deborah, 126
Desire, 171, 173
mrs. James E., 51
Jane, 125, 126
John, 125, 126, 173
Samuel, 125, 172
William, 171–173
SHIRLEY, SHERLEY James, 2, 109, 110
SHUNTUP, Henry, 148
SHURTLEFF, SHIRTLIFF William, 167
SIMMONS, SIMONS Moses, 186, 188
William Stearns, 127
SIMPKINS, John, 242
SIMPSON, John, 137
SKELDING, mrs. Arthur Bertram, 254
SKERRY, Amory Thompson, 254
SKIFF, SKIFFE James, 95
justice, 226
SLAPP, captain, 237
SMALL, Warren W., 52
SMALLE, Bethiah, 182
Zachariah, 182
SMITH, Abigail, 71, 140
Asaph, 200
David, 141
Dean, 184, 200
Elizabeth, 33, 182
Esther, 184, 200
Goldwin, 105
Hannah, 33, 72, 140, 141
mrs. Henry M., 190
Isaac, 142
mrs. James, 44
Jeremiah, 140, 141
Jesse, 142
Joanna, 32
John, 33, 88, 137, 247
Jonathan, 73, 74, 142
Marion A., 190
Mary, 141, 142, 223
Mercy, 140, 249
Nathan Holt, 51, 58
Nathaniel, 71
Ralph, 141, 210, 211
Rebecca, 141
Samuel, 229–232
mrs. Samuel F., 190
Sarah, 33, 73
Susanna, 71, 74
Thomas, 32, 135, 141, 142
SNOW, Aaron, 178, 248
Anna, 141
Anthony, 162, 163, 256
David, 177, 248
Deborah, 207
Ebenezer, 175, 245
Edward, 32, 247, 248
Elizabeth, 175
Grace, 32
Hannah, 175–178, 245, 247
Isaac Burrows, 58
Jabez, 32, 176, 247
Jane, 245
Jonathan, 177, 207, 248
Joshua, 207
Josiah, 125, 175
Lydia, 177, 178, 207, 246
Mark, 207
Martha, 247
Mary, 33, 175, 177, 178, 248
Mercy, 176, 247
Nathaniel, 207, 248
Nicholas, 207
Phebe, 207
Prence, 176, 177, 207, 247, 248
Rebecca, 125, 126, 247, 254
Ruth, 178, 248
Samuel, 176, 178, 247
Sarah, 30, 32, 207
Thankful, 207
Thomas, 32, 175, 177, 178, 245–249
William, 254
SOULE, SOUL Abigail, 21
Benjamin, 113

SOULE / SOUL *cont'd* } Deborah, 113
George, 45, 56, 62, 63, 98, 100, 127, 128, 159, 186, 187, 191, 192, 239, 252, 253, 256
Hannah, 113
Hester, 159
Horace Homer, 51, 55
James, 27, 241
John, 27, 29, 159, 160, 192, 239
Joseph, 161
Julius E., 62
Lydia, 24, 27
Martha, 72
Nathan, 64
Nathaniel, 256
Rachel, 160
Rebecca, 160
Sarah, 21, 64, 113, 160, 192, 239,
Zachariah, 113
Zeruah, 44
SOUTHER / SOWTHER } Nathaniel, 130, 132
SOUTHWORTH, Constant, 132, 186, 187
Nathaniel, 125, 165, 166
Thomas, 119, 186, 187, 215
SOWASHAN, indian, 220
SPALDIN, sergeant, 149
SPARROW, ——, 116
Jonathan, 180
Patience, 209
Richard, 116, 117
SPRAGUE, Francis, 186, 188
mrs. Francis P., 56, 190
Grace, 72
Samuel, 16, 17, 25, 29, 40–42, 67, 150, 152, 166, 167, 172, 174, 193, 194, 196–198
SPROUT, Robert, 256
Thankful, 73
STAFFORD, mrs. Edward Orr, 253
STANDISH, Alexander, 171, 256
Barbara, 119
Charles Dana, 60
Ichabod, 69
Mary, 69
Moses, 73
Myles, 7, 45, 51–53, 55, 57, 62, 82, 83, 85, 86, 92, 93, 102, 114–117, 127, 171, 186, 187, 191, 252, 254, 256
Phebe, 69
Rachel, 73
STANFORD, Robert, 172
STAPLES, Mary, 71
STARK, William M., 58
STARR, Comfort, 82
STEELE / STEEL } Ashbel, 101
Melatiah, 145
Mercy, 145
Thomas Sedgwick, 127
STEPHENS / STEVENS } Abigail, 32
Benjamin F., 55
Edward, 113, 172
George H., 190
James, 149
Phebe, 113
Richard, 32
William Burdick, 56
STETSON / STUDSON } Annabel, 60
mrs. George R., 62
Robert, 132
STEVENS, see STEPHENS
STEWART / STEWARTT / STEWARART / STUART / STUARD } Abigail, 199
James, 199
Joseph, 199, 201
Lydia, 185
Mary, 199, 201
Samuel, 183–185, 198–200
Temperance, 201
STILLMAN, William Maxson, 254
STONE, Achsah, 249
Eunice, 248
Heman, 246
Kezia, 245
Nathan, 247
Nathaniel, 242, 244, 249
Ralph, 60
Reliance, 245
Thankful, 247
STRAUSS, ——, 107
STRICKLAND, Helen Josephine, 191
STRONG, William J. H., 60
STROUT, Hannah, 32
Mary, 30
Sarah, 140
STUART, see STEWART
STURMEY, Dennis, 114
Elizabeth, 114
Rebecca, 114
Thomas, 114
STURTEVANT, Charles, 22
John, 165, 167
Joseph, 167
Lucy, 20
Priscilla, 20
Ruth, 22
Samuel Stafford, 20
Sarah, 20, 21
Thomas, 21
SUMERS, Elizabeth, 125
John, 125
SWAIN, ——, 135
SWAN, Robert T., 56
William, 138
SWANN, Josephine Ward, 57
SWEAT, Benjamin, 229

SWIFT / SWYFT } mrs. Edward Y., 128
Elizabeth, 24, 27
Joane, 168
Thomas, 24
William, 168, 170

TABER / TABOR } Mary, 22, 24, 27
Thomas, 22, 27
TALBOT / TALBOTT } Archie Lee, 60
Peter, 95
TAYLOR / TAYLER } Abigail, 142
Ann, 223
Daniel, 69
Desire, 182
Elizabeth, 67, 69
John, 67, 69, 142
Mary, 224
Mathes, 182
Robert, 67
TERRY, mrs. Charles H., 51
John Taylor, 50
Marion Jane, 191
Roderick, 52, 53, 57
THATCHER / THACHER } ——, 223
Franklin N., 190
John, 154, 156, 220
Peter, 71–73
Thomas C., 251
THAYER, Deliverance, 71
Ephraim, 202, 206
Isaac, 71
Sarah, 204
THOMAS, Abigail, 72
David, 44, 71
Deborah, 126
Dorothy, 126
Edward, 72
Elisha, 69
Elizabeth, 69, 71, 72
Ephraim, 69
Hannah, 71, 72
Israel, 69
Jedediah, 73
Jeremiah, 71
John, 3, 237
Joseph, 240, 241
Lois, 73
Lydia, 73
Mary, 71, 126
Mercy, 125
Miriam, 71
Nathaniel, 126, 146, 147, 159, 161
Samuel, 125
Sarah, 69
Thankful, 71
William, 69, 72, 138
THOMPSON / TOMSON } Abigail, 73

THOMPSON / TOMSON / *cont'd* } Amasa, 68
mrs. Andrew, 252
Elizabeth, 24, 70, 72
Esther, 22, 24
Huldah, 20
Isaac, 20
Jacob, 23–27, 29, 70, 72, 73, 160
James, 111
John, 22–29, 72
Joseph, 111
Lucian Bisbee, 190
Lucy, 20, 21
Lydia, 21, 24, 27
Mary, 22, 24, 27, 68, 123
Mercy, 24, 27, 72
Peter, 23–27, 29, 111
Sarah, 24, 27, 111
Thomas, 23–27, 29, 68
THORP, Joseph, 185
Mehitable, 185
Thomas, 185
THRASHER, Damaris, 70
TILDEN / TILDIN } John Newel, 50
Thomas, 162
TILLEY, Elizabeth, 217
TILSON, Edward, 82, 83
TINKER, Joseph Wescot, 127
TINKHAM / TINKAM / TINKCOM / TINCOM / TINCOME / TINCUM } Abijah, 68, 70
Bathsheba, 21
Caleb, 111
Ebenezer, 73, 74, 111, 123
Elizabeth, 74
Elkiah, see Helkiah
Ephraim, 122–124, 167, 254
Hannah, 69, 70, 110
Helkiah, 110, 111, 123
Isaac, 68, 70, 123
Jacob, 110, 111
Jeremiah, 74
Joanna, 72
John, 69, 70, 111, 123
Lydia, 110
Martha, 69
Mary, 69–71, 110, 111, 122, 123, 254
Mercy, 70
Noah, 68
Patience, 70, 74
Peter, 69, 111, 123
Priscilla, 74
Ruth, 110, 111
Samuel, 69–71
Sarah, 111
TITUS, mrs. Nelson V., 51
TOBA, negro, 237
TOBEY, Rufus B., 190

TOMLIN, ——, 31
TOMPKINS, Hamilton B., 51
TORREY, ——, 214
Anna, 112
Joseph, 112
Mary, 112
William, 112, 134, 135
TOTA, indian, 219
TOWER, Charlemagne, 58
TRACY / TRACYE / TRASIE } John, 27, 29
Stephen, 95, 186, 187
TRAFTON, mrs. Francis E., 190
TREAT, Abigail, 32
Joanna, 32
John, 229
Nathaniel, 229
Samuel, 30, 32, 140, 142, 217
TREWANT, Mehitable, 126
Morris, 126
TROW, Mary, 127
TROWBRIDGE, Edward A., 190
John, 172
TUCKER / TUKER } Benjamin, 70
Elizabeth, 184, 249
Eunice, 184
Hannah, 184
John, 184
Keziah, 184, 249
Samuel, 184, 248, 249
Sarah, 70
Thankful, 184, 249
TURNER, Charles Peaslee, 58
Elizabeth, 73
Ezekiel, 18
Frederic Alonzo, 45
mrs. Frederic A., 55
Hannah, 72, 73
Japheth, 73
John, 18
Mary, 18
Philip Foster, 60
Sarah, 18
TURRELL, mrs. Herbert, 58
TUSPAQUIN, indian, 29
TWINING / TWINNING } Abigail, 34
Barnabas, 142
Eleazer, 34
Elizabeth, 142
Hannah, 142
John, 34
Katrina, 182
Mercy, 34, 142
Nathaniel, 34
Ruth, 142
Stephen, 34
Thankful, 142
William, 142
TYLER, mrs. Joseph H., 190
William Seymour, 254
USHER, Gerard, 2

VAILL, Charlotte F. S., 60
Edward Griswold, 60
Frederick Sturdivant, 51, 60
Julia Cornelia, 60
VAN DYKE, Harry Weston, 52
VASSALL / VARSSALL } William, 86
VAUGHAN, Deborah, 68
Ebenezer, 68
Elisha, 75
Faithful, 68
George, 68, 74
Huldah, 20
Jabez, 68
Jerusha, 70
John, 70
Joseph, 72, 75, 160
Mercy, 72
Nathan, 68
Rebecca, 74
Samuel, 20
Thomas, 75
VENABLES, colonel, 2
VEZEY, Solomon, 206
VICKERY, Joanna, 32
VINAL, Alvin A., 190
VINCENT, Hannah, 210
John, 210
Sarah, 136
VINSEN, Sarah, 223

WADSWORTH / WADDESWORTH } ——, 66
Christopher, 82
Elisha, 147
John, 67
WALDO, captain, 150
WALKER, sergeant, 149
WALLEY, ——, 214
WALLIS, Thomas, 170
WALTER, mrs. Joel C., 190
WALTON, John Whittlesey, 50
WARD, mrs. Charles Albert, 59
Joseph Walter, 190
WARE, Francis A., 190
WARNER, Charles Dudley, 51, 53
WARREN, Abigail, 113
Anna, 161
Benjamin, 15, 16
Caroline B., 51
Daniel Frederick, 50–53, 57
Eleanor, 68
Elizabeth, 16, 152, 156, 188
Hannah, 113
James, 40
John, 113
Joseph, 14–17, 100
Mercy, 15
Nathaniel, 113
Patience, 16
Priscilla, 14–17

WARREN *cont'd* } Richard, 14, 45, 47, 56, 57, 60, 62, 128, 152, 161, 191, 252, 254
Ruth, 113
Samuel, 68
Sarah, 68, 113
Susanna, 113
Winslow, 1, 51, 52, 55
WASHBURN, mrs. Charles Francis, 252
Henry S., 126
Mary, 70
Miriam, 252
Nehemiah, 70
William Sherman, 59
WATERHOUSE, ——, 171
WATERMAN, Anne, 24, 25
Deborah, 20
Elisha, 20
Hannah, 21
Jabez, 21
Joanna, 21
John, 162, 164
Joseph, 21, 70, 164
Joshua, 70
Lucy, 21
Martha, 20
Patience, 70
Phebe, 20
Sarah, 21
William, 20
WATSON, George, 234
WEAD, mrs. Leslie Clark, 127, 190
WEBB, Benjamin, 204–206
general, 149, 238
Jonathan, 204, 205
Ruth, 204, 206
Susanna, 204, 205
WEBBER, Maria G., 51
Richard, 140
mrs. Samuel G., 51
Sarah, 140
Sarah S., 51
WEEKS, Abigail, 249
Andrew G., 190
Deborah, 249
George, 249
WELCH, A. R., 51
Ashbel, 51, 52, 58
WELD, ——, 126
WELLS, captain, 235, 237
WESCOAT / WASTCOAT } Cornelius, 69
Hannah, 72
James, 69
Joanna, 69
Mary, 69
Richard, 69
Thomas, 72
WESEN, Elizabeth, 182
WESTON, Edmund, 160
Rebecca, 160, 161
Thomas, 87–90, 92
WETHERHEAD, see WITHERHEAD
WETS, sergeant, 148
WHEATON, mrs. Loyd, 58
WHELDEN / WHILDEN } Joseph, 220
WHETSTON, John, 158
WHITAKER, Ann, 71
Richard, 71
WHITCOMB, Lawrence, 127
WHITE, Peregrine, 1, 86, 191
Resolved, 86
mrs. Stephen V. C., 51, 52
William, 45, 62, 191
WHITMAN, Josiah, 20
Samuel, 21
Sarah, 20, 21
WHITMARSH, John, 131
WHITNEY, Thomas, 97
WHOORY, Ralph, 130
WICKER, Cassius M., 51
WIGHT, Charles Henry, 51
Martha Cobb, 60
WILE, Moses, 229
WILEY, corporal, 237
WILKINSON, mrs. Henry W., 190
WILLARD, James Le Baron, 50
Susan Barker, 51
WILLETT / WILLET } Mary, 36
Thomas, 35–37, 83, 84, 86, 117, 118, 130
WILLIAMS, Anna, 138
Hannah, 33
mrs. Horace P., 190
Joseph, 71
Margaret, 71
mrs. Robert A., 60
Roger, 13, 101, 106, 107
WILLIAMSON, mrs. Chalmers Meek, 127, 190
George, 229–231
Timothy, 173
•WILLIS, John, 82
WILSON / WILLSON } Edmund, 2
Henry, 185
Mary, 185
WING / WINGE / WHING } Bethiah, 249
Daniel, 170
John, 234, 249
Rachel, 249
WINPENNY, mrs. J. Bolton, 62
WINSLOW / WINSLOWE / WINSLO } ——, 246
Edward, 1–3, 12, 45, 48, 57, 62, 63, 82, 87, 88, 90, 92, 93, 102, 239
Elizabeth, 2
Hannah, 248
Isaac, 239, 241
John, 97
Josiah, 2, 164, 239, 256

WINSLOW / WINSLOWE / WINSLO *cont'd* } Kenelm, 246, 248
Mary, 1, 44, 246
Mary Russell, 44
Thomas, 182
WINSOR, Joseph, 170
Justin, 102
WINTER, Christopher, 35
WINTHROP, John, 6, 256
WISWALL / WISEWALL / WISEWALLE } Ichabod, 65, 67
Priscilla, 65, 67
WITHERHEAD, John, 20
Submit, 20
WIXAM, Elizabeth, 32
WOOD / WOODS } Abial, 71
Abijah, 70
Ann, 71
Elnathan, 68
Ephraim, 68
Esther, 74
Eunice, 20
Glenn, 253
Hannah, 70, 71
Henry, 29, 70, 74
Jabez, 71
Jedediah, 68
Jemima, 68
Jerusha, 70
Lydia, 68
Mary, 68, 70, 74
Mercy, 71
Rebecca, 74
Samuel, 74, 123
Susanna, 71
Thomas, 70
Zephaniah, 70
WOODCOCK, Charles W., 60
WOODWARD, Theron Royal, 58
WORMALL, Grace, 72
Josiah, 72
Mary, 72
WORTHINGTON, Harry Cushman, 58
WRIGHT, Adam, 160, 161, 165, 167, 192, 239–241
Boardman, 254
Esther or Hester, 165, 192, 239, 240
Isaac, 240
James, 240
John, 239
Mary, 165, 240
Mehitable, 192, 239–241
Moses, 240
Nathan, 240
Rachel, 240
Richard, 165–167, 239
Samuel, 240
Sarah, 160, 192, 239, 240
William George, 254
mrs. William George, 254

YERGASON, Henry C., 59
YOUNG / YOUNGE } Abigail, 34
Barnabas, 229
Benjamin, 229
Dinah, 183, 202
Elizabeth, 226
Israel, 229
Jennet, 33
Joanna, 33
John, 183, 202, 229
Jonathan, 229–232
Lydia, 33
Mercy, 33
Patience, 226
Rebecca, 142
Robert, 33
Zipporah, 182, 183

INDEX OF PLACES.

ACUSHENA, 187
AGGAWAM, 15
AMERICA, 5–7, 12, 84, 100–102, 107
ASSAWAMSETT, 23, 29, 160
ASSONET, 160
ATLANTA, GA., 252
AUGUSTA, ME., 60

BACON'S BROOK, 157
BALTIMORE, MD., 191
BARNSTABLE, MASS., 44, 48, 120, 153, 181, 214, 217, 221, 231, 256
BARNSTABLE COUNTY, MASS., 48, 61–63, 179, 256
BEDFORD, ENG., 103
BELOIT, WIS., 60
BILLERICA, MASS., 133
BILLINGSGATE, 227, 228
BINGHAMTON, N. Y., 191
BOSTON, MASS., 1, 3, 4, 9, 13, 35, 36, 43–46, 55, 56, 64, 82, 100, 126, 127, 134, 158, 189, 190, 202, 205, 206, 213, 234, 235, 251
BRAINTREE, MASS., 202, 205, 206
BREWSTER, MASS., 242, 251, 256
BRIDGEWATER, MASS., 15, 20, 21, 48, 56, 70, 72, 73, 131, 150–152, 254, 256
BRISTOL, ENG., 109
BRISTOL COUNTY, MASS., 48, 61–63
BRITISH COLUMBIA, 44
BROOKLINE, MASS., 127
BROOKLYN, N. Y., 58, 191, 253
BUFFALO, N. Y., 191, 253
BURLINGTON, VT., 59

CANAAN, CONN., 149
CALIFORNIA, 43
CAMBRIDGE, ENG., 102
CAMBRIDGE, MASS., 44, 138
CAPE ANN, 88
CAPE COD, 3, 144, 242, 250
CARVER, MASS., 20
CHARLES RIVER, 133
CHARLESTOWN, 64, 87, 94, 129, 132, 133, 135–140
CHATHAM, MASS., 182, 198, 248, 256
CHATHAMPORT, MASS., 251
CHICAGO, ILL., 58, 59, 253
CINCINNATI, O., 59, 191
CLARK'S ISLAND, 3, 52
CLEVELAND, O., 59
COAKSETT, 187
COLCHESTER BROOK, 40, 41, 240
COLORADO, 44
CONNECTICUT, 44, 237
CORN HILL, 52
CROWN POINT, N. Y., 148, 149

DAMARIS COVE, 88, 89
DARTMOUTH, MASS., 48, 122, 123, 125, 185, 186, 256
DEDHAM, MASS., 56
DEERFIELD, MASS., 18
DENVER, COL., 253
DETROIT, MICH., 60
DIGHTON, 72
DISTRICT OF COLUMBIA, 44
DORCHESTER, MASS., 93
DOTY'S MEADOWS, 41, 194
DOVER, N. H., 213
DROITWICH, ENG., 1
DUXBURY, MASS., 25, 28, 39, 45, 48, 52, 65, 66, 72, 75, 91, 95, 103, 144, 151, 159, 160, 214, 256

EAST BREWSTER, MASS., 251
EAST DENNIS, MASS., 251
EASTHAM, MASS., 29, 30, 32–34, 48, 140–142, 181, 195, 210, 211, 216, 227–232, 248, 251, 256
EASTON, MASS., 21
EDINBURGH, SCOT., 105
EEL RIVER, 97
ENGLAND, 1, 2, 5, 10, 13, 93, 101–103, 106–109, 135
EUROPE, 6
EVANSTON, ILL., 59, 253

FITCHBURG, MASS., 56
FLORIDA, 44
FORT CHRISTINA, NEW SWEDEN, 85
FORT EDWARD, N. Y., 234, 236, 238
FORT WAYNE, IND., 127
FORT WILLIAM HENRY, N. Y., 238
FREETOWN, MASS., 71

GAINSBOROUGH, ENG., 126, 189
GETTYSBURG, PA., 105
GLENCOE, MINN., 253
GLENDALE, O., 191
GROTON, CONN., 64

HALF MOON, 238
HALIFAX, MASS., 20–22, 48, 256

HANOVER, MASS., 21
HARDWICK, MASS., 21
HARTFORD, CONN., 189, 193
HARWICH, MASS., 48, 175, 182, 207, 242, 245, 256
HAWAII, 44
HERRING POND, 24, 28
HILLSDALE DISTRICT, N. Y., 18
HINESDALE, PA., 252
HINGHAM, MASS., 131
HISPANIOLA, W. I., 1, 2
HOLLAND, 1, 6, 12, 100, 102–105, 107, 108, 136
HOOP PLACE FIELD, 15
HOQUIAM, WASH., 253
HOUSTON, TEX., 253
HUDSON, N. Y., 59
HUMBOLDT, IOWA, 252
HYANNIS, MASS., 44, 251

ILLINOIS, 43
INDIANA, 44
IOWA, 43
IPSWICH, 93
ISLES OF SHOALS, 88

JACKSON, MISS., 127
JAMAICA, W. I., 1
JERSEY, 150
JONES RIVER, 35, 38, 66, 91, 96, 97, 118, 130

KENTUCKY, 44
KINGSTON, MASS., 21, 44, 45, 47, 52, 53, 65

LAKE CHAMPLAIN, 64
LAKE GEORGE, 149
LAWRENCE, N. Y., 127
LEYDEN, 1, 6, 11, 101, 102, 108, 136
LONDON, ENG., 1, 2, 7, 87, 89, 101, 109
LOUT SWAMP, 194
LYME, CONN., 18
LYNN, MASS., 39, 44, 56

MADISON, WIS., 60
MAINE, 43, 60
MAJOR'S PURCHASE, 23, 28
MANILA, P. I., 58, 253
MANOMET, 15, 127
MARION, IND., 17
MARQUETTE, MICH., 253
MARSHFIELD, MASS., 2, 48, 52, 86, 125, 161, 163, 164; 171, 173, 174, 214, 256
MARYLAND, 44, 236
MASHPEE, 216
MASSACHUSETTS, 1, 4, 6–9, 13, 43, 88, 92, 93, 104, 131, 133, 134, 197, 236–238, 250, 256
MATTAPOISETT, 83, 84, 86
MEDFORD, MASS., 190, 251
MERRIMAC RIVER, 133
MICHIGAN, 43, 54
MIDDLEBOROUGH, MASS., 15, 20–22, 25, 27, 28, 39, 48, 67, 70–73, 122, 123, 125, 138, 151, 160, 194, 195, 256
MILTON, MASS., 21
MILWAUKEE, WIS., 60
MINNESOTA, 44, 54
MISSOURI, 44
MONHEGAN, 88, 92, 93
MONOMOY, 247
MONPONSET, 24, 123
MONTCLAIR, N. J., 254
MONTVILLE, CONN., 64
MORRIS, CONN., 18
MORRISTOWN, N. J., 252
MT. HOLLY, N. J., 253
MUNUSCASSET, 170
MYSTIC RIVER, 133, 137

NACOOKE BROOK, 133
NAMASKET, 39
NAMASSAKET, 162, 163
NAMATAKEESET, 151
NECKATAY, 187
NEW ENGLAND, 1, 2, 4, 5, 87, 88, 90, 99, 102, 105–109, 133, 135
NEW HAMPSHIRE, 43
NEW JERSEY, 44
NEW LONDON, CONN., 58, 252
NEW SWEDEN, 84, 85
NEW YORK, 43
NEW YORK, N. Y., 50, 57, 58, 191, 192, 252
NINE PARTNERS, N. Y., 64
NORFOLK, VA., 253
NORTH CAROLINA, 44
NORTH RIVER, 83
NORWELL, MASS., 190
NORWICH, CONN., 64, 144, 254
NOVA SCOTIA, 44

OBLONG, N. Y., 64
OGDENSBURG, N. Y., 127
OHIO, 43
OMAHA, NEB., 192
ORANGE, N. J., 254
OREGON, 44
ORLEANS, MASS., 29, 48, 140, 256
OSHKOSH, WIS., 60
OXFORD, ENG., 235
OYSTER BAY, L. I., 64

PAPASQUASH NECK, 156
PENNSYLVANIA, 43, 236,
PHILADELPHIA, PA., 58, 59, 128, 252, 253
PISCATAQUA, 93
PLAINFIELD, N. J., 254
PLYMOUTH, MASS., 2–4, 9, 12–17, 20, 25, 35–42, 45, 47, 48, 50, 52, 53, 64, 65, 67, 71, 82, 83, 85–110, 114, 117–119, 122–125, 128–130, 132, 133, 136, 143, 144, 146, 147, 150, 152–154, 159, 161–163, 165–167, 182, 185–187, 193–195, 197, 198, 212, 213, 217, 231, 233, 234, 239, 254, 256

PLYMOUTH COLONY, 1, 6, 8, 12, 35, 47-49, 61, 62, 75, 82, 101, 103, 105, 109
PLYMOUTH COUNTY, 16, 48, 61-63
PLYMPTON, MASS., 20, 21, 48, 71-73, 239, 241, 256
POCASSET, 164
POINT PERIL, 187
POLLAPODY COVE, 195
PORTLAND, ME., 56
PRINCETON, N. J., 57
PROVIDENCE, R. I., 192, 235
PROVINCETOWN, MASS., 3, 250, 251
PUNKATEST, 85

RADNOR, PA., 253
RAYNHAM, MASS., 20
REHOBOTH, MASS., 71, 83, 161
RHODE ISLAND, 43, 54, 85, 99, 107, 235-237
ROCHESTER, MASS., 22, 71, 248
ROCHESTER, N. Y., 191
ROCKY NOOK, 130
ROME, ITALY, 5
ROSEMONT, PA., 252
ROUND POND, 149
RUSSIA, 44

SALEM, MASS., 5, 107, 128
SAN DOMINGO, W. I., 1
SANDWICH, MASS., 15, 35, 152, 158, 168, 215, 254
SAN FRANCISCO, CAL., 190, 191
SANTA BARBARA, CAL., 253
SARATOGA, N. Y., 149, 237
SCITUATE, MASS., 35, 48, 83, 85, 256
SCOTLAND, 101, 128
SCROOBY, ENG., 6, 100, 102
SECUNK, 36
SHARON, MASS., 127, 190
SIXTEEN SHILLING PURCHASE, 23, 29, 39, 160
SMITH'S ISLANDS, 88
SNIPETUIT POND, 23, 29
SOUTH BAY, 149
SOUTH PURCHASE, 160
SOWAMSET, 36, 83, 84, 86
SPAIN, 6
SQUANTUM, MASS., 45
STILLWATER, N. Y., 237
ST. LOUIS, MO., 18
STOCKBRIDGE, MASS., 149
STONY BROOK, 144
STONY COVE, 157
SUDBURY, MASS., 170, 171
SWANSEA, MASS., 153, 215
SWEDEN, 84
SWITZERLAND, 44

TAUNTON, MASS., 20, 70, 85, 164
TEXAS, 44
TOLEDO, O., 127
TRURO, MASS., 52, 211
TWENTY-SIX MEN'S PURCHASE, 160, 161

VERMONT, 44
VIRGINIA, 13, 44

WASHINGTON, D. C., 59, 253
WELLFLEET, MASS., 227, 251, 256
WELLINGSLY, 96, 97
WELLS' CREEK, 157
WESSAGUSSET, 87, 90-93
WESTWOOD, MASS., 252
WEYMOUTH, MASS., 131, 132, 214
WHETSTONE VINEYARD BROOK, 123
WILMINGTON, N. C., 254
WINNATUXET, 26, 28, 39, 54, 240
WISCONSIN, 43
WOLLASTON, MASS., 190
WOODSTOCK, CONN., 235
WORCESTER, MASS., 252

YARMOUTH, MASS., 48, 116, 153, 154, 182, 188, 220, 246, 247, 256
YORKTOWN, VA., 105

500 SETS

...OF...

Bowman's Ancestral Charts

HAVE BEEN PRESENTED TO THE

Massachusetts Society of Mayflower Descendants

TO BE SOLD FOR THE BENEFIT OF THE

COLONIAL RESEARCH FUND

For conditions of sale, see next page.

[REDUCED FACSIMILE OF A COMPLETED CHART]

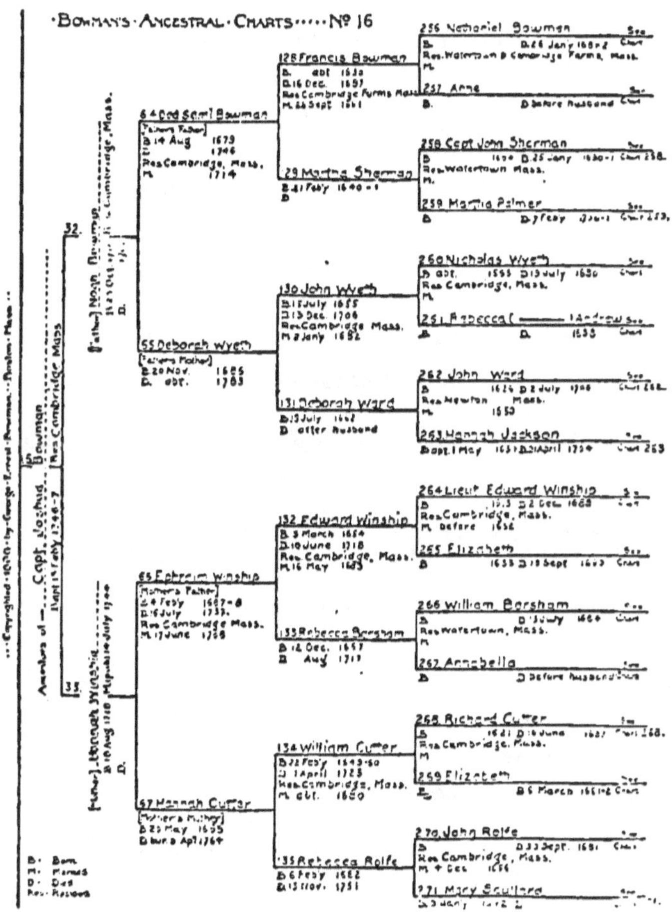

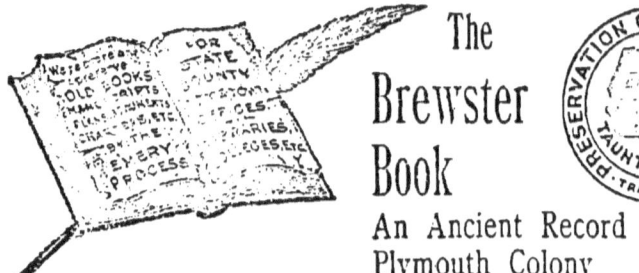

www.ingramcontent.com/pod-product-compliance
Lightning Source LLC
Chambersburg PA
CBHW030818230426
43667CB00008B/1271
* 9 7 8 3 3 3 7 7 1 2 9 7 6 *